Out of Turmoil:
Catalysts for Re-learning, Re-Teaching, and Re-imagining History and Social Science

A Volume in:
Social Science Education Consortium Book Series

Series Editors:
Gregory L. Samuels
Amy J. Samuels

Social Science Education Consortium Book Seriesy

Series Editors:
Gregory L. Samuels
Amy J. Samuels
University of Montevallo

Books in This Series:

Fostering Diversity and Inclusion in the Social Sciences (2021)
Amy J. Samuels & Gregory L. Samuels

*The Divide Within:
Intersections of Realities, Facts, Theories, and Practices* (2021)
Tina L. Heafner, Laura K. Handler, & Tracy C. Rock

*Democracy at a Crossroads:
Reconceptualizing Socio-Political Issues in Schools and Society* (2019)
Amy J. Samuels & Gregory L. Samuels

Out of Turmoil:
Catalysts for Re-learning, Re-Teaching, and Re-imagining History and Social Science

Dean P. Vesperman
Anne Aydinian-Perry
Matthew T. Missias
Whitney G. Blankenship

IAP

INFORMATION AGE PUBLISHING, INC.
Charlotte, NC • www.infoagepub.com

Library of Congress Cataloging-In-Publication Data

The CIP data for this book can be found on the Library of Congress website (loc.gov).

Paperback: 979-8-88730-075-7
Hardcover: 979-8-88730-076-4
E-Book: 979-8-88730-077-1

Copyright © 2023 Information Age Publishing Inc.

All rights reserved. No part of this publication may be reproduced, stored in a retrieval system, or transmitted, in any form or by any means, electronic, mechanical, photocopying, microfilming, recording or otherwise, without written permission from the publisher.

Printed in the United States of America

CONTENTS

Acknowledgments ix

Introduction xi
Dean P. Vesperman, Anne Aydinian-Perry,
Matthew T. Missias, and Whitney G. Blankenship

PART 1
CRITICAL EDUCATION IN TIMES OF TURMOIL

1. Approaching Critical Literacy With a Critical Race
   Theoretical Approach to Encourage Reflective
   and Just Democracy 3
   Amy J. Samuels and Gregory L. Samuels

2. What Do We Need to Know Now? Racial and Technological
   Pedagogical Content Knowledge for Discussing Race in Online
   History Classrooms 21
   Lightning Peter Jay

3. Preparing White Students for a Multiracial World 41
   Antony Farag and Bailey Verdone

PART II
PEDAGOGIES OF CHANGE

4. Teaching Social Studies in a Time of COVID-19: An
   Examination of Contradictions in Activity 57
   Dean P. Vesperman and Mariah Pol

5. Re-Imagining Citizenship Education Through Critical-
   Transformational Human Rights Education 73
   Ian M. McGregor, Glenn Mitoma, and Sandra Sirota

6. The Three Cs for Teaching in Contentious Times 91
   Debby Shulsky and Sheila Baker

7. Un-Learning, Re-Learning, And Re-Imagining Together: Early
   Career Teachers Engaging in Collaboration Toward Racial
   Literacies Development 109
   Mary Adu-Gyamfi, Joey Laurx, Trustin Dinsdale, and Rylie Kever

PART III
GLOBAL RESPONSES TO TURMOIL

8. A Tumultuous Tale of Socially Just Teaching: A Migrant Asian
   Australian Teacher's Critical Autoethnographic Account of
   Guiding White Bodies Through an Asian Ethnoburb 129
   Aaron Teo

9. Engaging With National Histories and Settler Colonial Master
   Narratives to Foster an Anti-Racist and Culturally Responsive
   Citizenry: The Pedagogy of Critical Ethical Nationalism in the
   Shadow of National Statues 143
   Mary Frances O'Dowd

10. How is Racism a Global Issue? Connecting Critical Global
    Education to the Teaching of Race 167
    Hanadi Shatara and Gerardo Aponte-Safe

PART IV
RECONCEPTUALIZING CURRICULUM

11. Centering Indigenous Voices: A Book and Film Study in a
    University Social Studies Content Course 183
    Linda Doornbos

12. Journey Box Projects for a Post-Pandemic World: How the
    Experiences of Teacher Candidates Invite the (Re)imagination
    of Culturally Relevant Social Studies Education 201
    Kaitlin E. Popielarz

13. African American History and Its Visual
    Portrayal in Textbooks 221
    Tina L. Heafner and Antoinette M. L. Rochester

14. Re-imagining Heroes and Holidays: Possibilities for
    Folkloristics in History and Social Science Education 243
    Mark E. Helmsing

Biographies 259

ACKNOWLEDGMENTS

We dedicate this book to the teachers and teacher educators who have worked tirelessly during this time of turmoil to transform education. Education has been shocked by the pandemic, the continued resistance to systemic racism and other forms of oppression, and the attempts to censor and silence teachers. It is in the midst of this turmoil we must be co-conspirators in the resistance to these challenges and we are grateful for the authors who joined us.

We would like to thank the contributors to this volume who worked tirelessly to advance the field of education in a time of turmoil. The authors of the various chapters of this book provide numerous frameworks by which we can resist the call to return to normal, which perpetuated systems of inequity. Without their dedication to transformative education, this book would not be possible.

We believe that as Ladson-Billings (2020) has urged us, we "must resist a return to 'normal'" and that this is our time to think about ways in which we can re-learn, re-teach, and re-imagine history and social sciences. The goal of this book is to provide researchers, teacher educators, and teachers with new visions of how we can disrupt the call to "return to normal" for it is clear that the old normal did not meet the needs of all people.

Out of Turmoil: Catalysts for Re-learning, Re-Teaching, and Re-imagining History and Social Science, pages ix–x.
Copyright © 2023 by Information Age Publishing
www.infoagepub.com
All rights of reproduction in any form reserved.

Lastly, we would like to thank our series editors Amy and Greg Samuels and our partner in publishing this book, Information Age Publishing (IAP) founder George Johnson and his team for publishing this volume.

—Dean P. Vesperman
University of Wisconsin-River Falls

—Anne Aydinian-Perry
University of Houston

—Matthew T. Missias
Grand Valley State University

—Whitney G. Blankenship
San Antonio College

—*Series Editors*
Amy Samuels
Greg Samuels

INTRODUCTION

Dean P. Vesperman, Anne Aydinian-Perry,
Matthew T. Missias, and Whitney G. Blankenship

It is not difficult to argue that the social sciences are in a period of transition. Since the United States saw its first Black President leave office, our day-to-day lives have been marked by uncertainty as our social lives have vacillated wildly between highs and lows, tensions between fellow citizens have heightened along ideological fault lines, and educators have been placed squarely at the center of public discourses about what—and how—we should be teaching. In the last two years alone we have lived through: the political, social, and medical effects of the COVID-19 pandemic; a public struggle for civil rights highlighted by disquieting moments of injustice; a renewal of workers asserting power through collective bargaining and organizing; social upheaval enabled by gross wealth disparity greater than the Gilded Age; and the crucial and urgent necessity to address systemic racism. By any measure, we are living in a time where every moment seems to be rife with high stakes realities that must be navigated. While some look to our nation's experts to understand how to examine the world in which we live, others have blindly—seemingly intentionally—buried their heads in the proverbial sands, choosing to eschew what have been commonly held beliefs and norms. We are living through a major paradigm shift in how the social sciences were taught

Out of Turmoil: Catalysts for Re-learning, Re-Teaching, and Re-imagining History and Social Science, pages xi–xiii.
Copyright © 2023 by Information Age Publishing
www.infoagepub.com
All rights of reproduction in any form reserved.

and learned, and educators are challenged to rethink how teaching and learning can help us navigate how we understand an increasingly tumultuous world.

We are up to the task. Ladson-Billings (2020) called on educators to reimagine education and contest the notion of a "return to normal." Additionally, Greene argued:

> To commit to imagining is to commit to looking beyond the given, beyond what appears unchangeable. It is a way of warding off the apathy and the feelings of futility that are the greatest obstacles to any sort of learning and, surely, to education for freedom. (as cited in Love, 2019, p. 102)

In the current highly polarized context where we see multiple competing narratives, rather than promoting a "return to normal" or "business-as-usual" approach, we argue that educators must use the lessons of the last two years, as well as draw on what we have learned from history and the social sciences. By asking ourselves how we might interrogate and inform current social landscapes and the challenges that arise from them, we have the opportunity to take leadership in fostering innovation, building solidarity, and re-imagining the teaching and learning of history and the social sciences.

This volume was crafted in the spirit of engaging social educators in the pedagogical imperative of leadership in our social discourses. The chapters in this volume seek to explore how educators and researchers have (a) attended to and proactively addressed existing challenges and inequities in teaching history and social sciences; (b) adapted teaching practices to prioritize the interests of students and families with fewer resources; (c) re-imagined the teaching of history and the social sciences toward diversity, inclusion, equity, and justice; (d) resisted calls to limit the academic freedom of history and social science educators; and (e) re-learned and re-examined historical narratives of the past and applied them to today. Collectively, the chapters in this volume provide spaces for us to immerse in critical conversations about the world around us, and how our teaching and learning practices must fundamentally shift in order to better engage with the realities of our world as all humans experience it. We recognize that humans live in multiple complex communities that include intersectional identities; relationships with power, agency, and discourses; and lived realities that are as unique as they are divergent. Consequently, the task of educators, and the goal of this volume, is to provide a clarion voice to a dynamic, relational, and undeniably human social world.

Each of the four sections outlined below provides a voice to the ways that educators can both embrace the complexity of our social world and make pedagogical choices that privilege a form of social education that seeks to understand the world in all of its turmoil and nuance. To accomplish this, the editors have divided the text into four themes concerning how education emerges from this time of turmoil. The first section engages in conversations about critical approaches to education, especially in a time of reaction to the continued struggle to address systemic racism in the United States and globally. The second section focuses on how teachers reconceptualize teaching in response to the global COVID-19 pandemic and recent political events. The third section addresses global responses to the turmoil that has wracked teaching and learning over the last several years. Lastly, the fourth section devotes attention to how the intersection of curriculum and teaching during a time of turmoil offers educators space to rethink their practice.

Education is never static, nor is it unresponsive to the community contexts from which it derives. Transformational teaching and learning, rather, is fundamentally predicated on the reality that we are ever evolving and ever changing in a social world and understanding that world from any curricular context requires us to be present and informed citizens. This volume stems from the concept that even in times of great turmoil, social upheaval, and considerable dimensions of injustice, we have a pedagogical imperative to be catalysts for influencing positive outcomes in society, to be innovative in the choices we make as educators, and to be responsible for the consequences of our decisions. Times of turmoil, in the myriad ways they position individual humans, give us a moment to assume leadership in being the impetus of change, and to take seriously our responsibility to re-learn, re-teach, and re-imagine History and Social Sciences.

PART 1

CRITICAL EDUCATION IN TIMES OF TURMOIL

CHAPTER 1

APPROACHING CRITICAL LITERACY WITH A CRITICAL RACE THEORETICAL APPROACH TO ENCOURAGE REFLECTIVE AND JUST DEMOCRACY

Amy J. Samuels and Gregory L. Samuels
University of Montevallo

In recent months, over thirty state legislatures and state school boards, including those in Alabama, Arizona, Florida, Georgia, Idaho, Iowa, New Hampshire, Oklahoma, South Carolina, Tennessee, and Texas, have passed legislation or official policies that (essentially) ban the teaching of critical race theory (CRT) in K–12 schools and several other states are currently debating whether to take similar action (Stout & Wilburn, 2022). Specifically, in Alabama, with a vote divided along political party lines, a resolution was adopted by the State Board of Education in October 2021. While the Alabama policy does not explicitly mention critical race theory, the related commentary about the issue consistently emphasizes the academic perspective. The resolution titled "Preservation of Intellectual Freedom and Non-Discrimination in Alabama Public Schools" states:

Out of Turmoil: Catalysts for Re-learning, Re-Teaching, and Re-imagining History and Social Science, pages 3–19.
Copyright © 2023 by Information Age Publishing
www.infoagepub.com
All rights of reproduction in any form reserved.

concepts that impute fault, blame, a tendency to oppress others, or the need to feel guilt or anguish to persons solely because of their race or sex violate the premises of individual rights, equal opportunity, and individual merit, and therefore, have no place in professional development for teachers, administrators, or other employees of the public educational system of the State of Alabama, and WHEREAS, for the same reasons, such concepts should not be taught to students in the public educational system of the State of Alabama. (Alabama State Board of Education, Action Item G.2.o)

The resolution continues by proclaiming, "that the Alabama State Board of Education affirms that we will not support, or impart, any K–12 public education resources or standards intended to indoctrinate students in social or political ideologies that promote one race or sex above another" (Alabama State Board of Education, Action Item G.2.o).

Governor Kay Ivey, who serves as the president of the Alabama State Board of Education, confirms that critical race theory is not being taught in Alabama classrooms (Moseley, 2021) and the Alabama state school superintendent Eric Mackey affirms that the state has never received any complaints about critical race theory being taught by any teachers in Alabama schools (Nexstar Media Inc., 2021). Yet, there was a heightened sense of urgency among the Alabama Board of Education to pass the resolution just months after it was first introduced in the state. Furthermore, immediately after the resolution was passed, the Governor took to Twitter to proclaim, "We have permanently BANNED Critical Race Theory in Alabama. We're focused on teaching our children how to read and write, not HATE" (Ivey, 2021).

The resolution in Alabama was seemingly inspired by the Executive Order issued by President Trump in September 2020, which was later revoked by President Biden, that banned federal contractors from conducting antiracist professional learning or racial sensitivity training that drew on critical race theory or other "race-based ideologies" or promoted the idea that "the United States is an inherently racist or evil country or that any race or ethnicity is inherently racist or evil" (Executive Order No. 13950, 2020). Similar in language, the second draft of the Alabama resolution stated, "The Alabama State Board of Education believes the United States of America is not an inherently racist country, and that the state of Alabama is not an inherently racist state" (Crain, 2021). Executive Order 13950 (2020) underscored principles of merit and individualism, rejected racialized views of the United States or any consideration of how race operates in our thoughts, conceptualizations, and actions, and disregarded how racist laws, ordinances, and policies shaped (and continue to shape) current disparities and inequalities.

Yet, in Alabama, a state with a nearly 250-year history of legalized slavery and another 100 years of legalized, oppressive Jim Crow laws, Section 256 of the state constitution still states that "separate schools shall be provided for white and colored children, and no child of either race shall be permitted to attend a school of the other race" (Mzezewa, 2021). Additionally, interracial marriage was not legalized in Alabama until 2000, even though The U.S. Supreme Court ruled in *Loving v. Virginia* (1957) that laws banning interracial marriage violate the Equal Protection and Due Process Clauses of the Fourteenth Amendment to the U.S. Constitution (Mzezewa, 2021). Furthermore, notwithstanding the fact that Alabama is the nation's fifth poorest state, Black residents of the state still experience higher rates of poverty and lower median household income than white residents. While 28.4% of Black Alabamians live at or below the poverty index, only 12.2% of white people do, and while white people in Alabama have a median household income of $55,690, Black people have a median household income of $32,188 (Alabama Possible, 2020). Moreover, Black students in Alabama are less likely to have access to quality pre-K than their white peers, more likely to attend schools in districts that spend less money per pupil, and, although Black students comprised 32 percent of the enrollment in the state's schools, they accounted for 62 percent of suspensions in 2017 (Crain, 2017; Rothwell, 2016). As such, borrowing from the ideas of Dr. Martin Luther King, Jr., while it would be a huge feat for human rights if a person was truly judged and provided access and opportunities based on the content of their character, rather than the color of their skin, persistent disparities and inequalities that continue to be perpetuated in various sociocultural contexts suggest we are not, yet, there. While the propositions of merit and individualism might seem appealing, to overlook the complex impact and consequences of years of legal segregation and discrimination in economic, educational, sociocultural, and sociopolitical contexts on structural racism and institutional racial inequalities (and enact policies to eliminate the study of such topics in schools) is not only shortsighted but unprincipled and unethical.

The resistance we are witnessing currently are not acts of novelty. When reflecting on multicultural education, and its evolution, it didn't come without resistance and backlash, where opponents viewed critical multicultural approaches as controversial, divisive, and polarizing. Nieto (2017) stated, "This is because, at its core, multicultural education is a direct challenge to public education's Eurocentric focus and curriculum, as well as to the starkly uneven outcomes of education that have been particularly onerous for children whose race, ethnicity, native language, and social class differ from the majority group" (p. 2). Therefore, as we draw parallels and consider the resistance to critical race theory, we must also consider approaches for counter-resistance.

Although the Alabama resolution is vague and does not explicitly name critical race theory or concepts related to diversity, equity, and inclusion, there are incontrovertible ramifications for teaching and learning in restricting discussions of racism, sexism, and biases in classrooms and educator training and professional learning. And, while critical race theory is not intended to be taught as a specific theoretical framework in K–12 settings (Ladson-Billings, 2021), there is great value in using a critical race theoretical approach to inform educational practices and drive educational research, particularly as it relates to understanding curricular exclusions, examining educational inequalities, and promoting increased educational justice. Many proponents of the current legislative and policy initiatives assert critical race theory is an evil and poisonous ideology that promotes division and drives people apart; however, we believe it serves to advance increased understanding, awareness, and informed action, as it acknowledges and centers the construct of race and its powerful and persistent role in society.

Rather than quelling hard conversations, for fear or discomfort with what might arise during the dialogue, threatening to enforce financial penalties, or withholding funding from schools that do not comply with vague and subjective mandates, education policy must allow districts, schools, and teachers to provide students the appropriate spaces, resources, and tools to develop a critical understanding of the world around them and work to reconcile the complexities of the past, even when the topics are unpleasant, unsettling, or potentially uncomfortable. In doing so, students will be better positioned to assess the current state of affairs, examine power dynamics and hegemonic systems, interrogate how power sustains privilege and oppression, including inequalities and injustices, and draw from multiple perspectives and narratives to inquire about historical (and current) actions, decisions, events, and policies.

Given the intensifying resistance to teaching for democracy and justice being witnessed across the United States, educators must be equipped with the skills, knowledge, and dispositions to effectively counter the escalating resistance, that is often based on uninformed mass hysteria, and advance systems to promote teaching and learning that is historically accurate, representative, and inclusive. Additionally, at a time when polarization, nationalism, and blind patriotism are heightened, there is a critical need for social science classrooms to skillfully encourage hard conversations, encourage analysis of current events, and facilitate learning about the historical implications of race and how racialized inequalities developed and were sustained. As argued by Educating for American Democracy (2021):

> We are responsible for cultivating in ourselves and the young the reflective patriotism needed to navigate the dangerous shoals we now face as we chart a course between cynicism and nostalgia. To those who believe in America's principles and promise, what we have inherited is painfully imperfect. It is our task not to abandon but to improve it. (p. 22)

Given the uninformed mass hysteria and the negative ramifications surrounding critical race theory, we argue critical literacy, informed by a critical race theoretical approach, can provide a framework to encourage teaching and learning committed to educational justice by equipping and empowering students to engage in dialogue, activism, and seek the truth even in the face of criticism. As such, in this chapter, we explore critical race theory and critical literacy, as both theories and pedagogical practices, and discuss how critical literacy, informed by a critical race theoretical approach, can be used as a strategy to promote reflective democratic thinking and increased educational justice.

CRITICAL RACE THEORY

Critical theory addresses the dynamics of power and oppression and explores strategies to advance society in a more equitable direction by examining and evaluating power relations and highlighting nuanced questions such as: (a) who controls power, (b) what constitutes power, and (c) how is power utilized to maintain current social standings (Lynn et al., 2006). As underscored by Delgado and Stefancic, highly-esteemed legal scholars, "The critical race theory (CRT) movement is a collection of activists and scholars engaged in studying and transforming the relationship among race, racism, and power" (Delgado & Stefancic, 2017, p. 3). CRT is a theoretical perspective that carefully and systematically examines the construct of race by first establishing racism as a structural precursor to legal oppression and identifying race as the key component in social inequalities (Delgado & Stefancic, 2017; Lynn, 1999; Lynn et al., 2006). Ladson-Billings (1998) underscores that "Critical race theory begins with the notion that racism is normal in American society" (p. 7) as it was created and sustained by legal principles (Delgado & Stefancic, 2017; Ladson-Billings, 2021). Additionally, critical race theorists argue race is an influential and significant factor in examining and understanding inequalities in the U.S. because the disparities and inequalities are "logical and predictable results of a racialized society in which discussions of race and racism continue to be muted and marginalized" (Ladson-Billings, 2021, p. 17).

Although CRT is interdisciplinary, it can be used to explore various educational components and provide a framework to challenge the dominant discourse on race, racism, and cultural deficit theories (Solórzano & Yosso, 2001). Seeking to disrupt current educational patterns, that perpetuate racialized disparities for students of color, proponents suggest CRT supports such efforts by establishing a foundation that focuses on the central tenets of CRT: (a) racism is endemic; (b) race is socially constructed; (c) racialized concepts change over time; (d) interest convergence is beneficial for social progress; (e) inclusion of counterstories is critical for underscoring alternative perspectives; and (f) intersectionality supports understanding how various identity components such as race, ethnicity, gender, and sexuality influence experiences, perceptions, and positionings (Abrams & Moio, 2013).

The application of CRT in educational research began to surface in the mid-1990s through the work of Gloria Ladson-Billings and William F. Tate IV (Ladson-Billings, 1998, 1999; Ladson-Billings & Tate, 1995; Tate, 1997). They argued that race remained untheorized in education and saw CRT as a framework that "provided a robust theoretical understanding of race" (Ladson-Billings, 2021, p.3). Utilizing CRT in educational discourse places race and racism, as well as the voices and experiences of people of color, at the center of the discussion and positions race as central in the analysis of educational inequalities (Ladson-Billings, 2021; Lynch, 2006). As maintained by Solórzano and Yosso (2000):

> CRT in education is defined as a framework or set of basic perspectives, methods, and pedagogy that seeks to identify, analyze, and transform those structural, cultural, and interpersonal aspects of education that maintain the marginal position and subordination of African American and Latino students. CRT asks such questions as: What role do schools, school processes, and school structures play in the maintenance of racial, ethnic, and gender subordination? (p. 42)

When considering analysis of curriculum, instruction, assessment, school funding, disproportionality, or desegregation, employing the tenets of CRT can be beneficial in accounting for educational inequalities in access, opportunities, and outcomes, because "it exposes the seeming neutrality of societal norms that must be addressed if we are to reach the full equality promised by the Constitution" (Ladson-Billings, 2021, p.3). For example, regarding curriculum, "it is not just the distortions, omissions, and stereotypes of school curriculum content that must be considered, it also is the rigor of the curriculum and access to what is deemed 'enriched' curriculum via gifted and talented courses and classes" (Ladson-Billings, 1998, p. 18). It examines course offerings, teacher quality, curricular representation, and resource selection. In the case of instruction, CRT can be applied in research to examine why instruction of African American students is often founded on the idea that students are academically deficient and takes a remedial approach (Ladson-Billings, 1998; Solórzano & Yosso, 2001). As argued by Ladson-Billings (1998), "Adopting and adapting CRT as a framework for educational equity means that we will have to expose racism in education and propose radical solutions for addressing it" (p. 22).

Critical race theory establishes that racism is endemic in U.S. society. As such, when we apply it as a framework for examining educational disparities, we evaluate the impact of U.S. race laws and policies on systems and structures, not simply the mindsets and behaviors of individuals. So, it's not about merit, it's not about individualism, but rather it is about the existing access and opportunities and the impact of history and law on the said access and opportunities. CRT encourages us to explore who is (was) granted access? Who isn't (wasn't)? Then, consider, how does (did) that access and those opportunities impact outcomes? In Derek Bell's early work in critical legal studies, he argued, "Diversity is not the same as redress...it could provide the appearance of equality while leaving the underlying machinery of inequality untouched" (Cobb, 2021). This idea can be expanded and applied to inform our understanding of continued racial disparities and inequalities in educational contexts. While attempts have been made that suggested the appearance of equality, for example, school desegregation with the passing of *Brown v. Board of Education* (1954), when those attempts were reversed or retracted, the foundation of the inequality was left undisturbed, thereby allowing the inequalities and disparities to persist (Delgado & Stefancic, 2017; Ladson Billings, 2021). To truly address the issue, and influence systemic change, we must address the foundation. We must expose the roots. We must examine the impact of laws and policies throughout the course of history and reimagine structures, systems, and institutions.

Applying a Critical Race Theoretical Approach in K–12 Contexts

When applied to education, CRT deepens our understanding of educational barriers faced by people of color in both real-world contexts and curricular representations. Extending beyond educational research, when considering how CRT can be used to inform and approach K–12 teaching and learning, specifically as it relates to the social sciences, we argue all tenets of CRT can be applied in various ways; however, for the purposes of this chapter, we will focus specifically on the permanence of racism and the need to include and promote counterstories.

Permanence of Racism

Derrick Bell, considered by many to be the father of CRT, proclaimed that "racism lies in the center, not the periphery; in the permanent, not the fleeting; in the real lives of black and white people, not in the caverns of the mind" (2002, p. 37). Consequently, educators would be doing a vast disservice to students by adopting a culture of silence and avoidance in relation to racial dialogue (as suggested by current legislative and policy efforts). Yet, when we consider whose knowledge is visible, voiced, valued, and validated in the curriculum, the "master narrative" that has developed in the social sciences emphasizes and sustains a Eurocentric perspective, while misrepresenting or ignoring perspectives and experiences of minoritized groups, and neutralizing or invalidating concepts related to race and racism (An, 2020; Au et al., 2016; Dunbar-Ortiz, 2015; Hannah-Jones, 2021; King, 2014; Loewen, 2018; Takaki, 2008). The racial script that has transpired underscores a Eurocentric, exclusive narrative while systematically omitting or distorting the voices, stories, and experiences of people of color (Ladson-Billings, 2003). As such, the hegemonic structures and social hierarchies that have developed in the socio-cultural realms of the U.S. have also found their way into the walls of the schools and the written curriculum.

As Ladson-Billings (2003) highlights, "CRT examines the way racism is made invisible through the curriculum" (p. 9); thereby exposing systematic exclusion and disenfranchisement. Misrepresentation, distortion, and complete lack of representation of the experiences of people of color in the curriculum encourages a belief, either implicitly or explicitly, that suggests people of color are insignificant in the history and development of the United States (King, 2020; Takaki, 2008). As Carter G. Woodson (1933) asserted nearly a century ago in *The Mis-Education of the Negro*, silence and inaccuracies negatively impact those who are misrepresented and "mis-educated" "by making him feel that his race does not amount to much and never will measure up to the standards of other peoples" (p. xiii). To disrupt the exclusionary historical narratives focused on Eurocentric perspectives, educators must take issue with and confront the invisibility and silence of people who have traditionally been placed on the margins. Busey and Vickery (2018) detailed increased attention in recent years to matters of race in the social sciences but cautioned educators to reflect on how race is contextualized and positioned in the curriculum and be steadfast in centralizing the experiences, perspectives, and voices of people of color in the facilitation of race dialogue.

To challenge the permanence of racism, not only must educators counter the lack of racial diversity and racial dialogue in many curriculums, but also provide students opportunities to explicitly examine the unique role of race and racism in society, particularly how race-based laws, ordinances, and policies have shaped economic, political, and social spheres. While little focus in most formal curriculums is directed to Asian American perspectives in history, outside of the experiences of Chinese in the 1800s or Japanese Americans during World War II, the problem is further compounded when curricular and supplementary resources frame a picture of victimization and disregard Asian American activism and resistance during these times (An, 2016, 2020; Rodríguez, 2019). For example, in learning about Japanese incarceration (often described as internment) during World War II, educators should (re)frame the purpose of the historical narrative. Rather than emphasizing Japanese American compliance to an Executive Order designed to enhance safety and security in the United States, learning should promote exploration of activism and resistance, and encourage discourse on the contradiction of who was "interned" (German Americans or Italian Americans were not subjected to the same "internment" policy), and draw connections between Japanese American incarceration and contemporary events (Rodríguez, 2019). Additionally, to underscore the dynamic of power in the legal incarceration of Japanese Americans, *who had committed no crimes*, learning should also explore aspects related to privilege and oppression and the related impacts. For example, (a) who had the power to limit rights, (b) who had the power to take away possessions, (c) who had the power to remove property, (d) who had the power to exclude from ownership, (e) who was subjected to limited rights and property removal, (f) how did the limitations and restrictions serve to empower some while disempowering others, and (g) in what ways did the limitations and restrictions impact future access and opportunities? To promote a more inclusive and coherent representation of historical events, teachers must also emphasize that events do not occur in a vacuum. For example, the incarceration of Japanese Americans was not a discrete event limited to people who were incarcerated from 1942 to 1945, but rather multiple generations were impacted by the historic tragedy.

Counterstories

Delgado and Stefancic (2017) explain that "Critical race theorists have built on everyday experiences with perspective, viewpoint, and the power of stories and persuasion to come to a deeper understanding of how Americans see race" (p. 45).

Counterstories (also referred to as counter-narratives by some) serve to challenge a singular, monolithic perspective of the world and counter dominant narratives that have been created and sustained by those in positions of power (Delgado & Stefancic, 2017). Counterstories are often framed as first-person accounts that communicate the experiences, perspectives, and realities of marginalized people (Ladson-Billings, 2021). They highlight alternate viewpoints by providing situational and interpretive context to increase the voice of those who have traditionally been placed on the margins and examine how structures and systems "work to re-inscribe racism and deny people of their full rights" (Ladson-Billings, 2021, p. 53). "Powerfully written stories and narratives may begin a process of correction in our system of beliefs and categories by calling attention to neglected evidence and reminding readers of our common humanity" (Delgado & Stefancic, 2017, p. 15). In addition, they may provide a form of validation and affirmation for people in racialized communities, reinforcing the idea that their experiences are not isolated events, because they give "voice and reveal other people have similar experiences" (Delgado & Stefancic, 2017, p. 51).

As King (2014) states, "The African proverb, 'Until the lions have their historians, tales of the hunt shall always glorify the hunter,' is used to metaphorically describe how dominant groups inscribe power through historical narrative" (p.2). To challenge the "master narrative" that has developed in the social sciences that emphasizes and sustains a Eurocentric perspective and misrepresents (or silences) perspectives of minoritized groups (An, 2020; Au et al., 2016; Dunbar-Ortiz, 2015; King, 2014; Loewen, 2018; Takaki, 2008), it is essential for curricular and supplementary materials to be inclusive and ensure representation of multiple perspectives, particularly perspectives and experiences of those who have historically been placed on the margins. This requires thoughtful revision of the historical narrative to present a holistic and accurate representation of the social sciences that highlights the contributions of minoritized people, characterizes their unique and complex positions as citizens, and counters the idea of "Whiteness as the quintessential and normalized idea of citizenship" (King, 2014, p. 8). Representation is critical not just to present an accurate and inclusive view of history, but because when students see themselves in the curriculum, learning becomes more purposeful and worthwhile; they have a more favorable perception of the subject (Busey & Russell, 2016) and demonstrate a greater commitment to the overall schooling experience (Antrop-Gonzàlez, 2006).

Busey and Walker (2017) called "for nuanced iterations of racialized citizenship in social studies curricula and research" (p.3) as they problematized the sanitized, scattered, and incoherent ways in which Black patriotism is presented in elementary social studies standards. They found "physical resistance, political thought and activism, and intellectual agency by Black people were sacrificed in favor of the master narrative of U.S. history and citizenship" (p.21). Consequently, as underscored by the CRT tenet of counterstories, it is imperative to consider how we best (re)frame narratives to counter the sanitized and incoherent representation in dominant narratives and expand the purview of the story of the United States so perspectives, experiences, and realities of racialized people are woven throughout the fabric of the story, not isolated to the margins (Takaki, 2008). Additionally, since counterstories are first-person accounts of people of color (Delgado & Stefancic, 2017; Ladson-Billings, 2021), in the re(framing) it is essential to ensure depictions of history and related fields are broadened to delineate histories, not just *about* people, but rather histories that are explicitly told through the voices, viewpoints, and experiences of people of color (Busey & Walker, 2017; King, 2016).

Many news outlets directed attention in late May and early June of 2021 to report on the 100th anniversary of the Tulsa Race Massacre. During this time many Americans expressed their disbelief over not knowing about the destruction that occurred in the Greenwood District during that time. We argue; however, the lack of awareness of the destruction of "Black Wall Street" is not at all surprising because the Tulsa Race Massacre receives limited attention or is completely excluded from most secondary social studies curricula (Samuels & Berson, 2012), regardless of the fact that hundreds of people were killed, thousands were left homeless, and generations of wealth were destroyed (Equal Justice Initiative, n.d.). Not only does the silence alienate students of color, it continues to perpetuate the singular, monolithic Eurocentric narrative of the United States, and results in an incomplete (and inaccurate) representation of United States history. As such, when (re)framing the narrative to embrace a critical race theoretical approach, while most curriculums quickly transition from WWI to the Roaring Twenties, educators should include counterstories that illustrate the rise in racial tension in the United States, which included the re-emergence of the Ku Klux Klan and heightened racialized violence, such as the horrific tragedy in Tulsa, where "none of the white rioters were convicted of any crime for their violent attack, and survivors of the violence received no compensation for lost property (Equal Justice Initiative, n.d.).

Counterstories: What It Is Not

When using a critical race theoretical approach in the social sciences, educators should reflect on how to (re)frame curriculum to include multiple perspectives and points of view, but also consider how the presentation of narratives is influenced and shaped by power. In October 2021, Gina Peddy, director of curriculum and instruction for Carroll Independent School District in Texas, drew national attention when she stated that teachers who have books about the Holocaust in their classroom should also have books from an "opposing" perspective (Hixenbaugh & Hylton, 2021). According to a recording, Peddy stated:

> Just try to remember the concepts of [House Bill] 3979," Peddy said in the recording, referring to a new Texas law that requires teachers to present multiple perspectives when discussing "widely debated and currently controversial" issues. "And make sure that if you have a book on the Holocaust," Peddy continued, "that you

have one that has an opposing, that has other perspectives. (Hixenbaugh & Hylton, 2021)

While the comment was vague and the administrator did not mention Holocaust denial, it is important to note many would consider Holocaust denial to be an opposing viewpoint of the Holocaust. Consequently, we must remember the danger in promoting false equivalences (Collins, 2019) when presenting opposing viewpoints, particularly when the event is a verified historical atrocity or precisely documented genocide. When teaching hard history, not only must educators provide students with context, they must also "make power dynamics visible" (Collins, 2019), providing opportunities to explore how privilege serves to empower some and tragically disempower others. Additionally, students should have opportunities to examine how oppressive and discriminatory policies, ordinances, and laws resulted in economic, political, and social disenfranchisement and, in the event of the Holocaust, the murder of six million Jewish men, women, and children in a systematic, state-sponsored genocide.

CRITICAL LITERACY

Like critical race theory, critical literacy is grounded in critical theory, which addresses the dynamics of power and oppression and explores strategies to advance society in a more equitable direction (Lynn et al., 2006). Critical literacy is an extension of critical pedagogy, which emphasizes critique of power structures, underscores the importance of praxis, and calls for increased equity and justice for people and communities who have been placed on the margins (Freire, 1993; Freire & Macedo, 1987).

Critical literacy is a pedagogical approach infused throughout courses of study that fosters the development of skills that utilize literacy to promote principles of democracy and social justice (Freire, 1993; Freire & Macedo, 1987; Riley, 2015) by encouraging the application of a critical lens to engage with texts and consider how texts and views are historically, culturally, and politically situated (Kang & Kline, 2020). Critical literacy encourages students to interrogate the relationship between language and power in texts and historical narratives, consider the socially constructed nature of power dynamics, take into account multiple perspectives, and contemplate actions that can be employed to promote increased justice (Lewison et al., 2015). Since the social norms and values of dominant groups are embedded in master narratives, critical literacy asserts the need to promote "reading the word and reading the world" (Kang & Kline, 2020, pp. 2–3) to deliberate how texts and historical narratives are socially constructed and positioned; thereby challenging claims of neutrality and universal truth (Freire, 1993; Freire & Macedo, 1987; Luke, 2012). It underscores how language is used to create, sustain, and interrupt power, inequality, and injustice in human relationships (Kurniawati et al., 2020); thereby providing students space and resources to make better sense of the world in which they live. Through engagement, inquiry, dialogue, and activism, students and teachers work in partnerships (Freire, 1993), where there is a reciprocal exchange of funds of knowledge drawn from the classroom, students' homes, and students' communities to facilitate learning that builds bridges between personal and educational spaces, thereby increasing the relevancy of the content (González et al., 2005).

Employing a critical lens to construct meaning, critical literacy can be used not only to assess the purpose and reliability of information (Kunnath & Jackson, 2019) but also to encourage analysis of what is being said, as well as what is *not* being said. "Students are challenged to look beyond the literal message, read between the lines, question the text, observe present and missing information, and consider the influence of the author's context and structure on the reader" (Kunnath & Jackson, 2019, p. 54), which makes critical literacy useful for evaluating biases based on the perspective and experience of the producer of the text or narrative (Giselsson, 2020; Luke, 2012). Accordingly, similar to critical race theory, critical literacy advances the need to incorporate multiple perspectives and examine how texts portray the life worlds and experiences of the learner (Luke, 2012). Additionally, complimenting the critical race theory tenet of counterstories, critical literacy asks how we consider "the possibility of using new literacies to change relations of power, both peoples' every-day social relations and the larger geopolitical and economic relations" (Luke, 2012, p. 9).

Using a Critical Race Theoretical Approach to Inform Critical Literacy

As Hannah-Jones (2021) emphasizes, "But while history *is* what happened, it is also, just as important, how we *think* about what happened and what we unearth and choose to remember about what happened" (p. xxvi). When shaping learning experiences to prepare students to think critically about the world, they should have the opportunity to critically examine texts, explore multiple perspectives to inform a more inclusive understanding of situations and events and be empowered to use their life experiences as text (Stribling, 2008). Such representation influences "a sense of ownership of, belonging in, and influence over the American story" (Hannah-Jones, 2021, p. xxiv) particularly when reading from a resistant perspective and using counter-texts that underscore marginalized experiences and social action (Behrman, 2006).

To actively counter historical visions that delineate people of color as "inconsequential" or "invisible" (Hannah-Jones, 2021, p. xviii), we support an approach to critical literacy that is informed by critical race theory to ensure race is centered in the discourse and examination of (in)equity and (in)justice. Let us position critical thinking and critical literacy in a way that takes "into account the deeply rooted racism that defines and delimits life in the United States" (Ladson-Billings, 2021, p. 3). Let us focus the lens so students not only consider how texts and views are historically, culturally, and politically situated (Kang & Kline, 2020), but how racialized views have shaped and sustained power structures and influenced what knowledge is visible, voiced, valued, and validated in the story of the United States. This is not to say educators should avoid or discount how other forms of oppression (ableism, antigay dispositions, anti-Semitism, classism, Islamophobia, or sexism, for example) have shaped and influenced history, but rather to ensure we foster inclusive representation and do not overlook (implicitly or explicitly) the complex, layered histories and legacies of both oppression and resistance connected to race and racism.

As we work to (re)frame historical narratives, King (2020) encourages us to consider how to challenge a "singular historical consciousness, which centers white people as the main protagonists and Black people and other non-Blacks as outliers of the American narrative" (p. 336). How do we acknowledge multiple perspectives and consider the insidious impact of racism in a way that decenters whiteness and centers the voices and perspectives of people of color? King (2020) emphasizes the need to teach "*through* Black history," not just "*about* Black history" (p. 336). He argues for the promotion and facilitation of Black historical consciousness, which "is an effort to understand, develop, and teach Black histories that recognize Black people's humanity. It emphasizes pedagogical practices that seek to reimagine the legitimacy, selection, and interpretation of historical sources" (p. 337). To promote reflective democratic thinking that underscores principles of equity and justice, curriculum must be reshaped and redefined to ensure the voices and experiences of Asian Americans, Black Americans, Hispanic Americans, and Native Americans are not just included, but positioned in a way that their complexity is valued and informs understanding of multidimensional historical narratives.

CONCLUSIONS

In *The Souls of Black Folk* (1903/2014), W. E. B. DuBois perceptively proclaimed, "the problem of the Twentieth Century is the problem of the color line" (p.3). Although DuBois originally wrote these words in 1903, we continue to bear witness to the insidious and deeply embedded implications of racial oppression and injustice in the United States as evidenced in educational opportunity gaps, employment discrimination, wage gaps, wealth disparities, home ownership, access to health care, mass incarceration, and police brutality (Sensoy & DiAngelo, 2017). Yet, currently, increased awareness of racialized disparities and injustices continues to be challenged by those who want to ignore or refuse to look into the "Veil" (DuBois, 1903/2014, p.3). As Hannah-Jones (2021) cautions in her discussion about the history and residual consequences of slavery, "The legacy of 1619 surrounds us, whether we acknowledge it or not" (p. xxix). To progress, as Stevenson (2021), founder and executive director of the Equal Justice Initiative in Montgomery, Alabama, contends, "we are at one of those critical moments in American history when we will either double down on romanticizing a false narrative about our violent past or accept that there is something better waiting for us, if we can learn to deal honestly with our history" (p. 282).

Racism is part of the history of the U.S; therefore, teaching history and related social sciences while avoiding, denying, or silencing this reality is not only incomplete, inaccurate, and dishonest, but serves as, yet, another form of institutionalized racism. As such, educators must not just promote diversity, equity, and inclusion in their classrooms, but rather rethink and reimagine educational justice. And we argue that employing a critical race theoretical approach to education, that centers the study of the permanence of racism and gives authentic voice to people and communities who have traditionally been placed on the margins, can serve as a strategy to actively counter the ringing of the silence and empower students to change the system. Let us foster collective responsibility to build the capacity of teachers and educational institutions to engage historically accurate and inclusive representation, actively counter misinformation and blind patriotism, and transform educational spaces to foster knowledge, skills, and dispositions to encourage reflective and just democracy.

REFERENCES

Abrams, L., & Moio, J. (2013). Critical race theory and the cultural competence dilemma in social work education. *Journal of Social Work Education, 45*(2), 245–261. doi:10.5175/JSWE.2009.200700109

Alabama Possible. (2020, May 21). *2020 Barriers to prosperity data sheet: 800,000 Alabamians live in poverty; Alabama fifth poorest state*. https://alabamapossible.org/2020/05/21/4480/

Alabama State Board of Education. (2021, August 12). *Preservation of intellectual freedom and non-discrimination in Alabama public schools*. Action Item G.2.o.

An, S. (2016). Asian Americans in American history: An AsianCrit perspective on Asian American inclusion in state U.S. history curriculum. *Theory & Research in Social Education, 44*(2), 244–276. doi:10.1080/00933104.2016.1170646

An, S. (2020). Learning racial literacy while navigating White social studies. *The Social Studies, 111*(4), 174–181. https://doi.org/10.1080/00377996.2020.1718584

Antrop-Gonzàlez, R. (2006). Toward the school as sanctuary concept in multicultural urban education: Implications for small high school reform. *Curriculum Inquiry, 36*(3), 273–301.

Au, W., Brown, A., & Calderón, D. (2016). *Reclaiming the multicultural roots of U.S. curriculum: Communities of color and official knowledge in education*. Teachers College Press.

Behrman, E. H. (2006). Teaching about language, power, and text: A review of classroom practices that support critical literacy. *Journal of Adolescent & Adult Literacy, 49*(6), 480–488.

Bell, D. (2002). Learning the three "I's" of America's slavery heritage. In P. Finkelman (Ed.), *Slavery and the Law* (pp. 29–42). Rowman & Littlefield.

Brown v. Board of Education. (1954). 347 U.S 483, 492.

Busey, C. L., & Russell, W. B. (2016). "We want to learn": Middle school Latino/a students discuss social studies curriculum and pedagogy. *Research in Middle Level Education, 39*(4), 1–20.

Busey, C. L., & Vickery, A. E. (2018). Black like me: Race pedagogy and Black elementary social studies teacher educators. In. S. B. Shear (Ed.), *(Re)Imagining elementary social studies: A controversial issues reader* (pp. 25–48). Information Age Publishing.

Busey, C. L., & Walker, I. (2017). A dream and a bus: Black critical patriotism in elementary social studies standards. *Theory & Research in Social Education, 45*(4), 456–488. http://doi:10.1080/00933104.2017.1320251

Cobb, J. (2021, September 13). The man behind critical race theory. *The New Yorker.* https://www.newyorker.com/magazine/2021/09/20/the-man-behind-critical-race-theory

Collins, C. (2019). *Why "both sides" of a story aren't enough.* Learning for Justice. https://www.learningforjustice.org/magazine/why-both-sides-of-a-story-arent-enough

Crain, T. P. (2017, March 6). *Suspensions feed the achievement gap in Alabama schools.* AL.com. https://www.al.com/news/2017/08/the_discipline_gap_why_suspens.html

Crain, T. P. (2021, June 11). *Alabama state school board: Keep critical race theory out of the classroom.* AL.com. https://www.al.com/news/2021/06/alabama-state-school-board-keep-critical-race-theory-out-of-classroom.html

Delgado, R., & Stefancic, J. (2017). *Critical race theory: An introduction.* New York University Press.

DuBois, W. E. B. (1903/2014). *The souls of Black folk.* Millennium.

Dunbar-Ortiz, R. (2015). *An indigenous peoples' history of the United States.* Beacon Press.

Educating for American Democracy (EAD). (2021). *Educating for American democracy: Excellence in history and civics for all learners.* iCivics, March 2, 2021. www.educatingforamericandemocracy.org

Equal Justice Initiative. (n.d.). On this day Jun 01, 1921: White mob in Tulsa destroys Black community; kills hundreds. *Equal Justice Initiative.* https://calendar.eji.org/racial-injustice/jun/1

Executive Order No. 13950. (September 22, 2020). https://www.federalregister.gov/documents/2020/09/28/2020-21534/combating-race-and-sex-stereotyping

Freire, P. (1993). *Pedagogy of the oppressed: New revised 29th anniversary edition.* Continuum.

Freire, P., & Macedo, D. (1987). *Literacy: Reading the word and the world.* Bergen & Garvin.

Giselsson, K. (2020). Critical thinking and critical literacy: Mutually exclusive? *International Journal for the Scholarship of Teaching and Learning, 14*(1), 5.

González, N., Moll, L.C., & Amanti, C. (2005). *Funds of knowledge: Theorizing practices in households, communities, and classrooms.* Lawrence Erlbaum Associates.

Hannah-Jones, N. (2021). Origins. In N. Hannah-Jones, C. Roper, I. Silverman, & J. Silverstein (Eds.), *The 1619 project* (pp. xvii–xxxiii). The New York Times Company.

Hixenbaugh, M., & Hylton, A. (2021, November 12). *Southlake school leader tells teachers to balance Holocaust books with 'opposing' views.* NBC News. https://www.nbcnews.com/news/us-news/southlake-texas-holocaust-books-schools-rcna2965

Ivey, K. (2021, October 21). *We have permanently BANNED Critical Race Theory in Alabama. We're focused on teaching our children how to read and write, not HATE.* [Tweet @kayiveyforgov]. Twitter. https://twitter.com/kayiveyforgov/status/1450880750665048067

Kang, G., & Kline, S. (2020). Critical literacy as a tool for social change: Negotiating tensions in a pre-service teacher education writing course. *Journal of Language and Literacy Education, 16*(2), 1–16.

King, L. J. (2014). When lions write history: Black history textbooks, African-American educators, & the alternative Black curriculum in social studies education, 1890–1940. *Multicultural Education, 22*(1), 2–11.

King, L. J. (2016). Black history is more than skin color. *Social Studies Journal, 36*(1), 72–78.

King, L. J. (2020). Black history is not American history: Toward a framework of Black historical consciousness. *Social Education, 84*(6), 335–341. https://www.socialstudies.org/sites/default/files/view-article-2020-12/se8406335.pdf

Kunnath, J., & Jackson, A. (2019). Developing student critical consciousness: Twitter as a tool to apply critical literacy in the English classroom. *Journal of Media Literacy Education, 11*(1), 52–74.

Kurniawati, N., Sugaryamah, D., & Hasanah, A. (2020). Proposing a model of critical literacy program for fostering Indonesian EFL students' critical thinking skills. *Journal of Education and Learning, 14(*2), 234–247.

Ladson-Billings, G. (1998). Just what is critical race theory and what's it doing in a nice field like education? *Journal of Qualitative Studies in Education, 11*(1), 7–24.

Ladson-Billings, G. (1999). Preparing teachers for diverse student populations: A critical race theory perspective. *Review of Research in Education, 24*, 211–247.

Ladson-Billings, G. (2003). *Critical race theory perspectives on the social studies: The profession, policies, and curriculum.* IAP.

Ladson-Billings, G. (2021). *Critical race theory in education: A scholar's journey.* Teachers College Press.

Ladson-Billings, G., & Tate, W. F. (1995). Toward a critical race theory of education. *Teachers College Record, 97*(1), 47–68.

Lewison, M., Leland, C., & Harst, J. C. (2015). *Creating critical classrooms: Reading and writing with an edge* (2nd ed.). Routledge.

Loewen, J. (2018). *Lies my teacher told me: Everything your American history textbook got wrong.* NEW PRESS.

Loving v. Virgina, 388 U.S. 1 (1967).

Luke, A. (2012). Critical literacy: Foundational notes. *Theory into Practice, 51*(1), 4–11.

Lynch, R. V. (2006). Critical-Race educational foundations: Toward democratic practices in teaching "other people's children" and teacher education. *Action in Teacher Education, 28*(2), 53–65.

Lynn, M. (1999). Toward a critical race pedagogy: A research note. *Urban Education, 33*(5), 606–627.

Lynn, M., Williams, A. D., Park, G., Benigno, G., & Mitchell, C. (2006). Critical theories of race, class, and gender in urban education. *ENCOUNTER: Education for Meaning and Social justice, 19*(2), 17–25.

Moseley, B. (2021, August 16). Alabama state school board passes resolution banning critical race theory. *Alabama Political Reporter.* https://www.alreporter.com/2021/08/16/alabama-state-school-board-passes-resolution-banning-critical-race-theory/

Mzezewa, T. (2021, September 19). Alabama begins removing racist language from its Constitution. *The New York Times.* https://www.nytimes.com/2021/09/19/us/alabama-constitution-racist.html

Nexstar Media Inc. (2021, October 14). *Alabama State Board of Education permanently bans critical race theory from being taught in public schools*. News 19: https://whnt.com/news/alabama-state-board-of-education-permanently-bans-critical-race-theory-from-being-taught-in-public-schools/

Nieto, S. (2017). Re-imagining multicultural education: New visions, new possibilities. *Multicultural Education Review,* 1–10.

Riley, K. (2015). Enacting critical literacy in English classrooms: How a teacher learning community supported critical inquiry. *Journal of Adolescent & Adult Literacy, 58*(5), 417–425.

Rodríguez, N. N. (2019). "Caught between two worlds": Asian American elementary teachers' enactment of Asian American history. *Educational Studies, 55*(2), 214–240.

Rothwell, J. (2016, June 29). *Brookings. Social mobility memos. Black and Hispanic kids get lower quality pre-K*. https://www.brookings.edu/blog/social-mobility-memos/2016/06/29/black-and-hispanic-kids-get-lower-quality-pre-k/

Samuels, G., & Berson, M. (2012). Uncovering marginalized topics using WebQuests: From Atlanta to the Zoot Suit Riots. *The Councilor: A Journal of the Social Studies, 73*(2), 5.

Sensoy, O., & DiAngelo, R. (2017). *Is everyone really equal: An introduction to key concepts in social justice education*. Teachers College Press.

Solórzano, D., & Yosso, T. (2000). Towards a critical race theory of Chicano and Chicana education. In C. Tejada, C. Martinez, & Z. Leonardo (Eds.), *Charting new terrains in Chicana(o)/Latina(o) education* (pp. 35–66). Hampton Press.

Solórzano, D., & Yosso, T. (2001). From racial stereotyping and deficit discourse toward a critical race theory in teacher education. *Multicultural Education, 9*(1), 2–8.

Stevenson, B. (2021). Punishment. In N. Hannah-Jones, C. Roper, I. Silverman, & J. Silverstein (Eds.), *The 1619 project* (pp. 275–283). The New York Times Company.

Stout, C., & Wilburn, T. (2022, February 1). CRT map: Efforts to restrict teaching racism and bias have multiplied across the U.S. *Chalkbeat*. https://www.chalkbeat.org/22525983/map-critical-race-theory-legislation-teaching-racism

Stribling, M. (2008). Using critical literacy practices in the classroom. *The NERA Journal, 44*(1), 34–38.

Takaki, R. (2008). *Different mirror: A history of multicultural America*. Back Bay Books.

Tate, W. (1997). Critical Race Theory and education: History, theory, and implications. *Review of Research in Education, 22*, 195–247.

Woodson, C. G. (1933). *The miseducation of the Negro*. Africa World Press.

CHAPTER 2

WHAT DO WE NEED TO KNOW NOW?

Racial and Technological Pedagogical Content Knowledge for Discussing Race in Online History Classrooms

Lightning Peter Jay
Binghamton University

Honest discussion has never been more difficult or more important. In 2020, COVID-19 forced many schools to impose remote-learning mandates, making the human act of talking to students a technological puzzle. That summer, the protests mourning George Floyd and decrying the long history of systemic racism in the United States made it clear that conversations about race, history, and the future of the country will not wait for a more convenient time. The twin pandemics of American racism and COVID-19 demand that social studies teachers rethink how and what they teach. This chapter looks at the expertise of one teacher endeavoring to maintain a pedagogy of discourse about race and the past in the face of jarring changes in the present.

Out of Turmoil: Catalysts for Re-learning, Re-Teaching, and Re-imagining History and Social Science, pages 21–39.
Copyright © 2023 by Information Age Publishing
www.infoagepub.com
All rights of reproduction in any form reserved.

Social Studies Discourse

Even under normal circumstances, classroom discussion is rare. Evidence that discussion supports a range of critical outcomes including the development of students' reasoning (Kohlmeier & Saye, 2019), identities (Brown et al., 2017; Goldberg, 2013), democratic citizenship (Parker & Hess, 2001), and subject matter knowledge (Engle & Conant, 2002; Goodwin et al., 2020) has almost always been accompanied by the caveat that most classrooms are not having substantive student-centered discussions (e.g., Bain, 2006; Cazden, 2001; Nystrand et al., 2003; Reisman, 2015). Teachers struggle to ignite discourse in every subject and discipline (e.g., Inagaki et al., 1998; Nystrand et al., 2003), but they appear particularly reluctant to engage students in discussion around race (Brown et al., 2017; SPLC, 2018). The avoidance of race talk is particularly concerning when considered alongside the fact that students of color and low-income students are less likely to experience high-quality discussions than their more affluent white peers (Campbell, 2008; Knowles, 2018), a trend that diminishes their learning opportunities and forecloses their capacity to investigate their own histories in class. Many teachers, especially White teachers, lack the racial literacy to navigate the stress of discussing race in the classroom (Stevenson, 2014), often resorting to "color muteness" and avoidance (Pollock, 2004). Increasingly, scholarship is interrogating how racial avoidance serves to sustain racial educational inequalities and can become integrated within the identity of White teachers (e.g., Crowley, 2016; Jupp et al., 2016).

Race in Social Studies

Race and education are newly omnipresent on the front page of newspapers, thanks in part to the national attention garnered by the protests against police violence and the moral panic about critical race theory, but they have long been fixtures in journals of social studies research. The aims of social studies are inextricable from understanding race, as learning about the past and the present, participating in deliberative democracy, and developing participatory social identity in the United States all demand frank discussion of race (Ladson-Billings, 2003; Nagda et al., 2003; Zúñiga et al., 2014). The bulk of the research to-date has been dedicated to outlining the deficiencies of existing practices for helping students develop a critical antiracist understanding of the world. In curriculum materials (Brown & Au, 2014; Ladson-Billings, 2003, Woyshner & Schocker, 2015), standards (Anderson & Metzger, 201; King & Chandler, 2016), and pedagogy (Chandler & Branscombe, 2015; Reisman et al., 2020; Wills, 2019), there is a surfeit of literature demonstrating the ways educators fail to teach about race. Less developed, however, is investigation into how teachers successfully engage in productive teaching about race. Hawkman (2019) called teachers' situated instructional actions regarding teaching race *racial pedagogical decision making*. This terminology draws attention to ways that students' opportunities to learn about race emerge in relationship to teachers' classroom actions, a framing that acknowledges that teachers' enactment extends beyond the boundaries set by curriculum (Reisman & Jay, In press; Remillard, 2005). Teachers' resources and lesson plans provide a limited view into how their teaching unfolds. Research exploring how teachers who are successful in teaching about race reveals that powerful teaching emerges from identities (Crowley, 2016; Salinas & Castro, 2010; Vickery, 2015), knowledges, (e.g., Castro et al., 2015) and pedagogical practices (e.g., Martell, 2015; Parkhouse, 2018) that distinguished these teachers from their colormute colleagues. This body of research is growing and increasingly being connected to teacher education (e.g., Demoiny, 2018; Hughes & Marhatta, 2021). Further research is still needed; however, both to extend our knowledge of how teachers do race in social studies and how the professional body of knowledge that undergirds antiracist teaching operates in situations when teachers undergo contextual changes, such as those brought on by the twin pandemics.

Online Learning

Unlike teaching about race and racism, online learning is a new domain of research in social studies, one that the field has just begun to examine. To date, research on technology use in social studies education has either focused on technology as tools for (e.g., research on digitized primary sources including Rodriguez et al., 2020) or objects of instruction (e.g., research on developing students' online civic reasoning including McGrew, 2021). Like these empirical studies, most of the existing theoretical frameworks for technology use in social studies position technology as an element within a traditional classroom (e.g., Bolick, 2017; Hammond & Manfra, 2009; Hicks et al., 2014), rather than a medium through which instruction takes place. Examination of online instruction is rare. Some work has occurred in higher education (e.g., Kireev et al., 2019) or in the use of online tools to facilitate short-term distance learning experiences (e.g., Freedman et al., 2018), but this research is preliminary and it is unclear how it might translate to K–12 settings where instruction primarily occurs online. In short, there is a dearth of research preparing social studies to shift to virtual instruction. In one of the first articles to discuss COVID era social studies, Manfra et al. (2021) reported that establishing classroom environments capable of sustaining academic dialogue was one of the greatest challenges facing teachers as they journeyed online. This study steps into that challenge and examines an experienced teacher's pedagogy to understand the overlapping forms of knowledge undergirding her work to facilitate antiracist online discussions.

Theoretical Framework

Teachers' instructional choices during classroom discussions have long been theorized as an expression of their *pedagogical content knowledge* (PCK), "that special amalgam of content and pedagogy that is uniquely the province of teachers" (Shulman, 1987, p. 8). PCK has proven durable because its broad categories describe a wide variety of teaching situations and domains of teacher knowledge (Ball et al., 2008). But some social studies scholars have contended that PCK is too broad. Its colorblind language may elide precisely the kinds of knowledge required for anti-racist teaching (Dyches & Boyd, 2017; King & Chandler, 2016). *Racial pedagogical content knowledge* (RPCK) injects critical race theory into PCK and explicitly calls for teachers to have "a working *racial* knowledge of how race operates within social science, from [critical race theory] perspectives" (Chandler, 2015, p. 5, italics in original). Within this framework, teachers' capacity to help students understand contemporary discussions about policing, the differential effects of the coronavirus, or any other way that race shapes our social and political lives, reflects not only their knowledge of the topics and generic skill as pedagogues but also their knowledge about race. Teachers' decisions about what to discuss and how to facilitate those discussions reveal their RPCK.

RPCK alone is not enough. While the lurch towards remote instruction caused by COVID-19 may have placed a spotlight on the necessity of technological fluency, even teachers in traditional classrooms work with an array of technology, ranging from laptops and digital whiteboards to old-fashioned paper and pencil. Just as RPCK articulates teachers' racial literacies, *technological pedagogical content knowledge* (TPACK) specifies the knowledge teachers draw upon to integrate technology tools into their instruction (Koehler & Mishra, 2009; Mishra & Koehler, 2006). TPACK research has explored the way that teachers' knowledge of technology is in continuous conversation with their knowledge of pedagogy and content (Archambault, 2016; Baran et al., 2017; Chai et al., 2013). Because teaching occurs with and through technology, teachers' capacity to imagine pedagogical strategies is inextricable from their facility with technology. Comfort with technology appears to open cognitive space for teachers, allowing them to devote greater attention to instruction (Willermark & Pareto, 2020). Yet, teachers' preparedness to utilize technology is profoundly variable, and many, perhaps even most, are not prepared to deploy new technologies flexibly (Farjon et al., 2019; Kim et al., 2013). In an online schooling context where technology becomes the medium of instruction, even teachers with the greatest RPCK must possess TPACK for their teaching to reach students.

RPCK and TPACK are emergent frameworks. Not only has their relationship never been studied, but most research on these frameworks has primarily worked in cognitive terms, rarely focusing on enacted knowledge, and generally relying on teachers' self-reported knowledge (Willermark, 2018). As it stands, RPCK and TPACK formulate their critique of PCK in terms of content, naming concepts that PCK does not explicitly state, but this approach may replicate some of the existing shortcomings of PCK. Scholars have taken issue with PCK for its treatment of knowledge "as information without sufficient regard for how it manifests itself as action" (Settlage, 2013, p. 9). Teaching is an enacted profession. TPACK has also been criticized for not attending to issues of equity, justice, and race (Voithofer &

Nelson, 2020), making it all the more important that it be placed in conversation with RPCK. For RPCK and TPACK to meet their explanatory potential, they must illustrate knowledgeable action as well as thought.

This study follows one expert teacher as she engaged her students in classroom discussions about racialized history in an online setting. Her decision-making and enacted practice exist at the intersection of PCK, RPCK, and TPACK. I ask, how did this teacher adjust her pedagogy around racialized history to fit an online environment? And what does this decision-making reveal about the body of professional knowledge required to engage in this kind of teaching?

METHODS

Data Collection and Sources

This case study follows the work of an expert teacher of African American history, who I will call Alexandra. Philadelphia is one of the only cities to require that high school students take African American history (Sanders, 2009). This history course provides a rare opportunity to center and explore race over the course of the year, but offers minimal curricular support, guidance, or oversight (Toliver, 2014). Perhaps even more than other courses, African American history relies on teachers' expertise and Alexandra is an expert. Prior to COVID, Alexandra's career had been remarkably stable. She spent the first eight years of her career in a single charter management organization teaching the curriculum to the same grade level. In that time, she had been recognized as an expert teacher. In addition to teaching the course, Alexandra had trained new teachers, won grants from national education agencies, and been named the "content lead" by her network, sharing her materials and leading professional development (PD) with the roughly dozen other teachers covering the same curriculum at the network's other high schools.

Alexandra loved teaching African American history. She called the curriculum her "second child" and spoke at length about the importance of the course for her students, whom she characterized as "99.9% Black of African descent," and for herself as a "mixed" woman with a Black Trinidadian father and White mother. Alexandra's own identity was an important presence in the class. Every year she started her first day of class with the story of her childhood memory of being called the "n-word" by a White friend's grandmother. That experience, her first time being labeled with that slur, motivated Alexandra. She wanted to make sure students had "the knowledge so that when they face racism in the world, they have a better understanding of it." Sharing that story allowed students to understand the vision for the course as well as Alexandra's positionality. After telling her story, she invited students to share their own experiences with racism. That personal connection was the heart of her teaching. When asked if she could imagine teaching other subjects, Alexandra quickly dismissed the idea saying, "I don't want to talk about White people."

In 2020, her ninth year of teaching, Alexandra was required to radically redesign her teaching to respond to the shift to online instruction, the changes in the national consciousness about race and history, and the consequence of her network's decision to hold history classes twice per week instead of daily. I observed four of Alexandra's classes during the 2020–2021 school year and interviewed her twice. The interviews bookended the observations and focused on Alexandra's pedagogical decision-making in response to instructional dilemmas (Lampert, 1985). Course sessions were selected for observation based on Alexandra's recommendation that they would feature substantial episodes of student-centered discussion. The first class I observed was devoted to discussing the 2020 murder of Breonna Taylor and the exoneration of the police officers who killed her. This class was the second of two days studying Taylor's death and part of a recurring segment in which every quarter Alexandra assigned students an essay responding to a contemporary problem of race. The second and third classes I observed were part of a four-session arc culminating in a mock trial of Nat Turner. I observed the initial introduction of the mini-unit and the trial day. The final class I observed was a stand-alone day on the 1857 Dred Scott decision. This class utilized materials from the previous year that Alexandra had developed as part of a PD I led on text-based historical inquiry (Jay, 2020). As part of that PD, she had filmed her in-person instruction of that lesson, which allowed for pre-and post-pandemic comparison.

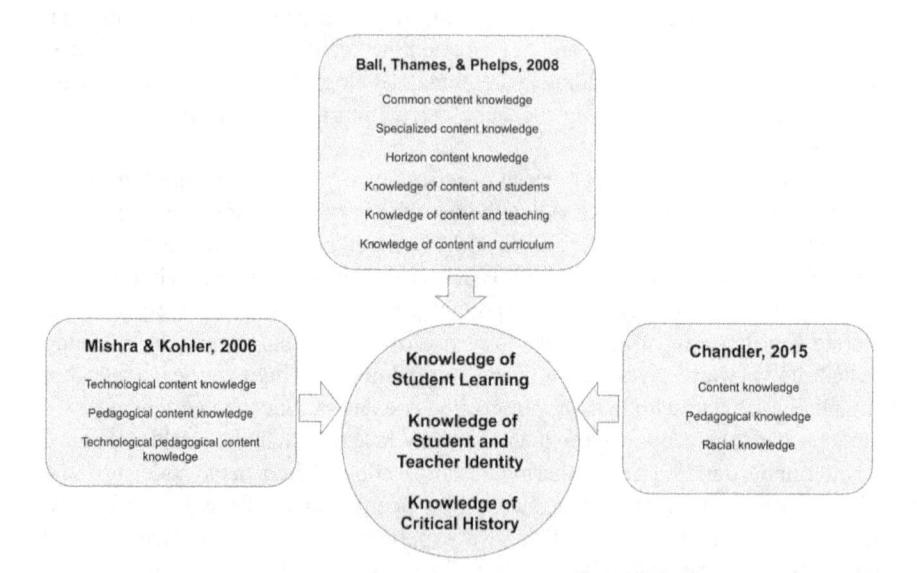

FIGURE 2.1. Transformation of a Priori Domains of Pedagogical Content Knowledge to Inductive Codebook.

Data Analysis

Data analysis crosswalked codes from existing descriptions for PCK (Ball et al., 2008), RPCK (Chandler, 2015), and TPACK (Koehler et al., 2014) to identify intersections in descriptions of teacher knowledge (Figure 2.1). The emergent codes from this analysis were applied to transcripts of Alexandra's interviews in an iterative coding process to determine how Alexandra expressed the dimensions of her knowledge (Miles et al., 2018). That coding, in turn, informed a secondary coding system for the observational videos highlighting how these domains of knowledge were enacted in the classroom. This process yielded three prominent domains of knowledge that recurred across observations and interviews: *knowledge of student learning, knowledge of student and teacher identity,* and *knowledge of critical history* (Table 2.1). These knowledge domains surfaced in each of the courses and interviews. In the findings below I illustrate how these domains

TABLE 2.1. Codebook

Domains of Knowledge	Definition	Example
Knowledge of student learning	Teacher comments demonstrating an awareness of students' learning experiences within the classroom including an attention to the roles of both technology and race as mediators.	"I actually changed my research paper question because I just struggled with teaching this unit online." "I also think it's really important to talk about resistance because kids get so sick of hearing about slavery all the time. I like to talk about Black people fighting back" "There are some kids…[who] love virtual learning…but like, for me by now, I would know, with certain kids, if they struggled with reading, they struggled with note taking…It's also like really weird to get to know these kids pretty personally."
Knowledge of student and teacher identity	Teacher comments demonstrating an awareness of student and teacher identities as raced, classed, gendered, and otherwise inscribed in social hierarchies.	"I'm mixed. My dad's Trinidadian." "I think I've had kids share in class about family members who have been locked up, about negative experience they've had with the police. I think it would be different if I was teaching it to a group of White children. But I'm not. The circumstances are I'm teaching it to a population that's 99.9% Black of African descent."
Knowledge of critical history	Teacher comments demonstrating an awareness of critical perspectives on history including an attention to the connection between the past and contemporary inequality.	"Every report period, we just like, pause like learning about history every day. So like, I want them to develop strategies to confront the issue, issues of race. So that's why they wrote about how to fix the probation system." "The kids should be learning more about the history of institutional racism and focusing on the fact that the court said Black people were property, that they had no rights, and called them inferior."

of knowledge emerged in Alexandra's online instruction. Because Alexandra indicated that "the cutting of the content" was the hardest part of transferring her teaching online, I interpreted online instruction as a form of forced-choice that heightened the significance of Alexandra's decision-making, placing her in a position where each decision about what and how to teach was, at least in part, an indicator of her instructional priorities.

FINDINGS

Lightening the Load

Alexandra had to ask her students to do less. Moving from five days a week to two days a week gave her no choice. Beyond deciding which days of class were essential, Alexandra pared down the instruction within each class. Her decision-making about what to keep hinged on Alexandra's *knowledge of student learning*. Alexandra's class on the Dred Scott decision illustrated the tough choices she faced. In the year prior to the pandemic, her class moved swiftly. In under three minutes, Alexandra introduced the landmark 1857 case and prompted students to predict whether the court would grant the enslaved Scott's petition for emancipation (they were certain the court would rule against Scott). By minute five, students were reading the text of Supreme Court Chief Justice Taney's decision. Ten minutes into the class, Alexandra had confirmed students' basic comprehension of the text, emphasized the far-ranging consequences of the court's decision to deny Scott's standing to bring the case on the grounds that people of African ancestry could not be citizens of the United States, and prompted students to engage in a turn and talk completing the sentence stem "This decision is horrible because…" If the efficiency with which Alexandra brought students into an explicit critique was not an already effective display of her RPCK, her next set of moves showed the depth of her knowledge. After ensuring that students were appropriately outraged, she presented students brief biographies of the justices who ruled on the decision. Once students realized that most of the justices were born in northern "free" states, the remaining half-hour of class centered on the question, "What does this tell us about the North?" The bulk of the lesson then centered on a robust critique of the North's complicity in southern racism.

Alexandra's online version of the same lesson took students in a different direction. Again, she asked students to anticipate the court's ruling and prompted them to read the same excerpt from the court decision. This time, however, Alexandra decided to spend more time giving the class background information before reading and asked students to read aloud instead of independently. As they read, she peppered them with comprehension questions. They finished reading the text 36 minutes after the start of class, leaving only 24 minutes for discussion. Alexandra chose not to introduce the biographies of the justice, instead asking students "Which claim is the most important" and "Why did the Dred Scott decision cause more tension between the North and South?"

The difference between the two versions of the lessons stems from Alexandra's TPACK and influences her RPCK. The primary change to the lesson is the amount of scaffolding afforded to the online students. They received more in-class background knowledge, were supported during the act of reading, and asked questions that were more directly related to comprehending the text. Alexandra did not make these modifications because she knew her students were worse readers than their peers from the year before, she made them because she simply did not know. The shift online had given her less time with each student, by virtue of reducing the frequency of the course sessions and prevented her from circulating around the room to check in with every student as they read as she would have in a normal year. Although this class took place in January, Alexandra did not feel confident in her assessment of each student's capacity. She had a clear mental model for how students learn, a schema for *knowledge of students' learning,* but her capacity to enact that knowledge was hampered by her circumstances. The following sections will explore how Alexandra was able to keep the critical dialogue of her course alive despite the limitations of moving online.

Caring for the Kids

Alexandra retooled her class by focusing on students' emotions. She mastered the technological tools that allowed her to connect with kids, fluidly switching between private and public chats, sharing music and videos of her son to brighten the mood, and kept class dynamic by altering the means of participation between chatting, polls, and vocal participation. She scrapped tools that did not facilitate that connection, for instance, she stopped using breakout rooms a few weeks into the semester because she felt they fostered a space of disconnect that she couldn't access. Those technological adaptations reflected the breadth of Alexandra's *knowledge of students' identities*. Alexandra fulfilled her commitment "to incorporate more moments of joy and like really build a sense of community" by building around Black culture. She had students curate playlists of Black artists, read African folk tales at the start of class, and rename their classes with names drawn from Black history and culture, such as "The Freedom Riders" and "The Woo."

Alexandra understood the cultivation of joy as a necessary element of her teaching, particularly given her curriculum and context. She said, "I think racial stress is a real thing. And for kids who are already in communities of trauma, asking them to then study it deeply is a big ask on top of that." While her routines worked to create a joyful atmosphere and validate students' Black identities, Alexandra had a harder time making the content of her course joyful. As she pared down her course to move online, Alexandra made sure to maintain her most fun lesson: the mock trial. In the past, she had held trials of George Washington, Abraham Lincoln, and Kanye West (charged with the reckless endangerment of Black history and culture). This year, she placed Nat Turner on trial and asked students to take on a variety of roles (including witnesses, prosecution, and defense) as the class investigated the extent to which Turner could be considered guilty for his role in leading a rebellion against slave owners in Virginia in 1831. Alexandra promised students the trial would be "so much fun" and encouraged them to use accents, dress up, or create props such as painting a tissue red to make a "bloody" handkerchief.

Alexandra's introduction to Turner and the trial was playful, even jocular. After asking students whether they would participate in a slave rebellion, Alexandra polled the class on whether it was ever right for an enslaved person to murder a White baby. The ethical question quickly became personal as students speculated and Alexandra prodded about whether they would personally murder White babies. Modeling, Alexandra mused, "A lot of Black children died during slavery. So, for White people to lose just a few babies. You know, that's maybe nothing in comparison. They could. They could lose a couple babies." Titters and accusations of ruthlessness followed. After class, Alexandra reflected, "I just do whatever I can to get kids engaged...When you're like, 'Whoa, killing a White child,' even a kid in the back corner of zoom [is going to sit up]." The trial simultaneously demonstrated Alexandra's commitment to joy and the pedagogical limitations that come into view as the boundary between playful and inappropriate is approached. Asking Black students to role play as slave owners, joke about murder, and potentially condemn the leader of a rebellion might be seen as undermining students' learning or exposing them to distress. Alexandra was aware of the tension here, "Teaching African American history, am I doing it in a positive enough way? I always feel like I am not. But then I'm like, What do I cut from the curriculum? . . . What else possibly could I teach in addition to that, so that kids walk away feeling good? I feel like, I don't know."

The trial was fun and engaging. It broke up the parade of oppression that can mark the history of slavery, but joy is only one of the emotions that need cultivation within an African American history. Alexandra's *knowledge of student and teacher identity* included understanding her own positionality in relationship to students and content. She strategically offered emotional disclosure to foster connection and make a space for the pain and anger that arose during her class. Alexandra's choices to share her taste in music, retell adorable stories about her toddler, and join in students' laughter during the silly moments of the trial were in-line with common teacher disclosures. Her decision to be open about her emotional reaction to the class's content; however, was unusual. When she read the Dred Scott verdict, she told students that the court's decision caused her to "get in my feels...[reading this] makes me want to close my door and curse." When she discussed Breonna Taylor's death, she told students, that this case prompted "my anger and what pisses me off. Killer cops. This is going to piss you off." Alexandra's disclosure built a connection between her own positionality vis-à-vis the content and her students. It allowed her to anticipate and validate students' emotions even without demanding that they publicly share online. Students recognized and reflected on that disclosure. At one point, an administrator visited the class, which prompted one student to let Alexandra know, "There are White people here!" Alexandra was not concerned about administrators seeing her teaching, but her students' mock concern demonstrated an understanding that Alexandra was an insider to their conversation. Despite teaching through a screen, Alexandra ensured that her students could see her and be seen by her. Alexandra's pedagogy of care was a form of radical authenticity welcoming students' whole selves.

Keeping it Current

As Alexandra built her curriculum out of students' lives and experiences, she committed to connecting the course to the present. Although the School District of Philadelphia does not require the African American history course to cover content past the Civil Rights Movement, Alexandra maintained "the year-long goal is for students to come up with strategies to address issues of race today." She made that explicit for students by assigning quarterly essays about contemporary issues. In the quarter I observed, students' quarterly essays stemmed from two lessons about the murder of Breonna Taylor. The first class was largely dedicated to building background knowledge about the circumstances that led police officers to fire dozens of shots into Taylor's home as she slept. The second class focused on the aftermath of Taylor's killing, the indictment of a single officer for wanton endangerment, the payment of $12 million to Taylor's family, and the promise and problems of police reform.

Teaching Taylor was not an easy choice. Creating and teaching the lesson demonstrated Alexandra's *knowledge of critical history*, and her capacity to help students use history to interpret and engage in the present from a critical perspective. The present is often tricky terrain for history teachers. There is no curriculum for current events and, for students of African American history, no cap on calamity. As Alexandra introduced the mini-unit, her students offered challenges and suggestions, saying, "Why are we talking about Breonna Taylor and not George Floyd, Walter Wallace or Ahmed Arbery?" and "Let's talk stop talking about all the bad stuff. Let's talk about something good." Faced with contradictory requests to cover a multitude of murders and to avoid trauma, Alexandra assured the class that "I specifically picked Breonna Taylor because I think the case is really interesting. I want to talk about a female life being taken," and promised that students could vote on the current event to study next quarter. Over the course of the period, Alexandra worked to position students as change-makers, asking them "What should the justice system do to prevent an unnecessary death like Breonna Taylor's?" and prompting them to evaluate a list of possible options ("A. Getting rid of no-knock warrants; B. Better police training; C. Allowing tougher charges to be brought up against police officers…; F. Something else."). At the same time, this optimism abutted students' own experiences with law enforcement, such as the student who related a long anecdote from her personal experience that began "I've seen plenty situations, situations or like witnessed plenty situations where if someone got caught…," as well as Alexandra's personal content knowledge about the history of policing in the United States. When the concept of the police's duty to serve and protect arose, Alexandra commented,

> I 97.9% agree...the police is supposed to, like de-escalate and protect you. As an African American history teacher, though, knowing the history of the police...The police was not formed to protect Black people. The police was formed to chase down enslaved African Americans that ran away. That was their initial job, the exact opposite of protecting Black people. So it is no surprise to me, as time goes on, we still don't have police officers that put Black people's lives first to protect them.

Her interjection highlighted the delicate balance Alexandra was negotiating. She was attempting to turn the talk over to students while maintaining foundational knowledge about policing. She was trying to support an interpretation of the present without introducing uncertainty about the past. And she was trying to support students' emotions without shying away from painful truths. All of this is feeding into an essay where students can extend the conversation further.

Alexandra's teaching is ambitious as it is difficult. Most history classes avoid the present. Placing this class prior to the Nat Turner and Dred Scott classes, Alexandra reversed the typical chronological march of history classes. She worked from the present towards the past, just as she worked from her students towards the social. This instructional design mirrored her decision to begin the course with her own personal experience with racism. Alexandra's *knowledge of critical history* applied the past to the present, asking students to understand the plight and imagine progress.

DISCUSSION

An expert teacher engaged in challenging work, Alexandra opened the door to the digital classroom. The first lesson of her class is that engaged, student-centered, critical discourses about race that connect past to present can occur in an online class. Looking further, we can see that Alexandra possessed complex bodies of knowledge about technology, teaching, and racial history that enabled her teaching. Supporting other teachers in building similar bodies of knowledge will require further articulation and exploration to see how the various concepts interact and manifest in teacher enactment.

The social studies literature offers a number of languages to describe Alexandra's teaching. We might call her teaching an example of leveraging multiple "resource pedagogies" to affirm students' identities and extend their critiques of the social structures that surround them (Castro, 2021). Her fluid incorporation of the histories of oppression, joy, African continuity, and resistance could be understood to embody a Black historical consciousness (King, 2020). Or we might focus on Alexandra's capacity to name, question, and demystify as exemplifying critical history pedagogy (Parkhouse, 2018). What the literature lacks, however, is a comprehensive framework that situates the various bodies of professional knowledge in relationship to one another. PCK once purported to be that umbrella term, but it may not be sufficient to capture Alexandra's knowledge of learning, students and self, and critical history.

The three domains of knowledge that I identified in Alexandra's teaching expose the uneasy relationship between PCK, RPCK, and TPACK. Ball et al. (2009) had theorized "knowledge of content and students" as an element of PCK. What I call *knowledge of students' learning* is analogous but highlights the ways that Alexandra's knowledge of students was mediated by RPCK and TPACK as technological limitations impinged upon Alexandra's ability to engage in discourse around racial history. The category *knowledge of student and teacher identity* also has some relationship to the "knowledge of content and students" category but highlights how Alexandra was attentive to the explicitly racialized elements of students' identity. It also indicates that Alexandra's understanding of her own positionality is a critical element of her professional knowledge. Neither PCK, RPCK, nor TPACK have previously named teachers' knowledge of self as part of their professional knowledge. *Knowledge of critical history* draws near some of Ball, Thames, and Phelps' content knowledge categories, but the connection to the present defies the tradition of connecting PCK to academic disciplines, as academic historians are wary of "presentism" (Wineburg, 2001). TPACK has no comment on the content of instruction and RPCK does not name current events as a domain of content knowledge (Chandler, 2015), although Chandler and Hawley's (2017) exploration of intersections between inquiry pedagogy and RPCK might open a space for connecting past to present from an RPCK perspective.

In positing the above categories, I do not mean to comprehensively describe all that Alexandra knows about teaching. Like other profiles of ambitious teachers (e.g., Castro, 2021; Parkhouse, 2018), it is important to remember that this portrait is incomplete. The four hours I spent observing Alexandra's class are a small fraction of the time she spent with students over the course of the year. Her teaching is contextualized within her specific time, place, person, and school, and what works for her may not travel seamlessly to other teachers and students. Rather, I believe these categories highlight how much about teacher knowledge is still unknown.

Even the framing of Alexandra's work as "knowledge" may be misleading. PCK has been criticized for portraying knowledge as static and intellectual (Settlage, 2013). RPCK seems to verge on recreating the same critique. Its perspectives on the content of social studies and the historical processes of the social sciences constitute a new alternative content knowledge, but the RPCK framework does not explicitly name how this knowledge would appear in enactment. If this knowledge were to be codified in a way that certified a "correct" understanding of the past, it might have the effect of foreclosing some areas of student exploration. In some writing, the authors of RPCK appear to be shifting to call RPCK a "stance" (Chandler & Hawley, 2017), which suggests some wariness about reducing RPCK to intellectual content knowledge. Other scholars have offered "racial pedagogical decision making" (Hawkman, 2019) as a frame to highlight what teachers do rather than know. TPACK, however, appears to conceptualize knowledge differently. In Alexandra's work TPACK manifests as a kind of technical proficiency. Rather than knowledge of something, it is a means towards an end. Koehler and Mishra (2009) articulated TPACK as the intersection of technological knowledge and pedagogical content knowledge, but it remains unclear what kind of knowing TPACK describes, how it intersects with other knowing like RPCK, and how it can be observed beyond self-report (Willermark, 2018).

Yet, despite the potential limitations of discussing teaching in terms of knowledge, it is clear that Alexandra is knowledgeable. Her teaching was guided by a coherent instructional philosophy that included both an understanding of the relationships between the history of American racism and present social experiences and a vision for how opportunities for inquiry, analysis, and argumentation prepared students to confront the world. Alexandra's professional knowledge was not purely intellectual, it was embodied and enacted. Her success does not come from simply understanding her positionality or caring about her students and content. She was successful because she exposed her positionality and demonstrated her care. If Alexandra's enactment is an expression of her knowledge, it offers hope for teacher education. Knowledge can be shared, refined, and extended.

Alexandra's instruction suggests three recommendations for creating critical caring classrooms. First, focus on connection. Technology tools are often prized for their capacity to deliver content efficiently or to prompt independent thinking (Hammond & Manfra, 2009), but Alexandra's classroom came alive when she centered student voice, identity, and inquiry. Inquiry pedagogy (Chandler & Hawley, 2017) and authentic intellectual work (Chandler et al., 2015) offer starting points for integrating RPCK into student-centered teaching. Beginning with students' ideas, safety, and circumstances opens the online classroom and makes discourse and learning possible. Second, teachers should center critique. Starting with students cannot mean coddling them. Even for a teacher as experienced Alexandra, finding the appropriate balance between care and challenge was tricky, but keeping her course critical and contemporary was an essential element of her pedagogy. Her willingness to confront difficult emotions in the past and the present made social studies meaningful. Alexandra's students reciprocated her trust in demonstrations of care and in their willingness to engage with the materials. The best instruction, online and in-person, lets students grapple with the problems of the past and generate solutions for the future. Finally, teachers hoping to capitalize on Alexandra's example ought to embrace enactment. They might ask themselves how they make their own positionality visible and accessible to students in class? How do they express their care for students? How do they ensure that students are getting chances to take ownership of the course's big ideas? These values are not unique, but they can get stuck in teachers' heads. To be meaningful, they must reach students by coming to life in physical and digital classrooms. Future research can further articulate and evaluate the domains of professional knowledge, but the work of developing that knowledge begins with teachers doing their work in the present.

REFERENCES

Archambault, L. (2016). Exploring the use of qualitative methods to examine TPACK. In M. C. Herring, M. J. Koehler, & P. Mishra (Eds.), *Handbook of technological pedagogical content knowledge (TPACK) for educators* (pp. 65–86). Routledge.

Bain, R. B. (2006). Rounding up unusual suspects: Facing the authority hidden in the history classroom. *The Teachers College Record, 108*(10), 2080–2114.

Ball, D. L., Thames, M. H., & Phelps, G. (2008). Content knowledge for teaching: What makes it special. *Journal of Teacher Education, 59*(1), 389–407.

Baran, E., Bilici, S. C., Sari, A. A., & Tondeur, J. (2019). Investigating the impact of teacher education strategies on preservice teachers' TPACK. *British Journal of Educational Technologies, 50*(1), 357–370. https://doi.org/10.1111/bjet.12565

Bolick, C. M. (2017). The diffusion of technology into the social studies. In M. Manfra and C. M. Bolick (Eds.), *The Wiley handbook of social studies research* (pp. 499–517). Wiley and Sons.

Brown, A. L., & Au, W. (2014). Race, memory, and master narratives: A critical essay on U.S. curriculum history. *Curriculum Inquiry, 44*, 358–389.

Brown, A. L., Bloome, D., Morris, J. E., Power-Carter, S., & Willis, A. I. (2017). Classroom conversations in the study of race and the disruption of social and educational inequalities: A review of research. *Review of Research in Education, 41*(1), 453–476. https://doi.org/10.3102/0091732X16687522

Campbell, D. E. (2008). Voice in the classroom: How an open classroom climate fosters political engagement among adolescents. *Political Behavior, 30*, 437–454.

Castro, A. J., Hawkman, A. M., & Diaz, J. (2015). Teaching race in high school social studies: Lessons from the field. In P. T. Chandler (Ed.), *Doing Race in social studies: Critical perspectives* (pp. 127–152). Information Age Publishing.

Castro, E. (2021). The case for leveraging multiple resource pedagogies: Teaching about racism in a secondary history classroom. *Teaching and Teacher Education, 109*(1). https://doi.org/10.1016/j.tate.2021.103567

Cazden, C. B. (2001). *Classroom discourse: The language of teaching and learning* (2nd ed.). Heinemann.

Chai, C. S., Koh, J. H. L., & Tsai, C. C. (2013). A review of technological pedagogical content knowledge. *Journal of Educational Technology & Society, 16*(2), 31–51.

Chandler, P. T. (2015). What does it mean do "do race" in social studies? Racial pedagogical content knowledge. In P. T. Chandler (Ed.), *Doing race in social studies: Critical perspectives* (pp. 61–87). Information Age Publishing.

Chandler, P. T., & Branscombe, A. (2015). White social studies. In P. T. Chandler (Ed.), *Doing race in social studies: Critical perspectives* (pp. 1–10). Information Age Publishing.

Chandler, P. T., Branscombe, A., Hester, L. (2015). Using authentic intellectual work and critical race theory to teach about race in social studies. In P. T. Chandler (Ed.), *Doing race in social studies: Critical perspectives* (pp. 153–169). Information Age Publishing.

Chandler, P. T., & Hawley, T. S. (2017). Using racial pedagogical content knowledge and inquiry pedagogy to re-imagine social studies teaching and learning. In P. T. Chandler & T. S. Hawley (Eds.), *Race lessons: Using inquiry to teach about race in social studies* (pp. 1–16). Information Age Publishing.

Crowley, R. M. (2016). Transgressive and negotiated White racial knowledge. *International Journal of Qualitative Studies in Education, 29*(8), 1016–1029.

Demoiny, S. B. (2018). Social studies teacher educators who do race work: A racial-pedagogical-content-knowledge analysis. *Social Studies Research and Practice, 13*(3), 330–334.

Dyches, J., & Boyd, A. (2017). Foregrounding equity in teacher education: Toward a model of social justice pedagogical and content knowledge. *Journal of Teacher Education, 68*(1), 476–490.

Engle, R. A., & Conant, F. R. (2002). Guiding principles for fostering productive disciplinary engagement: Explaining an emergent argument in a community of learners classroom. *Cognition and Instruction, 20*(4), 399–483.

Farjon, D., Smits, A., & Voogt, J. (2019). Technology integration of pre-service teachers explained by attitudes and beliefs, competency, access, and experience. *Computers and Education, 130*(1), 81–93. https://doi.org/10.1016/j.compedu.2018.11.010

Freedman, E. B., Willigan, L., Glading, R., & Rainville, K. N. (2018). Social studies without walls: Engaging students in online collaboration across district lines. *Social Studies Research and Practice, 13*(2), 254–269.

Goldberg, T. (2013). "It's in my veins": Identity and disciplinary practice in students' discussions of a historical issue. *Theory & Research in Social Education, 41*(1), 33–64. https://doi.org/10.1080/00933104.2012.757265

Goodwin, A. P., Cho, S. J., Reynolds, D., Silverman, R., & Nunn, S. (2020). Explorations of classroom talk and links to reading achievement in upper elementary classrooms. *Journal of Educational Psychology, 113*(1), 27–48. https://doi.org/10.1037/edu0000462.

Hammond, T. C., & Manfra, M. M. (2009). Giving, prompting, making: Aligning technology and pedagogy within TPACK for social studies instruction. *Contemporary Issues in Technology and Teacher Education, 9*(2), 160–185.

Hawkman, A. M. (2019). "Let's try and grapple all of this": A snapshot of racial identity development and racial pedagogical decision making in an elective social studies course. *The Journal of Social Studies Research, 43*(3), 215–228.

Hicks, D., Lee, J., Berson, M., Bolick, C., & Diem, R. (2014). Guidelines for using technology to prepare social studies teachers. *Contemporary Issues in Technology and Teacher Education,* 14(4), 433–450. https://citejournal.org/volume-14/issue-4-14/social-studies/guidelines-for-using-technology-to-prepare-social-studies-teachers

Hughes, R. E., & Marhatta, P. (2021). Disrupting narratives of racial progress: Two preservice elementary teachers' practices. *The Journal of Social Studies Research, 46*(3), 185–208. https://doi.org/10.1016/j.jssr.2021.09.004

Inagaki, K., Hatano, G., & Morita, E. (1998). Construction of mathematical knowledge through whole-class discussion. *Learning and Instruction, 8*(6), 503–526.

Jay, L. P. (2020). Contextualizing Octavius Catto: Studying a forgotten hero who bridges the past and present. *Social Education, 84*(6), 342–347.

Jupp, J. C., Berry, T. R., & Lensmire, T. J. (2016). Second-wave white teacher identity studies: A review of white teacher identity literatures from 2004 through 2014. *Review of Educational Research, 86*(4), 1151–1191.

Kim, C., Kim, M. K., Lee, C., Spector, J. M., & Demeester, K. (2013). Teacher belief and technology integration. *Teaching and Teacher Education, 29*(1), 76–85. https://doi.org/10.1016/j.tate.2012.08.005

King, L. J. (2020). Black history is not American history: Toward a framework of Black historical consciousness. *Social Education, 84*(6), 335–341.

King, L. J., & Chandler, P. T. (2016). From non-racism to anti-racism in social studies teacher education: Social studies and racial pedagogical knowledge. In A. R. Crow & A. Cuenca (Eds.), *Rethinking social studies teacher education in the twenty-first century* (pp. 3–23). Springer.

Kireev, B., Zhundibayeva, A., & Aktanova, A. (2019). Distance learning in higher education institutions: Results of an experiment. *Journal of Social Studies Education Research, 10*(3), 387–403.

Knowles, R. T. (2018). Teaching who you are: Connecting teachers' civic education ideology to instructional strategies. *Theory & Research in Social Education, 46*(1), 68–109.

Koehler, M., & Mishra, P. (2009). What is technological pedagogical content knowledge (TPACK)?. *Contemporary Issues in Technology and Teacher Education, 9*(1), 60–70.

Koehler, M. J., Mishra, P., Kereluik, K., Shin, T. S., & Graham, C. R. (2014). The technological pedagogical content knowledge framework. In J. M. Spector, M. D. Merrill, J. Elen, & M. J. Bishop (Eds.), *Handbook of research on educational communications and technology* (pp. 101–111). Springer

Kohlmeier, J., & Saye, J. (2019). Examining the relationship between teachers' discussion facilitation and their students' reasoning. *Theory & Research in Social Education, 47*(2), 176–204. https://10.1080/00933104.2018.1486765

Ladson-Billings, G. (2003). Lies my teacher still tells: Developing a critical race perspective toward the social studies. In G. Ladson-Billings (Ed.), *Critical race theories perspectives on social studies: The profession, policies, and curriculum* (pp. 1–11). Information Age Publishing.

Lampert, M. (1985). How do teachers manage to teach? Perspectives on problems in practice. *Harvard Educational Review, 55*(2), 178–195.

Manfra, M., & Grant, M., Turcol, K., Boop, L., Beller, D., Grow, M., & Grondziowski, A. (2021). Issues and opportunities in the digital transformation of social studies instruction. *Social Education, 85*(2), 93–97.

Martell, C. C. (2015). Learning to teach culturally relevant social studies: A White teacher's retrospective self-study. In P. T. Chandler (Ed.), *Doing race in social studies: Critical perspectives* (pp. 41–60). Information Age Publishing.

McGrew, S. (2021). Bridge or byway? Teaching historical reading and civic online reasoning in a US history class. *Theory & Research in Social Education*, 1–30. https://doi.org/10.1080/00933104.2021.1997844

Miles, M. B., Huberman, A. M., & Saldaña, J. (2018). *Qualitative data analysis: A methods sourcebook*. Sage publications.

Mishra, P., & Koehler, M. J. (2006). Technological pedagogical content knowledge: A framework for teacher knowledge. *Teachers College Record, 108*(1), 1017–1054.

Nagda, B. A., Gurin, P., & Lopez, G. E. (2003). Transformative pedagogy for democracy and social justice. *Race, Ethnicity and Education, 6*(2), 165–191. https://doi.org/10.1080/13613320308199

Nystrand, M., Wu, L. L., Gamoran, A., Zeiser, S., & Long, D. A. (2003). Questions in time: Investigating the structure and dynamics of unfolding classroom discourse. *Discourse Processes, 35*(2), 135–198.

Parker, W. C., & Hess, D. (2001). Teaching with and for discussion. *Teaching and Teacher Education, 17*(1), 273–289.

Parkhouse, H. (2018). Pedagogies of naming, questioning, and demystification: A study of two critical US history classrooms. *Theory & Research in Social Education, 46*(2), 277–317.

Pollock, M. (2004). *Colormute: Race talk dilemmas in an American school.* Princeton University Press.

Reisman, A. (2015). Entering the historical problem space: Whole-class, text-based discussion in history class. *Teachers College Record, 117*(2), 1–44.

Reisman, A., Enumah, L., & Jay, L. (2020). Interpretive frames for responding to racially stressful moments in history discussions. *Theory & Research in Social Education, 48*(3), 321–345.

Reisman, A., & Jay, L. (In press). Teaching racial history: Curriculum enactment in discretionary spaces. *Journal of Curriculum Studies.* https://doi.org/10.1080/00220272.2022.2049883

Remillard, J. T. (2005). Examining key concepts in research on teachers' use of mathematics curricula. *Review of Educational Research, 75*(2), 211–246.

Rodriguez, N., Brown, M., & Vickery, A. (2020). Pinning for profit? Examining elementary preservice teachers' critical analysis of online social studies resources about Black history. *Contemporary Issues in Technology and Teacher Education, 20*(3), 497–528.

Salinas, C., & Castro, A. J. (2010). Disrupting the official curriculum: Cultural biography and the curriculum decision making of Latino preservice teachers. *Theory & Research in Social Education, 38*(3), 428–463.

Sanders, F. C. (2009). *A curricular policy forty years in the making: The implementation of an African American History course in the Philadelphia School District* (Unpublished doctoral dissertation). Pennsylvania State University, State College, PA.

Settlage, J. (2013). On acknowledging PCK's shortcomings. *Journal of Science Teacher Education, 24,* 1–12.

Shulman, L. (1987). Knowledge and teaching: Foundations of the new reform. *Harvard Educational Review, 57*(1), 1–23.

Southern Poverty Law Center (SPLC). (2018). *Teaching hard history: American slavery.* Southern Poverty Law Center.

Stevenson, H. (2014). *Promoting racial literacy in schools: Differences that make a difference.* Teachers College Press.

Toliver, R. (2014). What are the children who grow up to become police officers learning in school? *The New Republic.* Retrieved from https://newrepublic.com/article/119593/surprising-lessons-philadelphias-african-american-history-course

Vickery, A. E. (2015). It was never meant for us: Towards a black feminist construct of citizenship in social studies. *Journal of Social Studies Research, 39*(1), 163–172.

Voithofer, R., & Nelson, M. J. (2020). Teacher educator technology integration preparation practices around TPACK in the United States. *Journal of Teacher Education,* 1–15. https://doi.org/10.1177/0022487120949842

Willermark, S. (2018). Technological pedagogical and content knowledge: A review of empirical studies published from 2011 to 2016. *Journal of Educational Computing Research, 56*(3), 315–343.

Willermark, S., & Pareto, L. (2020). Unpacking the role of boundaries in computer-supported collaborative teaching. *Computer Supported Cooperative Work (CSCW), 29*(1), 743–767.

Wills, J. S. (2019). Silencing racism: Remembering and forgetting race and racism in 11th grade US History classes. *Teachers College Record, 121*(4), 1–44.

Wineburg, S. (2001). *Historical thinking and other unnatural acts: Charting the future of teaching the past.* Temple University Press.

Woyshner, C., & Schocker, J. (2015). Cultural parallax and content analysis: Images of Black women in high school history textbooks. *Theory & Research in Social Education, 43*(4), 441–468. doi:10.1080/00933104.2015.1099487

Zúñiga X., Lopez, G., & Ford, K. (2014). *Intergroup dialogue: Engaging difference, social identity and social justice.* Routledge.

CHAPTER 3

PREPARING WHITE STUDENTS FOR A MULTIRACIAL WORLD

Antony Farag and Bailey Verdone
Westfield High School

On December 15, 2021, Florida Governor Ron DeSantis stood in front of a podium and addressed the press regarding a bill entitled the *Stop Woke Act*. This bill allows parents to sue school districts if they teach critical race theory (CRT) in their classrooms (Atterbury, 2021). It represents just one volley in the culture wars surrounding the identity of the United States. According to *Newsweek* magazine, as of June 2021, in addition to Florida, Arkansas, Idaho, and Oklahoma have officially banned the theory with many other states in the process of debating it (Dutton, 2021). While these states are generally considered Republican-dominated enclaves, in Democratic-leaning states, such as New Jersey, CRT has become a hotbed of discussion, especially in predominantly white[1] suburbs. However, what exacerbates these discussions is a fundamental misunderstanding of CRT and a conflation of it with every theory, practice, or policy that intends to shed light on racial inequities in systems and the history of racial inequality in the United

---

[1] Given the concepts discussed within this chapter, we have deliberately chosen not the capitalize "white" due to its historically recent construction as a racial signifier (Nayak, 2007) and to align with the approach of CRT to critically deconstruct race as a social construct.

Out of Turmoil: Catalysts for Re-learning, Re-Teaching, and Re-imagining History and Social Science, pages 41–54.
Copyright © 2023 by Information Age Publishing
www.infoagepub.com
All rights of reproduction in any form reserved.

States. The resistance to CRT attempts to undermine a theoretical lens that allows teachers to dismantle barriers to equity and empower their students.

In predominantly white districts, these political arguments, and how they impact school curricula and teacher pedagogy, manifest themselves as a zero-sum game in which if CRT is explicitly discussed in class, certain people gain power while others lose it. This framing is problematic as it presupposes that the only discussions surrounding race and inequality involve a critical understanding of only the United States and its racial politics. In an increasingly globalizing and multiracial world, CRT can empower students in predominantly white districts to understand the complexity of race on a global scale, which will, in turn, more accurately contextualize U.S. politics as such politics cannot be separated from global politics and economics. This reaction to CRT only serves to disempower students who will graduate from their respective schools in a more interconnected world than the adults who are advocating for its ban ever experienced.

In this chapter, two experienced teachers of color who teach in the predominately white suburban school district of Westfield, NJ will discuss navigating teaching in such turmoil through research, experience, theory, and practice. First, we will discuss recent research surrounding the demography of teachers in predominantly white schools in New Jersey and their dispositions toward CRT will be discussed (Farag, 2020). Secondly, we will share our experiences teaching in predominantly white schools throughout the socio-political turmoil surrounding race and describe controversies in the Westfield school district that made local, statewide, and national news. Finally, as so many discussions surrounding CRT are being defined by media narratives, we will discuss theoretical approaches to facilitating conversations about CRT, and other topics, with predominantly white students through an analysis of the interdisciplinary course that we teach entitled *The Global Citizen*. As media narratives hyper-sensationalize issues and further polarize society, it becomes increasingly important for academia, especially in public schooling, to continue to inform students about the complexities of racism in the United States through a theoretical and research-based standpoint.

PREDOMINANTLY WHITE SCHOOLS AND CRT

The history of racial segregation in the United States has impacted both White, Black, Indigenous, and people of color students for decades. White students, specifically those in suburbs, have been disadvantaged by this systemic racism by limiting their education and awareness of a multiracial, globalizing world. The politicization of CRT and its subsequent "banning" in many states, threatens to further disadvantage these students. Many will graduate their high schools rarely interacting with people of color in positions of power while being censored from having the benefit of a systematic and research-based way to understand a multiracial world in which they are a minority (United Nations, n.d.).

CRT has been a controversial topic in recent years mostly due to its politicization and not because of its aim or content. Former President Trump railed against it during his campaign (Adams, 2021), it has been banned in many school districts in states across the country (Vock, 2021), and teachers have been fired for using it in their classrooms (Tolson, 2021). In fact, the approval of a course we developed along with others at Westfield High School in New Jersey caused both local and national controversy (Glackin, 2019; Woodson, 2020) and was only approved after major resistance from members of the board of education (Farag, 2021). Despite the resistance, and maybe because of the resistance, we argue that CRT is an extremely useful tool to deconstruct the barriers to racial equity.

What has been seen as "controversy" is, in fact, a fundamental misunderstanding. CRT directly examines institutions and power, not individual people and their prejudices. Detractors argue that it is a Marxist idea that targets people who identify as white and is fundamentally anti-American. Despite some critical race theorists being Marxists, a chief distinction lies in the leading construct that CRT targets. Marxism is critical of capitalism whereas CRT is critical of white supremacy and, according to renowned Marxist, Cole, CRT is "basically incompatible with Marxism" (Cole, 2009). CRT also does not attack white people but rather systems of oppression that hold all Americans back from reaching each person's individual potential. In education, it can be used to help students of European ancestry to better understand their own identities as Irish, Italian, German, Polish, etc. Americans rather than as a conflation of identities called "white." Finally, CRT is fundamentally pro-American in that it seeks to extract the cancer of racism that has been dividing and weakening the country for centuries. Once this cancer has been removed, U.S. American society can better focus on rebuilding the country as it recovers from the global pandemic of COVID-19.

Social Studies Teachers in Predominantly White Schools Through a CRT Lens

Social studies teachers, particularly those in predominantly white schools, can have a major impact on helping white students navigate this multiracial world. One quantitative study (Farag, 2020), conducted by an author of this chapter, examined these teachers. Data was collected and analyzed months before the murder of George Floyd and the subsequent sensationalization of CRT and can shed light on understandings of CRT before sensationalized media narratives fixated on it. The study sought to inform the landscape upon which social studies teachers are both understanding the theory and their role as educators in these tumultuous times. The participants were 104 secondary education social studies teachers in predominantly white public schools (> 68% white) across New Jersey. These teachers filled out a survey that included a demographic questionnaire and CRT questionnaire along with other scales measuring their critical competency and critical consciousness.

This research showed that social studies teachers in predominately white districts are themselves products of racial segregation. Demographic results showed that the majority (94.2%) identify as white and grew up in predominantly white towns (M = 86.7%, SD = 12.5). Most of the teachers studied (89.9%) grew up in town towns that had a 70% or higher white population, with 62.3% growing up in towns that had a 90% or higher white population. The majority (82.7%) never had a high school social studies teacher of color while only 3.8% had more than one social studies teacher of color. The vast majority are white, grew up in white towns, and rarely had a social studies teacher of color. Prior research (Boyd et al., 2005; Geiger, 2018; Orfield et al., 2017; Reininger, 2012; Stroub & Richards, 2013) described teaching as a profession in which people stay close to or in similar towns to where they grew up. Demographic data collected reflected the same practice with an emphasis on social studies teachers. Coupled with New Jersey's historical and current state of racial segregation (Orfield et al., 2017), the effect of segregation can be seen in the demographics of current social studies teachers in predominately white high schools. This can lead to continual segregation as white students will rarely have a social studies teacher of color, then proceed to teach in similar schools in which they were taught.

Social Studies Teachers' Understanding of CRT

Institutional racism affects all of society, including the white population of the United States. Exposure to CRT is imperative for white students if schools are to be forces of resistance to inequality. Ladson-Billings (2003) described social studies as the field in which institutional racism needs to be discussed. The majority, 62.5% of teachers studied, reported that they had no knowledge of CRT, had varying levels of comfort with the premises of CRT, and received varying levels of support from their respective districts in implementing the basic concepts surrounding CRT. Even more (64.4%) did not know enough about CRT to infuse it into their pedagogy while only 9.6% either agreed or somewhat agreed that they are comfortable infusing CRT in their pedagogy. However, when asked if they agree with the specific premises of CRT derived from Ladson-Billings (1998), they responded in various ways. The most striking finding involved a fundamental purpose of the origination of CRT.

The majority of teachers agreed with a premise that contradicts the main purpose of CRT. Teachers surveyed agreed that racism and racial discrimination can be solved over time through incremental changes which is a fundamental antithesis to the purpose of CRT. This may be because they study and teach about the progress made surrounding race relations, however, social studies teachers play an important role in accelerating that progress. CRT originated from the frustration of incremental progress of Civil Rights legislation (Delgado, 2017). This should concern anyone dedicated to using education as a means to promote racial equity. More importantly, given that it has been decades since the Civil Rights movement and race relations across the United States continue to divide the country, the lack of using CRT as a lens to educate students may have a causal relationship with the lack of progress. When we developed a course explicitly framed by CRT in our predominantly white district of Westfield, NJ, it caused a national controversy.

FROM LOCAL TO NATIONAL TO LOCAL

The course we developed, entitled *Power, Privilege, and Imbalance in American Society*, is framed by CRT and the continuous local discussion surrounding its approval reflects its controversial nature on the national level. We designed it to be an elective course offered to 11th- and 12th-grade students. Discussing theorists including Michel Foucault and Pierre Bourdieu, the course is structured to examine the role power plays in constructing institutions—specifically how it can create privileges and imbalances within those institutions through identifying different forms of capital. It also addresses intersections among systems of power (e.g., race, gender, social class) and how differing contexts shape power dynamics. One underlying theme is that everyone in a society suffers when systems of oppression create imbalances and that in order for everyone to reach their full potential, these imbalances need to be addressed (Farag, 2021).

In the spring of 2018, the course was introduced to a committee formed by the Board of Education of Westfield. In December of 2019, in a publicly held board meeting, the course was approved in a contentious 6–3 vote. Critics of the course accused it of being divisive liberal indoctrination and even anti-Semitic (Chiarello, 2019) while proponents of the course, including the Dr. Martin Luther King, Jr. Association of the town (Wolf, 2019), argued that it was a necessary addition to the many electives the school offers to its students. Over the subsequent weeks, the course gained national attention (Schow, 2019) in both news and social media.

Even after the course was approved, the controversy didn't end. *The Wall Street Journal* published an opinion piece by Civil Rights activist Robert Woodson who took issue with the course for promulgating a "lethal message of despair and distortion of history" (Woodson, 2020, para. 12). While Woodson's contributions to the Civil Rights movement cannot be overstated, it's important to recognize that CRT is not focused on individuals and their successes but on institutions. Although individuals from marginalized groups can avoid despair and express their agency within an oppressive system, they may be less able to freely and equally do so than others. It is through examining institutional policies and their effects, which CRT encourages, that productive conversations about race can occur (Farag, 2021).

On May 25, 2020, George Floyd's death was recorded and millions of people across the country watched an African American man lose his life while being pinned to the ground by a white American police officer. The national debate surrounding whether he was murdered, the subsequent protests both violent and nonviolent, and the responses by major institutions and billion-dollar corporations, put CRT back on the national stage. In response to local protests in Westfield, which included direct critiques of the school system and curricula, the school district hailed the course as evidence of its proactive response to discussing the racial discrimination that protesters believed to be inherent within law enforcement and throughout the rest of society (Chiarello, 2020). In the following months, the national discussion about race and continued protests of institutionalized racism was heightened as the country got closer and closer to a contentious election, all while dealing with the COVID-19 pandemic. On September 4, 2020, shortly before the school year began, former President Donald Trump sent a memo regarding CRT which further fueled national controversy and, in turn, filtered into local politics (Farag, 2021).

Schools Grappling With CRT

"Critical Race Theory is the latest attempt to inculcate us to a Socialist ideology whose goal is a Totalitarian Communist state! Knowing this begs the question of those who embrace CRT: are they closet Communists or simply unwitting dupes?" concludes Bruce Baker from Lakewood, NJ in his piece entitled "Reader Takes Issue with CRT, Reading List Choices for Kindergartners" published in *The Westfield Leader*, Westfield, NJ's local newspaper (Baker, 2021, p. 4). This piece speaks to the anti-intellectual assault on teachers and school leaders premised upon blatant inaccuracies and Cold-War era troupes. The key point of his editorial was that the children's book *Our Skin: A First Conversation About Race* (Madison et al., 2021) has major historical inaccuracies including his assertion that race was historically constructed by whites to justify genocide against blacks. Notwithstanding the fact that nowhere in the book does it address genocide, the fallacy of "whataboutism" guides Baker's argument. This was not lost on readers of the newspaper. One week later, a resident of Westfield, Robert J. Anderson responded to Baker's piece calling it "extreme and inaccurate" while stating,

> Rather than attributing racism to particularly nasty individuals (although of course they exist), racism is understood as an aspect of our very culture…Indeed, it is not an issue of taking blame in any particularly individual manner; it is a duty to understand how we got this way and see what can be done to make it better. (Anderson, 2021, p. 4)

One effect of the national discussions surrounding CRT is that public misconceptions of its nuance would make it so that any attempt to teach social justice-themed topics would be misconstrued as CRT. In addition, diversity, equity, and inclusion (DEI) policies and initiatives have also been under attack with those against such initiatives believing that they are simply CRT in disguise. As Stephan Sawchuk, of *Education Week*, writes,

> Thus, there is a good deal of confusion over what CRT means, as well as its relationship to other terms, like "anti-racism" and "social justice," with which it is often conflated. To an extent, the term "critical race theory" is now cited as the basis of all diversity and inclusion efforts regardless of how much it's actually informed those programs. (Sawchuk, 2021, para. 11)

These misunderstandings can have a reverberating effect throughout school districts including that of Westfield, NJ where an active website, *Westfield Public Schools Transparency,* exists directly attacking school leaders and educators. The website attempts to organize parents to speak out at board of education meetings against what they term "Racial Literacy, Social Justice, Anti-Racism, Diversity, Equity and Inclusion (DEI) [and] Social Emotional Learning (SEL)" arguing they are all CRT in disguise (WPS Transparency, 2021).

School leaders, hoping to avoid confrontations in which they feel both powerless and ill-prepared, can curtail or water down DEI initiatives. In-service teachers, especially those without tenure, may be more apprehensive toward teaching topics that could be misconstrued by a given student (or their parent/guardian). In November of 2021, the New Hampshire governor was forced to condemn a tweet that offered a bounty for any parent that perceives CRT being taught in their children's classroom (Ramer, 2021).

NAVIGATING TURMOIL THROUGH PHILOSOPHY

In 2016, shortly after Donald Trump was elected president, *The Washington Post* published a column entitled "Ayn Rand-acolyte Donald Trump Stacks His Cabinet with Fellow Objectivists." In the column, author James Hohmann looked into the histories and prior statements from Trump himself, Rex Tillerson, Andy Puzder, and Mike Pompeo. Trump even went so far as to say that Rand's book *The Fountainhead*, "'relates to business, beauty, life and inner emotions. That book relates to…everything'" (Hohmann, 2016, para. 2). Ayn Rand is credited as being the founder of the philosophy of objectivism which is premised upon "a conception of metaphysical realism, rationality, ethical egoism (rational self-interest), individual rights, *laissez-faire* capitalism, and art" (Stanford Encyclopedia of Philosophy, 2020, para. 1). With regard to politics and objectivism, Rand defines

> Capitalism [as] the only political-economic system compatible with this philosophy because it is the only system based on respect for human beings as ends in themselves. The free-market libertarian political movement…draws great inspiration from her moral defense of the minimal state, that is, the state whose only *raison d'être* is protection of individual rights. (Stanford Encyclopedia of Philosophy, 2020, para. 2)

On the opposite side of the philosophical spectrum is constructivism (Murphy, 1997, p. 5) and when applied to society, labeled *social constructivism*. According to Burr (2015),

> The key tenet of social constructionism is that our knowledge of the world, including our understanding of human beings, is a product of human thought rather than grounded in an observable, external reality…the philosophers Kant, Nietzsche, and Marx all took this view. (p. 222)

Social constructivism is the philosophical foundation of many social theories, including CRT. It is also a common reason why CRT is continuously labeled as Marxist by its detractors. Regarding our pedagogical experiences, we employ a basic understanding of social constructivism and objectivism and use them in developing curricula, unit, and lesson plans.

To effectively navigate teaching through turmoil, teachers and school leaders need to understand the epistemological roots involving political controversies in order for them to ask accurate questions that help guide pedagogy and policies. More specifically, most major political questions surrounding racial inequality can be reduced to the question of whether the government should solve societal problems or should it allow the free market to solve such problems. In other words, to what extent should the government solve racial inequalities? And its corollary, to what extent should the government allow the free market to solve racial inequalities? A social constructivist would gravitate toward the idea that the government, being a construct itself and inherently manifesting collective action, should solve racial inequality. Whereas an objectivist would argue that these inequalities were formed by the government itself and that free-market capitalism can solve such inequalities over time. Public school policies and initiatives framed by CRT are essentially taking the social constructivist view and many of those against it base their arguments on an objectivist view. Using this framework, teachers can avoid media and political narratives that seek more to cloud the issue around sensationalist headlines than address inequalities in a productive manner.

Reducing discussions surrounding racial inequality to that fundamental question has proven to be a highly effective method in teaching students in a predominately white school. Here, we will share our experiences teaching the course we developed entitled *The Global Citizen* which is an interdisciplinary course, fulfilling a 4th-year English requirement, taught to seniors at Westfield High School. Its underlying aim is to prepare graduating seniors who have lived in a predominantly white suburban town with the goal of developing a conceptual understanding of a globalizing, multiracial world.

THE GLOBAL CITIZEN

To address these contentious issues that divide our community, in 2014 we designed a course in which the objective is to explore discourse surrounding politicized social constructs with our predominantly white students. With our students, what we have found effective in discussing politicized issues is framing them as social constructs to be analyzed with their efficacy consistently evaluated in class. With this framing, students can examine these issues more objectively without taking sides. As a year-long theme, we introduce the concept of social constructs using Plato's "Allegory of the Cave." We utilize this extended metaphor to analyze media, schooling, government, race, class, and gender. The "Allegory of the Cave" can be used to conceptualize many different topics in different disciplines and this metaphor is especially appropriate for students who have been raised within the "cave" of suburban America. We use it to discuss the continuous interaction between social constructivism and objectivism when applied to society and government. Students use the Socratic method in discussions which allows them to analyze and critique government as a construct and the laissez-faire capitalism at the core of objectivist philosophy. Students who are framing their political identities around social constructivism are exposed to the ways in which government intervention in society has historically caused inequities as well as attempted to solve them. In contrast, those students who are framing their political identities around objectivism are exposed to ways in which the free market has exacerbated inequities and address the ways it has helped to solve them. By shaping lessons this way, we discuss "shadows on the wall" as constructs while at the same time validating the objectivist viewpoint as continually "exiting the cave" using reason to grasp a deeper reality. This method engages students who are continually forming their political identities and allows us to discuss controversial topics in an academically productive way.

To further develop their capacities in forming their political identities, we also employ aspects of analytic philosophy, namely that of informal logic. Students are exposed to logical methods of thinking and become proficient at identifying fallacies and the rhetorical techniques of ethos, pathos, and logos. In addition, we further discuss epistemology using modern philosophy, history, literature, and science to understand and identify the soundness and cogency of arguments. This has become especially helpful in discussing the nuances of many socio-political issues including the global climate crisis and the United States and world response to the COVID-19 pandemic. In this way, we attempt to help students approach controversial topics from a logical standpoint, rather than personal feelings and opinions, which allows them to analyze and critique media and political narratives surrounding controversial topics such as race. However, discussing race as a construct and its impact on society requires multiple steps, especially for students in a predominately white school.

Step 1: Global White Supremacy and Nazi Germany

Before addressing the history of racial discrimination in the United States we study global white supremacy and use Nazi Germany as a case study. One unique adaptation of CRT is that we analyze 19th- and early 20th-century European imperialism and the global white supremacy that accompanied it before addressing white supremacy within the United States. As CRT is primarily used to deconstruct white supremacy when teaching white students in the United States, it is important to understand the global roots that stem from European Imperialism in early 20th-century global politics. As a case study, we examine how the German people democratically voted the Nazis into power, the manner in which the Nazis used logical fallacies and unsound arguments in their propaganda and policymaking, the events of World War II, and its continuous impact on global politics, and finally the Holocaust. In a school that has had multiple incidents of anti-Semitic hate crimes over the years, enough that these incidents made state-wide news (*News 12* Staff, 2021), a thorough discussion of Holocaust education and its connection to democratic governments becomes imperative. This allows students to have a strong foundation regarding not only discussing the history of World War II but also its connection to race relations within the United States. One specific lesson compares the Nuremberg laws of Nazi Germany to the Jim Crow laws of the United States. This comparison sets up the connections between the history of racial discrimination in the United States (United States Holocaust Memorial Museum, n.d.).

Step 2: An Interdisciplinary Approach to Discussing Racial Discrimination

CRT is an inherently interdisciplinary theoretical framework (Ladson-Billings, 1998). In *The Global Citizen*, we weave together science, history, philosophy, and literature as we continue to analyze social constructs and adapt academic concepts to secondary education students. Using the documentary *Race: The Power of an Illusion* (Adelman, 2003) and its accompanying texts as a foundation, we discuss the scientific basis for the lack of biological justification to classify the human species with races. We then focus on the historical impact of constructing society based on an inaccurate social construct. Next, we identify the differences between personal racism and the institutional nature of racial discrimination. In a predominately white school, this distinction is crucial and allows for a more authentic exploration of racial discourse with this demographic.

By identifying the differences between personal and institutional racism, students can address the ways in which systems can be discriminatory and are better able to talk about racial discourse in an informed manner. Using a literature study and comparison of *To Kill a Mockingbird,* by Harper Lee (1960/2010) and Lorraine Hansberry's (1959/1997) *A Raisin in the Sun,* students are able to explore not only historical contexts of racial discrimination but also engage with the humanity of those affected by systemic racism. In *To Kill a Mockingbird*, Lee writes the protagonist Atticus Finch, as the personally non-racist individual, though still questionable through literature analysis, operating in a discriminatory justice system. However, in *A Raisin in the Sun*, Hansberry makes her protagonist the Younger Family, leaving the reader to empathize with the Younger family fighting institutional racism through segregated housing policies.

The juxtaposition of these texts enables students to identify the difference between an individual being personally non-racist but doing nothing to change a system and a deep examination of the systemic racism in housing discrimination. As much of racial discourse in the United States among white Americans involves being personally absolved from historical racism (DiAngelo, 2018), combining these texts forces students to question what role people have in maintaining or disrupting racist systems, even if they are not personally racist. Furthermore, *A Raisin in the Sun* taught in a predominately white school, will have students question why the Younger family has such trouble moving into a desirable (read: white) suburb. Students who identify as white also gain essential exposure to the nuance and complexity of engaging with a family of black characters who are a cohesive and dynamic family unit, whose characters go to college, have sibling rivalries, go on dates, have dinner at the kitchen table together, etc. This humanizing exposure enables us to help students further question the way race has been historically constructed in the United States and question the way different races, specifically African Americans, are portrayed through media and literature. Exposed to philosophical, historical, scientific, and humanizing content and literature, students gain a foundation for understanding the complexity of the world that they are entering after they graduate.

Step 3: Preparing Students for a Globalizing, Multiracial World

The 2020 U.S. census showed that the United States is increasingly a diverse society (U.S. Census Bureau, 2021), while global demographic projections continue to predict people of European descent decreasing in population compared with the rest of the world (United Nations, n.d.). White students need to be prepared to navigate a country and a world that looks and operates very differently than it has in the past. One of the founders of CRT, Derrick Bell, coined the concept of *interest convergence*, which critiques the motivations of white Americans and argues that whites only promote civil rights only when it aligns with their self-interest (Bell, 1995). Although it is intended as a critique, interest convergence can be used to frame CRT as an effective method of understanding the multiracial world. This method allows for both social constructionist and objectivist learning students to engage with social justice and anti-racist issues. In our course, we frame fighting inequities as beneficial for all Americans and not as a zero-sum game that takes opportunity away from whites and gives it to non-whites.

One highly effective activity involves an adaptation of the recycle bin activity intended to teach about privilege. Common versions of this activity place a garbage can at a certain point in the room where students sit in various places around the classroom. Some students may be closer to the recycle bin while others further away. This activity was initially meant to employ white privilege pedagogy, which has been shown to have flaws (Crowley, R., & Smith, W., 2020). Instead, we tell students to write down on a piece of paper what they hope to contribute to society throughout their lives. Some may write that they want to become doctors, scientists, teachers, a good parent, etc. Then we allow our students to crumple up the paper and attempt to toss the crumpled paper into the recycle bin from where they sit in the classroom. The structure of the classroom will allow some students to have an easier shot than others and we make this idea analogous to some people having more opportunities than others in an inequitable society. We emphasize the idea that everyone loses when not everyone has an equal chance of contributing to a given society (Rose, 1996) as students directly see the contributions they lost out on when students miss the recycle bin, i.e., a good father, an innovative doctor, etc. If global economies, along with the United States, continue to discriminate based on race, all of humanity loses, even those not typically targeted by racial discrimination. From this standpoint, we discuss the complexity and nuance of globalization and emphasize the importance of developing a global consciousness (Stegar, 2017) that first begins with a theoretical understanding of race as a construct that CRT can inform.

CONCLUSION

The controversy surrounding CRT threatens the civil rights advances of people of color across the United States. It also threatens to disempower white Americans by leaving them less prepared for a globalizing multiracial world. Misunderstandings and misrepresentations of CRT cloud the issue further. Research shows that the majority of social studies teachers in predominantly white schools in NJ had never heard of CRT before the controversy (Farag, 2020) yet they are on the frontlines of socio-political conflicts about it in their classrooms and local school board meetings. The controversy occurs at both the local and national level of politics. In this chapter, we detailed a step-by-step model for engaging predominantly white students with CRT and using it as a lens to effectively analyze race as a construct and prepare white students for a globalizing multiracial world. As controversies about the identity of the United States continue to occur, it is the role of teachers, school leaders, and academics to make sure students are taught in the most accurate and empowering manner devoid of sensationalist media headlines and the self-serving motives of politicians.

REFERENCES

Adams, C. (2021, May 11). *How Trump ignited the fight over critical race theory in schools.* NBCNews.com. https://www.nbcnews.com/news/nbcblk/how-trump-ignited-fight-over-critical-race-theory-schools-n1266701.

Adelman, L. (2003). *Race: The power of an illusion.* [Video]. Produced by California Newsreel in association with the Independent Television Service.

Anderson, R. (2021, December 9). Letter on CRT was extreme and inaccurate. *Westfield Leader.* https://s3.amazonaws.com/simplecirc-cdn/publications/1308/21dec09-WF.pdf

Atterbury, A. (2021, December 15). *DeSantis pushes bill that allows parent to sue schools over critical race theory.* Politico PRO. https://www.politico.com/states/florida/story/2021/12/15/desantis-targets-critical-race-theory-with-bill-that-evokes-texas-abortion-bounties-1400102

Baker, B. (2021, December 2). Reader takes issue with CRT, reading list choices for kindergarteners. *Westfield Leader.* https://s3.amazonaws.com/simplecirc-cdn/publications/1308/21dec02-WF.pdf

Bell, D. A. (1995). Who's afraid of critical race theory. *U. Ill. L. Rev., 893.*

Boyd, D., Lankford, H., Loeb, S., & Wyckoff, J. (2005). The draw of home: How teachers' preferences for proximity disadvantage urban schools. *Journal of Policy Analysis and Management, 24*(1), 113–132.

Burr, V. (2015). *Social constructionism.* Routledge.

Chiarello, R. (2019, December 4). *Westfield school board splits in approval of course on race, power imbalance.* Tap into Westfield.

Chiarello, R. (2020, June 14). *Promises from Westfield schools after students' George Floyd protest draws thousands.* Tap into Westfield.

Cole, M. (2009). The color-line and the class struggle: A Marxist response to critical race theory in education as it arrives in the United Kingdom. *Power and Education, 1*(1), 111–124.

Crowley, R., & Smith, W. (2020). A divergence of interests: Critical race theory and white privilege pedagogy. *Teachers College Record, 122*(1), 1–24.

Delgado, R., & Stefancic, J. (2017). *Critical race theory: An introduction* (Vol. 20). NYU Press.

Diangelo, R. (2018). *White fragility: Why it's so hard for white people to talk about racism.* Beacon Press.

Dutton, J. (2021, June 11). Critical Race Theory is banned in these states. *Newsweek.* https://www.newsweek.com/critical-race-theory-banned-these-states-1599712

Farag, A. (2020). *Structured whiteness: A study of social studies teachers who teach in predominately-white public school districts* [Doctoral dissertation, Rutgers Graduate School of Education, Rutgers University, New Brunswick, New Jersey]. ProQuest Dissertations Publishing.

Farag, A. (2021). The fear of multiple truths: On teaching about racism in a predominantly white school. *Phi Delta Kappan, 102*(5), 18–23.

Geiger, A. (2018, August 27). *Public school teachers much less racially diverse than students in US.* http://www.pewresearch.org/fact-tank/2018/08/27/americas-public-school-teachers-are-far-less-racially-and-ethnically-diverse-than-their-students/ on 12.26.2018

Glackin, J. (2019, November 14). Proposed WHS class causes debate at BOE meeting. *Westfield Leader*, 46–2019.

Hansberry, L. (1997). *A raisin in the sun.* Modern Library. (Original work published 1959).

Hohmann, J. (2016, December 13). The Daily 202: Ayn Rand-acolyte Donald Trump stacks his cabinet with fellow objectivists. *Washington Post.* Retrieved December 22, 2021, from https://www.washingtonpost.com/news/powerpost/paloma/daily-202/2016/12/13/daily-202-ayn-rand-acolyte-donald-trump-stacks-his-cabinet-with-fellow-objectivists/584f5cdfe9b69b36fcfeaf3b/

Ladson-Billings, G. (1998). Just what is Critical Race Theory and what's it doing in a nice field like education?. *International journal of qualitative studies in education, 11*(1), 7–24.

Ladson-Billings, G. (Ed.). (2003). *Critical race theory perspectives on the social studies: The profession, policies, and curriculum.* IAP.

Lee, H. (2010). *To kill a mockingbird.* Arrow Books. (Original work published 1960).

Madison, M., Ralli, J., & Roxas, I. (2021). *Our skin: A first conversation about race (first conversations).* Rise x Penguin Workshop.

Murphy, E. (1997). *Constructivism: From philosophy to practice.* Reproduced by EDRS, ED 444 966 SP 039 420.

Nayak, A. (2007). Critical whiteness studies. *Sociology Compass, 1*(2), 737–755.

News 12 Staff. (2021, December 9). Officials: Swastikas found twice in Westfield HS bathrooms in less than a week. *News 12—New Jersey.* Retrieved December 22, 2021, from https://newjersey.news12.com/officials-swastikas-found-twice-in-westfield-hs-bathrooms-in-less-than-a-week

Orfield, G., Ee, J., & Coughlan, R. (2017, November). *New Jersey's segregated schools: Trends and paths forward—The Civil Rights Project at UCLA.* New Jersey's Segregated Schools. Retrieved December 22, 2021, from https://www.civilrightsproject.ucla.edu/research/k-12-education/integration-and-diversity/new-jerseys-segregated-schools-trends-and-paths-forward

Oxford Dictionaries. (2016). *Word of the year 2016.* https://languages.oup.com/word-of-the-year/2016/

Ramer, H. (2021, November 18). *Governor condemns tweet offering a "bounty" on teachers.* AP NEWS. Retrieved October 8, 2022, from https://apnews.

com/article/education-race-and-ethnicity-racial-injustice-new-hampshire-b231854bde76495a806d76355991857d

Reininger, M. (2012). Hometown disadvantage? It depends on where you're from: Teachers' location preferences and the implications for staffing schools. *Educational Evaluation and Policy Analysis, 34*(2), 127–145.

Rose, L. R. (1996). White identity and counseling White allies about racism. *Impacts of racism on White Americans, 2*, 24–47.

Sawchuk, S. (2021, September 21). What is Critical Race Theory, and why is it under attack? *Education Week.* https://www.edweek.org/leadership/what-is-critical-race-theory-and-why-is-it under-attack/2021/05

Schow, A. (2019, December 10). *Power, privilege and imbalance in American society' course that teaches 'Critical Race Theory' is coming to a New Jersey high school.* Retrieved September 12, 2020, from https://www.dailywire.com/news/power-privilege-and-imbalance-in-american-society-course-that-teaches-critical-race-theory-is-coming-to-a-new-jersey-high-school

Stanford Encyclopedia of Philosophy. (2020, July 13). *Ayn Rand (Stanford Encyclopedia of Philosophy).* Retrieved December 22, 2021, from https://plato.stanford.edu/entries/ayn-rand/

Steger, M. B. (2017). *Globalization: A very short introduction*(vol. 86). Oxford University Press.

Stroub, K. J., & Richards, M. P. (2013). From resegregation to reintegration: Trends in the racial/ethnic segregation of metropolitan public schools, 1993–2009. *American Educational Research Journal, 50*(3), 497–531.

United Nations. (n.d.). *Shifting demographics.* Retrieved December 22, 2021, from https://www.un.org/en/un75/shifting-demographics

Tolson, P. (2021, May 22). *Florida teacher gets fired over CRT ban, but parents still concerned over textbooks.* www.theepochtimes.com. https://www.theepochtimes.com/florida-teacher-gets-fired-over-crt-ban-but-parents-still-concerned-over-textbooks_3824057.html.

United States Holocaust Memorial Museum. (n.d.). *Nazism and the Jim Crow South—United States Holocaust Memorial Museum. Nazism and the Jim Crow South.* Retrieved December 22, 2021, from https://www.ushmm.org/collections/bibliography/nazism-and-the-jim-crow-south

U.S. Census Bureau. (2021, August 17). *Local population changes and nation's racial and ethnic diversity.* The United States Census Bureau. https://www.census.gov/newsroom/press-releases/2021/population-changes-nations-diversity.html.

Vock, D. C. (2021, May 25). *Attempts to ban teaching on 'critical race theory' multiply across the U.S.* NC Policy Watch. http://www.ncpolicywatch.com/2021/05/24/attempts-to-ban-teaching-on-critical-race-theory-multiply-across-the-u-s/

Wolf, E. (2019, November 27). *Letter: Westfield MLK Association endorses new course at high school.* Tap into Westfield.

Woodson, R. L. (2020, January 17). The left forgets what Martin Luther King stood for. *Wall Street Journal.* https://www.wsj.com/articles/the-left-forgets-what-martin-luther-king-stood-for-11579304166

WPS Transparency. (2021, October 11). *CRT is here in Westfield.* https://wpstransparency.org/issues/crt/crt-is-here-in-westfield/#crt-has-many-names

PART II

PEDAGOGIES OF CHANGE

CHAPTER 4

TEACHING SOCIAL STUDIES IN A TIME OF COVID-19

An Examination of Contradictions in Activity

Dean P. Vesperman
University of Wisconsin-River Falls

Mariah Pol
Indiana University

The COVID-19 (SARS-CoV-2) pandemic led to the unprecedented shuttering of schools and the transitioning from face-to-face to virtual teaching at unparalleled speed and scale (Bombardieri, 2021; Brown Center Chalkboard, 2021; Pokhrel & Chhetri, 2021; World Bank Group, 2020). The pandemic created a significant disruption to the human activity of teaching due to numerous, rapid shocks to education systems (World Bank Group, 2020). This disruption of the activity led to a "paradigm shift in the way educators deliver quality education" (Pokhrel & Chhetri, 2021, p. 134). In the early days of the pandemic this paradigm shift manifested itself in multiple ways from remote e-learning, melding synchronous and asynchronous learning, and the incorporation of new educational technologies (Bombardieri, 2021; Education Week, 2020; Harris, 2020).

Out of Turmoil: Catalysts for Re-learning, Re-Teaching, and Re-imagining History and Social Science, pages 57–72.
Copyright © 2023 by Information Age Publishing
www.infoagepub.com
All rights of reproduction in any form reserved.

The origins of this study began with phone conversations with two of the participant-researchers on how they reacted to the announcement of massive school closings and the movement of teaching social studies to an online format. The rapid transformation of the activity led the primary researcher to consider some fundamental questions: what effect will this change have on teachers? How will the changes in teaching social studies manifest over time in the Spring of 2020? These conversations led to the realization that the activity of teaching social studies was going to change rapidly. This led to the research question of how contradictions would manifest in the activity of teaching social studies.

THEORETICAL FRAMEWORK

To analyze the change that occurred in teaching social studies due to the pandemic, data was analyzed using cultural historical activity theory (CHAT), specifically second-generation activity theory (Engeström, 1987, 1990). This theoretical frame posits activity is collective, artifact mediated, and object-oriented (Elmberger et al., 2019; Engeström, 1987, 2001, see Figure 4.1). Next, activity arises from and comprises a multiplicity of views, traditions, and cultures (Elmberger et al., 2019; Engeström, 1987, 2001; Vesperman & Leet-Otley, 2021). The totality of activity is CHAT's primary focus (Engeström, 1987); for this study, we focus on the activity of teaching social studies.

Subsequently, CHAT allows for the examination of the interactions between the subject and the activity. As the subject moves toward the object of an activity,

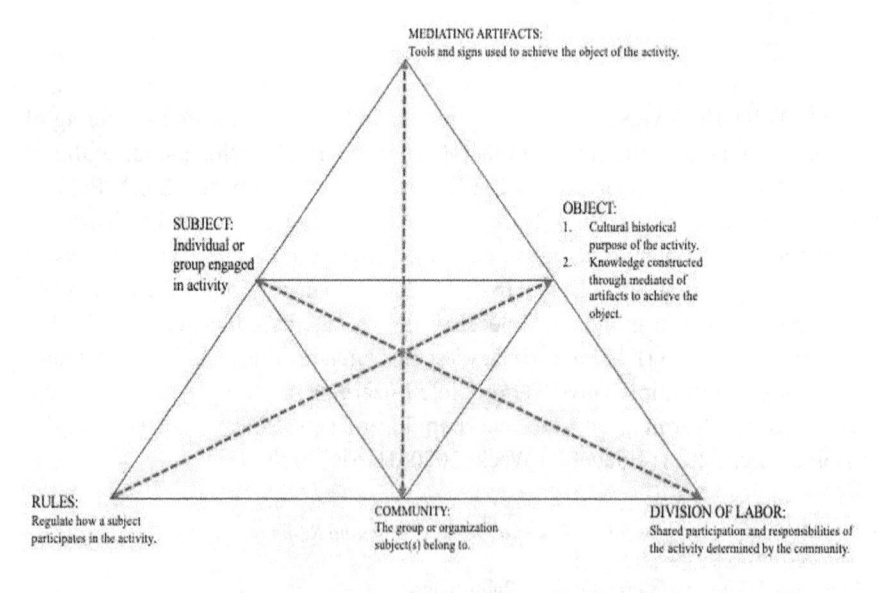

FIGURE 4.1. Second Generation Mediational Triangle (Engeström, 1987,1990)

they interact with the culturally mediated artifacts, the division of labor, community, and the rules of human activity to achieve a particular outcome (Engeström, 1987, 1990) (see Table 4.1). Next, the mediation of the subject with the various loci creates an ever-evolving complex activity that changes over time and promotes expansive learning (Engeström, 1987, 1990; Roth & Lee, 2007). This allows for an examination of the historicity of the activity and the evolution of the activity due to mediated action. Furthermore, CHAT allows for the critical analysis of the evolution of any human activity (Cole & Engeström, 1993), including teaching social studies; thus, revealing the qualitative transformations of the activity (Engeström, 1987, 1990, 2001). It is important to note that qualitative transformations cannot be classified as being positive or negative (Engeström, 1987).

This research is also guided by CHAT's conception of contradictions (Engeström, 1987, 1990, 2001). Contradictions arise in activity when the interplay of activities causes an imbalance due to opposing forces inside and outside a particular activity (Engeström, 1987, 1990, 2001; Foot, 2001; Yamagata-Lynch & Haudenschild, 2009). It is for this reason that contradictions are the motivating catalyst for the transformation of activity (Engeström, 1987, 1990, 2001). Next, Engeström and Sannino (2011) noted three important rules about analyzing contradictions. First, the concept of contradiction is not synonymous with "paradox, tension, inconsistency, conflict, dilemma or double bind" (Engeström & Sannino, 2011, p. 370). Contradictions are "dynamic tensions between opposing forces in an activity system," which build up over time, and are a source for qualitative transformations of the activity (Karanasios et al., 2017, p. 2). Next, contradictions

TABLE 4.1. Key Definitions—Second Generation Activity Theory (Engeström 1987, 1990) and Description of Loci for This Study

Second-Generation Activity Theory—Loci of Activity (Engeström 1987; 1990)	Definition of Loci (Engeström 1987, 1990)	Description of Loci for This Study
Subject	Individual or individuals who engage in mediated activity	Social studies teachers/participant-researchers
Object	Goal of the activity	Purpose for teaching social studies
Culturally mediated artifacts	The tools and signs used in mediated action in the activity	The tools and signs used by the teacher in teaching social studies
Rules	Regulate a subject's participation in an activity	How the activity of teaching social studies is regulated
Division of Labor	Shared responsibilities in participation in the activity	The responsibilities of the social studies teacher in the activity
Community	The group or organization the subject belongs	Social studies teachers

must be examined within their historical development. Engeström and Sannino (2011) argued that since contradictions are "historically emergent and systemic phenomena, in empirical studies, we have no direct access to them" (p. 371). Thus, contradictions can only be viewed through their manifestations in the actions and words of the subject. Lastly, "developmentally significant contradictions cannot be effectively dealt with merely by combining and balancing competing priorities" (p. 371). The reason is that as contradictions appear they reveal the tensions, imbalances, and conflicts between competing forces, which cannot be easily resolved (Foot, 2001). This revelation of a contradiction provides opportunities for creative innovations in the structure or function of the activity; thus, resulting in qualitative transformations of the subject or the activity (Engeström, 2001). Furthermore, subjects in resolving a contradiction may differ in their resolution of the contradiction due to various factors inside and outside an activity (Yamagata-Lynch & Haudenschild, 2009).

Next, Engeström (1987) described four levels of inner contradictions that appear within an activity (see Table 4.2). For the purpose of this study, the authors focused solely on secondary contradictions. Secondary contradictions occur when a new element from outside an activity conflicts with an old element (rules or division of labor) which leads to conflict (Engeström, 1987, 1990; Yamagata-Lynch & Haudenschild, 2009). For example, the introduction of a new element such as a co-teacher (Roth & Tobin, 2002), created inconsistencies between the goals of new professional development and the rules and regulations for teaching (Yamagata-Lynch & Haudenschild, 2009), resulting in conflicting opinions about feedback that was provided to students by a new instructor and teaching assistant (Gedera, 2016) leading to a rise in secondary contradictions. These new outside elements (co-teacher, professional development, instructor) led to conflicts with the existing rules or division of labor of the activity.

TABLE 4.2. Engeström's (1987) Four Levels of Inner Contradictions in Activity Systems.

Contradiction Level	Engeström's (1987) Definition
Level 1: Primary contradiction	When activity participants encounter more than one value system attached to an element within an activity that brings about conflict.
Level 2: Secondary contradiction	When activity participants encounter a new element of an activity, and the process of assimilating the new element into the activity brings about conflict.
Level 3: Tertiary contradiction	When activity participants face conflicting situations by adopting what is believed to be a newly advanced method for achieving the object.
Level 4: Quaternary contradiction	When activity participants encounter changes to an activity that result in creating conflicts with adjacent activities.

It is clear that COVID-19 changed the rules and the division of labor for teaching social studies with the rapid transition from face-to-face to synchronous and asynchronous instruction. It is important to note that other contradictions might have arisen due to the rapid transformation of the classroom; however, the significant role that COVID-19 plays as a significant new element in the activity of teaching, the researchers decided to focus solely on secondary contradictions.

METHODOLOGY

Given the rapid onset of the pandemic and the expansive qualitative transformations that might occur because of this crisis, several methodological decisions were made. This included convenience sampling of social studies teachers acquainted with the primary researcher, participants as participant-researchers, the use of semi-structured interview methodology, and selective coding of data.

Participants

Participant-researchers in this case study were selected through convenience sampling. All participant-researchers selected were acquainted with the primary researcher. Four of the participants had been preservice teachers who studied methods of teaching social studies with the primary researcher. One participant had been a colleague of the primary researcher at a summer program for gifted and talented students. The last participant-researcher was a college friend of the primary researcher, who recently began teaching. All participants-researchers were currently teaching social studies at the secondary level: two teachers taught middle school, two teachers taught high school, one teacher taught middle school students as part of a homeschool program, and the last teacher taught both middle and high school students. Next, participant-researchers taught in diverse schools: two taught in rural Midwest communities, two taught in an exurb of a large metropolitan area: Midwest and West Coast, one taught in an urban New England private school, the last teacher taught in a socio-economically and racially diverse Midwest suburb. Four of the participant-researchers are women, two are men. Five are Anglo-European/White and one participant is Latino/a. Four of the participants are in their 20s and the other two were in their late 40s.

Participant-Researcher

A key aspect of this case study is that participants were an essential part of the research from its formulation to the presentation of findings (Bergold & Thomas, 2012; Chase, 2017; Hall, 2005; Cohen et al., 2017). This intentional decision to include teachers as participant-researchers was founded on the desire that participants should have a role in the joint creation of knowledge. Therefore, participants would be more involved in the research than in the use of a traditional member check of data (Bergold & Thomas, 2012; Chase, 2017). As Chase (2017) noted this process might stimulate reflection on social practices; thus, revealing to all participants the qualitative transformations that were occurring in the activity. To achieve this principle, mediational triangles were shared with participant-researchers to analyze, reflect, and when needed correct findings to create a dialectical process of dialogue over the time of the research following the principles of participatory research (Bergold & Thomas, 2012). For example, several participant-researchers modified the description of culturally mediated artifacts, rules for their activity, or the division of labor. This allowed participant-researchers to examine their conception of the activity of teaching social studies before and after the completion of the academic school year.

The next key aspect of achieving this goal was the use of the fundamental principles of participatory research (Bergold & Thomas, 2012). First, participants-researchers aided in shaping the research questions and aims of the research to increase the democratic nature of this participatory research. During our initial interviews participant-researchers discussed their goal of participating in the research, concerns they had about the research included what data should and should not be analyzed, and suggestions of other teachers to be participant-researchers for this study.

The second principle was to provide a safe space to share their views (Bergold & Thomas, 2012) of the pandemic and its effects on their classroom practices. To achieve this objective, full transcripts of the interviews were only analyzed by the primary and one participant-researcher who co-wrote this chapter. Participant-researchers determined what data would be included and excluded from the study. Discussions of students, school administration, and other political issues were not to be analyzed nor included in the study. Participant-researchers decided data only related to the transformation of the activity of teaching social studies were analyzed. Lastly, all data and findings were shared with participant-researchers. Next, each participant-researcher was assigned a random number, which is used when displaying all data.

The last principle was that participants were self-defined in the community of social studies teachers and members of participatory research. As part of the community, participants-researchers determined their own level of participation in this study. For instance, all participant-researchers examined and commented on their mediational triangles. Only one participant-researcher desired to participate in the coding of data and writing of this paper. Participant-researchers were also given the opportunity to co-present the findings of the study. This allowed participant-researchers to be active in the collection and analysis of qualitative data and determine their own role in the study.

Data Analysis

Qualitative data was collected during three 30–45-minute interviews that were conducted during the first week of the pandemic, four weeks later, and after the conclusion of the six participant-researcher's spring semesters. Interviews were conducted using an interview guide approach/semi-structured interview (Drever, 1995; Patton, 1980). Prior to the first interview, participant-researchers were provided a basic second-generation mediational triangle (see Figure 4.1), which provided a general outline and sequence of questions. Next, providing participant-researchers a sample triangle preserved a conversational and situational pattern to the interviews (Patton, 1980, see Table 4.1). Qualitative data from the first interviews were coded and mapped onto the aforementioned second-generation triangles (Engeström, 1987, 1990) using a selective coding method (Strauss & Corbin, 1990) based on core categories of activity theory (see Table 4.1). The initial participant-researchers' mediational triangles provided a base from which possible manifestations of contradictions could be analyzed. As noted, contradictions manifest themselves in the historical context of the activity and in the words and actions of participant-researchers. Thus, the initial interviews were used to monitor the qualitative transformations resulting from the appearance of contradictions in subsequent interviews.

Data from the second and third interviews were also immediately coded using the same selective coding method as the initial interview (Strauss & Corbin, 1990, see Table 4.1). Using the same iterative process, data was mapped onto a second-generation mediational triangle. This revealed the qualitative transformations of the activity of teaching social studies.

Following the conclusion of all interviews and the return of all mediational triangles, data from the second and third interviews were then analyzed to uncover overall patterns of qualitative transformations across all participant-researchers. This process required a second round of selective coding using a constant comparison method (Strauss & Corbin, 1990). This revealed patterns in the qualitative transformations of the activity of teaching social studies across all six participants. This process resulted in numerous findings (see Table 4.3); however, the primary researchers focused on two significant qualitative transformations of the activity (see Table 4.4).

TABLE 4.3. Patterns of Qualitative Transformations From Second and Third Interviews

Loci	Qualitative Transformation
Object	• Media literacy (teacher 1 and 4) • Creation of personal history –connection to current events (teacher 1, 2, 3, and 6)
Community	• Historians of past and present
Culturally mediating artifacts	• Teleconferencing software • Crash Course videos, TED Talks, other digital media • Asynchronous activities • Media literacy • Personal connection to current events

TABLE 4.4. Significant Qualitative Transformations

Loci	Qualitative Transformations
Object	1. Media literacy (teacher 1 and 4)
	2. Creation of personal history—connection to current events (teacher 1, 2, 3, and 6)
Culturally mediated artifacts	1. Online news disinformation game, scientific reading of the news, viewing current events through multiple lenses
	2. Coronavirus Blog, free write in an online document about current events and the past, Problem based learning project

FINDINGS

The pandemic caused rapid changes to the rules and the division of labor of teaching social studies. This led to the rapid rise of secondary contradictions and qualitative transformations of the activity. While primary researchers uncovered numerous qualitative transformations especially to the mediated artifacts of teaching social studies (increased use of technology and student driven learning, shorter lessons/activities, and the implementation of asynchronous teaching), the focus of this chapter is on the unique qualitative transformations that occurred. The most significant were the appearance of new objects of activity: media literacy and personal connection to history and current events appeared. Consequently, the appearance of new objects generated new culturally mediating artifacts (see Tables 4.5 and 4.6).

Media Literacy

Teachers one and four both added a new object to their activity of teaching social studies due to the pandemic; the need for students to develop media literacy (see Table 4.5). For both teachers' controversies surrounding the pandemic and

TABLE 4.5. Qualitative Transformations of Teacher 1 and 5: New Object of Activity—Media Literacy

Teacher	Pre-COVID Object	New Object
#1	1. Better understanding of the world: multiple perspectives	1. Better understanding of the world
	2. Improve critical thinking skills	2. Improve critical thinking skills
		3. Media literacy
#4	1. Building better global citizens: Understanding of the world	1. National and global citizenship
		2. Democratic citizenship—active citizenship
	2. Create good individuals—Civic efficacy	3. Media literacy

TABLE 4.6. Qualitative transformations of teacher 2, 3, and 6: New object of activity—Personal connection to current events/history

Teacher	Pre-COVID Object	New Object
#2	1. Breadth of knowledge—Topics and subjects 2. Essential skill sets—citizens	1. Check-in with students 2. Cover the content—Focus on key events—importance 3. To see change over time—personal connection
#3	1. Critical analysis of the world around them. 2. Better citizen—democratic citizens 3. Global citizens	1. Students are openminded to different perspectives. 2. Citizenship 3. Personal connection to current events
#6	1. Social justice PBL 2. How they matter as people—citizens 3. Anti-racist citizens	1. Connecting children to history—meaningful history 2. Real history—not the romantic past/present 3. Anti-racist citizens—Answering tough questions

the transformation of the activity gave rise to a new object and culturally mediated artifacts.

Object

For two of the participant-researchers, media literacy became a new object of their activity of teaching social studies (see Figure 4.2). Teacher one stated, "I want my students to learn about what's going on in the world. I want them to improve their critical thinking skills. I want them to improve their media literacy skills" (second interview). In the final interview, teacher one stated, "Coronavirus did really bring out a lot of conspiracy theories, so it was timely, and relevant to start ... with what they were seeing in the world." Thus, teacher one expanded their initial object of "students having a better understanding of the world they live in" (first interview) to include media literacy as a key aspect of learning about the world. Media literacy was now more than a tool to be used, it was a goal of the course. Similarly, teacher four expanded their object of the activity to include media literacy. Initially, teacher four noted that a key goal was active global and domestic citizenship, and a key mediating artifact was using current events to achieve this object. Teacher four stated,

> Almost being able to, you know, just read all the information that's coming to us. You know there's so much. Coming out of the media and people are really confused and I just, I feel like I've done a lot of [asking students].

"How do you interpret that?" "How do you feel about that?" (second interview). They added,

> If you have one source, if you're concerned that looking at those sources, you know you've got where that information came from. You know they're calling it a place like Snopes. You don't go there and look up what they're saying about it. [If] It's information about the number of infected people, the number of deaths go to the Johns Hopkins site. Don't rely on a single source of information in these times. Try to get multiple sources of information. You try to identify the facts, try to separate the spirit or bias of whatever it is that you're looking at. Then you don't make decisions for yourself based on the information that's out there but don't get that information based on one source (second interview).

They later noted,

> The students were consuming a lot more news than they had been previously. Part of that was just being at home all the time. I think in the pre-COVID-19 situation, I had to push them to go to the news. It had to be part of the class [pre-COVID-19]. Then I had to set time [after the start of the pandemic] aside and really try to discuss what they were all consuming and were they getting it from multiple places. (third interview)

Thus, the pandemic required students to develop media literacy. For teachers one and four the pandemic led to the new object of media literacy.

Culturally Mediating Artifacts

The appearance of the new object for teacher one and four led to the appearance of new culturally mediating artifacts the teachers were to use. For example, teacher one stated "Yes I still have had them do some research projects. I've sort of ramped up my use of media literacy type training" (second interview). They added,

> One of the things I did recently, I had previously found and been planning to use. [It is an] Online game where you get to personify someone who is trying to spread disinformation and create click bait. This basically teaches you all the tools and tricks that they [fake media] use to get followers and grab attention. In the hopes of helping students be able to recognize it better when they encounter clickbait. It's a great game. (second interview)

Teacher one also noted,

> Then I've done a couple of assignments where they're looking at the same topic through the lens of right leaning media versus left leaning media. And so that's another sort of take on [it], both media literacy as well as perspective taking. (second interview)

Through research projects, an online game, and new activities of examining topics through multiple lenses, teacher one hoped to achieve the new object of teaching social studies.

Similarly, teacher four added new mediating artifacts. He noted, "The textbook that we use for government had a section on how to read a newspaper. So I use[d] that as a starter. So they read through the chapter on it" (second interview). After including this new artifact, teacher four added a new artifact—reading scientifically:

I had them go to a TED Talk about how to scientifically read the news. Then walked them through all of that and then we had a discussion. I asked them to pick an article from a news source and then go through and answer some questions about it [the article]. (second interview)

This activity then expanded to students using their new media literacy skills to examine the pandemic. Teacher four stated,

I didn't, you know, just walk in here and then [start] comparing and contrasting because all five articles were about COVID-19 [from] very different perspectives. Five different sources of information and we were able to compare and contrast. Who they interviewed? And what they did? And why didn't they? Why didn't one source interview the same source? (second interview)

Thus, the chapter on media, the method of scientifically reading the news, and the comparing and contrasting of articles about the pandemic served as new mediating artifacts to achieve the new object of media literacy.

The new object in teaching social studies for teachers one and four was media literacy. The appearance of this new object was tied to the desire that students understand the impacts of the pandemic and the effects this event was having on them and their community. This new object led to the manifestation of new culturally mediating artifacts including the use of an online game on disinformation, the use of a scientific method of reading the news, and the examination of the news through multiple lenses.

Personal History of Current Events

The second significant qualitative transformation was the appearance of another new object for three of the teachers (teachers two, three, and six): personal history of current events. While this new object and subsequent culturally mediating artifacts resulted from the rapid changes to the division of labor and rules, the object was connected to the pandemic and the civil rights protests of the spring of 2020. Prior to COVID-19, three teachers focused on helping students grow as citizens (see Table 4.6). The transformations of the activity due to COVID-19 led to the addition of a new related object to the activity of teaching social studies.

Object

Three of the teachers developed another new object for the activity of teaching social studies: students constructing a personal history of current events due to changes to the rules and division of labor. They argued that given the events of the spring of 2020 this required students to learn how to construct their own personal history of these events. For example, teacher three stated, "I want students to connect how things from the past are today...I want them to see themselves as a primary source of history" (second interview). They added they wanted students to be "their own primary source" (second interview). This sentiment was mirrored by teacher six, who stated, "With our current climate, I just wanted to connect kids to history and make it as meaningful as possible" (second interview). They added,

> Well why would a kid right now in the middle of a pandemic care about what people decided in the late 1800s about how to reform the country? Well right now with everything going on it's [the] perfect time to breathe modern life into the Reconstruction and show them all the different injustices that are going on in our country. How those really took root at the very beginning of our country. (second interview)

In a similar fashion, teacher two noted, "I think that it's important because I want my students to see themselves in the history that they study" (second interview). They added,

> I think it's important for them [students] and maybe they don't realize that maybe they do but for them to see themselves in the history that they're reading and to see it as this was not that long ago and this is still very recent history and it's important to learn from it [because how the past has shaped current events]. (second interview)

Students were to create a personal connection to history and see themselves in the events that were reshaping their lives.

Culturally Mediated Artifacts

In a similar fashion a new object of students constructing a personal history of current events led to the appearance of new mediating artifacts. Teachers argued that students needed to move beyond just examining how the past influenced the present but that students needed to explore their own role in creating history.

Two of the teachers used writing as a culturally mediated artifact to achieve the new object of teaching social studies. COVID-19 shifted the paradigm, from having students analyzing primary sources and practicing empathy when they learn about the past. Students were no longer examiners of the past but recorders of their own personal history. This manifested in the practice of "daily journaling during e-Learning," using an online platform, called "Coronavirus Blogs" (teacher three, second interview). Students were asked to answer "If you were there" questions and primary source analysis questions. Teacher three explained that

> blogs concerned how their [students] lives had changed because of the Coronavirus. Students wrote in them three times a week. They had to write in their blogs about "What went on that day? What did they hear happen in the news? How is this going to affect them?" (second interview)

Teacher three wanted students to be "Their own primary source" (second interview) and to aid them in this process,

> I also tried to do lessons since that related to past pandemics and what similarities could we see from like the Spanish influenza in 1918 to today. What were some of the ways people responded and was there a backlash to the things that the government was trying to do to keep people safe. (second interview)

Next, teacher three had students use digital tools including social media apps (TikTok, Snapchat, Instagram) for students to upload materials such as photos and videos to their blog to document their experiences. Teacher three stated, "[they] wanted students to imagine seventh and eighth graders one hundred years from now using their blogs as primary sources to learn about life in 2020" (second interview). Similar to teacher three, teacher two also used various activities to have students construct a personal history. Teacher two stated they wanted their students to see themselves as part of history and current events. They stated,

> Civil Rights, I feel like are things that are obviously seen today [George Floyd protests], and I've wanted to give as much of their [student] choice in how they went about that [project]. With you know responding to a paragraph or responding to a Google form. (second interview)

Students were provided space to write about the Civil Rights Movement and current events in the Spring of 2020.

Teacher six modified an existing pedagogy, problem-based learning, to aid students in constructing a personal history of current events. A key object before the pandemic was to create an anti-racist community. This included students doing projects based on connecting historical and current events using problem-based learning. They described that students would "create campaigns to educate their fellow Americans to care and help with causes" (teacher six, first interview). Given the changes to the division of labor and rules melded her existing object to the new object of students creating personal history with new culturally mediated artifacts. Teacher six created a project connecting their "unit on Reconstruction with the Black Lives Matter movement and the events of Spring 2020" (second interview). Students were tasked with creating "a virtual artifact project showing the roots of Reconstruction ideas in modern American history" (second interview). As part of this project, students explored current events affecting their lives. For instance, teacher six noted, "So I already have a couple of kids asking about the different killings that have happened [in neighboring cities and states]" (second interview). Students were analyzing the past by exploring the present and developing a personal history of current events by examining multiple perspectives and developing personal empathy to how events of the past relate to present events.

For these three teachers (teachers two, three, and six), the secondary contradiction manifested in a new object: personal connection to current events. This new object was clearly tied to the existing object of citizenship but moved beyond connecting the past to the present. For two of the teachers, it was important that students write about current events and how it influenced their lives. For the third, it was essential for students to engage in a problem-based learning project to achieve the new object.

DISCUSSION

As noted by Engeström (1987, 1990), the introduction of an outside element which changes the rules or division of labor of an activity produces secondary contradictions. The closing of schools for face-to-face instruction due to COVID-19 resulted in dramatic and dynamic changes to the rules and the division of labor in the activity of teaching secondary social studies. Teachers had to rapidly move from face-to-face instruction to teaching synchronously and asynchronously with the precipitous reduction of the amount of time for teachers to interact with students; therefore, the rules of teaching social studies and how labor was divided in the activity changed. Thus, COVID-19 gave rise to secondary contradictions.

Next, as Engeström (1987, 1990) argued, contradictions are manifested in the words and actions of the subject. The participant-researchers described that the activity of teaching social studies had changed in profound ways, which led to transformations of the object of their teaching. All six teachers noted they relied more on technology, applied more strategies for synchronous and asynchronous learning, and found creative ways of teaching social studies with decreased time for interactions with students. While the degrees of transformations differ in magnitude from teacher to teacher; the most significant transformations occurred with the appearance of new objects of the activity. Two participant-researchers found a new object in guiding students in expanding their media literacy, which resulted in new mediating artifacts the teachers used to achieve the new object. Next, three participant-researchers developed a new object of ensuring that students were building a personal connection to current events (COVID-19 pandemic and the civil rights protests). This also resulted in the creation of new culturally mediated artifacts. The transformation of the rules and division of labor led to the creation of these new objects came new or modified culturally mediating artifacts.

Next, as predicted by Engeström (2001) and Yamagata-Lynch & Haudenschild (2009) the participant-researchers differed in how they resolved contradictions. Each participant-researcher responded to the turmoil caused by COVID-19 to re-imagine their class including creating new objects of the activity with new culturally mediating artifacts. Participant-researchers developed similar new objects and culturally mediated artifacts. These new objects and culturally mediated artifacts were shaped by how the participant-researcher re-imagined the activity of teaching social studies.

CONCLUSION

COVID-19 radically changed the rules and the division of labor of the activity of teaching social studies due to the tensions, imbalances, and competing forces it unleashed. This led to the rise of contradictions because of the opposing forces inside and outside the activity. The appearance of the secondary contradiction manifested in the actions and words of the participant-researchers. They clearly responded to the tensions and turmoil that arose from the rapid transformation of the rules and division of labor of teaching social studies. As predicted, these tensions were not easily resolved (Engeström, 2001; Foot, 2001) by the participant-researchers in this study, but it provided opportunities for creative innovations to re-think the structure and function of the activity. Participant-researcher responded to the tensions created by the rapid transformation of teaching social studies by altering the activity.

Participant-researchers increased the use of technology, shifted to more student-driven/asynchronous learning, shortened the length of lessons, and increased use of digital media (see Table 4.3). The most significant qualitative transformations that occurred was the appearance of new objects of the activity and subsequent culturally mediated artifacts (see Table 4.4). The appearance of these new objects and culturally mediated artifacts were in response to the rise of secondary contradictions. It is clear that COVID-19 changed the rules and the division of labor for teaching social studies with the rapid transition from face-to-face to synchronous and asynchronous instruction. This transformation led to a re-thinking and re-imaging of the object of teaching social studies; consequently, leading to new culturally mediated artifacts.

REFERENCES

Bergold, J., & Thomas, S. (2012). Participatory research methods: A methodological approach in motion. *Historical Social Research/Historische Sozialforschung*, 191–222.

Bombardieri, M. (2021, April 15). Covid-19 changed education in America—Permanently: It's been a school year like no other. Here's what we learned. *Politico*. https://www.politico.com/news/2021/04/15/covid-changed-education-permanently-479317

Brown Center Chalkboard. (2021). *Coronavirus and schools: Reflections on education one year into the pandemic* [Policy brief]. Brookings Institute: Brown Center on Education Policy. https://www.brookings.edu/blog/brown-center-chalkboard/2021/03/12/coronavirus-and-schools-reflections-on-education-one-year-into-the-pandemic/

Chase, E. (2017). Enhanced member checks: Reflections and insights from a participant-researcher collaboration. *The Qualitative Report*, *22*(10), 2689–2703.

Cohen, L., Manion, L., & Morrison, K. (2017). *Research methods in education*. Routledge.

Cole, M., & Engeström, Y. (1993). A cultural-historical approach to distributed cognition. In G. Salomon (Ed.), *Distributed cognitions: Psychological and educational considerations*. Cambridge University Press.

Drever, E. (1995). *Using semi-structured interviews in small-scale research. A teacher's guide*. Scottish Council for Research in Education.

Education Week. (2020, June 2). Classroom technology: How did COVID-19 change your teaching, for better or worse? See Teachers' responses. *Education Week*. https://www.edweek.org/technology/how-did-covid-19-change-your-teaching-for-better-or-worse-see-teachers-responses/2020/06

Elmberger, A., Björck, E., Liljedahl, M., Nieminen, J., & Laksov, K. B. (2019). Contradictions in clinical teachers' engagement in educational development: an activity theory analysis. *Advances in Health Sciences Education*, *24*(1), 125–140.

Engeström, Y. (1987). *Learning by expanding: An activity-theoretical approach to developmental research*. Orienta-Konsultit Oy.
Engeström, Y. (1990). *Learning, working and imagining: Twelve studies in activity theory*. Orienta-Konsultit Oy.
Engeström, Y. (2001). Expansive learning at work: Toward an activity theoretical reconceptualization. *Journal of Education and Work, 14*(1), 133–156.
Engeström, Y., & Sannino, A. (2011). Discursive manifestations of contradictions in organizational change efforts. *Journal of Organizational Change Management, 24*(3), 368–387.
Foot, K. A. (2001). Cultural-historical activity theory as practice theory: Illuminating the development of conflict-monitoring network. *Communication Theory, 11*(1), 56–83.
Foot, K. A., & Groleau, C. (2011). Contradictions, transitions, and materiality in organizing processes: An activity theory perspective. *First Monday, 16*(6), 1–9 https://doi.org/10.5210/fm.v16i6.3479
Gedera, D. S. (2016). The application of activity theory in identifying contradictions in a university blended learning course. In *Activity theory in education* (pp. 51–69). Brill Sense.
Hall, B. (2005). Breaking the monopoly of knowledge research methods, participation and development. In R. Tandon (Ed.), *Participatory research: Revisiting the roots* (pp. 9–21). Mosaic.
Harris, D. N. (2020). *How will COVID-19 change our school in the long run?*. Brown Center on Education Policy. https://www.brookings.edu/blog/brown-center-chalkboard/2020/04/24/how-will-covid-19-change-our-schools-in-the-long-run/
Karanasios, S., Riisla, K., & Simeonova, B. (2017). *Exploring the use of contradictions in activity theory studies: An interdisciplinary review*. Presented at the 33rd EGOS Colloquium: The Good Organization, Copenhagen, July 6-8th.
Patton, M. Q. (1980). *Qualitative evaluation methods*. Sage
Pokhrel, S., & Chhetri, R. (2021). A literature review on impact of COVID-19 pandemic on teaching and learning. *Higher Education for the Future, 8*(1), 133–141.
Roth, W. M., & Lee, Y. J. (2007). "Vygotsky's neglected legacy": Cultural-historical activity theory. *Review of educational research, 77*(2), 186–232.
Roth, W. M., & Tobin, K. (2002). Redesigning an" urban" teacher education program: An activity theory perspective. *Mind, Culture, and Activity, 9*(2), 108–131.
Strauss, A., & Corbin, J. (1990). *Basics of qualitative research*. Sage publications.
Vesperman, D. P., & Leet-Otley, J. (2021). *Primary contradictions: Qualitative transformations of White social studies teacher identity*. In T. Haefner, L. Handler, & T. Rock (Eds.),*The divide within: Intersections of realities, facts, theories, & practices* (pp. 111–132). Information Age Publishing.
World Bank Group. (May, 2020). *World Bank Group: Education report: The COVID-19 Pandemic: Shocks to education and policy responses*. World Bank Group. https://www.worldbank.org/en/topic/education/publication/the-covid19-pandemic-shocks-to-education-and-policy-responses
Yamagata-Lynch, L. C., & Haudenschild, M. T. (2009). Using activity systems analysis to identify inner contradictions in teacher professional development. *Teaching and Teacher Education, 25*(3), 507–517.

CHAPTER 5

RE-IMAGINING CITIZENSHIP EDUCATION THROUGH CRITICAL-TRANSFORMATIONAL HUMAN RIGHTS EDUCATION

Ian M. McGregor
University of Nevada, Reno

Glenn Mitoma
University of California Santa Cruz

Sandra Sirota
University of Connecticut

Citizenship education has been a contentious field since early public educators set out to prepare young people for life in a democratic society. Citizenship education policies and curriculum have traditionally promoted a nationalist ideology of citizenship that creates conforming, obedient citizens to the exclusion of others and the denial of the pluralistic lives of young people. Amidst our current democratic crisis and a renewed interest in citizenship education among educators, academics, policymakers, federal agencies, and activists (Educating for American Democracy Initiative, 2021), we have the opportunity to re-imagine citizenship education through a human rights education framework in which transformative

Out of Turmoil: Catalysts for Re-learning, Re-Teaching, and Re-imagining History and Social Science, pages 73–90.
Copyright © 2023 by Information Age Publishing
www.infoagepub.com
All rights of reproduction in any form reserved.

models of human rights education (Bajaj, 2011a, 2011b), critical human rights education (Zembylas & Keet, 2018, 2019) and action civic curricular models (Levinson, 2014) may promote transformative agency (Bajaj, 2018) in young people. Re-imagined through a human rights education framework, citizenship education has potential to be a model that is characterized by young people:

- critiquing, rearticulating, adopting, and applying global human rights principles and standards in dialogue with peers,
- examining identities, loyalties, and solidarities,
- identifying sites and experiences of formal, non-formal, and informal learning for citizenship,
- learning about, developing, and implementing activist strategies that challenge barriers to the full realization of equal dignity for all,
- analyzing interconnectedness of civil, political, social, economic and cultural domains and developing an understanding of solidarity and collective agency across borders,
- enacting diverse roles, positions, strategies, and agency at the local, national, regional, and global levels, and
- engaging in reflexivity in which continued learning and transformational agency are supported.

CITIZENSHIP EDUCATION AND HUMAN RIGHTS EDUCATION

Preparing young people for citizenship has long been recognized as an essential function of public education and is reflected in prominent national organizational position statements and U.S. federal educational policy (see Educational Policies Commission, 1940; National Commission on Excellence in Education, 1983; NCSS, 2013a, 2013b). The National Council for the Social Studies (NCSS), the largest U.S. professional association devoted to social studies education, places a specific emphasis on preparing students for civic life. The College, Career, and Civic Life (C3) Framework for Social Studies State Standards, which many state education systems and school districts have used as a model, highlights the central role of social studies education in preparing students for the responsibilities of citizenship (NCSS, 2013a). Within the C3 Framework, the importance of citizenship education is evident. It appears as both a core objective of all social studies inquiry, noting that the "goal of knowledgeable, thinking, active citizens [...] is universal" (p. 4); and that as "civics," citizenship education constitutes one of the four primary "disciplines" of social studies, alongside economics, geography, and history.

Despite being centered, in principle, by the NCSS, in practice, public education in the United States has largely neglected citizenship education and civics. The recent report by the Educating for American Democracy Initiative (2021) notes that decades-long reliance on high-stakes testing (which generally does not include social studies) and emphasis on STEM fields have meant a steady erosion of citizenship education at all levels. Almost a decade after the publication of the C3 Framework, the authors of the report conclude, "Generations of students have not received the high-quality education in history and civics that they need, and deserve, to prepare them for informed and engaged citizenship" (p. 10).

Where and when it is pursued, citizenship education is often based on a citizenship transmission model in which the purpose of social studies education is to promote student acquisition of specific American and/or democratic values through teaching and learning of discrete, factual pieces of information drawn primarily from Western thought and culture (Ross & Marker, 2005a, 2005b). The citizenship transmission model promotes a nationalist version of citizenship organized around the nation-state, which learner-citizens are assumed to have a natural affinity for and identity with (Apple, 2004; Chappell, 2010; Osler, 2011). This nationalist citizenship is characterized by an ideological commitment to American exceptionalism (Loewen, 2007; Tyrrell, 1991), the fostering of a homogeneous, exclusive national identity (Chappell, 2010), patriotic commitments to the nation (Kahne & Middaugh, 2008; Westheimer, 2007, 2019), and a focus on passive, obedient, individualistic acts (Johnson & Morris, 2010; Veugelers, 2007; Westheimer & Kahne, 2004). Nationalist citizenship does not allow for the pluralistic lives and multiple loyalties learner-citizens may hold, nor was it designed to do so. Moreover, nationalist citizenship is set in opposition to other nations, invoking an "us" vs. "them" identity-by-exclusion. As an in-group, citizens are supposed to share identical values, culture, and language that set them apart from (and usually above) the out-group (see Kymlicka, 2017). According to Westheimer (2019), "Currently, the vast majority of school programs that take the time to teach citizenship emphasize good character, including the importance of volunteering, helping those in need, and following the law" (p. 7). Citizenship education in the United States largely asks students to be "good citizens" by following the rules, being obedient, attending to individual moral responsibilities, and having a patriotic commitment to the nation. This version of citizenship education has been subject to sustained critique by scholars (see Banks, 2009; Fernekes, 2016; Johnson & Morris, 2010; Kymlicka, 1995, 2011; Ladson-Billings, 2004; Lister, 2003; Osler, 2011; Osler & Starkey, 2003, 2005, 2018; Rosaldo, 1994, 1999), yet remains largely in place in many classrooms throughout the United States.

In contrast to the more common citizenship education programs in the United States that reinforce the type of nationalist citizenship described above, this paradigm of citizenship education is challenged by the emergent field of human rights education (HRE). While still marginal to social studies as compared to citizenship education, HRE has expanded in recent years. As of 2016, 42 out of 50 U.S. states included human rights topics in their K–12 social studies standards as either required content or as an example of a history or civics standard (The Advocates for Human Rights, 2016). Further, the NCSS has called for HRE to be integrated into social studies classrooms, and civic education specifically (NCSS, 2014, 2021). As HRE becomes more prevalent, human rights education frameworks are disrupting nationalistic conceptions of citizenship. HRE promotes global human rights ideals and civic action grounded in a pluralistic notion of citizenship (Banks, 2009; Fernekes, 2016; Osler, 2011; Osler & Starkey, 2003, 2005, 2018). Over the past 30 years, HRE has achieved increasing recognition at the international level, and in many European, Latin American, and a select few other countries. These countries have developed complementary curriculum materials (Council of Europe, 2009; Osler, 2008; Starkey, 1991; Waldron & Ruane, 2010) and have integrated HRE into curriculum standards (Sirota, 2017; Stone, 2002; The Advocates for Human Rights, 2016) and textbooks (Meyer et al., 2010; Russell & Suárez, 2017; Russell et al., 2017; Suárez, 2007). This growing legibility is tied to HRE's potential for fostering a broader culture of human rights. As defined by the United Nations:

> Human rights education and training comprises all educational, training, information, awareness-raising and learning activities aimed at promoting universal respect for and observance of all human rights and fundamental freedoms and thus contributing, inter alia, to the prevention of human rights violations and abuses by providing persons with knowledge, skills and understanding and developing their attitudes and behaviors, to empower them to contribute to the building and promotion of a universal culture of human rights. (United Nations General Assembly, Dec. 2011, p. 3)

As such, it encompasses:

a. Education about human rights, which includes providing knowledge and understanding of human rights norms and principles, the values that underpin them and the mechanisms for their protection;
b. Education through human rights, which includes learning and teaching in a way that respects the rights of both educators and learners;
c. Education for human rights, which includes empowering persons to enjoy and exercise their rights and to respect and uphold the rights of others. (United Nations General Assembly, Dec. 2011, p. 3)

Human rights education warrants involvement in all forms of education (not just schooling) and draws attention to the differentiated processes of teaching about, through, and for human rights (Tibbitts, 2017). Through studying *about* human rights and human rights violations, young people have the opportunity to develop the necessary knowledge about their community and the wider world as a basis for civic engagement. As Barton (2015) noted, "consideration of human rights thus plays a crucial role in helping students evaluate policies related to a wide range of contemporary social concerns, including globalization, migration, genocide, warfare, security, economic development, sustainability and the expansion of human potential" (p. 49). Teaching *through* human rights asks educators to model and apply human rights practices as part of their pedagogies and classroom management strategies, ensuring that young people have the opportunity to see themselves as rights-holders with agency in and out of the school context. Of particular note is the need to teach *for* human rights, where HRE aims to empower the learner with the means of analyzing, naming, and addressing violations of human rights and proactively advancing human dignity for all (Starkey, 2010). Education *for* human rights places emphasis on skills that resemble forms of critical citizenship (see Johnson & Morris, 2010), and can be developed by integrating the practices of action civics (Levinson, 2014). Education *for* human rights asks students not to be passive, obedient citizens, but rather learner-citizens that are active and engaged with communal and societal life.

Action Civics

For citizenship education to be effective, it must engage students in the "deeper learning" of active sense-making and deliberation; ideation, revision, strategic thinking, and planning; implementing action plans individually and in coordination with others; and evaluating and reflecting on outcomes and impacts (Levine & Kawashima-Ginsberg, 2015). Regular opportunities for young people to engage in civic learning activities is essential to cultivating a commitment to democratic participation (see Guilfoile et al., 2016; Kahne & Sporte, 2008; Levine, 2013; Levinson, 2012; Youniss, 2011). Drawing from Youth Participatory Action Research (YPAR; Levinson, 2014), action civics curricular models have emerged as an approach that goes beyond traditional civics programs by combining learning and practice (Circle Staff, 2013). Young people are positioned not as future citizens but as current citizens with voice and agency, and, as such, action civics is politically engaged, challenging young people "to take on a social justice orientation as they reflect upon their lived experiences and the actions they propose to take" (Levinson, 2012, p. 226).

In Levinson's (2014) model, action civics often encompasses six steps: 1) examine your community; 2) choose an issue; 3) research the issue and set a goal; 4) analyze power; 5) develop strategies; and 6) take action to affect policy. These steps are designed to make civics authentic to the experience and environment of students and to foster their capacity to participate in democratic life, rather than simply present a fixed curriculum of governmental institutions and processes. In this way, young people move from being passive observers of democracy to being "viewed as assets who possess knowledge and insight that will help them make positive contributions and act as agents of change in their communities" (LeCompte et al., p. 128).

HUMAN RIGHTS EDUCATION AS A MODEL FOR CITIZENSHIP EDUCATION

Given the ways human rights education is in disharmony with nationalist models of citizenship, we have the opportunity to re-imagine human rights education as a new model for citizenship education. By combining transformational models of HRE (Bajaj, 2011a, 2011b; Bajaj et al., 2016; Spreen et al., 2018; Tibbitts,

2017), transformative agency (Bajaj, 2018; Hantzopoulos et al., 2021), and critical HRE (Zembylas & Keet, 2018, 2019) with action civics curricular models (see LeCompte et al., 2019; Levinson, 2014; Pope et al., 2011), human rights education has the potential to engage young people to learn and practice meaningful human rights-informed civic action in their own schools and communities. The transformational approach of HRE requires that, in addition to learning about human rights, students are treated with dignity and respect in the learning environment, have the opportunity to engage with others in the planning and implementation of meaningful human rights action, and participate in dialogue and reflection throughout the process (Bajaj et al., 2016). This combination of knowledge gained, an environment of respect and dignity, and the opportunity for action, dialogue and reflection in community with others may result in a transformative experience in which the learner may gain advocacy skills and recognize their own agency for the first time. Echoing Freire's (1970) conception of critical consciousness, transformative agency is "the ability to act in the face of structural constraints to advance individual and collective goals related to positive social change" (Bajaj, 2018, p. 7). Transformative HRE fosters and supports transformative agency, both for students and for educators, in ways that lead to civic action.

Critical-Transformational HRE

While human rights education frameworks grounded in the *UN Declaration on Human Rights Education and Training* open up the potential for approaches to citizenship education that cut against the tradition of nationalist citizenship, Keet (2015) and others have long cautioned against a "declarationist" approach to HRE which would center international documents like the *Universal Declaration of Human Rights*, accepting them without critique, at the expense of critical, localized co-constructions of human rights ideas and practices. An overemphasis on the international dimensions of human rights risks reinforcing the idea that human rights are about sad, deprived lives of distant others in foreign lands and not about the interconnected challenges of advancing justice for all. Such an approach might ironically reproduce nationalist tropes of "us" vs. "them" or the "savage, victim, savior" metaphor (Mutua, 2001) through the discourse of human rights. However, HRE must stand in a critical relationship with human rights universals (Zembylas & Keet, 2019) to be truly transformational.

In opposition to declarationist approaches, Michalinos Zembylas and André Keet (2019) argue HRE should view human rights universals not as authoritative, but rather as part of critical analyses within HRE. They note including 'critical' adds the

> necessary distance between HRE and human rights universals that allows for a reflexivity capable of questioning, from a social justice perspective, the assumptions, premises and suppositions of human rights itself and how and why these are exported into the praxis of HRE in the way that they are. The 'critical' is regenerative,

aimed at perpetual transformation of, in this case, HRE. (Zembylas & Keet, 2019, p. 26)

This is not to suggest human rights universals should be discarded, but rather acknowledged as contingent political and discursive constructions in which various power-knowledge relations are embedded (Zembylas & Keet, 2019). They define critical HRE as:

> a pedagogical formation that: first, stands in a critical relationship with human rights universals; second, perpetually revisits the receivable categories of human rights praxes; third, advances a social-justice-oriented human rights practice; and fourth, emphasizes human critiques to enrich human rights understandings. (Zembylas & Keet, 2019, p. 28)

In conversation with transformative models of HRE, critical human rights education has the potential to open conceptual spaces to the lived experiences of young people grounding HRE in the context of needs, compassion, and solidarity. The focus is placed on addressing human wrongs, the "instinctive registration of a negative and degrading human experience," as opposed to noncompliance with stated regulatory principles (Zembylas & Keet, 2019, p. 29). The critical stance assumes that young people are more likely to have transformative experiences when examining their own lived experiences in relation to human wrongs in the context of local civil, political, social, economic, and cultural power structures as compared with technical regulatory principles.

Human Rights Informed Citizenship Education

Combining a critical-transformational model of human rights education with action civics has the potential to reconstruct citizenship education in ways that can strengthen American democracy. Cultivating student agency through critical engagement with human rights principles, collaborative inquiry into human wrongs, and scaffolded opportunities for authentic action can empower young people to cocreate and participate in a diverse democratic society. We suggest that when young people are provided the opportunity to collaboratively think critically about, envision, and practice human rights ideals and democratic skills, they can contribute to the realization of human rights and the building of more just and democratic communities. Specifically, we propose an updated model of citizenship education that centers HRE and allows young people to:

- critique, rearticulate, adopt, and apply global human rights principles and standards in dialogue with peers,
- examine their own identities, loyalties, and solidarities,
- identify sites and experiences of formal, non-formal, and informal learning for citizenship,

- learn, develop, and implement activist strategies that challenge barriers to the full realization of equal dignity for all,
- analyze interconnectedness of civil, political, social, economic and cultural domains and develop an understanding of solidarity and collective agency across borders,
- enact diverse roles, strategies, and agency at the local, national, regional, and global levels, and
- engage in reflexivity in which continued learning and transformational agency are supported.

Each of these stages of a citizenship education models informed by critical and transformational HRE are not meant to be sequentially enacted, but rather are a dynamic feedback loop encouraging continual learning, engagement, and reflexivity (see Figure 5.1).

Often the study of human rights begins with an introduction to and examination of the Universal Declaration of Human Rights (UDHR). Citizenship education informed by critical and transformative HRE aims to disrupt this initial experience

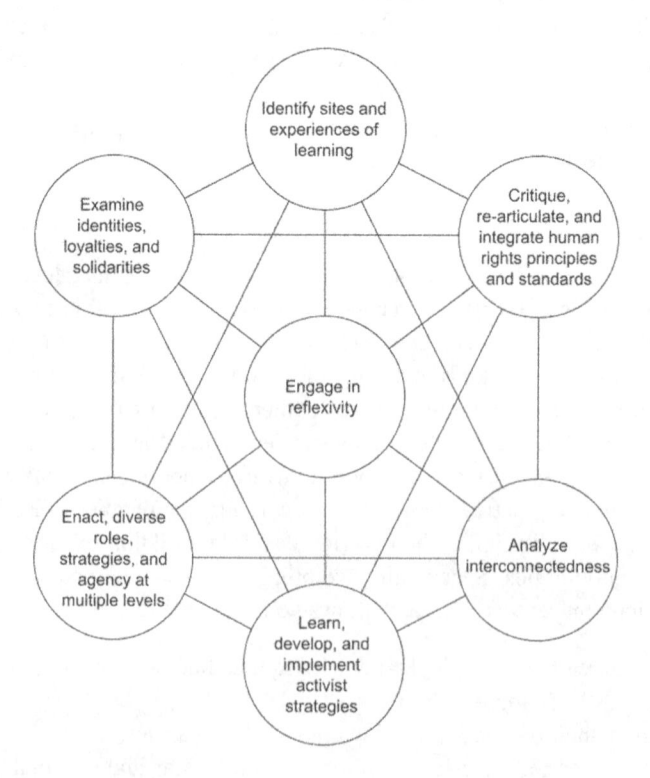

FIGURE 5.1. Characteristics of HRE Informed Citizenship Education

and conceptual space by asking young people to examine the UDHR through a critical and decolonizing lens (Sanchez, 2020; Zembylas & Keet, 2018, 2019). In dialogue with peers in which lived experiences center the conversation, young people are provided space to critique the assumptions, premises, and suppositions of human rights universals. This practice in critical-transformational HRE aims to encourage and support reflexivity. Students are asked to critique the UDHR and other global human rights universals and consider how these principles and standards may be changed to ensure dignity to all. Moreover, this practice in critical-transformational HRE allows young people to question other principles and standards closer to home that may be shaping their identities and loyalties. Traditionally, citizenship education in the United States has assumed blind obedience from young people to the principles and standards found in local and national constitutions and other foundational legal documents—Loewen (2007) aptly calls textbook's coverage of the U.S. federal government "anti-citizenship manuals—handbooks for acquiesce" (p. 220). When informed by transformational and critical HRE, citizenship education allows students to reexamine local principles and standards, taking a reflexive approach in examining how they have been influenced by them (See Table 5.1). Teachers might ask students to reexamine national legal documents such as the U.S. Constitution as a document deeply rooted in the historical context in which it was created and how the assumptions, premises and suppositions found in the U.S. Constitution have continued and impacted their lived experiences. This exercise would help bridge the often sterile environment found in civic education with the realities young people are exposed to daily.

Through this iterative process of examining how assumptions, premises, and suppositions found in domestic and global universals, principles, and standards may or may not apply to their lived experiences, young people are provided space to explore their own identities, loyalties, and solidarities. This exploration may force a serious reconsideration of national identity formation that is currently carried out in citizenship education. No longer would the classroom space and experiences be the central place in which civic identity is developed. Everyday lived experiences of young people and the inclusion of action civics curricular models would allow young people to practice activist strategies outside of the classroom. The classroom becomes one of many sites of learning and experience as young people reorient themselves as learner-citizens with agency in the spaces they take action in. Teachers must take care to give space and time for young people to reflect and dialogue on these experiences outside of the classroom in order to cultivate trust, inviting young people to decide the focus and level of engagement of their work.

Although action civics can adopt a social justice approach, alone, it is agnostic to any particular political orientation or values. Conceptually, action civics has the adverse potential to provide space for young people to take action based on anti-democratic principles. Combining action civics with critical and transformational HRE ensures that citizenship education is oriented toward justice and democracy

TABLE 5.1. Nationalist Citizenship Education Compared to Human Rights Informed Citizenship Education

Characteristics	Nationalist Citizenship Education	Human Rights Informed Citizenship Education
Purpose	To promote student acquisition of specific American and/or democratic values. To promote patriotic attachment to symbols of American nationalism. To promote social reproduction. To promote individual responsibility.	To disrupt traditional conceptions of citizenship education. To bridge learner-citizens multiple loyalties and identities across local, national, regional, and global contexts. To promote transformational agency in which actions aim to promote and protect rights and dignity for all humans.
Core assumptions	Democratic life requires a cohesive and stable society. To participate in democratic life, students must learn factual, discrete pieces of information drawn from the cultural heritage of the dominant society. Schools and teachers must maintain strict political neutrality with respect to issues, ideals, and outcomes.	Democratic life requires active engagement of all community members to solve problems and improve society. To participate in democratic life, students must learn about societies around the world and in relation to their own society and utilize their own agency to protect the rights of themselves and others. Schools and teachers must uphold fundamental human rights principles and adhere to democratic processes
Example pedagogical practices	Teacher-centered. Banking method/transmission model (e.g., lecturing, using textbooks as essential sources of information).	Student-centered pedagogies. YPAR. Action civics. Engaging pedagogies (e.g., problem-based learning, service learning, experiential learning, project-based learning, inquiry oriented learning).
Example learning outcomes	Students are able to identify key governance institutions and laws. Students understand basic governance processes. Students understand formal mechanisms for citizen participation in governance. Students express loyalty to the United States.	Students value human dignity and human rights. Students have knowledge and critical understanding of democratic institutions and processes. Students have collaborative inquiry and critical thinking skills. Students take individual and collective action in support of human rights.
Sites and experiences of learning	Experiences in the classroom.	Daily lived experiences in all spaces.

in addressing issues and barriers associated with equal dignity for all across local, national, regional, and global contexts. In utilizing a human rights focused action civics model, young people are expected to identify human rights issues, develop plans of action, and enact the plan. This student-centered orientation offers democratic instruction as students decide on the issues they wish to focus on. It allows young people to define issues relevant to their lives (Gingold, 2013), in dialogue with the discourse of human rights and global frames of reference. Young people are exposed to a pedagogy in which they are encouraged to act on their own initiative, to learn through enacting novel forms of citizenship (Levinson, 2014) rather than learning about a static, often obedient and passive, model of citizenship (Westheimer, 2019).

Young people need not only have authentic civic experiences in promoting and protecting human rights and dignity, but also understand the interconnected forces at play in perpetuating human wrongs (Fernekes, 2016). Through the examination of the interconnectedness of civil, political, social, economic, and cultural domains, young people unpack, examine, and analyze the social controversies that arise in a democratic society situated in local, national, regional, and global contexts (Fernekes, 2016). HRE informed citizenship education builds on young people's experiences, identities, multiple loyalties, and solidarities, rather than focusing on individualistic loyalty to a nation-state. Through this process, it has the potential to prepare young people for interdependence and diversity and in understanding our collective agency in promoting and protecting human dignity.

As a pathway for young people to help build and participate in a diverse, interdependent, democratic society, HRE informed citizenship education recognizes that individual and collective actions towards addressing human wrongs are grounded in lived experiences within the constraints of social structures and systems. This is not to suggest that individual and collective actions cannot take place within these boundaries, but rather in complex relationships with them: sometimes in opposition to them, sometimes enabled by them, and sometimes in spite of them. HRE informed citizenship education aims to acknowledge and develop the agency young people hold in diverse roles and positions and the strategies that can be implemented at different scales of society. For young people, human rights advocacy and civic action too often are positioned as the domains of others, whether it be advocates privileged enough to tackle human rights issues in faraway countries or those provided the right to vote and run for and hold office. By engaging in authentic action civic experiences, young people experience the diverse ways in which their agency can be empowered towards addressing human wrongs.

Lastly, engaging in HRE informed citizenship education encourages reflexivity, not only around beliefs and judgements on human rights principles and standards, but laying open the process, action taking, and efficacy young people experience. For young people to have a transformative experience, they must dive into the complexities of processes unfolding in action taking, examining their agency in the context of a rapidly changing world. Transformational agency is a continuous process in which agency invariably changes as young people have new experiences, hold different roles and positions, and unpack changing identities, loyalties, and solidarities. This reflexive process supports each part of HRE informed citizenship education in empowering young people to make change in the world in ensuring dignity for all.

Through critical-transformational human rights education, HRE informed citizenship education will situate young people as current citizens with voice, power, and agency. By including young people in our current society rather than in an envisioned future society, young people increasingly have the potential to recognize their agency for change at different scales of society. Nationalist citizenship continues to disenfranchise young people by positioning agency as a characteristic of future citizenship. Recognizing the human rights and citizenship young people hold is a first step towards centering human rights in citizenship education.

CONCLUSION

Human rights education includes citizenship education. However, citizenship education must adopt a critical-transformational stance grounded in HRE that employs curricular models providing young people opportunities to engage in civic action. A vision of citizenship education that does not adopt a critical-transformational stance invites reinforcement of the status quo in which young people continue to be framed as future citizens void of agency in the present and educational experiences are marked by learning factual, discrete information. The framework we present here offers a foundation in which citizenship education might be used in social studies classrooms to address criticisms of nationalist citizenship. Many interactional forces shape how young people develop as citizens, but the positioning of human rights at the center of citizenship education provides young people opportunities to practice full citizenship with the intent of promoting transformational agency. This framework aims to provide educators a means to address issues of nationalist citizenship and frame citizenship education in a manner consistent with human rights ideals and civic actions.

In a time when teachers are being pressured to retreat from engaging with action-oriented pedagogies such as YPAR and action civics and with controversial or difficult curriculum such as human rights in the United States, the work of adopting a vision of citizenship education grounded in human rights is becoming increasingly more difficult. Nonetheless, HRE informed citizenship education cuts across disciplines, providing a concrete language to empower learner-citizens. Students can use basic math skills to examine issues related to food scarcity, raising further reflexive questions around food security in their communities and associated human rights issues such as freedom of movement (Izard, 2018). Employing a critical literacy lens can examine underlying positions, power, and discursive constructions that exclude and dehumanize (Campano et al., 2016). Further, these types of investigative pedagogies align with the inquiry arc found in the NCSS C3 Framework (NCSS, 2013a). However, naming injustices is only half the work. Partnerships with community-based organizations, such as museums, libraries, universities, and other non-profit organizations may help teachers increase their students' engagement with human rights issues locally, nationally, regionally, and globally. Community partnerships "can create place-based experiential opportunities for young people that localize issues of equity and collaborative civic agency" (Hartman & Kahn, 2017, p. 7).

Future research might utilize this framework to examine a number of questions. Except for a handful of small studies, it is yet to be seen what effective classroom practices teachers may be employing towards supporting transformational agency in students in the United States. Beyond action civics curricular models, what micro instructional and curricular choices teachers are making towards promoting HRE informed citizenship education is understudied. Further, when presented with this framework, what challenges and anxieties do teachers face in implementing HRE informed citizenship education? As others have noted, instructional and curricular choices are not arbitrary but politically and ideologically motivated (Knowles, 2018; Westheimer & Kahne, 2004). Moreover, teachers' concerns and anxieties over teaching difficult histories and controversial topics (Barton, 2019; Walsh et al., 2017) associated with HRE (Mitoma, 2017) may lead to their reliance on safe, traditional curriculum and methods of instruction that are underpinned by traditional, conservative, nationalist notions of citizenship. To move teacher praxis towards one that aligns with HRE informed citizenship education, more research is needed that acknowledges teachers' values, experiences, and political and ideological identities (Knowles, 2018) in relation to citizenship education. Lastly, longitudinal studies are needed to understand if students are continuing to engage in transformative agency post K–12 education. Pedagogical practices that align with HRE informed citizenship education promise more long-term engagement in reforms, but more empirical data is needed to support this.

REFERENCES

The Advocates for Human Rights. (2016). *Human rights in state social studies standards: An analysis*. Report prepared for Human Rights Educators USA.

Apple, M. (2004). *Ideology and curriculum* (3rd ed.). Routledge Falmer. https://doi.org/10.4324/9780203487563

Bajaj, M. (2011a). Human rights education: Ideology, location, and approaches. *Human Rights Quarterly, 33*(2), 481–508. https://doi.org/10.1353/hrq.2011.0019

Bajaj, M. (2011b). *Schooling for social change: The rise and impact of human rights education in India*. Bloomsbury Publishing USA.

Bajaj, M. (2018). Conceptualizing transformative agency in education for peace, human rights, and social justice. *International Journal of Human Rights Education, 2*(1), 13.

Bajaj, M., Cislaghi, B., & Mackie, G. (2016). *Advancing transformative human rights education: Appendix D to the report of the global citizenship commission*. Open Book Publishers. http://dx.doi.org/10.11647/OBP.0091.13

Banks, J. (2009). Human rights, diversity, and citizenship education. *The Educational Forum, 73*, 100–110. https://doi.org/10.1080/00131720902739478

Barton, K. C. (2015). Young adolescents' positioning of human rights: Findings from Colombia, Northern Ireland, Republic of Ireland and the United States. *Research in Comparative and International Education, 10*(1), 48–70. https://doi.org/10.1177/1745499914567819

Barton, K.C. (2019). Teaching difficult histories: The need for a dynamic research tradition. In M. Gross & L. Terra (Eds.), *Teaching and learning difficult histories: Comparative perspectives* (pp. 11–25). Routledge. https://doi.org/10.4324/9781315110646

Campano, G., Ghiso, M.P., Rusoja, A., Player, G. D., & Schwab, E. R. (2016). "Education without boundaries": Literacy pedagogies and human rights. *Language Arts, 94*(1), 43–53.

Chappell, D. (2010). Training Americans: Ideology, performance, and social studies textbooks. *Theory & Research in Social Education, 38*(2), 248–269. https://doi.org/10.1080/00933104.2010.10473424

Circle Staff. (2013). *Civic learning through action: The case of generation citizen.* The Center for Information & Research on Civic Learning and Engagement (CIRCLE). https://civicyouth.org/wp-content/uploads/2013/07/Generation-Citizen-Fact-Sheet-July-1-Final.pdf

Council of Europe. (2009). *Human rights education in the school systems of Europe, Central Asia and North America: A compendium of good practice.* Warsaw, Poland: OSCE Office for Democratic Institutions and Human Rights.

Educating for American Democracy (EAD). (2021). *Educating for American democracy: Excellence in history and civics for all learners.* iCivics. www.educatingforamericandemocracy.org

Educational Policies Commission. (1940). *Education and the defense of American democracy.* Washington, DC: National Education Association of the United States, and the American Association of School Administrators.

Fernekes, W. R. (2016). Global citizenship education and human rights education: Are they compatible with U.S. civic education? *Journal of International Social Studies, 6*(2), 34–57.

Freire, P. (1970). *Pedagogy of the oppressed.* Continuum.

Gingold, J. (2013). *Building an evidence-based practice of action civics: The current state of assessments and recommendations for the future* (CIRCLE Working Paper No.78). The Center for Information & Research on Civic Learning and Engagement (CIRCLE). http://www.civicyouth.org/wp-content/uploads/2013/08/WP_78_Gingold.pdf.

Guilfoile, L., Delander, B., & Kreck, C. (2016). *Guide book: Six proven practices for effective civic learning.* Education Commission for the States. https://www.ecs.org/six-provenpractices-for-effective-civic-learning/

Hantzopoulos, M., Rivera-McCutchen, R. L., & Tyner-Mullings, A. R. (2021). Reframing school culture through project-based assessment tasks: Cultivating transformative agency and humanizing practices in NYC public schools. *Teachers College Record, 123*(4), 1–38. https://doi.org/10.1177/016146812112300404

Hartman, S., & Kahn, S. (2017). Start local, go global: Community partnerships empower children as scientists and citizens. *Social Studies and the Young Learner, 29*(4), 3–7.

Izard, B. (2018). Teaching human rights through mathematics. Mathematics *Teachers, 112*(2), 114–119.
Johnson, L., & Morris, P. (2010). Towards a framework for critical citizenship education. *The Curriculum Journal, 21*(1), 77–96. https://doi.org/10.1080/09585170903560444
Kahne, J., & Middaugh, E. (2008). *Democracy for some: Civic opportunity gap in high school* (CIRCLE Working Paper No. 59). The Center for Information & Research on Civic Learning and Engagement (CIRCLE).https://civicyouth.org/PopUps/WorkingPapers/WP59Kahne.pdf
Kahne, J., & Sporte, S. E. (2008). Developing citizens: The impact of civic learning opportunities on students' commitment to civic participation. *American Educational Research Journal, 45*(3), 738–766. https://doi.org/10.3102/0002831208316951
Keet, A. (2015). It is time: Critical human rights education in an age of counter-hegemonic distrust. *Education as Change, 19*(3), 46–64. https://doi.org/10.1080/16823206.2015.1085621
Knowles, R. T. (2018). Teaching who you are: Connecting teachers' civic education ideology to instructional strategies. *Theory & Research in Social Education, 46*(1), 68–109. https://doi.org/10.1080/00933104.2017.1356776
Kymlicka, W. (1995). *Multicultural citizenship: A liberal theory of minority rights*. Oxford University Press. https://doi.org/ 10.1093/0198290918.001.0001
Kymlicka, W. (2011). Multicultural citizenship within multination states. *Ethnicities, 11*(3), 281–302. https://doi.org/10.1177/1468796811407813
Kymlicka, W. (2017). Citizenship education: From multicultural to cosmopolitan? In J. A. Banks (Ed.), *Citizenship education and global migration: Implications for theory, research, and teaching* (pp. xi–xvii). American Education Research Association.
Ladson-Billings, G. (2004). Culture versus citizenship: The challenge of racialized citizenship in the United States. In J. A. Banks (Ed.), *Diversity and citizenship education* (pp. 99–126). Jossey-Bass.
LeCompte, K., Blevins, B., & Riggers-Piehl, T. (2019). Developing civic competence through action civics: A longitudinal look at the data. *The Journal of Social Studies Research, 44*, 127–137. https://doi.org/10.1016/j.jssr.2019.03.002
Levine, P. (2013). *We are the ones we have been waiting for: The promise of civic renewal in America*. Oxford University Press. https://doi.org/ 10.16997/jdd.180
Levine, P., & Kawashima-Ginsberg, K. (2015). *Civic education and deeper learning. Students at the Center: Deeper Learning Research Series*. Jobs for the Future.
Levinson, M. (2012). *No citizen left behind*. Harvard Education Press. https://doi.org/10.4159/harvard.9780674065291
Levinson, M. (2014). Action civics in the classroom. *Social Education, 78*(2), 68–72.
Lister, R. (2003). *Citizenship: Feminist perspectives* (2nd ed.). New York University Press.
Loewen, J. (2007). *Lies my teacher told me: Everything your American history textbooks got wrong*. Touchstone.
Meyer, J. W., Bromley, P., & Ramirez, F. O. (2010). Human rights in social science textbooks cross-national analyses, 1970–2008. *Sociology of Education, 83*(2), 111–134. https://doi.org/10.1177/0038040710367936
Mitoma, G. (2017). Teaching the history and contemporary challenge of human rights through film. In J. Stoddard, A. S. Marcus, & D. Hicks (Eds.), *Teaching difficult history through film* (pp. 39–56). Routledge. https://doi.org/10.4324/9781315640877

Mutua, M. (2001). Savages, victims, and saviors: The metaphor of human rights. *Harvard International Law Journal, 42*, 201.

National Commission on Excellence in Education. (1983). Nation at risk: The imperative for education reform. *The Elementary School Journal, 84*(2), 112–130.

National Council for the Social Studies. (2013a). *The college, career, and civic life C3 framework for state social studies standards: Guidance for enhancing the rigor of K–12 civics, economics, geography, and history*. NCSS.

National Council for the Social Studies. (2013b). *Revitalizing civic learning in our schools: A position statement of National Council for the Social Studies*. https://www.socialstudies.org/positions/revitalizing_civic_learning

National Council for the Social Studies. (2014). *Human rights Education: A necessity for effective social and civic learning: A position statement of National Council for the Social Studies*. https://www.socialstudies.org/social-education/79/3/human-rights-education-necessity-effective-social-and-civic-learning

National Council for the Social Studies. (2021). *Human rights education: A position statement of National Council for the Social Studies*. https://www.socialstudies.org/position-statements/human-rights-education

Osler, A. (2008). Citizenship education and the Ajegbo report: Re-imagining a cosmopolitan nation. *London Review of Education 6*(1), 11–25. https://doi.org/10.1080/14748460801889803

Osler, A. (2011). Teacher perceptions of citizenship education: National identities, cosmopolitan ideals, and political realities. *Journal of Curriculum Studies 43*(1), 1–24. https://doi.org/10.1080/00220272.2010.503245

Osler, A., & Starkey, H. (2003). Learning for cosmopolitan citizenship: Theoretical debates and young people's experiences. *Educational Review, 55*(3), 243–254. https://doi.org/10.1080/0013191032000118901

Osler, A., & Starkey, H. (2005). *Changing citizenship: Democracy and inclusion in education*. Open University Press. https://doi.org/10.18546/LRE.06.1.10

Osler, A., & Starkey, H. (2018). Extending the theory and practice of education for cosmopolitan citizenship. *Educational Review, 70*(1), 31–40. https://doi.org/10.1080/00131911.2018.1388616

Pope, A., Stolte, L., & Cohen, A. K. (2011). Close the civic engagement gap: The potential of action civics. *Social Education, 75*(5), 265–268.

Rosaldo, R. (1994). Cultural citizenship and educational democracy. *Cultural Anthropology, 9*(3), 402–411. https://doi.org/10.1525/can.1994.9.3.02a00110

Rosaldo, R. (1999). Cultural citizenship, inequality, and multiculturalism. In R. D. Torres, L. F. Mirón, & J. X. Inda (Eds.), *Race, identity, and citizenship: A Reader* (pp. 253–261). Blackwell Publishers.

Ross, E. W., & Marker, P. M. (2005a). Social studies: Wrong, right, or left? A critical response to the Fordham Institute's where did social studies go wrong? *The Social Studies, 96*(4), 139–142. https://doi.org/10.3200/TSSS.96.4.139-142

Ross, E. W., & Marker, P. M. (2005b). (If social studies is wrong) I don't want to be right. *Theory & Research in Social Education, 33*(1), 142–151. https://doi.org/10.1080/00933104.2005.10473275

Russell, S. G., & Suárez, D. (2017). Symbol and substance: Human rights education as an emergent global institution. In M. Bajaj (Eds.), *Human rights education: The-*

ory, research, praxis (pp. 19–46). University of Pennsylvania Press. https://doi.org/10.9783/9780812293890

Sanchez, D. G. (2020). Transforming human rights through decolonial lens. *The Age of Human Rights Journal,* (15), 276–303. https://doi.org/10.17561/tahrj.v15.5818

Sirota, S. (2017). The inconsistent past and uncertain future of human rights education in the United States. *PROSPECTS,* 101–117.

Spreen, C. A., Monaghan, C., & Hillary, A. (2018). From transforming human rights education to transformative human rights education: Context, critique, and change. In M. Zembylas & A. Keet (Eds.), *Critical human rights, citizenship, and democracy education: Entanglements and regenerations* (209–224). Bloomsbury Academic. https://doi.org10.5040/9781350045668

Starkey, H. (Ed.) (1991). *The challenge of human rights education.* Cassell.

Starkey, H. (2010). The universal declaration of human rights and education for cosmopolitan citizenship. In F. Waldron & B. Ruane (Eds.), *Human rights education* (pp. 15–42). Liffey Press.

Stone, A. (2002). Human rights education and public policy in the United States: Mapping the road ahead. *Human Rights Quarterly, 24*(2), 537–557. https://doi.org/10.1353/hrq.2002.0029

Suárez, D. (2007). Education professionals and the construction of human rights education. *Comparative Education Review, 51*(1), 48-70. https://doi.org/10.1086/508638

Tibbitts, F. (2017). Evolution of human rights education models. In M. Bajaj (Ed.), *Human rights education: Theory, research, praxis* (pp. 69–95). University of Pennsylvania Press. https://doi.org/10.9783/9780812293890

Tyrrell, I. (1991). American exceptionalism in an age of international history. *American Historical Review, 96*(4), 1031–1055. https://doi.org/10.1086/ahr/96.4.1031

United Nations General Assembly. (December 2011). *Declaration on human rights education and training.* The United Nations.

Veugelers, W. (2007). Creating critical-democratic citizenship education: Empowering humanity and democracy in Dutch education. *Compare: A Journal of Comparative Education 37*(1), 105–119. https://doi.org/10.1080/03057920601061893

Waldron, F., & Ruane, B. (Eds.). (2010). *Human rights education: Reflections on theory and practice.* Liffey Press.

Walsh, B., Hicks, D., & van Hover, S. (2017). Difficult history means difficult questions. In J. Stoddard, A. S. Marcus, & D. Hicks (Eds.), *Teaching difficult history through film* (pp. 17–36). Routledge.

Westheimer, J. (2007). Politics and patriotism in education. In J. Westheimer (Ed.), *Pledging allegiance: The politics of patriotism in America's schools* (pp. 171–188). Teachers College Press.

Westheimer, J. (2019). Civic education and the rise of populist nationalism. *Peabody Journal of Education, 94*(1), 4–16. https://doi.org/10.1080/0161956X.2019.155358

Westheimer, J., & Kahne, J. (2004). What kind of citizen? The politics of education for democracy. *American Educational Research Journal, 41*(2), 237–269. https://doi.org/10.3102/00028312041002237

Youniss, J. (2011). How to enrich civic education and sustain democracy. In D. Campbell, M. Levinson, & F. Hess (Eds.), *Making civics count: Citizenship education for a new generation* (pp. 115–134). Harvard Education Press.

Zembylas, M., & Keet, A. (2018). *Critical human rights, citizenship, and democracy education: Entanglements and regenerations.* Bloomsbury UK. https://doi.org10.5040/9781350045668

Zembylas, M., & Keet, A. (2019). *Critical human rights education: Advancing social-justice-oriented educational praxes.* Springer Nature Switzerland. https://doi.org/10.1007/978-3-030-27198-5

CHAPTER 6

THE THREE Cs FOR TEACHING IN CONTENTIOUS TIMES

Debby Shulsky and Sheila Baker
University of Houston-Clear Lake

America was founded on the historically novel and radical premise that *conflict and tension, rightly held, are the engine, not the enemy, of a better social order.* By holding our differences with hospitality instead of hostility, we can act on that premise, rebuild our civic community and hold power accountable to the will of the people.

— *Parker J. Palmer,*
"A Season of Civility: Religion and Public Life"

Historically, Americans have often been divided on critical issues imperative to the defense of our democratic ideals. Contentious issues such as slavery, immigration, integration, and equal rights have posed critical inquiries about the complicated and often divisive work of aligning our institutions and policies with our constitutional ideals. Throughout each era, citizens have grappled with divisive issues—today is no different. Currently, we find ourselves in a highly politicized era; one in which the truth of the media is questioned, some politicians are profoundly polarizing figures, and vigorous activism abounds. Consequently, we, as a nation, should heed Palmer's (2012) sound advice regarding our role as citizens during

Out of Turmoil: Catalysts for Re-learning, Re-Teaching, and Re-imagining History and Social Science, pages 91–108.
Copyright © 2023 by Information Age Publishing
www.infoagepub.com
All rights of reproduction in any form reserved.

these contentious times. As educators, we have an opportunity to model, facilitate, and promote critical, yet civil classroom experiences that bridge the gap of difference to discover compromise, an ideal imperative to our democratic republic.

Inevitably, the issues society grapples with breach the schoolhouse doors. Classrooms can be spaces where learners make sense of societal conflicts, tragedies, and uncertainties; however, this is not always the case. For some, especially new teachers, addressing contentious issues with their students is avoided due to discomfort, lack of knowledge, or in concession to parents or guardians (Hess, 2008; Hinde, 2004; Journell, 2013a; Lintner, 2018). Accordingly, teacher educators must prepare teacher candidates to integrate the real-world hot topics that will surely enter their teaching spaces. Teachers must educate students on how to engage with divisive topics in ways that encourage discourse that honors differing perspectives and the discovery of new ideas and solutions. This chapter explores the Three Cs (3Cs) framework as a way to position curriculum throughout the school year to promote the foundational skills required to negotiate uncertain times. Each C, which includes critical thinking, critical literacy, and civil discourse, should be integrated across the K–12 curricula. The curricular examples in this chapter are grounded within the elementary context, as these are key foundational developmental years that set the stage for the deepening of these imperative skills throughout students' post-elementary education. This pathway will assure students' capacity to examine contentious issues over the course of their K–12 education with civility and a critical level of engagement focused on well-informed decision-making and action.

CONTEXTUALIZING SCHOOLS IN SOCIETY

Public education has often been the incubator for making sense of the challenges of any given era within the history of America. Educators have been and remain the sentries on the frontline, educating learners as directed by the zeitgeist of the time. In times when the ideas and values of America are questioned or challenged, schools serve as learning labs for the exploration and resolution of complex issues within society. Over time many issues impacting American society have crossed over the threshold of the schoolhouse door, such as a) the assimilation of large numbers of immigrants, b) the need for child-centered pedagogy, c) the accessibility of public education for all students, and d) the improvement of academic achievement to compete on the world stage (Graham, 2005). The lessons learned within the microcosm of American schools often provide insight for solutions beyond the educational context; however, the lessons learned are not always transferred to the macrocosm of society.

Currently, the merging of politics and education is undeniable. Within the context of recent years, riddled in social, political, and racial unrest, national attention has been focused on political conversations about race and injustice. Within a highly divisive time in history, concepts focused on racism and social justice have seemingly been commandeered and politicized. Currently, critical race theory (CRT) is at the forefront of such concepts. Not surprisingly, this issue has breached the schoolhouse door and educators are positioned as facilitators of hard conversations with learners as triggered by the events and debates prevalent in the national conversation. Adding an additional layer of complexity is a highly divisive political culture and a "widespread use and circulation of misinformation" (Kahne & Bowyer, 2017, p. 7). In this political milieu, schools, as public institutions, cannot be separated from politics (Freire, 1970/1992; Jenlink, 2017; Kincheloe, 2005).

THE CHALLENGE OF TEACHING CONTROVERSY

Critical race theory, the latest rally cry of the political bandwagon, poses challenges for educators. Boundaries sanctioned by political entities have engaged educators and communities in difficult inquiries. Is CRT really being taught in classrooms? How can educators differentiate their curricular approaches from CRT? How do Social Studies teachers address the layered narratives of American history amid the charged national debate regarding CRT? Ultimately, the answers to these questions could pose direct contradictions to Justice and Stanley's (2016) contention, "Public schools exist, in part, for the political purpose of instilling the principal values of a democratic republic, training students in the skills and knowledge requisite to healthy democratic life" (p. 38). This conversation is illustrative of a larger challenge for most teachers: teaching controversial issues.

Before continuing, a distinction must be made between hard history and controversial issues. Goldberg (2020) asserts that "difficult histories expose learners to historical suffering and victimization that constitute a collective trauma. The difficulty stems from the strong emotional reactions or ethical responses learners may evince, undermining their trust in security and morality of this world" (p. 130). Social studies curriculum is riddled with hard history (e.g. slavery, Japanese internment). In the shadow of the politicization of CRT, at least 28 states have or are taking steps to legislate restrictions on how teachers discuss divisive topics (Ray & Gibbons, 2021). Given that controversial issues give rise to discussions which generate opposing views, and the CRT debate has impacted approaches to hard history, hard history is a controversial issue.

Hren (2020) declares, "In the present era of alternative facts, teaching about current realities can be for some a slippery slope" (p. 5). A myriad of reasons supports the reality of teachers' struggles when addressing controversial issues in the classroom which can, ultimately, lead to teachers' avoidance of addressing such issues (Hess, 2005; Journell, 2013a). The most common reasons teachers avoid addressing controversy include teachers' lack of knowledge and training (Hinde, 2004; Journell, 2013b; Lintner, 2018; Oulton et al., 2004; Philpott et al., 2011), and fear of repercussions and pressure from stakeholders (e.g. school board, parents; Byford et al., 2009; Hinde, 2004; Journell, 2017; Lintner, 2018; Misco & Patterson, 2007). Additionally, the exclusion of contentious topics in the curriculum can be impacted by the level of self-awareness of the teacher regarding the regulation of bias (Hinde, 2004), limited access to meaningful teaching strategies that support discourse on such topics, justification for and adherence to the standards-based curriculum (Hinde, 2004), and concern for student sensitivity and unintended offense (Journell, 2017; Philpott et al., 2011).

Nearly a century ago, Charles Beard (1929) pointed to the essential need for the inclusion of controversy in the Social Studies curricula,

> It will be said that the growth of social studies places on teachers an impossible burden, it compels them to deal with controversial questions...They are in a different position from that of a teacher of Latin or mathematics...The subject matter of their instruction is infinitely difficult and it is continually changing. (p. 372)

The National Council for the Social Studies (NCSS) deepens the need for the inclusion of controversial issues as connected to the development of the skills required of a participatory citizen in a democratic society. The organization states, "The aim of social studies is the promotion of civic competence—the knowledge, intellectual processes, and democratic dispositions required of students to be active and engaged participants in public life" (NCSS, 2017, para. 3). More specifically, NCSS (2016) declares the integration of controversial issues within the social studies curricula pointedly cultivates the following skills and dispositions:

1. The desire and ability to study relevant problems and to make intelligent choices from alternatives;
2. The desire and ability to use rational methods in considering significant issues;
3. The willingness to recognize that differing viewpoints are valuable and normal;
4. The recognition that reasonable compromise is often an important part of the democratic decision-making process; and
5. The skill of analyzing and evaluating sources of information—recognizing propaganda, half truths, and bias. (p. 186)

With these skills in mind, it is undeniable that the nature of Social Studies, as a discipline, is inseparable from deep, challenging, and contentious inquiry. Lintener (2018) states,

> If the sweeping objective of using controversy in the classroom is to push students to develop deeper, layered, alternatively critical and empathic understandings while concomitantly raising civic awareness and action, there may arguably be no space more appropriately suited to do so than the Social Studies classroom. (pp. 15–16)

As stewards of civic education, social studies educators are challenged during contentious times when polarized views and highly charged topics dominate the national narrative. In such times, it becomes imperative that students are taught how to navigate discussions on hard topics and engage with others with respect, discover and articulate their own ideas after thoughtful deliberation, question claims of neutrality, and be comfortable with the potential lack of definite answers (Oulton et al., 2004; Philpott et al., 2011).

Scholars have discussed teaching controversial issues for decades, resulting in guidelines and suggestions for how to mindfully and purposely address controversial issues in the classroom. Hess and McAvoy (2015) suggest that an issue can be categorized as either settled or open. A settled issue is one that is not controversial, as it is based on general agreement and rational justification of a decision. Conversely, an open issue involves multiple evidence-based viewpoints and has yet to reach a settlement. Based on the collective literature, Journell (2017) offers three criteria for assessing the status of the controversiality of an issue: epistemic, political, and politically authentic. The epistemic criterion states that issues must be rationally and empirically supported. The political criterion makes a distinction between public and private values, asserting that public values cannot impose upon private values. The final criterion questions if the issue is politically authentic, exhibiting political traction. In other words, the issue is "appearing on ballots, in courts, within political platforms, in legislative chambers, and as part of political movements" (Hess & McAvoy, 2015, pp. 168–169).

The process of establishing whether an issue is settled or open is complex, as the criteria for identifying issues as settled or open are not always straightforward. Hess and McAvoy (2015) suggest that teachers use their professional judgment as they decide what is controversial and what is not regarding their curriculum. Their framework for professional judgment includes context, evidence, and aims. First, this level of decision-making requires the teacher to consider the context in which they teach (e.g. classroom, school, community), as well as their students' identities (Journell, 2017). Secondly, teachers need to be able to identify and evaluate public debates based on the presented evidence and identify well-reasoned claims prior to engaging students with an issue. Finally, pursuing a controversial issue should be guided by the goals and desired outcomes of the teacher's philosophical or curricular stance.

The challenge illuminated in the literature related to teaching controversial issues is that it is a very complex process that is inclusive of the dispositions and skills of the teacher, external pressures from the community, the emotionality innate in the discussion of controversial topics and, most currently, the concept of post-truth America (e.g. Journell, 2017; Lintner, 2018; NCSS, 2016; Philpott et al., 2011). Hess (2018) declares,

> In the face of intense political polarization, rising levels of inequality and the narrowing view of the mission of schools, we recognize that giving up on teaching young people about controversial issues is an ill-advised and damaging option. The stakes, after all, are exceptionally high: empowering young Americans to become active participants—and to co-exist peacefully—in a pluralistic society brimming with opposing views. (p. 306)

THE 3CS FRAMEWORK

Historically, controversy is threaded throughout the history of this country and, therefore, social studies. Teachers of every decade have faced challenges in teaching the various contentious topics aligned with the issues of the era. Currently, based on varied state legislation, there seems to be a movement toward an attempt to limit teachers' ability to engage in meaningful discussions around controversial topics where students can practice the skills needed to be an engaged and informed critical citizen (Ray & Gibbons, 2021).

The framework presented in this chapter offers a new paradigm to support meaningful engagement and inquiry across all grade levels and content areas when navigating contentious and highly divisive times. The 3Cs framework is presented in Table 6.1.

Critical Thinking

The ability to think critically is vital to the health of a democratic society. Shulsky and Hendrix (2016) support this notion in their statement, "In a country that depends upon an informed 'we the people,' the ideal of democracy is hinged upon the education of the individual " (p. 107). In order to step into the role of an informed citizen, the intentional cultivation of critical thinking is foundational, especially while navigating through highly divisive times. The body of research on critical thinking is vast, with a multitude of definitions and approaches. Chance (1986) defines critical thinking as, ."..the ability to analyze facts, generate and organize ideas, defend opinions, make comparisons, draw inferences, evaluate arguments and solve problems" (p. 6). The Institute of Critical Thinking (2007) denotes two dimensions of critical thinking: the ability to reason and the required disposition to do so. Brookfield (2012) states that critical thinkers: seek out assumptions (the deliberate quest to unearth unconsciously accepted beliefs); examine assumptions (effortful and reflective evaluation of the reliability and sensibility of our assumed beliefs); consider diverse viewpoints (openness to perspectives

TABLE 6.1. The Three Cs Framework

Component	Definition
Critical thinking	The process of careful and thoughtful inquiry about a topic for the purpose of forming a belief and engaging in action/problem solving (Burkhalter, 2016; Hitchcock, 2018; Scriven & Paul, 2003).
Critical literacy	A perspective through which one views the world with a focus on issues of social justice—questioning and analyzing what is presented and absent—with the goal of creating innovative action toward social healing (Shulsky & Hendrix, 2016; Wolk, 2003).
Civil discourse	Conversation intended to enhance understanding and support the good of society (Herbst, 2014).

divergent from one's own views); and take informed action (evidence-based action as a result of thoughtful and convincing analysis).

The deeply rooted skill of critical thinking allows citizens to purposefully examine issues and seek evidence-based solutions, remembering Burkhalter's (2016) statement, "It's [critical thinking] goal is to prevent thoughts from flowing unexamined through learners' minds and directly out of their mouths…This process prevents minds from going on autopilot, which often leads to making ill-considered decisions…" (p. 7).

Classroom Connections

It is never too early to begin seeding the skills of critical thinking. For young learners, a foundational starting point is the integration of activities that promote learners' abilities to question and consider multiple viewpoints. The activity in Table 6.2 is an example that may be modified for use in Kindergarten through grade 6. It allows young learners to explore, in age-appropriate ways, their assumptions and consider multiple perspectives using a beloved children's fairy tale.

This activity promotes the development of content specific skills connected to the objectives of the elementary curricula. Additionally, as stated in the College, Career & Civic Life (C3) Framework for Social Studies Standards (NCSS, 2015), this activity aligns with the ELAR Common Core Standards. Both sets of stan-

TABLE 6.2. Pig Tales and Other Perspectives

Lesson Plan Component	Description
Engage	Read a classic version of *The Three Little Pigs*. Ask students the following questions: Who is the hero of the story? Who is the villain? What evidence do you have to support your answer?
	Watch the *3 Pigs* Video (https://www.youtube.com/watch?v=4F8vWWcTPnE) or, as an alternative, read *The True Story of the Three Little Pigs*, by Jon Scieszka (1996). Ask students the following questions: Who is the hero of this story? What evidence do you have to support your answer? How are the stories the same? Different? Why do you think there are two versions of the same story?
	Complete a Venn diagram comparing the two versions of the story.
Explore	Assign one of the following characters to each table: 1) Pig #1- Brad the Brick; 2) Pig #2—Straw Dawg; and 3) Pig #3—Stix; 4) The Wolf—Wanda; 5) The Squirrel—Squeakers (Wanda's best friend); and 6) The Moon—Luna (Wanda's spiritual guide).
	The Scenario: The local Newspaper, *The Forest Gazette* has written an article reporting the events from *The Three Little Pigs*, almost word for word. Your assigned character reads this article and is outraged by the lack of accuracy and twisted slant of the story. Angry, you pen a letter to the editor setting the story straight.
	As their assigned character students write a letter to the editor clarifying what happened with the Pigs and the Wolf. Students share their letters with the entire class.

dards integrate the terms of argument, explanation, and point of view, providing easy integration of critical thinking into these two content areas.

Through the comparison of the classic version of *The Three Little Pigs* versus the video, students complete a graphic organizer to analyze and compare the two versions of the story. In doing so, students are challenged to seek the multiple perspectives of the characters and authors. More importantly, comparison of the stories engages students in critical inquiry that challenges them to question what is presented. This activity leads to the cultivation of their critical literacy skills, which are crucial as they move to the exploration of more advanced divisive topics.

In the scenario portion of the activity, students use the lens of an assigned character to articulate an evidence-supported stance to counter the paper's reporting of the story. In writing a letter to the editor, students must distinguish between opinions and supported arguments. Through analysis of evidence, students discern and support the position of their stance. Early development of these skills builds a foundation from which learning experiences in middle and high school can deepen. The curricula opportunities at the secondary level are unlimited; however, teachers should consider the questions in Table 6.3 when designing lessons and curricula that integrate critical thinking. Engagement in such activities throughout the K–12 experience allows students to mature into critically thinking adults who, at the very least, seek out evidence, question the accuracy of sources, and confidently articulate reasoned arguments.

Critical Literacy

Most recently, contention has centered upon issues of social justice. Are American institutions based in systemic racism? Do all people have equal access? Whose stories need to be included in the American narrative? The complexity of contentious times warrants the cultivation of a differentiated element of critical thinking—critical literacy. As a concept, critical literacy is complicated and holds many historical orientations, definitions, and pedagogical approaches (Comber, 2016; Friere 1970/1992; Vasquez et al., 2019). For this chapter, critical literacy is

TABLE 6.3. Questions for Consideration

Question Number	Question
1	Are multiple perspectives represented?
2	Does the activity encourage learners to generate higher-order questions?
3	How are learners being asked to reflect on their own thinking?
4	How can project-based learning be included in curricula that integrate critical thinking?
5	What activities can be created that teach learners how to ask questions?
6	Can learners identify connections between the content area and the world around them?

defined as a lens through which to view the world from a critical stance to interrogate issues of power, equity, and social justice for the purpose of changing the status quo. Teitelbaum (2011) reminds us that critical literacy is not a mere set of strategies or skills, but an ingrained mindset. Critical literacy, as a way of being (Shulsky et al., 2017; Vasquez et al., 2019), includes four dimensions: "disrupting the commonplace, interrogating multiple points of view, focusing on sociopolitical issues, and taking action and promoting social justice" (Lewison et al., 2002, p. 382). Lewison et al.'s (2002) dimensions are detailed in Table 6.4.

Amid tumultuous times when citizens are grappling with issues of social justice, critical literacy offers a vantage point dedicated to the rigorous exploration and discussion of obstacles and possible solutions. "Critical literacy can be a catalyst for the discovery of the grander power structures and institutions that socialize and influence individuals within a society...[critical literacy] practices provide the hope that learners will be inspired to act with the intent of exposing and transforming acts of injustice" (Shulsky & Hendrix, 2016, pp. 105–106).

Classroom Connections

At all levels of K–12 education, the inclusion of critical literacy may pose a challenge as it seeks to expose what is not explicitly stated and can disrupt the dominant narrative, causing contention. The integration of critical literacy within the classroom provides experiences for students to challenge the practice of blindly accepting the status quo. Table 6.5 provides questions to guide young learners as they read between the lines of any resource in an effort to hone their ability to question the explicit, question the implicit, and advocate for what is absent (adapted from Shulsky & Chvala, 2017).

These questions can be an extension of the Pig Tales and Other Perspectives activity to solicit a magnified reading of different versions of the classic story. Looking at various tellings of the story allows for inquiry and analysis of con-

TABLE 6.4. Directions of Critical Literacy

Dimensions	Definition
Disrupting the common place	A critical approach that looks beyond the status quo via analysis of constructed narratives and exposure of hidden narratives.
Interrogating multiple points of view	Rigorous questioning and inclusion of multiple and often contradictory perspectives, as well as historically marginalized perspectives which are often absent from the narrative.
Focusing on sociopolitical issues	Critical examination of how sociopolitical systems and power relationships influence personal responses and actions.
Taking action in promoting social justice	Reflecting on the knowledge gained from the previous dimensions, to engage in action to promote social justice and transform society at large.

TABLE 6.5. Read Between the Lines

Elements of Text	Questions
Context	• Who wrote the text? • Is the author an authentic voice for the portrayed characters? • When was the text written? • How is the era reflected in the text, theme, illustrations, vocabulary of the text?
The Message	• What is the message of the text? • Who is represented prominently in the text? • Who is not represented in the text? • How is the text message inclusive of all voices? Explain. • From varied perspectives, are there "hidden" messages within the text?
Illustrations	• Are there offensive images? Describe and discuss. • Are the illustrations accurate? Explain. • How is diversity depicted within the illustrations?
Voice	• Select three words that can be interpreted positively or negatively? • How are the voices of marginalized characters addressed? • How does the overall voice of the text respect diversity and value the contributions of all?

text, messaging, illustrations, and voice. These skills can be transferred to more complex texts that explore more difficult topics that highlight issues related to social justice (e.g., poverty, race). When selecting books for integration into the curricula, at any level, teachers should consider the questions in Table 6.6. Early exposure to critical literacy allows students to form a lens through which they can view and question the world with a commitment to acting towards the creation of a more socially just and equitable society.

Civil Discourse

The work of a democratic government requires collaboration, cooperation, and compromise to solve the complex issues of today's society. Most recently, the polarization of American politics has bled into all of society, causing a crisis in communication. Many people have placed themselves in rigid camps of thought,

TABLE 6.6. Questions for Consideration

Question number	Question
1	Are multiple voices represented? Whose voice is missing?
2	What are the underlying assumptions and biases of the given narrative?
3	Do the resources used present a balanced of gender and race?
4	Does the activity lead to the exploration of contradictory experiences or perspectives?
5	In what ways will the learner's lens expand or shift?
6	Does the activity lead students to engage in action to make a difference?

restricting their ability to engage in respectful dialogue with those who hold divergent beliefs. This division limits the ability to critically think about complex issues and seek solutions beholden to the common good. Civil discourse requires one to hear, honor, consider, and accept the views of others—skills which are not inherent, but cultivated. Such discourse moves beyond politeness (Shuster, 2009, 2016); it is dialogue grounded in goodwill and respect for others' views while separated from personal accusation (Catalano, et al., 2021). Oppositional views can be navigated with civility with the hope for a deeper understanding of a divisive issue (Henry & McBride, 2021). There are common characteristics of civil discourse highlighted across the literature (e.g. Catalano et al., 2021; Henry & McBride, 2021; Shuster, 2016). They include critical thinking, active listening, the art of argumentation, and critical conviction.

Foundational to civil discourse is the ability to critically think about the issues. Attention to the development of critical thinking that focuses on the teaching of a) effortful thinking guided by critical questions; b) analysis and synthesis of ideas; c) diverse viewpoints; d) identification and examination of assumptions; and e) evidence based-decision making, positions students to enter discourse with the knowledge to assuredly engage in civil discussion. The Pig Tales and Other Perspectives activity presented earlier in the chapter, provides an example of how these skills can be easily integrated into any grade level curricula.

An additional key component of civil dialogue is the skill of active listening. Such listening should be done with great intent for the purpose of understanding another and confirming what is heard while refraining from judgment and comment. The development of these skills requires intentionally designed learning experiences that provide opportunities for students to practice them. Any teacher understands the struggle and the need to focus on establishing good listening skills within their students. Teaching students how to listen attentively to understand is a mainstay of any classroom. Teachers can take students to the next level of listening by scaffolding activities and discussions that teach learners how to listen with inclusivity and discernment, and with an open mind and empathetic ear—very important dispositions for productive and thoughtful dialogue. For example, teachers can design a system for solving student conflict that is guided by a listening protocol that supports the "hearing" of all perspectives involved in the incident and results in a collaborative positive resolution.

The art of argumentation is an essential skill in assuring that discussions with those who hold different viewpoints are conducted in a respectful manner. This allows the discussants to respectfully share evidence in support of their positions and demonstrate a willingness to potentially learn. Teaching the art of argumentation to students provides them with the ability to articulate a reasoned stance. This stance includes clear evidence-based assertions. The goal of such an exchange encourages students to understand one another's viewpoints. An example of a framework for teaching the art of argumentation is presented in Table 6.7 and Table 6.8 in the next section.

A crucial element of civil discourse resides in the disposition of critical conviction. Informed by Anderson (2001) and Hanvey (1982), Shulsky and Hendrix (2016) present this mindset as being open to reconsider beliefs and positionalities during critical analysis and discourse. This disposition is directly linked to the cognitive process of accommodation which relates to altering or creating new schemas as a result of learning new information or engaging in new experiences (Zhiqing, 2015). In the classroom, critical conviction can be cultivated through activities that emphasize reflection on knowledge gained and openness to shifting schemas. The inflexibility that often accompanies divisiveness, may be countered by the intentional development of the skills (as noted above) and experiences that promote critical conviction.

Civil discourse provides access to compromise and the possible transformation of beliefs—all in hopes of discovering common ground from which to construct solutions for the benefit of the whole. This is most needed during times of turmoil as Bond reminds us, "We have to turn the tide to break through social pressures... and embrace opportunities to learn the skills to navigate courageous conversations with civility" (as cited in Students Taking Action Together, 2019, p. 3). This is crucial to the health and progress of society.

Classroom Connections

The art of argumentation is a process that can be integrated across grade levels and content areas. The cultivation and practice of argumentation allows learners to articulate their beliefs as supported with evidence. When engaged with those who disagree, this skill offers a protocol from which to listen, discuss, and consider the beliefs of another with respect. Consider the activities shared from the work of Shuster (2009, pp. 6, 12–13) as easy and adaptable ways to engage learners in the articulation of reasoned arguments and the ability to refute the stated arguments of others. The three parts of a well-structured argument (assertion, reasoning, and evidence [ARE]), are found in Table 6.7.

TABLE 6.7. Framework for Argumentation

Steps	Explanation
Assertion	This is a simple position statement. For example, extending the critical thinking activity, "The Big Bad Wolf is a villain."
Reasoning	This is the "because" part of an argument. (In the early grades, focus on the link between the assertion and the reason, as opposed to the validity of the reason). For example, "The Big Bad Wolf is the villain because he destroyed three pigs' houses."
Evidence	This is your proof. Teach the cue "for example." Such as, "The Big Bad Wolf is the villain because he destroyed three pigs' houses. For example, the illustration shows that Stix's house was blown to the ground."

TABLE 6.8. Framework for Refutation

Steps	Explanation
Restate	Repeat the argument of the other person. ("They say…")
Refute	State another side of the argument. ("But…")
Support	Reasoning and evidence. ("Because…")
Conclude	Summarize both sides. ("Therefore…")

Any argument is open to refutation. A well-structured refute has four steps. A possible refutation linked to *The Three Little Pigs* assertion, "The big bad wolf is a villain," might be:

> Amy says that the big bad wolf is a villain, but the big bad wolf accidentally blew the houses down because he had allergies. Therefore, blowing the houses down was only an accident, so the big bad wolf is not a villain.

See Table 6.8 for steps that structure a refutation.

Exposure to the art of argumentation via ARE and the four steps of refutation is in direct alignment with NCSS's (2015) C3 inquiry arc, specifically Dimension 3: Evaluating Sources and Using Evidence. NCSS (2015) notes, "Making and supporting evidence-based claims and counter-claims is key to student capacity to construct explanations and arguments" (p. 18). Dimension 4 within the inquiry arc engages students in the communication of the conclusions of their arguments allowing them to take informed action. As an instructional approach connected to the aims of the inquiry arc, the Inquiry Design Model (IDM) integrates the argumentation process through the development of Social Studies inquiries. Within the IDM blueprint, inquiries are driven by compelling questions and conclude

TABLE 6.9. Questions for Consideration

Question Number	Question
1	Are there established ground rules in the classroom for engaging in respectful conversations?
2	Is there intentional emphasis on the students' development of self-regulation practices?
3	Are there established guidelines for fairly and equitably facilitating discussions?
4	Is there a list of assertions to integrate into classroom curricula that will help student formulate arguments and refutations regularly?
5	Are there established routines to practice the skills required for civil discourse (e.g. evidence-based conversations)?
6	Are students offered an opportunity to reflect on the effectiveness and challenges of the discussion?

with a summative product that establishes an evidence-based argument addressing the compelling question (Swan et al., 2015). This model is one example of how teachers can infuse the skills of argumentation within their curricula. The inclusion of intentionally structured activities that incorporate the practice of argumentation prepares students to apply critical thinking skills. The ability to articulate a reasoned stance inclusive of relevant evidence-supported assertions can foster shifts in understanding of complex concepts, problems, issues, or situations. Table 6.9 offers questions for consideration as teachers design activities that address the key components of civil discourse, critical thinking, active listening, argumentation, and critical conviction.

CONCLUSION

The tumultuous times of the recent past inspired the proposed 3Cs framework. Although this contextualization began an inquiry which led to the design of this framework, the authors' hope is that the 3Cs will be a guide for the design of teaching practices that become foundational in K–12 schools and beyond. Additionally, the goal of this work is that the integration of the ideas connected to the 3Cs framework will alleviate teachers' avoidance and trepidation related to making sense of contentious issues/times with their students.

The practices of critical thinking, critical literacy, and civil discourse should be a common fixture in American education. The examples offered in this chapter are intentionally aimed toward young learners as these practices lay a foundation for the dispositions and skills required of tomorrow's leaders. However, the skills and practices suggested within the framework can be easily embedded in numerous content areas, as well as grades beyond elementary. Ultimately, we need both citizens and leaders who are committed to and comfortable with seeking cooperation, collaboration, and compromise—all competencies fostered by the 3Cs. To do so would honor the words of Martin Luther King III (2020),

> It's time for political leaders across the ideological spectrum to realize that, while partisanship is understandable, hyper-partisanship is destructive to our country. We need more visionary leaders who will earnestly strive for bipartisanship and find policy solutions that can move America forward (para. 11).

REFERENCES

Anderson, C. (2001). Global education in the classroom. *Theory Into Practice*, *21*(3), 168–176. https://doi.org/10.1080/00405848209543002

Beard, C. A. (1929). The trend in social studies. *Social Studies*, *20*(8), 369.

Brookfield, S. D. (2012). *Teaching for critical thinking: Tools and techniques to help students question their assumptions*. John Wiley & Sons.

Burkhalter, N. (2016). *Critical thinking now: Practical teaching methods for classrooms around the world*. Rowman & Littlefield.
Byford, J., Lennon, S., & Russell, W. B. III. (2009). Teaching controversial issues in the social studies: A research study of high school teachers. *Clearing House: A Journal of Educational Strategies, Issues and Ideas, 82*(4), 165–170. https://doi.org/10.3200/TCHS.82.4.165-170
Catalano, T., Ganesan, U., Barbici-Wagner, A., Reeves, J., Leonard, A. E., & Wessels, S. (2021). Dance as dialog: A metaphor analysis on the development of interculturality through arts and community-based learning with preservice teachers and a local refugee community. *Teaching and Teacher Education, 104*, 103369. https://doi.org/10.1016/j.tate.2021.103369
Chance, P. (1986). *Thinking in the classroom: A survey of programs*. Teachers College Press.
Comber, B. (2016). *Literacy, place, and pedagogies of possibility*. Routledge.
Freire, P. (1992). *Pedagogy of the oppressed.* (M. Ramos, Trans.). Continuum. (Original work published 1970)
Goldberg, T. (2020). Delving into difficulty: Are teachers evading or embracing difficult histories? *Social Education, 84*(2), 130–136.
Graham, P. (2005). *Schooling America: How the public schools meet the nation's changing needs.* Oxford University Press.
Hanvey, R. (1982). An attainable global perspective. *Theory into Practice, 21*(3), 162–167.
Henry, R., & McBride, C. (2021, October 27-30). *Crash the discord: Creating a learning environment that bolsters value appreciation and respect through civil discourse* [Paper]. American Association for Adult and Continuing Education 2020 Conference, Online, https://eric.ed.gov/?id=ED611629
Herbst, S. (2014). Civility, civic discourse and civic engagement: Inextricably interwoven. *Journal of Higher Education Outreach and Engagement, 18*(1), 5–10.
Hess, D. E. (2005). How do teachers' political views influence teaching about controversial issues. *Social Education 69*(Jan/Feb), 47–48.
Hess, D. E. (2008). Controversial issues and democratic discourse. In L. S. Levstik & C. A. Tyson (Eds.), *Handbook of research in social studies education* (pp. 124–136). Rutledge.
Hess, D. E. (2018). Teaching controversial issues: An introduction. *Social Education, 82*(6), 306.
Hess, D. E., & McAvoy, P. (2015). *The political classroom: Evidence and ethics in democratic education.* Routledge.
Hinde, E. (2004). Bones of contention: Teaching controversial issues. *Social Studies and the Young Learner, 17*(2), 31–32. https://doi.org/10.1080/1356251042000216624
Hitchcock, D. (2018). Critical thinking. *Stanford Encyclopedia of Philosophy.* https://plato.stanford.edu/entries/critical-thinking/
Hren, K. A. (2020). *Why should I close my eyes to reality? A qualitative study of controversial and sensitive photographs in the high school social studies curriculum.* [Doctoral dissertation, Aurora University]. ProQuest Dissertations & Theses Global.
The Institute of Critical Thinking. (2007). *Critical thinking and education.* The University of the West Indies. https://sta.uwi.edu/ct/ct-and-education

Jenlink, P. M. (2017). Democracy distracted in an era of accountability: Teacher education against neoliberalism. *Cultural Studies ↔ Critical Methodologies, 17*(3), 163–172. https://doi.org/10.1177/1532708616672676

Journell, W. (2012). Ideological homogeneity, school leadership, and political intolerance in secondary education: A study of three high schools during the 2008 Presidential Election. *Journal of School Leadership, 22*(3), 569–599. https://doi.org/10.1177/105268461202200306

Journell, W. (2013a). Learning from each other: What social studies can learn from the controversy surrounding the teaching of evolution in science. *The Curriculum Journal, 24*(4), 494–510. https://doi.org/10.1080/09585176.2013.801780

Journell, W. (2013b). What preservice social studies teachers (don't) know about politics and current events—And why it matters. *Theory & Research in Social Education, 41*(3), 316–351. https://doi.org/10.1080/00933104.2013.812050

Journell, W. (2017). Framing controversial identity issues in schools: The case of HB2, bathroom equity, and transgender students. *Equity & Excellence in Education, 50*(4), 339–354. https://doi.org/10.1080/10665684.2017.1393640

Justice, B., & Stanley, J. (2016). Teaching in the time of Trump. *Social Education, 80*(1), 36–41. https://www.socialstudies.org/social-education/80/1/teaching-time-trump

Kahne, J., & Bowyer, B. (2017). Educating for democracy in a partisan age: Confronting the challenges of motivated reasoning and misinformation. *American Educational Research Journal, 54*(1), 3–34. https://doi.org/10.3102/0002831216679817

Kincheloe, J. (2005). *Critical pedagogy.* Peter Lang.

King, M. L. (2020, January 19). Martin Luther King III on MLK legacy: Respect, reason work better than political insults. *USA Today.* https://www.usatoday.com/story/opinion/voices/2020/01/19/elect-constructive-candidates-to-honor-martin-luther-king-column/4509986002/

Lewison, M., Flint, A. S., & Van Sluys, K. (2002). Taking on critical literacy: The journey of newcomers and novices. *Language Arts, 79*(5), 382–392. https://uhcl.idm.oclc.org/login?url=https://www.jstor.org/stable/41483258

Lintner, T. (2018). The controversy over controversy in the social studies classroom. *SRATE Journal, 27*(1), 14–21. https://files.eric.ed.gov/fulltext/EJ1166700.pdf

Misco, T., & Patterson, N. C. (2007). A study of pre-service teachers' conceptualizations of academic freedoms and controversial issues. *Theory and Research in Social Education, 35*, 520–550. https://doi.org/10.1080/00933104.2007.10473349

NCSS (National Council for the Social Studies). (2015). *The College, Career, and Civic Life (C3) Framework for Social Studies State Standards: Guidance for enhancing the rigor of K–12 civics, economics, geography, and history.* National Council for the Social Studies. https://www.socialstudies.org/system/files/2022/c3-framework-for-social-studies-rev0617.2.pdf

NCSS (National Council for the Social Studies). (2016). *Academic freedom and the social studies educator* [Position statement]. *Social Education, 80*(3), 186. https://www.socialstudies.org/social-education/80/03/academic-freedom-and-social-studies-teacher

NCSS (National Council for the Social Studies). (2017). *National standards for the preparation of social studies teachers.* National Council for the Social Studies. https://www.socialstudies.org/standards

Oulton, C., Day, V., Dillon, J., & Grace, M. (2004). Controversial issues—Teachers' attitude and practices in the context of citizenship education. *Oxford Review of Education, 30*(4), 489–507. https://www.jstor.org/stable/pdf/4127162.pdf

Palmer, P. (2012, July 3). A season of civility: Religion and public life. *Huffpost.* http://www.huffingtonpost.com/parker-j-palmer/a-season-of-civility-religion-and-public-life_b_1641933.html

Philpott, S., Claybough, J., McConkey, L., & Turner, T. N. (2011). Controversial issues: To teach or not to teach? That is the question! *Georgia Social Studies Journal, 1*(1), 32–44.

Ray, R., & Gibbons, A. (2021). *Why are states banning critical race theory?* Brookings. https://www.brookings.edu/blog/fixgov/2021/07/02/why-are-states-banning-critical-race-theory/

Scieszka, J. (1996). *The true story of the three little pigs.* Puffin Books.

Scriven, M., & Paul, R. (2003). *Defining critical thinking: A draft statement prepared for the National Council for Excellence in Critical Thinking Instruction.* The Foundation for Critical Thinking. https://www.quia.com/files/quia/users/medicinehawk/1607-Thinking/defining.pdf

Shulsky, D., Baker S., Chvala, T. & Willis, J. (2017). Cultivating layered literacies developing the global child to become tomorrow's global citizen. *International Journal of Development Education and Global Learning, 9*(1), 49–63. https://files.eric.ed.gov/fulltext/EJ1167861.pdf

Shulsky, D., & Chvala, T. (2017, October 22–24). *Lens on literacy: Zooming in on critical literacy with EC-6 candidates.* 2017 Consortium of State Organizations for Texas Teacher Education (CSOTTE), Corpus Christi, Texas. https://2017csotteconference.weebly.com/

Shulsky, D., & Hendrix, E.Y. (2016) Rooting the literacies of citizenship: Ideas that integrate social studies and language arts in the cultivation of a new global mindset. In A. R. Crowe & A. Cuenca (Eds.), *Rethinking social studies teacher education in the twenty-first century* (pp. 101–119). Springer.

Shuster, K. (2016, April 15). Toward a more civil discourse [Blog post]. *Learning for justice.* http://www.tolerance.org/blog/toward-more-civil-discourse

Shuster, K. (2009). *Civil discourse in the classroom.* Teaching Tolerance. https://files.eric.ed.gov/fulltext/ED541263.pdf

Students Taking Action Together. (2019, Summer). *Civility and society.* SmartFocus on social and emotional learning. https://static1.squarespace.com/static/5b5882f8b98a78554648ca48/t/5d976fe4c5f7cb7b667f73ee/1570205669752/Rutgers+SECD+Lab+SmartFocus+Civility+and+SECD+final.pdf

Swan, K., Lee, J., & Grant, S. G. (2015). The New York State toolkit and the inquiry design model: Anatomy of an inquiry. *Social Education, 79*(6), 316–322. https://c3teachers.org/wp-content/uploads/2016/05/Swan-Grant-Lee_Anatomy_of_Inquiry.pdf

Teitelbaum, K. (2011). Critical civic literacy. In J. L. DeVitis (Ed.) *Critical civic literacy: A reader* (pp.11–23). Peter Lang.

Vasquez, V. M., Janks, H., & Comber, B. (2019). Critical literacy as a way of being and doing. *Language Arts, 96*(5), 300–311. https://hilaryjanks.files.wordpress.com/2020/09/vasquezjankscomber-cl_as_a_way_of_being_and-copy-3-1.pdf

Wolk, S. (2003). Teaching for critical literacy in social studies. *The Social Studies, 94*(3), 101–106. http://pedagogy21.pbworks.com/f/teaching%2Bfor%2Bcritical%2Bliteracy.pdf

Zhiqing, Z. (2015). Assimilation, accommodation, and equilibration: A schema-based perspective on translation as process and as product. In *International Forum of Teaching and Studies* (vol. 11, No. 1/2, p. 84). American Scholars Press, Inc. http://americanscholarspress.us/journals/IFST/pdf/IFOTS-2-2015/v11n2-art9.pdf

CHAPTER 7

UN-LEARNING, RE-LEARNING, AND RE-IMAGINING TOGETHER

Early Career Teachers Engaging in Collaboration Toward Racial Literacies Development

Mary Adu-Gyamfi
University of Missouri-Columbia

Joey Laurx
University of Northern Colorado

Trustin Dinsdale, and Rylie Kever
University of Missouri-Columbia

In the wake of growing racial justice movements across the globe aiming to center the experiences of Black, Indigenous, and people of color's (BIPOC) families and their children, engaging in our own learning and understanding, as White educators, around our students' backgrounds and histories is imperative before authentically and adequately educating children of all families. In this work, we aim to respond to the call put forth by Brown (2017): "The time has come where we can no longer wait until the 'just right time' emerges for us to address race and racism. We must create opportunities to do this work now" (p. 93). Thus, in addition

---

Out of Turmoil: Catalysts for Re-learning, Re-Teaching, and Re-imagining History and Social Science, pages 109–126.
Copyright © 2023 by Information Age Publishing
www.infoagepub.com
All rights of reproduction in any form reserved.

to outlining our focus on racial literacies[1] development (RLsD), our contexts and backgrounds, we explain the three phases of our collaborative work to *un-learn, re-learn,* and *re-imagine* our teaching. We also highlight resources we consulted, and name five integral elements of this collaboration that were most impactful in our learning.

Recognizing that RLsD is not prescriptive (Boutte, 2021), but is instead, based on and tailored to the educators' context, we hope to provide one example of how educators may not only address their own implicit biases and misunderstandings, but work together to set expectations for more culturally responsive teaching practices (Gay, 2010; Hammond, 2014). This is one method of collaborative work[2] educators can engage in to not only develop their racial literacies knowledge, but also practice and act on their new learning.

WHITE TEACHERS LEARNING AND TEACHING ABOUT RACE

With the title of his book—*We Can't Teach What We Don't Know*—Gary Howard (1999) issued a call for White educators to do the necessary work of learning in order to better serve all students. Not only do White teachers comprise the majority (approximately 80%) of the teaching workforce, but many are also culturally isolated (Howard, 1999). Due to such isolated and segregated backgrounds, White educators are often uncomfortable talking about race and racism (e.g., Winans, 2010). Research shows that talking about race, or even listening to conversations about race can bring out fear, anger, and guilt (Stevenson, 2014), which often lead to one's reacting with silence or deflection (Matias, 2016; Mazzei, 2008). A teacher reacting this way in the classroom does little to address and deconstruct race and racism but speaks volumes as it dehumanizes the historically marginalized and oppressed voices and experiences.

Numerous scholars have issued calls for teacher educators to engage in the work of educating their teacher candidates toward antiracist, anti-oppressive, and equity-focused practices (e.g., Sealey-Ruiz, 2011) to better prepare them for teaching their future students. However, teacher education in the United States seems to be caught up in "symbolic action" (Sealey-Ruiz, 2021, p. 281), adding courses such as "culturally responsive pedagogy" without addressing the racism

---

[1] As we developed this collaboration model, we attended specifically to our own contexts and backgrounds, as well as the contexts of our students and schools. In doing so, we came to an understanding echoed by Grayson's (2017) sentiments: there is a "need for instructors interested in developing racial literacies curricula to expand their conceptualization(s) of race to include those who do not identify as Black or White" (p. 159) in order to address the "problematic binary of American racial discourse" (p. 159). Such a limited view rejects the racialization of other minority groups (i.e., Indigenous peoples). Thus, we consider the term racial literacies to include all minority groups who have been historically racialized. Recognizing that the experience of racialized minority groups widely varies, it is important to attend to how race functions differently in diverse contexts, thus calling for multiple literacies.

[2] This presentation is intended to serve as a guide to how White teachers, or those who recognize their need for greater understanding of racial literacies, might take responsibility for their own learning.

embedded in the institutional structures in higher education. Simply having access to scholarly articles in such courses is insufficient for helping teachers engage in RLsD. While professional development (PD) can be a valuable asset for many teachers, there is a lack of effective PD around RLsD and, specifically, the practice (e.g., McCormack et al., 2006) in teaching in culturally responsive ways. Learning *what* is often presented in the PD sessions but learning *how* often comes from practice. This practice is often left to the teachers, without adequate feedback or continual support.

Furthermore, teachers are often not provided the support (Clandinin et al., 2015; Darling-Hammond, 2005) and practice that they need when expected to teach in racially literate ways. In fact, teachers are increasingly looking to non-traditional platforms for the support they seek (i.e., peer groups; Mercieca & Kelly, 2018). Scholarship has already illustrated the prevalence of teachers seeking support for engaging in critical conversations around race, ethnicity, or Indigeneity (e.g., Segall & Garrett, 2013).

In response to these needs, scholars have proposed strategies to help better prepare teachers. First, educators must engage in deep and critical reflection on their own racial socialization (Stevenson, 2014), identifying how they are positioned in society, and how that positioning has had direct impacts on their lives, past and present. King et al. (2018) also argue for developing a "common racial literacy" (p. 316) to prevent misunderstanding and confusion around race and racism. Perhaps one of the first steps teachers must engage in is developing the ability and skill of speaking about race and racism in informed ways by learning about what race and racism mean and how it functions in society. Another strategy named by Skerrett (2011) is for teachers to engage in collaborative PD where teachers can establish a "unified discourse and shared practices of racial literacy instruction" (p. 327). Such efforts can help bridge the gap between knowledge and practice.

We recognize that learning, in and of itself, is not enough. Among calls for White people to be coconspirators (Love, 2019) is the imperative for us to not only listen to people of color but act on our new learning. Change remains limited when the learning sits inside the minds of teachers. Instead, educators must push themselves to engage in antiracist and anti-oppressive action (Dover et al., 2020). Engaging in collaborative and participatory efforts like the model outlined in this paper, can provide the confidence, motivation, critical reflection, learning, and action necessary for educators to become more equitable and inclusive for all students. We hope this model may be a helpful place for aspiring allies to begin.

FOCUS ON RACIAL LITERACIES AND DEVELOPMENT

Racial Literacies

To boil it down to its simplest form, Price-Dennis and Sealey-Ruiz (2021) explain racial literacies as being the "ability to examine, discuss, challenge, and take anti-racist action in situations that involve acts of racism" (p. 19). This ability must involve examination of racism on many levels: the individual and relationship levels (Twine, 2004), institutional and systemic levels (Guinier, 2004), as well as through personal story (Stevenson, 2014). In our work with White, early career teachers, we take racial literacies scholarship into account in focusing on the following tenets:

- Understanding the social construction of race and racial identity;
- Recognizing that racism is not only a historical problem, but also a contemporary one;
- Recognizing the impact of racisms at the individual, institutional, and societal levels;
- Considering the ways race and racism are influenced by multiple factors (i.e., class);
- Developing language practices in and for discussing race, racism, and antiracism; and
- Practicing the reading of racial interactions and engaging in antiracist action.

In addition to these tenets, we also understand racial literacies to have certain characteristics. First, racial literacies are humanizing projects for all people (Price-Dennis & Sealey-Ruiz, 2021). Second, based on their contextual nature, racial literacies are not prescriptive (Boutte, 2021), but instead lead to tailor-made approaches for respective communities. Racial literacies must also be critical, which implies an unrelenting attention to power dynamics and structural racism (Boutte, 2021; Brown, 2017). Finally, racial literacies imply engagement in an ongoing journey, not a final outcome (Grayson, 2019). Considering these tenets and characteristics of racial literacies, it is important to acknowledge that developing toward greater racial literacies is very much a process. Thus, we specifically think of our collaborative work as moving toward greater RLsD and not a static knowledge set of racial literacies.

Racial Literacies Development

Because of our focus on our RLsD in a collaborative group setting, we also outline tenets of RLsD. We lean on Sealey-Ruiz's (2021) tenets. First, one must "question their assumptions about race, acknowledge their biases, and take the stance that much of what they 'assume to know' about race is faulty and incomplete" (p. 286). Second, one must "engage in critical conversations" (p. 286), focusing on how bias and racist attitudes manifest through language. Third, one must "practice reflexivity" (p. 286), engaging in a "cyclical process of (re)examining perceptions, beliefs, and actions relating to race" (p. 286). These are all resonant with the tenets of racial literacies as shown previously but provide a bit more tangible and concrete plan for moving forward.

In all, Price-Dennis and Sealey-Ruiz (2021) note that the natural progression for teachers engaging in RLsD is "(re)examination of what and how they are teaching, and a deliberate development of culturally responsive educational approaches in their classroom…[and] seek to decolonize their pedagogy and create a foundation for equitable practices in their classroom" (p. 22). Thus, we illustrate how this platform of racial literacies and RLsD has driven elements of this present and ongoing project.

CONTEXT OF THE STUDY

Participants

We are four White educators who identify as aspiring allies. At the time of this chapter, Mary was a teacher educator at a midwestern university and teaching an undergraduate teacher preparation course. Joey and Trustin were in their second year of teaching at a charter school in Colorado. Rylie was beginning her first year of full-time teaching in an elementary school in Missouri.

Trustin, Rylie, and Joey were formerly students in several of Mary's courses and were interested in continued collaboration with Mary after graduating from the program. As students in this midwestern institution, they took many of the same courses, which served as the groundwork for this collaboration toward RLsD. Three required courses focused on what cultural diversity means in the U.S. context—students' biases, teaching in diverse schools and communities, and teaching social studies—which involved readings and learning experiences such as Takaki's (2012) *A Different Mirror for Young People: A Multicultural History of America* to guide teacher candidates in exploring the histories of many historically marginalized populations in the United States. These three courses served as the launchpad from which we began this work to further, and more intentionally, engage in RLsD.

Approach

In our work, we followed a collaborative and participatory action design approach, making decisions and engaging in discussions and reflections in a collaborative manner. To put it simply, a participatory action research (PAR) approach engages "people in processes of reflection, education, and change" (McIntyre, 2008, p. 79). We attempted to build five specific areas of focus inherent in a participatory approach into our design: dialogic communication, power dynamics, iterative process, flexibility, and action.

Freire (1970/2000) claimed that this iterative process of dialogue can lead to critical consciousness, in which people learn to question, grow, and reflect in the collaborative meaning-making process. Regarding power dynamics, we tried to work together as equals, acknowledging that we each had different perspectives and experiences to contribute. This also compelled us to focus on how power was at play and needed to be addressed as we invited guest speakers. Third, we all had a responsibility to attend to contextual factors that informed and influenced our work and the relationships within the collective such as societal, economic, political, and identity factors. This required the group members to adapt to situations, sometimes changing course mid-way through the project. Participatory work also calls for an intervention to act on the strength of the relationships and the conviction brought by the new knowledge (i.e., Irizarry & Brown, 2014). With these five elements and the elements of RLsD, we designed our collaborative model.

COLLABORATIVE MODEL TOWARD RACIAL LITERACIES DEVELOPMENT

Following the design of Sealey-Ruiz's (2021) question, engage, and reflect, we designed a series of three phases toward RLsD (see Figure 7.1) to guide us from un-learning, to re-learning, and re-imagining.

Phase 1: Recruitment and Laying Groundwork

Topic and Purpose

Considering that PAR is dialogic and cyclical in nature, the initial purpose and topic that brought me (Mary) to this work remained fluid as I read more and work with my collaborators. I first came to this study through my growing interest and passion for educating my own multiracial and multiethnic children. This passion intersected with my role as a teacher educator. Because I did not have experience as an undergraduate in our current university context's teacher education program (TEP), I aimed to recruit those who completed the program as experts (see Figure 7.1). The growing awareness of my lack of experience with racialized and marginalized histories and literacies fueled my interest in pursuing this line of research, but it was my acknowledgement that the graduates were best positioned to help inform my own practice that laid the foundation for collaboration within this project.

Recruitment

In February of 2020, I reached out to nine of my previous students. These nine stood out in my mind as having great passion for the profession of teaching as well as deep commitments to their students. All nine agreed to an initial conversation

Recruit members → Establish common interest → Create plans

FIGURE 7.1. Phase 1 of Collaborative Racial Literacies Development

with me in which I asked them what they saw as gaps in their institution's TEP. At the end of each conversation, I asked if they saw specific gaps around the TEP's integration of marginalized and racialized ethnic and Indigenous backgrounds. After compiling commonalities among the nine responses, three had particularly strong leanings toward this desired focus. After meeting to establish a common interest, we created a plan for going forward.

Initial Meetings

Google, Zoom, and text messaging served as our means of communication and collaboration platforms due to distance. To build rapport within the group, we started by each sharing artifacts that spoke to our passion for education. I shared a brief overview of how I imagined our collaboration and participatory action would look, acknowledging that I expected things to shift as the group members learned more and interests shifted and narrowed. We also spent time discussing and reflecting on the following three questions:

- What are strengths around diversity, ethnicity, and Indigeneity in the TEP?
- What experiences do you bring with you to this work?
- What are your expectations?

Next, we discussed what this team project might produce in the end, such as workshops, presentations, or PD. Finally, to further establish a plan for going forward, we discussed what time commitments everyone felt comfortable with over the summer, as well as how we wanted to spend time learning about this topic before meeting again to discuss.

Although we began the creation of a plan in the first phase, we remained flexible and attempted to make shifts along the way. In our second group meeting that took place three weeks later, we attempted to refine our expectations for this collaboration. During our third meeting, we focused more on what goals we had for each of our teaching contexts. We afforded ample time to reflect on the learning we had done in the TEP around racialized ethnic and Indigenous histories and backgrounds, while considering what work we knew we still needed to do in order to be better educators to all students.

Phase 2: Learning Toward Racial Literacies

This second phase of the collaboration model consisted of the intentional learning towards becoming more culturally responsive teachers (see Figure 7.2). We engaged in weekly meetings throughout the summer with a goal to learn toward planning for enactment and implementation. Out of the nine summer meetings, we hosted seven scholars for 30- to 60-minute sessions to share their educational experiences as well as their research. We sought out speakers who wanted to share their experiences as being from marginalized and racialized identities. After sharing with them the work we were doing and the goals we had, each guest speaker

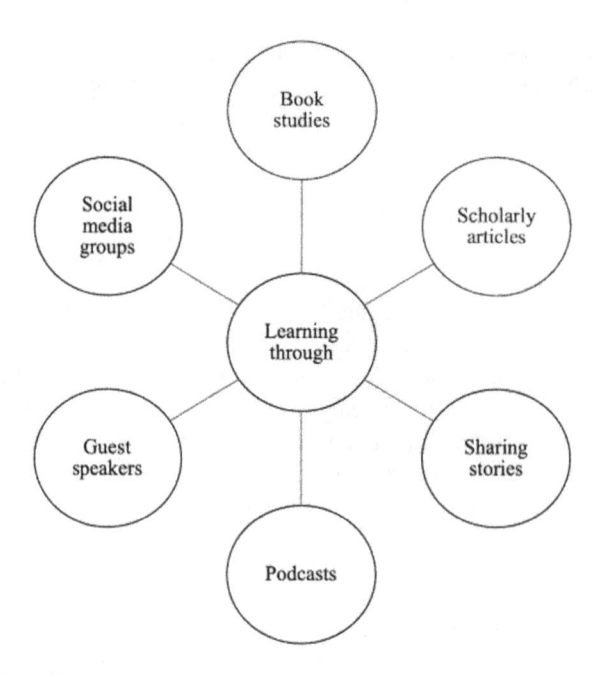

FIGURE 7.2. Phase 2 of Collaborative Racial Literacies Development

we reached out to accepted our invitation. We had guest speakers[3] who identified as Metis/Anishinaabe, Blackfeet, Kenyan, and Mexican-American/Latina. Being cognizant of needing to also learn from White scholars who had gathered knowledge from working with historically marginalized and racialized populations, we invited two White scholars who had several years of experience working in education research with marginalized knowledges and histories.

With each meeting lasting between 90 minutes to 2 hours, we spent the beginning of each meeting checking in with each other, seeking additional feedback about any learning toward RLsD that took place that week, as well as further thoughts about implementation in the classroom. After each guest speaker's visit, we spent the rest of our meeting time reflecting on what we learned from the visit and discussing ways we could implement what we learned from the speaker's unique perspective.

To account for time constraints in our group meetings and potential discomfort sharing in the whole group, Mary held individual interviews at the midpoint of the summer. This meeting gave each team member more time to discuss how they were processing their learning as well as develop plans for enactment in their specific teaching contexts.

---

[3] We would not have gained the knowledge and understanding about racial literacies without the investment of time and energy devoted by numerous persons of color who have personally shared their stories with us. In our presentation and teaching, we aim to learn from and honor their stories.

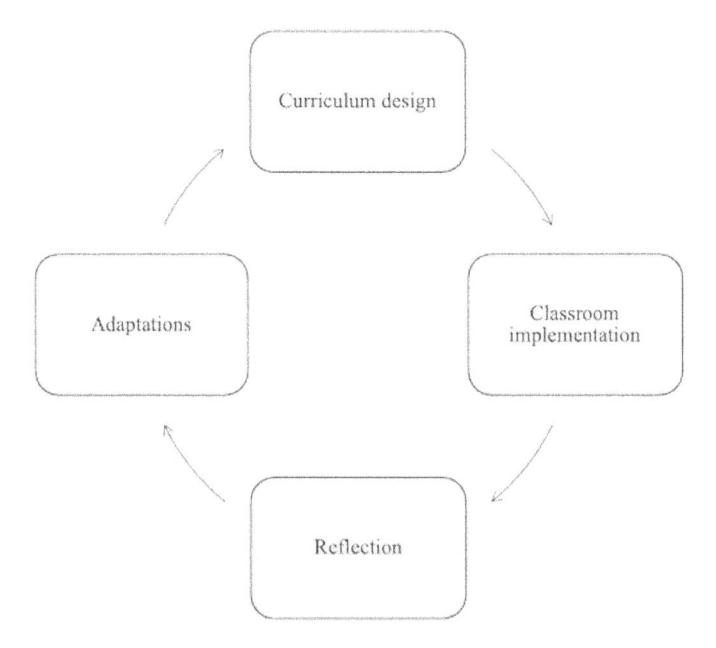

FIGURE 7.3. Phase 3 of Collaborative Racial Literacies Development

In addition to the guest speakers who graciously and passionately shared their stories with us, we sought resources including a range of podcasts, books, articles, films, picturebooks[4], and social media groups. Some were recommended by the guest speakers and some were found through other avenues. Each member of the group decided which texts they wanted to consult in their own personal time outside of our group meetings, then reported their new learning to the group. In these discussions, we shared what the resource stated as well as how the resource affected us personally.

Phase 3: Racial Literacies Implementation for Culturally Responsive Teaching

As we progressed, we each established areas in which we wanted to start implementing our learning. Recognizing we wanted to go beyond Banks' (1993) additive and contributive approaches to teaching curriculum, we picked a starting point to attain a more transformational and social-justice-action approach for both infusing our new RLsD throughout the curriculum and allowing it to change the structure of our teaching (see Figure 7.3).

---

[4] In this chapter, we purposely use the word "picturebook" in accordance with Sipe's (2001) thinking to represent the idea that the words and the pictures in a picturebook convey meaning together.

Rylie's goal was to address concepts of race, racism, and discrimination in her read-aloud times. Instead of using many of the books left by previous teachers, Rylie sought texts that featured characters and authors from various racial, ethnic, and Indigenous backgrounds. Although the majority of her second-grade students were White, she believed it was vital for all of her students to engage in discussions around race through picturebooks, as well as receive invitations to respond by writing about how a text made them feel or prompted them to make connections to their own lives.

Trustin and Joey aimed to infuse their science curriculum with Indigenous knowledges and histories. Considering they had a much more racially, linguistically, and ethnically diverse group of students, they wanted to do more to specifically feature the experiences of their students in the curriculum. Since both teach science at the fifth-grade level, they worked together to recreate the science curriculum.

In addition, Trustin set a goal to establish and cultivate an environment in his classroom in which sharing stories was normalized. While he started the school year by sharing more about himself to build rapport with his students, he invited a different student to share a story of their choice each morning. Over time, he hoped that students would build rapport with and respect for each other, thus affecting their engagement in learning.

In her language arts curriculum, Joey decided also to trade out the novel *Percy Jackson & The Olympians: The Lightning Thief* by Rick Riordan for a similar book by Kwame Mbalia, *Tristan Strong Punches a Hole in the Sky*. Instead of presenting Riordan's focus on Greek mythology, Mbalia's text focuses on West African Mythology and African American folklore. This was more relevant to the population of her students. Joey also did a read aloud of the book *Blended* by Sharon Draper, which focuses on a sixth-grade girl who is struggling with her identity because of her multiracial identity (White mom and Black dad) and her parent's divorce. Joey used this book to spark conversations in her classroom about identity, race, ethnicity, and racism.

Reflection

Reflection was an integral component of this project from the beginning. As Sealey-Ruiz (2021) states, reflecting on one's background, bias, and racialization is the key to RLsD. She notes that the *archaeology of the self* is not something that is ever complete but is vital to the beginning of the process. Numerous race scholars (e.g., Sealey-Ruiz, 2011) note the importance of critical reflection in one's ability to engage in race work, all the more so when the person is White because of the evasive nature of Whiteness (Lipsitz, 2006; Matias, 2016). Using the few courses in their TEP that emphasized the need for critical reflection as a launching point, we built time into the beginning and end of each of our meetings to process what we had learned—discussing things that surprised us, challenged us, and confused us. Once the school year started and the weekly meetings ended, we exchanged weekly text messages discussing how the implementation plan was going. These texts addressed feelings of discomfort and disappointments, signs of progress, and logistical difficulties.

This model or set of phases, in no way, constitutes an end. Instead, these phases serve as a proposition of how early career teachers and aspiring allies can begin the work of intentionally developing their racial literacies. Once begun, this process of resource diving, critically reflecting, collaborative planning, and implementation should be an ongoing project of life-long learning.

TEACHER TESTIMONIES

Central to this work was the acknowledgment and recognition that we are each at a different point in our RLsD, traveling in the same direction and yet at different points in our journey. As such, it is advantageous to give voice to each educator, highlighting how engagement in this together has transformed each one's thinking and teaching.

Rylie

Because I grew up in such a bubble, my preservice teacher education and my work within this group opened my eyes to the world beyond myself and my identity. I believe that it is my role as a teacher to share and validate all identities so that students can feel accepted and build upon their own schema to form understanding, generate beliefs, and make informed decisions. It is my job to provide these opportunities for learning to children, but I knew that I needed to provide them for myself first. I found stories to be a powerful way of explaining complex ideas in understandable ways. Listening, watching, and reading stories that were windows into another person's experiences gave me the push to start sharing these in my classroom.

As a primary educator, I view literacy simply as communication: written, visual, verbal, or even nonverbal. Because my students were still learning to read, I encouraged them to gain and communicate knowledge using all forms of communication. To me, racial literacy is the communication of what race is, how it functions, and where it originated. The perspectives and beliefs surrounding race depend on the communication that is consistently interpreted as true. I chose to use picturebook read-alouds as a means to communicate the different perspectives, beliefs, and experiences of cultures and communities that were misinterpreted or not consistently included in my classroom. I also hoped that providing students the opportunity to grow and alter their current schema to encompass more than just their own experiences would help them to build social skills.

I aimed to enact my own RLsD through more culturally responsive teaching practices such as through the use of stories and picturebooks to provide meaningful and engaging experiences for my students that were both windows into and mirrors of their own lives. I incorporated these stories and books into my everyday read-alouds and focus lessons as mentor texts. As I continued to engage in my own RLsD, I grew more conscious of my words, thoughts, and actions pertaining to cultural responsiveness.

Trustin

Growing up in rural Missouri, I was not exposed to much diversity. I came into college with an idyllic view of the world and no idea of the importance of being racially literate. Progressing through my education I was exposed to more and more diversity that shaped my view of education and the importance of diversity in the classroom. When Mary asked me to be a part of this group I was excited for what I could learn and how I could apply it to my own teaching. This group allowed me to step out of my own comfort zone and invest in my own racial literacies.

When we first started this group I began to read about culturally responsive pedagogy and the importance of racial literacies. This research widened my understanding of what teaching can be. I began to learn what it takes to create a culturally responsive classroom and the complexities surrounding that. Over the course of this project we discussed the importance of storytelling. This inspired me to use stories in my own classroom as a way of sharing a bit of our culture with our little community.

Each day I invited one student to share a story from their own life. As I implemented this I also stressed the importance of personal culture to all of my students. My goal was for the stories that we shared every day to create a bond between everyone in the classroom. It was my hope that the bond that we created also improved their ability to learn. Humans learn better when they feel safe so I worked to ensure that my classroom was a space where they felt heard.

I was very grateful for the opportunity to be a part of this project as it helped me to become a better teacher. The more that I invested in my own racial literacies, the easier it was for me to connect to my very diverse students. While I am far from being an expert on RLsD, I am still working towards a better understanding and bettering myself.

Joey

Since the day I realized I wanted to become a teacher, I knew I wanted to make a difference in the education and lives of students. When Mary asked me to be a part of this group, I was very excited about how this could make me a better teacher. Being knowledgeable about diverse populations and being a culturally responsive educator has been important to me since the time I started my teacher education program. This group gave me the space I didn't know I needed in order to become a more racially literate and culturally responsive teacher.

This group provided a place for me to learn from other teachers and professionals to not only improve my RLsD but use it. I gained many more resources for how to implement my new knowledge, which was a challenge for me previously. At my school, the administrators are very passionate about teaching teachers about Black Excellence through PD. While these PD's presented valuable information, we were often left wondering how to apply this learning in our own classrooms. With the help of the members of this group and guest speakers, I was able to discuss ideas regarding curriculum design and get insight about what would and would not work.

One idea I got from this group that I was most excited about was creating a more culturally responsive science curriculum. Through discussions with the others, readings, and listening to guest speakers, we came up with more inclusive connections (i.e., Indigenous) to science. For example, we connected our unit on human impact on Earth systems to Indigenous peoples and the importance of land and water. I began applying this approach in my language arts curriculum, including discussion of specific African and Indigenous people groups.

Although I would have considered myself racially literate before this experience, my knowledge and confidence in what I am teaching increased significantly as a result of this collaboration. These topics were still a challenge to teach and can still be very uncomfortable, but it was impactful to have this accountability group behind me, supporting each other through challenges. I know I still have a lot to learn and it is empowering to know that I have a place to continue that learning.

IMPLICATIONS

It is important to note that this collaborative model functions differently from professional and school-bound groups, such as a "professional learning team," in which grade-level teachers collaborate together for the purposes of planning or making resources for grade-specific instruction. In such groups, there can be an emphasis on remaining professional, rather than engaging in vulnerable conversations about big-picture issues such as how race functions in the classroom. In our collaborative model, we not only have the choice to participate, but we do so with the desire to learn and contribute with honesty and humility.

Thus, drawing from the experiences in the above sections, we highlight five elements of this collaborative model that have been most beneficial to our RLsD and could further guide others who begin collaborative groups of their own. We also note a few obstacles that collaborative team members may experience when undertaking similar work.

Accountability

Through data collection, we started each meeting with the space to share how the reading or resources added to our understanding, addressed implicit biases we held, or helped us imagine its application in our classrooms.

Meeting Frequency

Having frequent meetings encouraged and motivated us to actively look for ways in which we were letting implicit biases go unchecked or unchallenged. Establishing this routine began to normalize how we thought of racial literacies in our own lives.

Sharing

We had some shared experiences as White folks who grew up with certain privileges, but we each had unique experiences that positioned us with slightly different perspectives. These differences allowed us to share unique insights in reaction to our engagement with resources, share ideas, and push one another to think more deeply about teaching in racially literate ways.

Like-Minded Disposition

We aligned around the goal of attaining greater understanding of historically marginalized racial, ethnic, and Indigenous groups and individuals. Because we all came to the group knowing that we had much to learn, we also engaged in humility toward one another and towards those who were educating us. We intentionally positioned ourselves as novices and, in turn, positioned our guest speakers and other BIPOC authors and resource creators as experts on their perspectives.

Learning Through Story

We have found that learning through story has been especially impactful. In sum, each of the resources we consulted presented a story in different formats. We intentionally sought stories told and presented by BIPOC authors. An additional component of story was found in our own renderings of incidents of racism and evidence of systemic racism in our own contexts or about what we have learned through these other stories.

Potential Obstacles

As might be expected, there are a number of potential obstacles we faced both in implementing our learning in the classroom context and in participating in this collaborative group.

Classroom Implementation

First, while there are many ways teachers can implement new racial literacies knowledge into their practice (i.e., morning meeting, read-alouds) in the classroom, obstacles may arise. We found that attending to context was crucial. For example, we knew conversations in Rylie's predominantly White context would look and sound very different from Trustin and Joey's racially and linguistically diverse context. Joey and Trustin found that engaging in conversations around race and racism occurred naturally in their classrooms, while Rylie found it to be intimidating and unnatural to bring up concepts of race and racism in her classroom. As in Rylie's context, students seemed to have very little awareness of race or racism and perhaps did not feel prepared to have such conversations. Talking about such obstacles in a collaborative group can provide needed support for engaging in these classroom conversations. Veteran teachers, team teachers, or school administrators can also provide a wealth of support to help jumpstart these conversations as well.

Two more obstacles to classroom implementation are time and emotional investment. First, schools already expect teachers to cover so much material that it can be a challenge to implement anything in addition to the traditional curriculum. On top of this, the emotional investment can be steep. For example, Trustin noted being surprised by the extensive amount of groundwork that needed to be laid in creating an open environment in which students chose to engage in open dialogue around race or discrimination. He stated that educators must "give a lot for the students to give back." In a similar vein, Rylie noted how it is important sometimes to let go of some of those "professional boundaries" in order to connect with students and "make them feel loved." She noted that she was initially "scared to open up" because of the legal issues she learned about in her recent teacher education program regarding school law and policy. Certainly a teacher's lack of confidence or fear of backlash from parents or administrations can hamper a classroom engagement with topics such as race and racism, as well. For example, Joey recalled that, although implementing her learning helped engage her students, there were times when the students did not always take conversations seriously. In this case student behavior negatively impacted a teacher's confidence and stifle further engagement. With any of these classroom concerns, speaking to supportive teachers and administrators who are also trying to do the same work can be a tremendous help.

Collaborative Work

We also experienced a few obstacles related to engaging in a collaborative group. In our experience, the main obstacles involved constraints on our time, finances, and commitment. First, it took time to search for reputable resources for individual and group learning. While each member spent some time looking for resources, such as podcasts and books, Mary spent added time lining up guest speakers for the summer meetings. Each of these tasks takes extra time, but one way to address this time constraint is to instead take up opportunities that are already organized, such as the numerous online sessions or academic conferences being offered and advertised on social media and other platforms. However, saving time in this way may also contribute to financial pressures.

While some schools and organizations may offer funding for teachers' professional development (i.e., books, conference attendance), procuring such funding can be difficult and time-consuming. Asking about funding opportunities early on could be beneficial for informing next steps. In our experience, very little funding was available to help compensate guest speakers for their time. Because honoring the time and labor expended by our guest speakers was important to us, we offered compensation to each in the form of gift cards or donations to a cause of their choice. Considering our positioning in this work, this was non-negotiable.

With the pandemic not yet behind us, and with educators' jobs involving additional responsibilities (i.e., hybrid teaching), our commitment to engagement in this group naturally wavered. For example, we often felt like there were times we were more physically present than mentally present. Not to mention, each member of this group faced difficult and unforeseen situations during this time period, which warranted additional sensitivity. With time already being stretched thin, it was hard to engage in all that we wanted to (i.e., book club readings and discussions). Considering these stressors, we postponed a few of our regular meetings during the school year and, when we did meet, we spent the beginning of the meeting checking in with each other. Finally, considering we are all White teachers trying to engage in our own racial literacies development, we certainly had moments where we allowed our discomfort or vulnerability to keep us from engaging as we should have. We desired to identify these discomforts then target them by engaging further, even if it meant coming back to a topic or experience.

CONCLUSION

The model of sustained practice outlined here illustrates how early career teachers can engage in RLsD in a collaborative manner, joined together by a commitment to being and doing better for our students. These implications speak directly to White teachers entering into critical work, who fear doing harm to students by replicating the status quo yet hesitate (and rightfully so) when trying to enact antiracist work. Forming such a group of early career teachers, with its emphasis on teacher commitment to critical collaborative meaning making and RLsD, provides a viable model for implementation when attempting to become more equitable and inclusive educators. As Brown (2017) stated, we cannot wait. We need to find ways to engage in this work now. We hope that this model can be helpful as a starting place for others as it was for us.

REFERENCES

Banks, J. (1993). Multicultural education: Historical development, dimensions, and practice. *Review of Research in Education, 19*, 3–49. https://doi.org/1167339

Boutte, G. (2021). Critical racial literacy in educational and familial settings. *Oxford Research Encyclopedia of Education*, 1–17. https://doi.org/10.1093/acrefore/9780190264093.013.1570

Brown, K. D. (2017). Why we can't wait: Advancing racial literacy and a critical sociocultural knowledge of race for teaching and curriculum. *Race, Gender & Class, 24*(1–2), 81–96.

Clandinin, D. J., Long, J., Schaefer, L., Downey, C. A., Steeves, P., Pinnegar, E., Robblee, S., & Wnuk, S. (2015). Early career teacher attrition: Intentions of teachers beginning. *Teaching Education, 26*(1), 1–16. https://doi.org/10.1080/10476210.2014.996746

Darling-Hammond, L. (2005). Teaching as a profession: Lessons in teacher preparation and professional development. *Phi Delta Kappan*, 237–340. https://doi.org/10.1177%2F003172170508700318

Dover, A., Kressler, B., & Lozano, M. (2020). Learning our way through: Critical professional development for social justice in teacher education. *The New Educator, 16*(1), 45–69. https://doi.org/10.1080/1547688X.2019.1671566

Freire, P. (2000). *Pedagogy of the oppressed*. Continuum. (Original work published in 1970).

Gay, G. (2010). *Culturally responsive teaching: Theory, research, and practice*. Teachers College Press.

Grayson, M. (2017). Race talk in the composition classroom: Narrative song lyrics as texts for racial literacy. *Teaching English in the Two-Year College, 45*(2), 143–167.

Grayson, M. (2019). Racial literacy is literacy: Locating racial literacy in the college composition classroom. *Journal for Expanded Perspectives on Learning, 24*, 17–46.

Guinier, L. (2004). From racial liberalism to racial literacy: *Brown v. Board of Education* and the interest-divergence dilemma. *Journal of American History, 91*(1), 92–118.

Hammond, Z. (2014). *Culturally responsive teaching and the brain: Promoting authentic engagement and rigor among culturally and linguistically diverse students*. Corwin.

Howard, G. (1999). *We can't teach what we don't know: White teachers, multiracial schools*. Teachers College Press.

Irizarry, J., & Brown, T. (2014). *Humanizing research in dehumanizing spaces: The challenges and opportunities of conducting participatory action research with youth in schools. Humanizing research: Decolonizing qualitative inquiry with youth and communities* (pp. 63–80).

King, L., Vickery, A., & Caffrey, G. (2018). A pathway to racial literacy: Using the LETS ACT framework to teach controversial issues. *Social Education, 82*(6), 316–322.

Lipsitz, G. (2006). *The possessive investment in Whiteness: How White people profit from identity politics*. Temple University Press.

Love, B. (2019). *We want to do more than survive: Abolitionist teaching and the pursuit of educational freedom*. Beacon Press.

Matias, C. E. (2016). *Feeling White: Whiteness, emotionality, and education*. Sense Publishers.

Mazzei, L. (2008). Silence speaks: Whiteness revealed in the absence of voice. *Teaching and Teacher Education, 24*(5), 1125–1136. https://doi.org/10.1016/j.tate.2007.02.009

McCormack, A., Gore, J., & Thomas, K. (2006). Early career teacher professional learning. *Asia-Pacific Journal of Teacher Education, 34*(1), 95–113. https://doi.org/10.1080/13598660500480282

McIntyre, A. (2008). *Participatory action research* (pp. 61–69). SAGE Publications.

Mercieca, B., & Kelly, N. (2018). Early career teacher peer support through private groups in social media. *Asia-Pacific Journal of Teacher Education, 46*(1), 61–77. https://doi.org/10.1080/1359866X.2017.1312282

Price-Dennis, D., & Sealey-Ruiz, Y. (2021). *Advancing racial literacies in teacher education: Activism for equity in digital spaces*. Teachers College Press.

Sealey-Ruiz, Y. (2011). Dismantling the school-to-prison pipeline through racial literacy development in teacher education. *Journal of Curriculum and Pedagogy, 8*(2), 116–120. https://doi.org/10.1080/15505170.2011.624892

Sealey-Ruiz, Y. (2021). The critical literacy of race: Toward racial literacy in urban teacher education. In T. Howard & H. Milner (Eds.), *Handbook for urban education* (2nd ed., pp. 281–295). Routledge.

Segall, A., & Garrett, J. (2013). White teachers talking race. *Teaching Education, 24*(3), 265–291. https://doi.org/10.1080/10476210.2012.704509

Skerrett, A. (2011). English teachers' racial literacy knowledge and practice. *Race Ethnicity and Education, 14*(3), 313–330. https://doi.org/10.1080/13613324.2010.543391

Stevenson, H. (2014). *Promoting racial literacy in schools: Differences that make a difference*. Teachers College Press.

Takaki, R. (2012). *A different mirror for young people: A history of multicultural America*. Triangle Square.

Twine, F. W. (2004). A white side of black Britain: The concept of racial literacy. *Ethnic and Racial studies, 27*(6), 878–907.

Winans, A. (2010). Cultivating racial literacy in White, segregated settings: Emotions as site of ethical engagement and inquiry. *Curriculum Inquiry, 40*(3), 475–491. https://doi.org/10.1111/j.1467-873X.2010.00494.x

PART III

GLOBAL RESPONSES TO TURMOIL

CHAPTER 8

A TUMULTUOUS TALE OF SOCIALLY JUST TEACHING

A Migrant Asian Australian Teacher's Critical Autoethnographic Account of Guiding White Bodies Through an Asian Ethnoburb

Aaron Teo
The University of Queensland, Australia

It happened again at a preliminary gathering of young married couples who would later become close friends.

This gathering was held potluck style in the dining room of one of the couple's houses and was buzzing with a tangible excitement that stemmed from the anticipation of getting to know seemingly similar individuals in a similar phase of life.

My wife and I decided to be adventurous and had painstakingly seasoned, rolled, folded, and concocted a loosely pan-Asian offering for the potluck comprising of raw salmon nigiri, pork and chive guo tie and a chicken mie goreng.

As dinnertime approaches, the hosts call us to order, and, as the conversation dies down, request that each couple take a turn to introduce the dishes they had brought along.

Out of Turmoil: Catalysts for Re-learning, Re-Teaching, and Re-imagining History and Social Science, pages 129–142.
Copyright © 2023 by Information Age Publishing
www.infoagepub.com
All rights of reproduction in any form reserved.

As fate would have it, the host couple decide on an anticlockwise progression and so, I am the last to speak after all the other introductions. I take a quick second to gather my thoughts before stepping through what I know about the ingredients, origin and eating norms associated with each of the three dishes.

Just as I am about to conclude, I notice, from the corner of my eye, one of the other husbands—a white[1] Australian man—stood beside me leaning in.

"Wow, Aaron, your spoken English is *really* good. Where are you from?"

Despite having received similar "compliments" in the past, I am caught off-guard by Sterling's (pseudonym) racializing comment yet again. I respond instinctively by trying to read Sterling's face for any sign of malice or "jest."

I pause for a moment.

Nothing whatsoever—instead, a look of what seemed like genuine curiosity. I respond tentatively.

"Umm…Brisbane?"

"Oh yeah, but I meant originally, *before* that. As you were talking through all this Asian food so eloquently, it made me wonder…Like, where are you *really* from?"

***

Instead of continuing with my response to Sterling, I provide a quick note on my own positionality. I am a middle-class, heterosexual, able-bodied, male high school teacher. Before migrating to Australia for higher education, I was educated in two of Singapore's most elite private schools, and was privileged to have received consistent social, emotional, and financial support from both my friends and family. Consequently, the colour of my skin was never an issue. I was never quizzed about my origins, nor was my sense of national belonging ever questioned.

Since migrating, however, the colour of my skin has rendered me a racial minority who has experienced (and continues to experience) different forms of racism; and so, I write here as a political decision to engage in transformative practice (hooks, 1994); a writing steeped in a refusal to perpetuate settler-colonial logics (Cairns, 2021; Klippmark & Crawley, 2018). At the same time, I also realise that the above-mentioned privileges have limited my experience and as such, do not claim to represent the experiences of all Asian Australians or migrants of colour.

With that in mind, as I move along with this politically motivated writing, I now "come to theory" (hooks, 1994) as a way of autoethnographically connecting my personal experience to culture, society, and politics (Ellis, 2004). This

---

[1] In this chapter, I have been mindful of the terms used to represent different racial groups, starting with a deliberate choice to capitalise or leave in lower case. In particular, names of racial and ethnic groups of color have been capitalized as a sign of respect for groups who have been historically disempowered and marginalized. By the same token, I have deliberately chosen not to capitalise "white" as a representation of this chapter's role in critically interrogating whiteness (Halley et al., 2011).

autoethnographic approach is reflected in the chapter's format, where I intersperse aspects of literary writing (Ellis, 2004), seen in personal narrative containing dialogue-rich scenes, with more traditional academic prose (Bochner & Ellis, 2002), constantly shifting in and out of both voices as a-way of writing, and a "method for conducting and displaying research" (Vasconcelos, 2011, p.417).

For this chapter, I come to Asian critical race theory (AsianCrit), which, like its critical race theory (CRT) counterpart, emerged in the 1990s in the field of law (Lawrence & Matsuda, 1997). While AsianCrit differs from CRT in its understanding of racial oppression through the unique geopolitical, temporal-historical, and cultural contexts of Asians as a minority group (Chang, 1993), AsianCrit shares a similar political commitment to intersectionality, praxis, and subverting privilege and oppression (Iftikar & Museus, 2018).

In many ways, Sterling's question implicitly reflects the AsianCrit tenet of *Asianisation*, which concerns a uniquely Asian racialisation—a form of nativistic racism—based on an "intense opposition to an internal minority on the grounds of its [purportedly] foreign connections" (Chang, 1993, p. 1253). This results in Asians being homogenised as a monolithic "cultural" whole and inscribed with a deficit of *perpetual foreignness* [emphasis added] (Chang, 1993).

In the Australian context specifically, owing to increasing globalised flows of migration, this question of where one is from—a usually incessant and irritating inquiry into the origins for racial and ethnic "others" living in Australia (Ang, 2005)—has become an increasingly common occurrence (Ang, 2005). Indeed, implied in Sterling's question of where I was from "was always the expectation, the requirement even, that I would mention *another* space"—a space, somewhere in Asia that embodies the "mysterious, inscrutable other—presumably the 'natural' land for people with my 'racial' features" (Ang, 2005, p. 11).

It is this very Asianisation—a "stereotyping of Asia as 'out there' rather than Asia…being part of Australian society itself" (Curry, 2021, para. 16)—that results in "the inevitable positioning of [the Asian Australian internal minority] self as [a homogenised] deviant vis-à-vis the normal" (Ang, 2005, p. 30) and an acute awareness that such questions are asked on the assumed "denaturalisation of our status as coinhabitants of this country, and in the automatic assumption that because we don't fit the stereotypical image of the typical Australian, we somehow don't (quite) 'belong' here" (Ang, 2005, p. 144). Put simply, the "Where are you from?" phenomenon subsumes Asian Australians into the politics of discrimination, marginalization, and exclusion by the white (Australian) majority (Rizvi, 1990).

From an education perspective, schools and classrooms function as the principal location of knowledge construction and production (Rudnick, 2019), meaning that there is a germane opportunity—through what is taught in classrooms—to move away from this "culture of [racialized] domination" (hooks, 1994, p. 173) by reversing the rhetoric through politically transformative lessons (Breunig,

2016) that impact on values, attitudes and perspectives towards race and racism (Rudnick, 2019).

Rather concerningly, however, the Australian Curriculum—which "sets the expectations for what all young Australians should be taught, regardless of where they live in Australia or their background" (Australian Curriculum, Assessment and Reporting Authority [ACARA], 2021a, para. 1)—and its focus on Asia, and by extension, Asian Australia, contrives a very different story to the lived experiences of Asian Australians. Set against the context of three decades of Asia as the key driver of world economic growth and strategic contestation (Curry, 2021), as well as a force that will reshape the global distribution of power in the 21st century (Lowy Institute, 2019) a.k.a. the "Asian Century" (Zhang et al., 2020), Asia is positioned vis-à-vis Australia as "interdependent through linked histories and contemporary realities" (Curry, 2021, para. 9) and thus conceived in the Australian educational imaginary as highly beneficial to domestic economic growth through trade, international education, and migration (Curry, 2021). As a result, "engaging and building strong relationships with Asia" (Ministerial Council on Education, Employment, Training and Youth Affairs, 2008, p. 4) has remained a significant part of the Australian Curriculum.

As it currently stands, the Australian Curriculum is comprised of three dimensions, namely the various discipline-specific subject areas, general capabilities (also known as 21st century skills) and cross-curriculum priorities (CCPs; ACARA, 2021b). The focus of this chapter is one of the three CCPs, specifically, "Asia and Australia's Engagement with Asia" which was included in the Australian Curriculum for its contemporary relevance and supposed importance to Australia (Henderson, 2020).

Under this CCP, the politics of discrimination and exclusion (Rizvi, 1990) that stem from a cultural homogenisation (Chang, 1993) of those with racial minority status is invisibilized and silenced (Herzog, 2018). Instead, somewhat ironically, this CCP purportedly empowers students to "recognise the diversity within and between the countries of the Asia region" (ACARA, 2021c, para. 6) as well as the diversity of Asian "ethnic background[s], traditions, cultures, belief systems and religions" (ACARA, 2021c, para. 13), and in so doing, developing active and informed Australian citizens (ACARA, 2021c).

Beyond this obviously paradoxical relationship to the lived realities of Asian Australians, the Australian Curriculum's "Asia and Australia's Engagement with Asia" CCP is also fraught with its own internal inconsistencies. To begin with, at a national level there is no clear data or understanding about the conversations that may or may not be occurring between school leaders and educators about how best to implement this CCP, nor is there any clarity on what students learn about this CCP through their education, and its potential subsequent impacts (Curry, 2021). Even though there is an argument for the strength of how teachers enact curriculum documents—as opposed to the documents themselves (Cannadine et al., 2011)—its practical implementation is replete with difficulties (Henderson,

2020). Indeed, the CCP is there in principle, but "the reality is vastly different" (Curry, 2021, para. 4).

One aspect of this discrepancy is attributable in no small degree to the lack of understanding and context to effectively teach about the tremendous diversity (Curry, 2021) within the contested construct that is "Asia" (ACARA, 2021c). Indeed, it is unlikely that teachers emphasise curriculum components where they "lack specialist disciplinary knowledge" (Henderson, 2018, p. 129), or areas in which they have never studied, or are unfamiliar with (Henderson, 2020). On one hand, while this significant autonomy offers the possibility of engaging students in a variety of ways (Ormond, 2017), it is often the case that teaching Asia functions solely as a means of meeting a short-term curriculum accountability goal, as opposed to a considered incorporation of the broader significance of teachers' potentially transformative work (Biesta et al., 2015).

To exacerbate this situation, despite agreement on the contested nature of Asia (ACARA, 2021c), there is an absence of nuanced information around the descriptor "Asia" or "Asian" in the Australian Curriculum documents as well as a dearth of guidance in the curriculum elaborations about how and where to include Asian content as a CCP (Zhang et al., 2020). Overall, any content that is meant to support this CCP is unevenly dispersed across discipline-specific subject areas with a high degree of variability across Australian States and Territories in terms of the key ideas and resources used (Zhang et al., 2020).

As a result, the CCP is an inherently contested form of knowledge (Henderson, 2020) with its nebulous nature presenting a "challenging curriculum space for teachers to negotiate in practice" (Henderson, 2020, p. 19). That is, the "Asia and Australia's Engagement with Asia" CCP in the Australian Curriculum is a veritable "assemblage of contradictions" (Henderson, 2020, p. 19), nullifying the potential to operationalise any type of non-exclusionary, non-racist response externally to Asia (Zhang et al., 2020) and internally to Asian Australia.

While there is a slowly developing body of scholarship that explores how Australian in-service teachers have started to include an Asian focus in their work (Henderson & Jetnikoff, 2013; Salter, 2014), only one study by Salter (2014) explicitly acknowledged the "eminently political" nature of education (Giroux, 2010, p. 336) and curriculum (Zhang et al., 2020) in arguing that genuine "Asia literacy" stems from a "disruption of the dominant discourse of 'Asia' as a unitary construct" (Salter, 2014, p. 781).

Further to this, there is a distinct absence of scholarship around Asian-focused teaching in Australia that explicitly acknowledges that "schools and classrooms, as microcosms of society and as primary sites of knowledge construction and production, are key determinants of how we think, feel and talk about race and racism" (Rudnick, 2019, p. 217). On that basis, this chapter focuses on bridging this worrying gap by using the self-as-event to write story as research that is inherently political (Ellis, 2004); an intentional enmeshing of "the personal within the political and the political within the personal in ways that can…matter" (Holman Jones, 2005, p. 774).

***

As the lunch bell screeches, I quickly shoo my Senior Humanities students from class and make a beeline for the car park. I have half an hour to be at Market Square in Sunnybank, Brisbane's main Asian ethnoburb (Li, 2014) for a Junior Geography[2] excursion on Asian migration patterns in Australia. With 20 minutes of driving to get there and a usual scarcity of parking space, I wonder why I turned down having a replacement teacher for the Senior Humanities class that had just concluded.

I haul the driver's door shut and yank my seatbelt across my chest, growling frustratedly at each unsuccessful attempt at fastening the implement. It is on my fifth unsuccessful try that I simultaneously give up and slam both palms aggressively into the steering wheel.

I take a deep breath and eventually realise that my head and my heart are at war with each other. Rationally, I am a seasoned high school teacher and know the importance of the excursion I am heading to from a curricular perspective–I am aware of the "key requirement" that is Asia literacy (ACARA, 2021c). As a racial minority in a predominantly white institution, I am also keenly aware of the excursion's potential for transformative practice (hooks, 1994) and importance from a personal-political-pedagogical (Mackinlay, 2019) point of view. Despite this, I had absolutely no idea what exactly I was going to say to the students. I knew that the *construct* of Asia was a term that conflates a variety of places, spaces, cultures, histories, languages, societies and politics (Henderson, 2020), and earlier attempts to concoct some sort of script to highlight the importance of understanding Asian intragroup diversity had been thwarted by the still, small voice of self-doubt (Ellis, 2004)—after all, what gave *me* the right to speak for a group with such a wide heterogeneity of characteristics due to diverse class, ethnic, and immigrant experiences (Yu, 2006)? Alas, as a racial minority, I usually took what seemed like the easy way out by staying silent and smiling politely—as I had done in response to Sterling—in uncomfortable racialized situations, so who was *I* to be proclaiming some sort of antiracist pedagogy with such audacity? How would I even enact an antiracist, socially just pedagogy in this circumstance? Would the students (and teachers) take what I was going to say seriously? Would the presence of my non-white body make any sort of difference?

***

---

[2] This excursion was specifically for Year 8 students, who are typically 13 or 14 years old in the Australian context.

"Hey, I know you're just about the head back to work, but do you have time for a quick chat? I don't have much time anyway—the Year Eights are meant to be here for the excursion in the next five minutes or so."

"Yeah, sure, bub, what's up?"

Before responding, I nestle the phone between my right shoulder and right ear and straighten out the excursion worksheet I had been scrawling on since I arrived at Market Square.

"Okay, great. So, you know how I was still struggling to figure out what to say to the students on the excursion later?"

"Yeah, you looked pretty troubled about all of it even before leaving for work."

"Hmm... Maybe. I didn't realise it was showing..."

My wife interjects with the fact that I'm not fantastic at hiding my emotions.

"Right, well, anyway, I thought a bit more about what I might say on the drive in. Be honest and tell me if it sounds stupid, okay?"

***

"Alright, Year Eights, eyes on me in 5, 4, 3, 2, 1..."

As I bellow out the numbers, I let my right hand linger in the air as outstretched fingers drop in unison with my verbal countdown. This seems enough to momentarily quell the students' palpable excitement at being outside school during school hours.

Just as I am about to address them, I feel anxiety and self-doubt turn from a small, light tap on my shoulder to a large, heavy lump in my throat. As time stands still, I take a deep breath in an attempt to still my nerves and in that moment, replay my wife's encouragement at the end of the earlier phone call.

***

"Bub, weren't you telling me something that you read recently about your methodology being a 'courageous moral act' (Lapadat, 2017, p. 591)?"

"Yeah, but..."

"But what? Unlike the teachers who teach this subject that have a limited personal knowledge base of Asia's diversity to fall back on (Henderson, 2020), you were *born* there–you *are* 'Asian.' Fundamentally, you agreed to be involved in today's excursion because you wanted to speak back to the racism you've experienced and continue to experience, no? You're sick of people assuming you're part of this homogenous 'cultural' whole (Yu, 2006) with all its associated deficit assumptions (Chang, 2013), so, how is writing about it in your thesis any different from what you're about to do with the students? If anything, I'd argue that it's likely to have a more immediate impact!"

"Hmm... I suppose..."

"Of course, it will. So go on, set the scene, tell your story, share your experiences with the appropriate explanations and you'll be just fine (Holman Jones, 2005)!"

As time with the Year Eights resumes, I am spurred on into just "letting go, hoping [that my captive audience] will bring the same careful attention to [my words] in the context of their own lives (Holman Jones, 2005, p. 765)."

***

"Okay, Year Eights, thank you to those of you who have followed my instruction and have their eyes on me. Before we make our way around Market Square, I would like to make a few things clear. These are deeply important to me—in fact, some of you might know that I'm a Business, not Geography, teacher, and those of you who *do* take Business are aware that you've recently submitted your assignments. Normally, I would be marking those but instead, I've chosen to be here, so, please make sure you're listening closely."

I pause and scan to ensure that I have every student's full attention. This seems to be the case, and I notice my white teaching colleagues leaning in ever so slightly as well.

"Right, I know this excursion is all about Asian migration, and that we're aiming to use the range of predominantly Asian eateries here as evidence for that. BUT, before we get started, I think it's crucial for us to recognise that there's a *tremendous* amount of national diversity under that one label. How many of you know that Asia comprises 70% of the world's population, or that 75% of the world's largest economies are in Asia (Henderson, 2020)?"

The mixture of shaking heads and fascinated looks tells me that none of them do. I am not surprised.

"Interesting, hey? And if we look at Market Square alone, most of the restaurants here are mainly from East Asia—so China, Taiwan, Hong Kong, Korea, Japan—and Southeast Asia—like Vietnam, Thailand, Malaysia and so on. And guess what? That's not even *all* of the continent we know as Asia–Central, South and West Asia aren't even represented here! Why I'm telling you this is because even though I *am* 'Asian,' I'm aware that I can't speak for *all* 'Asian' experiences (Iftikar & Museus, 2018), with migration, or even food, for that matter–that would be rather reductive. What I can do though, is share *my* experiences and things that I've learnt from other people in the diaspora."

"I think it's so important to acknowledge this diversity because let's face it, many of us here who are white Australians can identify our heritage with *pride*— oh, I'm 50% Irish, 30% German, 15% South African and 5% milk bla bla…"

The more attentive students pick up on my joke and giggle to themselves.

"Unfortunately, it's not the same case for many non-white people I know—certainly not the case for me, or at least it *wasn't* the case for me. I know I found it tough to explicitly verbalise my Singaporean heritage straightway because it was just another reminder that because I'm not white Australian, I don't belong here (Ang, 2005). And on top of that, I think there's a real danger in lumping such a diverse group of individuals into this one…blob…because it conveys that their heritage is of less value (Iftikar & Museus, 2018). Does that make sense?"

The nodding heads indicate that I just might be getting through.

"That leads me to my second key point—besides national diversity, the other thing to note is that there is *huge* diversity even in which generation of migration someone might be part of. I say this because firstly, unless you're Indigenous Australian, you *are* a migrant. So really, it's important to note that there isn't one group of people that is more Australian than the other, or that has the right to tell someone else to 'go back to where they came from' (Klippmark & Crawley, 2018), unless you're Aboriginal, of course. To exclude someone in that way would be on this basis of completely arbitrary boundaries (Rizvi, 1997), really."

"So, yes, if there's anything I want you to remember, it's this idea of diversity—an incredibly rich diversity of peoples, environments, cultures (Henderson, 2020) and migration flows. Me—I'm a first-generation migrant; I moved here for university. But you all know Mr. C and Mr. H at school? See, they're second-generation migrants, meaning that they were *born* here. This brings me back to my point about not lumping people together just because they're not white—get to *know* the person instead of making lazy assumptions or stereotypes based on skin colour. Now, especially considering that as of 2019, 28 % of the Australian population was comprised of individuals born overseas, with Asian Australians constituting an ever-increasing presence in Australian society (Evans, 2019), I think this is absolutely crucial."

I pause to catch my breath.

"Does anyone have any questions with my little spiel?"

A handful of shaking heads tell me that there are no immediate questions, and the now-solemn demeanour from the rest of the students suggests that at the very least, they had heard me.

I take this as my cue to start the excursion proper. By this point, self-doubt seemed preoccupied elsewhere, and I am looking forward to talking about the eateries. I motion the group of students in front of a bubble tea shop and quiz them about the Taiwanese origins of bubble tea. I point out the shop's clearly Japanese name and décor and share how I used to be the bubble tea mixologist at a Vietnamese restaurant in my undergraduate days.

I then twirl towards the ostensibly Singaporean restaurant beside it, being mindful of asking the Cantonese waitress who is opening the restaurant what the owner's heritage is. She tells me that it was originally owned by a Malaysian but has since been taken over by a South Korean. I pass this on to the students and am thrilled to see them scribbling away furiously on their excursion workbooks.

As we pass a Vietnamese restaurant in Market Square, I share what I learnt about the Vietnamese language during my undergraduate mixologist days. In front of a cluster of Chinese-looking eateries, I distinguish Cantonese, Northern

Chinese, and Southern Chinese cuisine. With the assistance of the store owners, I allude to the geographical differences and rough migration trends (Henderson, 2020) in these regions that have shaped the style of these respective cuisines.

I continue in a similar fashion with the other establishments, relieved to see what looks like continued engagement from the students and staff.

***

"Hey bub, how did it go?"

I am excited to pick up my wife's call and proceed to animatedly regale her with a detailed report about the excursion.

"See, I told you it wouldn't be that bad! You sound like you had fun and it seems like they took what you were saying on board?"

"Look, considering the fact that some students couldn't even distinguish Taiwan from Thailand or the Korean script from the Mandarin Chinese one, coming on this excursion has definitely cemented that we cannot simply perpetuate the status quo by 'accept[ing] the prevailing [classroom] culture as normal' (Joseph, 2007, p. 284)."

"The way I ran it wasn't exactly what Mrs. O, the Head of Geography, asked me to do—God knows she'd be *very* unhappy if and when she finds out—so in that sense, it felt like an act of 'pedagogical risk-taking' (Breunig, 2016, p.5), but hopefully today's outing will help some of the students to start moving away from their 'fixed, customary modes of seeing' (Joseph, 2007, p. 284) Asia as this monolithic, unitary construct (Salter, 2014). I don't know if *all* of them were necessarily on board, or if I got through, but I think maybe today's excursion was a starting 'provocation that challenge[d] students to critically engage with the world' (Giroux, 2010, p. 336) around them. Maybe, just maybe, what I shared with them in terms of my experience with marginalisation and the concomitant dangers of making homogenising deficit assumptions about Asians just based on their skin colour was the first step in 'equip[ping] students with knowledge, behaviour and skills needed to transform society into a place where social justice can exist' (Ayers et al., 2009, p. 590). Or, at the very least, something that de-westernised their existing knowledge in favour of an alternative (Connell, 2009) and more cosmopolitan worldview (Iwabuchi, 2015) that can begin to 'resist ethnocentrism and simplistic binaries' (Cairns, 2021, p. 22)."

"I'm *so* cognisant that the curriculum has the ability to induct 'the younger generation into who is…[seen as] other' (Yates & Grumet, 2011, p. 242) and these sorts of moral and political practices vis-à-vis the curriculum can 'take them beyond their own experience' (Morgan, 2015, p. 14) to influence the values, knowledges and types of citizenship practices of the future (Zhang et al., 2020). Because of that, today's teaching moment was never really going to be anything final with a 'neat ending' (Mackinlay, 2019). If anything, given what we know about the contested and contradictory nature of the curricular focus on Asia (Henderson,

2020), I think there needs to be *much* more work in this space—work that is done in solidarity with other unabashedly anti-racist teachers and allies to 'build those coalitions, affiliations, and social movements capable of...promoting substantive social change' (Giroux, 2010, p. 339). I hope as well that this work is not just siloed to the Humanities, Social Sciences, and Languages, as has been the case up to this point (Curry, 2021)—after all, this sort of transformative work and 'deep shifts in consciousness' and subsequent action (Gorski, 2008, p. 517) cannot take place in isolation. I'd imagine this Asia focus *must* have multiple synergies with subject areas like the Arts, Economics, Sciences, and even Maths (Curry, 2021). I'd love to have a chat with some of the other subject teachers about this when I get the chance, and perhaps this can be the start of a productive conversation about the 'constraints of the dominant cultural and epistemological traditions of the social-historical milieu' in which we as teachers are located (Cairns, 2021, p. 22)."

"Of course, this work has to be done in a way that's specific to the context since each classroom is different and the corresponding strategies used must be changed and reconceptualised for each new teaching experience (hooks, 1994)—in that sense, what I did on the excursion today is less of a 'class plan for duplication... [as opposed to] a path to praxis' (Hinchey, 2008, p. 20). After all—and I would know this well—teachers do need the freedom and flexibility to bring this sort of important subject matter alive (Curry, 2021)!"

"I'm so sorry—I've been talking *at* you for ages. I just hope I helped make everyone a little more aware and perhaps, with that awareness, they can start to ask the right type of questions. I don't know if that makes sense—do you get where *I'm* coming from?"

REFERENCES

Ang, I. (2005). *On not speaking Chinese*. Taylor and Francis. https://doi.org/10.4324/9780203996492

Australian Curriculum, Assessment and Reporting Authority. (2021a). *About the Australian curriculum*. https://www.australiancurriculum.edu.au/about-the-australian-curriculum/

Australian Curriculum, Assessment and Reporting Authority. (2021b). *Structure*. https://www.australiancurriculum.edu.au/f-10-curriculum/structure/

Australian Curriculum, Assessment and Reporting Authority. (2021c) *Asia and Australia's engagement with Asia*. https://www.australiancurriculum.edu.au/f-10-curriculum/cross-curriculum-priorities/asia-and-australia-s-engagement-with-asia/#:~:text=An%20understanding%20of%20Asia%20underpins,social%2C%20intellectual%20and%20creative%20capital.

Ayers, W., Quinn, T. M., & Stovall, D. (2009). *Handbook of social justice in education*. Routledge.

Biesta, G., Priestley, M., & Robinson, S. (2015). The role of beliefs in teacher agency. *Teachers and Teaching: Theory and Practice, 21*, 624–640. https://doi.org/10.1080/13540602.2015.1044325

Bochner, A. P., & Ellis, C. (2002). *Ethnographically speaking: Autoethnography, literature, and aesthetics*. AltaMira Press.

Breunig, M. (2016). Critical and social justice pedagogies in practice. In M. Breunig, & M. A. Peters, (Eds.), *Encyclopaedia of educational philosophy and theory* (pp. 1–6). Springer.

Cairns, R. (2021). Recognizing, reproducing and resisting West as method discourse: An analysis of senior secondary Asia-related history curriculum enactment. *Journal of Curriculum and Pedagogy*, *18*(1), 21–24. https://doi.org/10.1080/15505170.2020.1764413

Cannadine, D., Keating, J., & Sheldon, N. (2011). *The right kind of history*. Palgrave MacMillan.

Chang, B. (2013). Voice of the voiceless? Multiethnic student voices in critical approaches to race, pedagogy, literacy and agency. *Linguistics and Education*, *24*(3), 348–360. https://doi.org/10.1016/j.linged.2013.03.005

Chang, R. S. (1993). Toward an Asian American legal scholarship: Critical race theory, post-structuralism, and narrative space. *California Law Review*, *81*(5), 1241–1323. https://doi.org/10.2307/3480919

Connell, R. (2009). *Southern Theory: The global dynamics of knowledge in social science*. Allen & Unwin.

Curry, H. (2021, May 20). *A letter to Australia: The Asia-Literacy conversation we're not having*. Asialink (The University of Melbourne). https://asialink.unimelb.edu.au/insights/a-letter-to-australia-the-asia-literacy-conversation-were-not-having

Ellis, C. (2004). *The ethnographic I: A methodological novel about autoethnography*. AltaMira Press.

Evans, G. (2019, 19 June). *Asian-Australians in the Asian century*. 2019 Asian Australian Foundation Oration, Melbourne. https://www.gevans.org/speeches/Speech697.htmlh

Giroux, H. A. (2010). Paulo Freire and the crisis of the political. *Power and Education*, *2*(3), 335–340. https://doi.org/10.2304/power.2010.2.3.335

Gorski, P. C. (2008). Good intentions are not enough: A decolonizing intercultural education. *Intercultural Education*, *19*(6), 515–525. https://doi.org/10.1080/14675980802568319

Halley, J., Eshleman, A., & Vijaya, R. M. (2011). *Seeing White: An introduction to White privilege and race*. Rowman & Littlefield Publishing Group.

Henderson, D. (2018). Seeking Asia literacy beyond and within: Examining the nature of future teachers' learning throughout mobility experiences in higher education. In H. Soong & N. Cominos (Eds.), *Asia literacy in the global world: An Australian perspective* (pp. 125–144). Springer.

Henderson, D. (2020). Some reflections on the challenges and opportunities of the CCP Asia and Australia's engagement with Asia in the Australian curriculum. *Geographical Education*, *33*, 18–28.

Henderson, D., & Jetnikoff, A. (2013). Exploring representations of Asian identities in films for the Australian curriculum. *English in Australia*, *48*(2), 33–44.

Herzog, B. (2018). Invisibilization and silencing as an ethical and sociological challenge. *Social Epistemology*, *32*(1), 13–23. https://doi.org/10.1080/02691728.2017.1383529

Holman Jones, S. (2005). Auto ethnography: Making the personal political. In N. K. Denzin & Y. S. Lincoln (Eds.), *Handbook of qualitative research* (pp.763–791). Sage.

hooks, b. (1994). *Teaching to transgress: Education as the practice of freedom.* Routledge.

Iftikar, J. S., & Museus, S. D. (2018). On the utility of Asian critical (AsianCrit) theory in the field of education. *International Journal of Qualitative Studies in Education, 31*(10), 935–949. https://doi.org/10.1080/09518398.2018.1522008

Iwabuchi, K. (2015). Foreword. In C. Halse, (Ed.), *Asia literate schooling in the Asian Century* (pp. xiv–xvii). Routledge.

Joseph, P. B. (2007). Seeing as strangers: Teachers' investigations of lived curriculum. *Journal of Curriculum Studies, 39*(3), 283–302. https://doi.org/10.1080/00220270600818481

Klippmark, P., & Crawley, K. (2018). Justice for Ms Dhu. *Social & Legal Studies, 27*(6), 695–715. https://doi.org/10.1177/0964663917734415

Lapadat, J. (2017). Ethics in autoethnography and collaborative autoethnography. *Qualitative Inquiry, 23*(8), 589–603. https://doi.org/10.1177/1077800417704462

Lawrence, C. R., & Matusda, M. (1997). *We won't go back: Making the case for affirmative action.* Houghton Mifflin Company.

Li, W. (2014). Ethnoburbs. In M. Y. Danico (Ed.), *Asian American society: An encyclopedia* (pp. 322–327). SAGE Publications.

Lowy Institute. (2019). *Lowy Institute Asia Power Index 2019.* https://power.lowyinstitute.org/

Mackinlay, E. (2019). *Critical writing for embodied approaches.* Springer International Publishing AG. https://doi.org/10.1007/978-3-030-04669-9

Ministerial Council on Education, Employment, Training and Youth Affairs. (2008). *The Melbourne declaration on agreed goals for schooling.* http://www.curriculum.edu.au/verve/_resources/National_Declaration_on_the_Educational_Goals_for_Young_Australians.pdf?msclkid=2cd7836bc23411ec85b967652aee650b

Morgan, J. (2015). Michael Young and the politics of the school curriculum. *British Journal of Educational Studies, 63*, 5–22. https://doi.org/10.1080/00071005.2014.983044

Ormond, B. M. (2017). Curriculum decisions—The challenges of teacher autonomy over knowledge selection for history. *Journal of Curriculum Studies, 49*(5), 599–619. https://doi.org/10.1080/00220272.2016.1149225

Rizvi, F. (1990). Understanding and confronting racism in schools. *Unicorn, 16*(3), 169–176.

Rizvi, F. (1997). Beyond the East-West divide: Education and the dynamics of Australia-Asia relations. *The Australian Educational Researcher, 24*(1), 13–26. https://doi.org/10.1007/BF03219638

Rudnick, D. L. (2019). Walking on eggshells: Colorblind ideology and race talk in teacher education. *Multicultural Education Review: Policy Influences and Practical Contributions of Multicultural Education in Diverse Contexts, 11*(3), 216–233. https://doi.org/10.1080/2005615X.2019.1644043

Salter, P. (2014). A reconceptualisation of knowing Asia in Australian education. *Discourse: Studies in the Cultural Politics of Education, 36*(6), 781–794. https://doi.org/10.1080/01596306.2014.967178

Vasconcelos, E. (2011). "I can see you": An autoethnography of my teacher-student self. *The Qualitative Report, 16*(2), 415–440. https://doi.org/10.46743/2160-3715/2011.1063

Yates, L., & Grumet, M. R. (2011). *World yearbook of education 2011: Curriculum in today's world: Configuring knowledge, identities, work and politics.* Routledge.

Yu, T. (2006). Challenging the politics of the "Model Minority" stereotype: A case for educational equality. *Equity & Excellence in Education, 39*(4), 325–333. https://doi.org/10.1080/10665680600932333

Zhang, H., Diamond, Z., & Zeng, S. (2020). A content study of cross-curriculum priority of Asia and Australia's engagement with Asia in the Australian curricula. *Asia Pacific Journal of Education,* 1–20. https://doi.org/10.1080/02188791.2020.1864288

CHAPTER 9

ENGAGING WITH NATIONAL HISTORIES AND SETTLER COLONIAL MASTER NARRATIVES TO FOSTER AN ANTI-RACIST AND CULTURALLY RESPONSIVE CITIZENRY

The Pedagogy of Critical Ethical Nationalism in the Shadow of National Statues

Mary Frances O'Dowd
Anti-Racist Pedagogy: Educational Consultant & Researcher

The chapter's focus is effective teaching through contested histories and racism and overcoming resistance and working with affect in learning. The roar of turmoil and protests in 2021 echoing, "Black Lives Matter" resonate with First Nations' struggles and speak back to the dreams of nations where equality was a foundational discourse. This chapter explores the shadows of national statues and the powerful racist imaginings that underlie them, through a discussion and analysis of the historiography of nationalism in *master narratives* (hereafter abbreviated to MNs [plural] and MN [singular]). It applies and adapts these ideas to the *settler colonial* (hereafter abbreviated to SC) contexts of Australia while making major comparative references to her older sister SC of the British Empire, the United States[1]. In this it names *Settler Colonial Master Narratives* (SCMNs), theorizes and discusses how they have a powerful role in history teaching *and* across disciplines. It indicates how to enable students to critically and ethically engage with national identity and racism and to foster a culturally responsive citizenry. The analysis, theory and reflection were reiterative and arose from a necessity to develop a pedagogy that overcomes resistance, conscious and below conscious racist views, and promotes the engagement of tertiary students with Indigenous Australian history—a subject that has generated overtly expressed racist views, White rage, anger, resentment, and overt, and passive resistance. The pedagogy, critical ethical nationalism, uses SCMNs to reduce resistance and fosters a deep engagement and ethical engagement with racism that is transformative.

MNs and their SCMN iterations are discussed as foundational to the endurance of racial and ethnic division. They require understanding and a specific educational focus to foster critical and ethical engagement, and an engagement with their affective power in cognition. Therefore, it is important to identify and understand their themes, and how they operate in fostering and maintaining racism in order to more effectively challenge racism, White privilege and non-Indigenous privilege. In SC contexts White privilege has moved over time into non-Indigenous citizenry privilege.

Throughout the chapter there is a deliberate and innovative attempt to engage the reader's intellect with affect, and to promote the use of affect in engaging with racism in learning. While the focus is racism in SCMNs, it also addresses directly ethnocentric settler colonial nationalism and Indigenous people[2,3]. The premises have equal relevance in addressing Whiteness that is foundational to the nation (Dozono, 2020; Garner, 2005).

The chapter (as far as can be ascertained) is the first naming and analysis of SCMNs and identification of their foundational role in racism. The theory and praxis have developed over a decade of the author's reiterative research and teaching practice in three universities in three States with national and international students, including those from the United States. Thus, this chapter builds on the work of historiography and makes an important contribution to anti-racist

---

[1] Wolfe (1999, 2006), defines describes SC colonies as nations where the settler colonizer has not gone home. He stresses that SC is a structure not an event.

[2] Guest (2006), Kolchin (2002), Orser (1998) and Valluvan (2019) indicated that a singular focus establishing a binary of White and Black has the danger of reinforcing the very difference of color it seeks to remove, and drawing attention away from class struggles. This is outside this chapter's focus, and such a discussion has a danger of manipulation to excuse and deflect the very urgent focus on MN, racism, and White supremacy

[3] In Australia Indigenous people were discussed by Whites as Black (among other labels); and many identify today as Black.

pedagogy, culturally responsive, and socially inclusive teaching of history and citizenship studies, and intertextually across disciplines (including literature, art, and geography). The pedagogy so created, is a pedagogy of critical ethical nationalism; it contributes a new important foundation to teaching anti-racism (Wagner, 2005) and culturally responsive pedagogy (as named by Ladson-Billings, 1995). It fosters a citizenry capable and ethical in an increasingly multiethnic, multicultural and interdependent world where racism, intolerance, threat of war, and war are serious dangers for humanity.

To do this the paper moves through sections that each consider affect and cognition beginning with the murder of George Floyd, then to the use of MN in understanding nationalism and racism; and then to a historiography of SCMN nations and their role in and overcoming White resistance and racism. This history and its intertextual embedding are considered. The chapter's conclusions draw together how understanding SCMN enables teaching through racism and turmoil with the pedagogy of critical ethical nationalism.

THE ROAR AND TIPPING POINT

Black Lives Matter protests roared through the streets of the United States following the murder of George Floyd on 25 May 2020 in Minneapolis. It was the tipping point in the context of ongoing frustration and protests about the deaths of Black people at the hands of police. The visual images of George Floyd's murder impacted intellect and affect. It brought the present into the past and the past into the present. It was a flashback to colonial abuse, slavery and its legacies that illuminated present racism. It shone spotlights into a possible future of enduring racism where institutions continue to protect White history and privilege.

The murder of George Floyd lasted nine minutes. Witnessing this murder was history, memory and the present: cognition and emotion combined. Newsflash of memory: Black people are 3.5 times more likely to die at the hands of police than White people in the United States (Statista, 2021). Stop. See. Breathe. Stop. A Black man handcuffed, pinned to the ground. Stop. Blood supply—breath cut off. Stop. Voice, "I can't breathe." Stop. White policeman's knee on his neck. Stop. "I can't breathe." Stop. Pinned by 3 police officers. Stop. Replay. Stop. Replay. Stop 8 times. Replay. "I can't breathe." No stop. "I can't breathe." No stop. 8 times. "I can't breathe." No stop. No replay. No stop. Yes 8 times "I can't breathe." No stop. Replay. A man on the ground, still. A man, dead, murdered. Officers of the law looking on. Officers of *our* law…or the Wild West, outlaws of an enduring White privilege?

The brutal killing in the context of a plea for life resulted in the largest protests in half a century in the United States. It drew millions of people internationally to protest about racism still embedded in the 21st Century: from the United States to Britain to Australia to Canada to Aotearoa/New Zealand, settler colonizer nations, and beyond. Statues were graffitied, some toppled and flung into rivers. The protests arose not merely from people's intellectual knowledge of the facts but also their interaction with the affective, including the visual images of a man brutalized, his cry for life, his plea, and then the silence, the stillness, the place of no return that is death. History and the present fused in 9 minutes, shouted and erupted. Protesters responded to death, and to themes they knew and felt (Pettit & Western, 2004; Western & Wildeman, 2009). Yet, the statues were not new, the knowledge was not new, police brutality was not new, and deaths in custody were an old story. The fire of affect burned the intellect into action. The protests drew attention to racism and its institutional curriculum emanating from statues that celebrated imperialism and empires of land and racism. These statues sang to White people's power to silence the history of the colonized and raced, usually people of color (but also the colonization of some White nations including Ireland (Barton & Levstik, 2004; Barton & McCully, 2003, 2005, 2007; O'Doherty, 2021).

Revised histories of colonization have been slow to penetrate the schools, academy, and the societies of Australia and the United States (Dunbar-Ortiz, 2014; Reynolds, 2000). The Stone and Iron statues (like dolman), reconfigured by murder and protest now spoke to curriculum where racism and minority histories are silenced, institutionalized. In the nations and classrooms of SC Australia and the United States the consequences of the protest enable questions, "What perspective is privileged?" and "What is silenced?" and expose these questions to ethical scrutiny and the why.

Yet many preservice teachers, when required to do units that engage with racism and Whiteness, feel threatened and demonstrate strong resistance to this education both in Australia (Aveling, 2002; Hollinsworth, 2014; O'Dowd, 2010; Quaid & Williams, 2021) and the United States (Cochran-Smith, 2000; Vaught & Castagno, 2008). The response is the same when it is mandated in teaching health sciences and social work (Micheal et al., 2021; Miller et al., 2004.); White citizenry (DiAngelo, 2011, 2018). It is similar for White peer academics of educators (Barrow & Judd, 2014). Teaching about race and White privilege is identified as troubling knowledge as it impacts the affective and cognitive (Zembylas, 2012, 2014) and requires not only learning but *unlearning* (Cochran-Smith, 2000). Where national history and identity weave together this unlearning becomes complex as such knowledges can and do challenge a student's sense of self-identity and its intersection with White national culture (O'Dowd, 2011). Reynolds' (2000) book titled *Why Weren't We Told*, in reference to Australia's Indigenous history, might have been better named, *Why Can't We (White People) Listen?* because the histories of brutality and dispossession as he revealed was known by significant numbers. It was not just silenced as Stanner (1969) suggested.

MASTER NARRATIVES & NATIONALIST HISTORIES: THE SHADOWS OF NATIONAL STATUES

Racism is not a mere silence, an information/knowledge gap to fill, as the literature cited above demonstrates. The insights of MNs have a key role in enabling deep critical engagement, "unlearning" (the useful concept of Cochran-Smith,

2000) and overcoming resistance. This section is necessarily a short overview of the literature to convey key ideas drawn on in the later sections. While the understanding of national history as a construction is not new (Hobsbawn, 1983), MN studies have demonstrated the pervasiveness of the idea of nation embedded not only in history but across socio-cultural locations including schools, media, film, as Ben-Yehuda's (1995) study of Israel illustrated.

Nationalist histories are a genre of history writing that became dominant in the late 18th and early 19th century (Berger, 2006). They are foundational histories of a nation and have a typicality (not a uniformity) of constructing national history and identity. National identity has been noted for its positive impacts, including fostering a cohesion which rarely exists in any natural form in a nation (Anderson, 2020). However, nationalist histories typically embed an explicit superiority of *one's own* nation and people over another nation (Berger, 2009). Common themes emerge from the study of national histories, including myths of origins with ideas of a pure stock from which the race developed; a golden age of the nation; the peasantry reflecting the incorruptible soul of the nation; and the idea of defending or saving the nation from enemies (Berger, 2009). A master narrative is "'the big story' told by the dominant group in a given society...Master narratives relate the mythic origins of the group (nation, class religion, race), define the identity of the we-community as well as that of its enemies" (Thijs, 2011, p. 60). The MN is the top of a narrative hierarchy and linked to social control (Thijs, 2011). Thus, MNs have social power over other narratives, including, Indigenous histories, and also hold power of manipulation to foster racism.

MNs make the national identity glorious. The MN justifies the existence (if not the greatness) of that nation (Berger & Conrad, 2015). As such, MN are not factual representations of the past but embody interpretations so that a neat distinction between myth and history is fraught (Berger, 2006) and the role of fiction and myth in national remembrance has no clear separation from facts (Rigney, 2008).

As I write, a Soviet Russian MN myth enables the invasion of Ukraine, not as *war* but as *liberating brothers*. Such nationalism reminds us that invasion, colonization and racism was predominantly, but not exclusively, White on Black, although some is/was White on White (Garner, 2009); and some People of Color on People of Colour (Straus, 2004; Yang, 1999)[4]. Colonization and its racism are strategies to achieve economic benefit (see Garner, 2009, 2015; Hund et al., 2015). The Irish were raced as primitive and ape-like under British colonization. The key ideas of nationalism and racism have been linked to strategies of marginalization, racialization and dehumanization. These ideas and practices, facilitating economic gain, sailed with the British Empire to Ireland, and with other European empires to Africa, Asia and the Americas establishing the White European colonization and its racist gaze (Said, 1995) as strategy.

---
[4] This is not to explain, excuse, or move away from the necessary focus on the prevalence, damage and power of White racism but to stress motivates, strategy and discourse in order to overcome racism.

MNs foster inclusion and exclusion between nations and within the nation (Berger & Conrad, 2015). MN may be used as images sold to the dominant group, adopted and fostered by governments for political purposes to foster political manipulation and ethnocentrism, to promote aggression, and have been used by leaders to take nations to war (Berger, 2005; Berger & Lorenz, 2011). Perhaps the best-known example is the use of a MN was by the Nazi regime where the Aryan's promotion as a super race was used to justify ethnic cleansing and murder (Berger, 2004, 2009). MNs and their nationalisms are created by historians who have been complicit in making deep commitments to the nation (Berger, 2015), but some historians also challenge them (Berger & Lorenz, 2008).

History is only one site of the construction and reinforcement of national identity, and the construction of the MN is intertextual (Berger, 2015; Rigney, 2008). This is demonstrated in the early popularization of national history using the novel (Eriksonas, 2008; Leerssen, 2013); the cinema also reinforced tropes and silences, reproducing the imaginings and silences of history (Collins & Davis, 2004; Frey, 2008[5]). MNs are replicated in silences by national fine and applied arts (Wintle, 2008), and popular culture, such as song (Bohlman, 2008) and jokes. These written, visual, and oral forms echo the his-stories[6] of history and enable an often taken for granted national identity with its exclusion of minorities.

MNs construct what is remembered and what is forgotten—in for example how particular history is privileged in national commemorations to enforce a particular remembering (Berger & Niven, 2014), and as such they are epistemic, embedding the taken for granted as *truth*. The idea of "memory cultures" links with MNs as sites of social control and manipulation (Thijs, 2011), embracing racism. Beattie (2013) identifies how racism may be conscious, unconscious, and below conscious, and MNs often embed and continue to foster conscious, unconscious, and below conscious nationalism, racism, and its dangers. Bloom (1996, p. xvi), reflecting on Jewish culture and history, stated that to reinforce a particular memory of the past creates habits of thought which, "is an enclosure, and to be enclosed is both a protection and a punishment" (Bloom, 1996, p. xxv); Yerushalmi (1996) also echoes the power of memory in creating a story as the history. MNs are affective, appealing, and flatter the self/nation with ideas of being a superior race/ nation. Thus, MNs have the potentiality, if uncritiqued and unconsidered, to be dangerous to peace and justice.

It is considered a difficult pedagogy to challenge such MNs because accepting *our* nation and *our* national identity as superior- period, is normalized. The mo-

---

[5] Cinema reinforced history as that great tale of the Civil War, Gone With the Wind, airbrushed slavery from that history—as Miss Scarlett was hair brushed—almost gone with the wind.

[6] His-stories is hyphenated here to emphasize the story (typically male focused [Berger, 2011]) crafted around selected facts, representations with deliberate silences in national histories and intertextually (Davies, 1991; Landow, 1990; Marcus, 1976). His-stories have an emphasis that challenges authority which is particularly relevant in the discussion of SCMNs as they are typically dominated by a White male focus.

tivation of German historiographers (such as Stefen Berger) is not only to understand the processes that explain why Germans became Nazis but to contribute to understanding how humans are manipulated into such beliefs, and become complicit, in order to reduce such possibilities. To consider and understand the self and nation's *racism* is an anathema to many people. To consider oneself capable of being a compliant worker in the Nazi regime, is difficult. A pedagogy engaging citizens with critical and ethical nationalism by engagement with MNs facilitates a nation's people to be more reflective and resistant to such political manipulation, more aware of racism and better able to see and challenge racism.

MNs embedded in national histories, national identity and its intersection with individual identity may be best conceptualized as a system of representation, a way power, thought and truth are constituted in taken for granted. In this sense MNs operate as a discourse. Discourse produces knowledge and is enmeshed with power (on Foucault; [Hall, 2001]). MNs penetrate the educational, social, cultural nation and self.

SCMN ENABLING TEACHING THROUGH TURMOIL & HISTORY WARS

The discussion above focused on racism, affect and MNs. These ideas and theory are taken into SC contexts where the genre of SCMNs is named and theorized here (to my research for the first time). They operate as an epistemic discourse to race and so *other* Indigenous (First Nation) peoples. Said (1995) indicated the idea of *other* sailed with Europeans. SCMNs defined the *we* community and created Indigenous people as *other*—outside the nation's history and identity. The other has typically been racialized, and/or religionized, and/or genderized and *then responded to* as inferior.

The ideas of contested history have only in recent decades slowly gained more than minimal attention in Australia and the United States (e.g. Macintyre & Clark, 2003; Sturgis, 2007). Australia like the United States (and Aotearoa/New Zealand and Canada) were White settler colonies-now-nations, founded by the British and as such they provide a foundation for a pedagogy to engage students.

The founding histories of British SC nations have established SCMNs that have a significant commonality, particularly the discourse of *settlement* rather than *invasion*. SCMNs were shaped by the privilege of the White non-Indigenous authors and, like MNs, operate in national histories, intertextually and rhizome-like through the structures of society, culture, and individuals. They are embedded in educational institutions' curriculum; contemporary history books; older school texts; and in foundational art, literature, music, and poetry; high and popular culture; as well in cinema, cinematographic and pictorial representations of the "founding" of the nation (O'Dowd, 2011). They create particular remembering and *forgetting*.

They are usefully conceptualized as an epistemic discourse that writes over the *othered* Indigenous people. SCMNs inscribed in a new geography of ownership,

White names over Indigenous names; imposing new boundaries by fences and state lines; and of course in the statues of famous White explorers, in the metal labels attached to rocks recalling pioneers passing by, and within the sites claimed as *pioneer parks*. There are epistemics embedded in commemorations (Columbus Day, Australia Day) that speak of the knowledge claims of the colonizers' ownership. Dispossession is inscribed in White law and its White privilege. They reflect social power, including the power to silence. The SCMNs of the United States, Australia, Canada and Aotearoa/New Zealand are White/ non-Indigenous foundational his-stories. There are four pillars of SCMNs identified here: (a) pioneers, (b) savages, (c) virgin land and wilderness, and (d) bringing civilization and progress. They create an imagining and an epistemic of remembering and forgetting as set out in Table 9.1: The Four Pillars of SCMNs. This table provides critical detail indicating how the SCMN is a discourse that produces an epistemic; each pillar is involved in creating a particular imagining providing how words lead to an epistemic. It has a cohesive internal conceptual logic that is cumulative; each pillar enables and justifies the SC nation and indicates how Indigenous people are placed out of nation, are relevant, and are cultural human beings.

The pioneer is his-storied (as Table 9.1 demonstrates) as the men (women are marginal; Dixson, 1976) who fought for, struggled, endured and earned the land by labor, so invasion is silenced and settlement privileged. The characterization and appearance of the pioneer is an idealized goodness—saint-like (McCreanor, 2000). Such a status makes pioneer abuses, and Indigenous histories of massacre and abuse, improbable if not impossible, at least until the SCMN identity is reflected on. In Australia, pioneers are mythologized as men who fought a tough wilderness. These lovely muscled pioneer men are in history and intertextual sites including national art, stories and film (see Table 9.1; O'Dowd, 2011, 2012a; Ward, 1958; White, 1981). They are *Aussie battlers*—who explored, sheared sheep, had a laugh, liked a drink, and in all their play and courage and representations are a discoursed *truth*, providing the foundation for the White nation's claims that gave a country an imagining that drifted into the Anzac soldier (Hirst, 1978). Pioneers who rightfully give, "the fruits of their labor" (Hudson, 1908a, p. 38, 1908b) to their descendants. You will have met a slightly later version of the Australian national man in the charming, witty, muscled Crocodile Dundee: competent in the bush and even in the wilds of an urban U.S. city. Mick Dundee's steely eyes, smiling face—an Aussie bloke, a loveable larrikin. The pioneers are juxtaposed with the second pillar, constructing of Indigenous people as *savages* (Russell, 2001; Vrasidas, 2019). Their nations are named *tribes*, so marginalized as sovereign owners: "savages" have no culture.

The internal logic pounds on: pioneers find savages, savages do not own land so the third pillar is thus discovery of virgin land and wilderness. This silences Indigenous peoples' presence and epistemic where at invasion there was no wilderness as every part was known—the land held history and knowledge (e.g. Patrick, 2015 on Warlpiri Country; Fletcher et al., 2021, Mar, 2010). The narrative so the epistemic of the fourth pillar is White arrival bringing civilization and progress. The idea of savages (people without a worthy culture) enables control and cultural erasure to be disguised as gifts of civilization, including education (boarding schools and stolen generations) and so leads to the aim of *re-form* (killing the Indian in the Indian (Fournier & Crey, 2006) and the associated SC practices (Maaka & Andersen, 2006).

The four pillars operate separately and intertextually through subjects and society. These four pillars operate consciously, and below consciously on cognition and affect to manipulate and be maintained across generations. They demonstrate that the SCMNs are a discourse. Hall (2001) observes that discourse is knowledge and is enmeshed with power and it is discourse not subjects that speak it, rather they are the bearers of such knowledge. Students and citizens of SC nations were inscribed with discourse of peaceful and/or rightful settlement. Indigenous Australians were created in the SCMN as a people who looked benignly at the arrival and colonization (Ward, 1958). They were constructed as a gentle stone-age people, a primitive culture who simply observed White civilizations' arrival (O'Dowd, 2012a). The idea of resistance and a war for land was not there. From 1788 to 1978 and beyond the White his- story was of settlement and foundation, not dispossession. In the United States, SCMN is the same epistemic journey of pioneers, virgin wilderness, savages and the arrival of civilization. Native Americans' fight for their homeland had them portrayed as savages, not as guerilla fighters against a much more powerful White invader. U.S. narratives in story and the films of the *Wild West* embed the SCMN discourse as *truth*.

After generations of a process of inscribing a national SC story with perhaps greater impact than the Bible, young people who want to be teachers (and other citizens) have an identity and history which is often a taken for granted truth. When the validity of the revised history[7] is challenged by influential people, including historians (Blainey, 1993), public figures (Windschuttle, 2002[8]), and even a Prime Minister (Brantlinger, 2004) they affirm and enable the desired SCMN discourse (so pleasant to Whiteness), and silence reaffirmed.

In Australia, a mandatory subject in Indigenous history reinforced the idea that racism is just an information gap. A critical ethical engagement with SCMNs' nationalism, racism, and exclusion is a very powerful means of engaging students prior to hearing a history they are ready to resist. Without this, White students do not understand the SC discourse of self and nation that has shaped them and taught them this *truth*. Hearing Indigenous history is perceived as an attack on

---

[7] It is beyond the scope of this chapter to discuss the content of the revisionary history that expands and challenges the SCMNs other than affirm its importance and note the contestation began a slow continuity from the 1970s in Australian history (e.g. Reynolds, 1981) and was gradually taken up by more historians (e.g. Connor, 2002; Peters-Little et al., 2004; Roberts, 2005). In the United States the pattern is similar (e.g. Brown, 1970; Berkhofer, 1979; O'Connor, 1993; Sawyer, 2013; Sturgis, 2007; Tate, 2020).

[8] This work is now strongly refuted (e.g. Manne, 2003).

TABLE 9.1. Four Pillars of SCMN: Illustrating Their Power via Imagining & Silence & Epistemic Erasure to Construct

The Four Pillars	NIP Language	Epistemic About IP	Epistemic of NI Remembering in Memory Culture	Epistemic Erasures/Silencing (E&S) by NIP
1. Pioneers	**Qualities:** Courageous, brave, heroic explorers, civilizing, productive, industrious, resilient through struggles, endurance, battlers (Australia), youth & vigor **Appearance:** Manly, handsome	Other & outside the nation & national identity's tropes. Other & inferior Direct juxtaposition to qualities of the pioneer (See savages, column 1) Other to the appearance of the pioneer	**Founders, and creators of the nation** Righteous, justified possession, & legitimate dispossession; NIPs remembering **Remembering Sites:** **Sites: Educational & scholarly:** Foundational history in curriculum and texts; museums. **Sites intertextual:** art galleries, school libraries, galleries in foundational art, literature (poetry), song, popular culture, including film (and their reiterations into the present). **Sites in Days** of National Commemoration & anthems e.g. Australia Day, Columbus Day **Sites in landscape/geography** inscription the land with commemoration privileging pioneers; explorers; and White naming over Indigenous naming; **Sites in politics:** representation refused/not provided **Sites in** *the* **national flag & anthem** that create silence **Sites of inscription on IP:** Caricatures of Indigenous people in high and popular culture and even jokes. **Site in discourse:** narrative hierarchy: IP a minor add-on the national narrative	**E&S history:** of invasion & dispossession of Ips **E&S** IPs culture, art, spirituality, languages, knowledges, ontology, epistemology, culture ignored **E&S** from respect in national memory in sites (see all sites in adjacent column) **E&S** of White/NI wrong, misuse of power **E&S:** by & in discourse hierarchy **E&S** by limited representation & voice in: politics, media, education **E&S** in the national flag **E&S** recognition of, & need for, restorative justice
2. Savages	**Other to pioneers:** savages, uncivilized, brutal, idle, primitive, childlike, unintelligent, sneaky, nomadic, nuisance, lawless	IP not fully human, a barrier to progress, cultureless/uncivilized without history. Tribes, not nations unworthy irrelevant savages	White power: legitimate presence IP savages out White/NI nation, not worthy in nation, unproductive, not fully human (White/NI); not entitled to voice; placed out of (full) human rights. IP a project to be inscribed and re-formed under, and as, a White possession; a project of White civilization (in all facets of the White/IN nation-state (language, culture, law, knowledge) NIP speak for and over IP	**E&S** IPs ownership (in custodianship) minimized or ignored. **E&S** positioned out of new nation of worthiness for nation; human rights limited. **E&S:** IP voice removed; IP a project to be inscribed and re-formed under, and as, a White possession (in all facets of the White/IN nation-state);

	White epistemic	Privileged epistemic	E&S
3. Virgin land and wilderness	Virgin Untouched, unexplored, un-named, empty, for the taking	No IP ownership: IP not legitimate sovereign people IP not engaged in rightful resistance.	**Privileged epistemic:** White discovery ; justified settlement; legitimate possession; unnamed land, Whites in an adversarial relationship with land and IP: both to be conquered, cleared NIP earned the land by toil Adversarial relationship with land & IP, both: wild, dangerous; to be tamed, cleared	**E&S:** IP as worthy in new nation, productive, fully human; voice & autonomy in nation; power & (full) human (White) rights. IP a project to be inscribed and re-formed under, and as, a White possession (in all facets of the White/IN nation-state); **E&S IPs:** Indigenous culture, art, spirituality, languages, knowledges: ontology, epistemology
4. Civilization & progress	Righteous foundation, establishing justice, truth & right, providing law.	As above all this column	Western/White civilization as the civilization: superior to othered nations. IP & society inferior, unworthy. IP to be reformed; culture to be eradicated.	E&S erasure: invasion, dispossession IP knowledge environment (As above all this column) As above all this column

The cumulative impact ON students and citizenry: Epistemic impact in students and citizenry: assumed truths; assumed knowledge; taken for granted facts about the other; below conscious and conscious racism; assumption of already being sufficiently informed; limited openness to understanding of or reflection on understanding of institutional racism. Assumptions of assault on self/ national identity & exposure to a leftwing political orthodoxy.
The educationalist has to enable a critical and ethical engagement with formative nationalism, national identity and the SCMN and its endurances. SCMN enables this. Building on much already known, and enabling this to be reconsidered. from the past, the recent present and its enduring issues and the future.

Note: Words abbreviated in the table: Indigenous people/s (IP/s); non-Indigenous people/s (NIP/s), and erasures & silencing (E&S).

self/nation identity as it indicates racism as foundational and its endurance. Ideas of systemic and institutional racism are often unknown and require explanation (O'Dowd, 2020; Salter et al., 2017). Many students in Australia and the United States are still unwilling to consider how they may be racist in views or ideas because their reflections are limited to the personal (Vaught & Castagno, 2008). They do not see or know the SCMN discourse. Being able to ignore the Indigenous peoples' social and political marginalization (e.g. as expressed in policing and imprisonment rates [Anthony & Baldry, 2017; Murphy & Cuneen, 2018] as part of the character of the *other* (see savages, NIP language, Table 9.1) is easier, self-congratulatory, and desirable, so restorative justice is then unnecessary, and irrelevant. White is right.

Contributing further to resistance is that racist and non-racist are set up as a binary: one is a racist or one is not. The SCMN demonstrates it is very difficult *not* to hold some racist understandings unconsciously (at the very least). Therefore, understanding MN and the SCMN as discourse, reflecting on its imagining and then considering its epistemic silences and erasures (see Table 9.1, the columns that move from words to epistemics, sites memory and forgetting) is critical.

Resistance & Affect in Teaching

Beginning in approximately 2008 (the dates varied across Australia as each state and territory auspices its own teacher education system) in order to gain registration, preservice teachers must complete and pass a mandated subject as a part of their teaching degree. They are of course mostly nice vibrant young people and typically White. Their studies to be a teacher were flowing along nicely at university until the introduction of a new mandatory subject, Indigenous history, and its troubling content. They listened to lectures on this history and were to reflect and consider it in tutorials. It was as if the students' hearing captured only staccato fragments that angered them, and academic references were blocked—heart-knowledge disabled reflection and engagement. Resistance throbbed to: land taken, land stolen, dispossession (Reynolds, 1981, 2000, 2006; Roberts, 2005) invasion—no peaceful settlement. No to news of "dispersing" (the pioneer sport of shooting Aboriginal people (Foster, 2009, p.68.6). Massacre/murder Stop. No treaty. PAUSE. Why no treaty? Stop. Stolen Generations. Pause. Forced assimilation. Stop. Enough! Disadvantage, no—laziness. Discrimination, no—discernment. *Othered* Indigenous—no. Then the bold and brave student rap: *they* with "chip on shoulder"—and are getting bolder. *They* make claims but have no aims. We're fair, they're- there. Pioneers have no fears. Pause. Stop. No more Indigenous history. Stop. Stop. Law for Whites. No!—true blue. Stop. Frontier war not peaceful settlement. Stop! As Foster (2009) says in his title, "Don't mention the war"

I, lecturer, see academic references floating away from meaning and substantiation. The academy's proof is pushed over head as a balloon named "just *that* version of *their* history." I see the balloon pushed airily toward the EXIT and it sails out the door with the end of the lecture, resisted and repelled.

Student voices: it does not matter what researchers' say. We/I know my nation. My truth. We/I know. I/we know. We/I are good. We/I worked hard. We do it tough too. Stop! Teichmann (2005) echoes positioning the truths of history as residing with "Normal Australians [who] judge their countrymen by mixing within their society and remembering their parent's attitudes, and quite often their grandparents...they know by direct acquaintance most Australians are neither racist nor callous and most settlers from other lands agree with them" (p.38). They are breathing heavily, angrily. This is NOT their history. They kick up and dismiss words and history And over the room glides the pioneer with angel wings, holy, an almost perfection. There he is embedded in wilderness, rising over savages, kissing earth into civilization. He blesses them. And all the while the other, that lecturer, spouts a left-wing orthodoxy, a political correctness and a history that is not that of the *Our* or, the *We*. This is not us! The lovely smiles of all the Crocodile Dundees and all the Davy Crocketts that they met, growing up and up into the shining White soul of SCMNs—smile on their nation-admiration. The subject's impact was the reverse of the intent. It was solidifying resistance.

I did not initially have the language of MN or SCMN. Two comments by students drew my attention to themes as I surveyed, researched, and struggled to understand—I had not entered the dreams which shaped them. One of my surveys asked, "Does it assist having a non-Indigenous lecturer?" One response had such clarity, "When the non-Indigenous lecturer does not give a non-Indigenous view, how does that help?" The comment conveyed the perception that Australian history was a non-Indigenous history. This captured the ideas in SCMN of good and greatness as Australian history. Indigenous Australian history was not part of *our* history in student imagining. Then there was a verbal comment, not said with any anger, which simply expressed the personal impact, "All I want to do after these lectures is go home. Have a glass of wine, take two Panadol and go to bed." This history was a headache, needed an anesthetic and ways to forget. I thought of Stanner (1969) and his well-considered Boyer Lecture in which he identified the great Australian silence where Indigenous people were almost totally omitted from the history of Australia. Stanner (1969) predicted that this silence would all be gone in 10 years' time—history would catch up by 1978. The absence of Indigenous history was framed by Stanner as some innocent knowledge gap solved by a knowledge of history. It was not a deliberate and desired forgetting.

This initial period of turmoil was eased with new strategies, particularly a focus on ethical reflection on history, stepping out of a raced-nation positioning in national identity to carefully work with the emotions generated (O'Dowd, 2010, 2012a, 2012b) and later to SCMN and a practice of the: pedagogy of critical and ethical nationalism. This enabled student engagement with foundational Whiteness and privilege through the historiography, moving into and from MNs, in Europe (including how these narratives have contemporary relevance, such as, but not only, Germany just before ad in World War II) This enabled understanding of how the MNs of Europe sailed from Europe evolved in SCMNs in nations, including Australia. This worked cognitively and affectively to foster students' capacity to distance emotion and reduce resistance; to see nationalist history and national identity as a genre- and the ego-flattering aspect of that identity (we are better than they). They then were able to focus on Australia. The supposedly unique qualities in the Australian national identity and their parallels to other countries make apparent the constructed nature of identity. It becomes easier to consider how many do not hold that identity (reflecting on their own life experience) and so they could engage with Indigenous Australian history. They explored sites (see sites, Table 9.1) such as national literature, history etc. They then were enabled to enter the cultural interface of Indigenous and non-Indigenous history and with courage and ethics. It is a task of exploration where students found the history books, the art of Australia's Heidelberg School, and the construction of the beautiful man. They sought representations and paintings of Indigenous people from colonization (Tasks a lecturer or teacher can guide using known resources such as online national and state galleries or books). They considered their education and explored the idea of a silence and its ethics. They were guided to identify or contest that the Australian SCMN is a knapsack of privileges. Acknowledging McIntosh's (1992, 2007) ideas of White privilege, students were to consider SCMNs as a similar "invisible package of unearned assets" (p.30). They reflected on how White privilege came in varying degrees/complicity to newer non-Indigenous migrants[9] (as argued persuasively by writers such as e.g. Khan et al., 2015; Upadhyay, 2019). New migrants arrive after the raw brutality ceased but the realities of ongoing social, legal, health and educational disadvantages of Indigenous people endure.

Thus students consider how settler colonialism may be understood and consider the SCMN as a discourse that embodies social power and narrative hierarchy. Revisionist history becomes part of a slow process of disruption of the SCMN. For example, they consider if and how there is textual hierarchy when Australian History is juxtaposed with Indigenous Australian history (just as American history is juxtaposed with Indigenous history of the United States [Dunbar-Ortiz, 2014]). The SCMN was their history. They reflected on how the *Indigenous* history is named but also on how within so-called American and Australian history the non-Indigenous perspective is not prefixed[10]. There is a textual hierarchy in each of the four pillars of SCMN, as Table 9.1 indicates (e.g. *pioneer* is privileged, not *invader*, Indigenous peoples are characterized as lazy and inferior; Berkhofer, 1979; Russell, 2001). A western epistemic is the normalized *truth* under colonialism (For further discussion see Mignolo, 2007a, 2007b, 2009; Quijano, 2000).

---

[9] United States history with Black Americans stands out as an important difference beyond the scope of this paper when considering non-Indigenous migrant privilege.

[10] E.g., There are no (found) national histories called, A Non-Indigenous history of America/Australia, but rather an inferred inclusiveness (a whole history). O'Dowd (2012b) started to explore the implications of this as othering in teaching.

AFFECT AND COGNITION IN NATIONAL ANTHEMS & NATIONALIST POETRY

Briefly, national anthems also may capture SCMN and its narration of nation. The Australian anthem up until 30 December 2021 included the words, "Australians of the world rejoice for we are *young* and free." On 1 January 2022, the word "young" was officially changed to "one" (Vickery & Dix, 2021). Thus, it recognized "young" which ignored Indigenous Australians who have the oldest continuing civilization of earth of at least 60,000 years. The anthem continues to sing over more complex questions of Indigenous people being *free* with enduring colonial structures, no voice to Parliament and no treaty. The U.S. national anthem, "The Star-Spangled Banner," has a rousing beat and the cheering final verse ends with, "the land of the free and home of the brave" (Key, n.d.). It is perhaps more uplifting than that of Australia but reflects a similar SCMNs of claim and silencing. It implicitly denies taking Native Americans' freedom.

Finally, SCMN poetry is briefly considered, comparing Walt Whitman's (1865) "Pioneers! O Pioneer!" to one poem of the minor Australian poet, Frank Hudson (1908a), "Pioneers." This might be audacious as Whitman is recognized as one of America's most influential poets; however it is not a comparison of quality but of the power of poetry to reinforce the SCMN and the use of affect.

Whitman was born in 1819 and as Folsom (1998) noted his life was framed by two defining events, the Trail of Tears in 1838–1839 and the Wounded Knee Massacre in 1890 (see Keenan, 2016 for details on massacres). Whitman's (1865) poem, a celebration of the courage and vigor of the pioneers 'Conquering, holding, daring, venturing as we go the unknown ways (line 23; See pioneers, Table 9.1). The poem is a discourse positioned in a narrative hierarchy as its assumed reader is *my* "Come my tan-faced children," the pioneers. Native Americans are not an assumed audience. Mignon (1998, entry 594) described how the poem sits between Whitman's "Song of the Universal" and "To You (whoever you are…)." The three poems are described as forming a sequence on the evolution of the human race, where the soul seeks its ideal; America seeks its destiny and pioneers are the symbol. In this the pioneer represented "a spiritual migration" (Mignon, 1998, entry 594). It is thus a poem that reflects and exalts the SCMN; it is about the pioneer as the future. Native Americans are positioned as an enemy and outside of courage and vision (not a people being dispossessed, whose homeland is being invaded). This poetic SCMN imagining of the implicit goodness of the enterprise operates to disable and silence the history of Native Americans including their dispossession. Whitman's (1865) pioneers are ready to attack (not negotiate) and so are aggressors, "get your weapons ready,/Have you your pistols?" (lines 2–3) and "Fresh and strong the world we seize" (lines 19–20). Such aggression is not at odds with implied spiritual journey (Mignon, 1998, entry 594). The imputation is a virgin land, "we the virgin soil upheaving,!" (line 27) and perhaps destruction, "We primeval forests felling" (line 25). The language of the poem is easily critically and ethically analysed; possession is celebrated but dispossession is not. It crafts killing Native Americans as an aside, casual, with no reflection on injuries and pain to be inflicted. Pioneers are not invaders of another's homeland. The pioneer presence is centered, loved and proclaimed, "O beloved race in all!" (line 37). The power of the meter is observed by Mignon (1998, entry 594) as "marching rhythms." The beat of the drum evokes affect into cognition. The themes march into mind and memory—of and who is not of the nation.

Hudson was born in 1913, just twelve years after the Federation of Australia, in outback Queensland. His life was also framed by extreme brutality to Indigenous people. In his home state Aboriginal people were dispossessed, rounded up and effectively imprisoned on reserves where the attempted genocide of their culture was in place (see Anti-Discrimination Commission Queensland, 2017, report). Yet Hudson's (1908a) poem also reflects the same celebratory imagining about pioneers. The simple rhyme is penetrating, so like Whitman's poem it is cognitive and affective. Hudson (1908a) also assumes his audience is non-Indigenous as he writes in the first person, as a pioneer, "We are the Old-world people,/ Ours were the hearts to dare" (p. 38). It conveys pathos for the pioneers; and notes their hard work aged them, "But our youth is spent, and our backs are bent, /And the snow is in our hair" (p. 38). He infers the Australian land as wilderness, "By the bush-grown strand of a wild, strange land,/ We entered—the pioneers…Our axes rang in the woodlands…/And we turned the load of our new found home" (p.38). Dispossession is ignored. The land is found. Yet he acknowledges, "we fought the black" (p.39), just as he objectifies Indigenous people as a color. The imputations are again of righteous toil and the children of pioneers as the heirs, "Take now the fruit of our labor,/ Nourish and guard it with care" (p. 39). Both poems are silent on the impact of the brutal colonization on Indigenous people. In rhythm and words, affect and cognition the discourse of the SCMN his-stories are enforced.

CONCLUSION

We live in nations and in an interconnected world. Much assumed knowledge and emotion comes into the classroom and embodies racism. Students have already learned imaginings of race and nation and taken for granted ideas that *other*. Students can become the citizens who can abuse, exclude or press their knee on the throat of a man and kill when he is *othered*. The chapter provides important conceptual understandings and ideas to bring to classroom practice in the first naming and analysis of SCMN as a discourse. It outlines theory and method to foster students' engagement (affective and cognitive) to critically and ethically reflect on the constructed nature of White history, nationalism and national identity. In the identification and discussion of four major pillars to SCMNs: (a) hardy honest pioneers, (b) virgin lands with wilderness, (c) "savages" (Indigenous people), and (d) the coming of civilization and progress, and their intertextuality (Table 9.1), the chapter engages and guides teachers and readers in pedagogy of critical and ethical nationalism where the imagining, and epistemic of remembering and forgetting in SCMNs are traced and exposed and resistance to Whiteness and minority history is scaffolded into curiosity and insights. The manipulative power of ego and race in nationalist histories become better understood. Whiteness as power is seen. The manipulative nationalism issued by politicians and enforced by nationalist historians, artists, and songs can be addressed effectively. Students engage with the necessary learning and un-learning to facilitate ongoing interaction in exciting exploration. Students' ethical reflection and rationale for a transformative vision in education, nation and world are fostered to encourage important insights for teaching and living together in our increasingly multicultural nations and globally dependent world.

In Leviticus (19:18) Moses conveyed the law for a Promised Land, to love God and love your neighbor as oneself (The New Community Bible, 2012). Jesus was asked what the greatest commandment was, and he responded as Moses (Matthew 22:39; The New Community Bible, 2012). The words speak to a way of being in nation and world to which an ethical deliberation on MNs & SCMNs and racism contribute. Let's teach to cognition and affect; let's teach to these statues and their shadowed power in intertextual locations. Let's teach to overcome racism and its appeal to human ego. Let us grasp the amnesia of nationalist history and history as more than history, and into narration of his-stories of the nation. Using SCMNs, as discussed, we foster a nationally and globally capable citizenry not blinded by Whiteness and its epistemics. Critical and ethical nationalism is a pedagogy founded on anti-racism to foster engagement with the multicultural and Indigenous nations in which we live; it enables ethics and hope. It engages student-citizens as a people of dreams and emotions to foster the good.

REFERENCES

Anderson, B. (2020). *Imagined communities: Reflections on the origin and spread of nationalism*. Routledge.

Anthony, T., & Baldry, E. (2017). "Fact check Q&A: Are indigenous Australians the most incarcerated people on Earth?," *The Conversation*, 6 June 2017. https://theconversation.com/factcheck-qanda-are-indigenous-australians-the-most-incarcerated-people-on-earth-78528

Anti-Discrimination Commission Queensland. (2017). *Aboriginal people in Queensland: A brief human rights history*. https://www.qhrc.qld.gov.au/your-rights/for-aboriginal-and-torres-strait-islander-people/Aboriginal-people-in-Queensland

Augoustinos, M., Tuffin, K., & Rapley, M. (1999). Genocide or a failure to gel? Racism, history and nationalism in Australian talk. *Discourse & Society, 10*(3), 351–378. https://doi.org/10.1177%2F0957926599010003004

Aveling, N. (2006). Student teachers' resistance to exploring racism: Reflections on 'doing' border pedagogy. *Asia-Pacific Journal of Teacher Education, 30*(2), 119–130. https://doi.org/10.1080/13598660220135630

Barrow, E., & Judd, B. (2014). 'Whitefellas at the margins': The politics of going native in post-colonial Australia. *International Journal of Critical Indigenous Studies, 7*(2) 1–15. https://doi.org/10.5204/ijcis.v7i2.111

Barton, K., & Levstik, L. (2004). *Teaching history for the common good*, Routledge.

Barton, K. C., & McCully, A. (2003). History teaching and the perpetuation of memories: The Northern Ireland experience. In E. Cairns & M. Roe (Eds.), *The role of memory in ethnic conflict* (pp. 107–124). Palgrave Macmillan.https://doi.org/10.1057/9781403919823_7

Barton, K. C., & McCully, A. W. (2005). History, identity, and the school curriculum in Northern Ireland: An empirical study of secondary students' ideas and perspectives. *Journal of Curriculum Studies, 37*(1), 85–116. https://doi.org/10.1080/0022027032000266070

Barton, K., & McCully, A. (2007). Teaching controversial issues... where controversial issues really matter. *Teaching history*, (127), 13–19.

Beattie, G. (2013). *Our racist heart?: An exploration of unconscious prejudice in everyday life*. Routledge. https://doi.org/10.4324/9780203100912

Ben-Yehuda, N. (1995). *Masada myth: Collective memory and mythmaking in Israel*. University of Wisconsin Press.

Berger, S. (2004). *Inventing the nation Germany*. Hodder Arnold.

Berger, S. (2005). A return to the national paradigm? National history writing in Germany, Italy, France, and Britain from 1945 to the present. *The Journal of Modern History, 77*(3), 629–698. https://www.journals.uchicago.edu/doi/abs/10.1086/497719

Berger, S. (2006). National historiographies in transnational perspective: Europe in the nineteenth and twentieth centuries. *Storia della storiografia, 50*, 3–26.

Berger, S. (2009). On the role of myths and history in the construction of national identity in modern Europe. *European History Quarterly, 39*(3), 490–502. https://doi.org/10.1177%2F0265691409105063

Berger, S. (2011). Fathers' and their fate in modern European national historiographies. In H. Paul (Ed.), *Fathers of history: Genealogies of the historical discipline* (Vols. 59–60, pp. 231–250). Special Supplement in Storia della Storiografia.

Berger, S. (2015). The past as history. In S. Berger & C. Conrad (Eds.), *The past as history: National identity and historical consciousness in modern Europe* (pp.viii–xi). Palgrave Macmillan.

Berger, S., & Conrad, C. (2015). *The past as history: National identity and historical consciousness in modern Europe*. Palgrave Macmillan.

Berger, S., Eriksonas, L., & Mycock, A. (Eds.). (2008). *Narrating the nation: Representations in history, media and the arts* (vol. 11). Berghahn Books.

Berger, S., & Lorenz, C. (2008). *The contested nation: Ethnicity, class, religion and gender in national histories*. Palgrave Macmillan.

Berger, S., & Niven, B. (Eds.). (2014). *Writing the history of memory*. A&C Black.

Berkhofer, R. F. (1979). *The white man's Indian: Images of the American Indian, from Columbus to the present* (vol. 794). Vintage.

Blainey, G. (1993). Drawing up a balance sheet of our history. *Quadrant, 37*(7–8), 10-15.

Bloom, H. (1996). Foreword. In Y. Yerushalmi (ed.), *Zakhor: Jewish history and Jewish memory* (pp. xiii–xxv). University of Washington Press.

Bohlman, P. (2008). The nation in song. In S. Berger, L. Eriksonas, & A. Mycock (Eds.) *Narrating the nation: Representations in history, media and the arts* (vol. 11, pp. 246–267). Berghahn Books.

Bonnett, A. (1998). How the British working class became white: The symbolic (re) formation of racialized capitalism. *Journal of historical sociology, 11*(3), 316–340.

Bonnett, A. (2002). How the British working class became white: The symbolic (re) formation of racialized capitalism. *Journal of Historical Sociology, 11*(3), 316–340. https://doi.org/10.1111/1467-6443.00066

Brantlinger, P. (2004). 'Black armband' versus 'White blindfold' history in Australia. *Victorian Studies, 46*(4), 655–674. http://www.jstor.org/stable/3829922

Brown, D. (1970). *Bury my heart at wounded knee: An Indian history of the American West.* Holt, Rinehart & Winston.

Cochran-Smith, M. (2000). Blind vision: Unlearning racism in teacher education. *Harvard Educational Review, 70*(2), 157–190.

Collins, F., & Davis, T. (2004). *Australian cinema after Mabo.* Cambridge University Press.

Connor, J. (2002). *The Australian frontier wars, 1788–1838.* UNSW Press.

Davis, R. (1991). History or his/story? The explorer cum author. *Studies in Canadian Literature, 16*(2), 93–11. https://journals.lib.unb.ca/index.php/scl/article/view/8143/9200

DiAngelo, R. (2011). White fragility. *International Journal of Critical Pedagogy, 3*(3), 54–70. http://libjournal.uncg.edu/ijcp/article/view/249/116

DiAngelo, R. (2018). *White fragility why it's so hard for White people to talk about racism.* Allen Lane, Penguin.

Dixson, M. (1976). *The real Matilda: Women and identity in Australia 1788 to 1975.* Penguin.

Dozono, T. (2020). The passive voice of White supremacy: Tracing epistemic and discursive violence in world history curriculum. *Review of Education, Pedagogy, and Cultural Studies, 42*(1), 1–26. https://doi.org/10.1080/10714413.2020.1721261

Dunbar-Ortiz, R. (2014). *An Indigenous peoples' history of the United States* (vol. 3). Beacon Press.

Eriksonas, L. (2008). Toward the genre of popular national history: Walter Scott after Waterloo. In S. Berger, L. Eriksonas, & A. Mycock (Eds.), *Narrating the nation: Representations in history, media and the arts* (vol. 11, pp.117–132). Berghahn Books.

Fletcher, M. S., Hamilton, R., Dressler, W., & Palmer, L. (2021). Indigenous knowledge and the shackles of wilderness. *Proceedings of the National Academy of Sciences, 118*(40). https://doi.org/10.1073/pnas.2022218118

Folsom, E. (1998). Native Americans [Indians]. In J. R. LeMaster & D. D. Kummings (Eds.), *Walt Whitman: An encyclopedia.* Garland Publishing. https://whitmanarchive.org/criticism/current/encyclopedia/entry_34.html

Foster, R. (2009). 'Don't Mention the War' frontier violence and the language of concealment. *History Australia, 6*(3), 68.1–68.15. https://doi-org/10.2104/ha090068

Fournier, S. & Crey, E. (2006). Killing the Indian in the child: four centuries of church-run schools. In R. Maaka & C. Andersen. (Eds.). (2006). *The indigenous experience: global perspectives* (pp. 141–150). Canadian Scholars Press Inc.

Frey, H. (2008). Cannes 1956/1979: Riviera reflections on nationalism and cinema. In S. Berger, L. Eriksonas, & A. Mycock (Eds.), *Narrating the nation: Representations in history, media and the arts* (vol. 11, pp. 181–205). Berghahn Books.

Garner, S. (2006). The uses of whiteness: What sociologists working on Europe can draw from US research on whiteness. *Sociology, 40*(2), 257–275. https://doi.org/10.1177%2F0038038506062032

Garner, S. (2009). Ireland: From racism without "race" to racism without racists. *Radical History Review, 2009*(104), 41–56. https://doi.org/10.1215/01636545-2008-067

Garner, S. (2015). The siminization of the Irish. In W. Hund, C. Mills, & S. Sebastiani. (Eds.), *Simianization: Apes, gender, class, and race* (pp. 197–221). Zurich Lit Verlag.

Hall, S. (2001). Foucault: Power, knowledge and Discourse. In. M. Wetherell, S. Taylor, & S. Yates (Eds.), *Discourse, theory and practice* (pp. 72–81). Sage.

Hirst, J. B. (1978). The pioneer legend. *Australian Historical Studies*, *18*(71), 316–337. https://doi.org/10.1080/10314617808595595

Hobsbawn, E. & Ranger, T. (Eds.). (1983). *The invention of tradition* (pp. 1–14). Cambridge University Press.

Hollinsworth, D. (2014). Unsettling Australian settler supremacy: Combating resistance in university Aboriginal studies. *Race ethnicity and education*, *19*(2), 412–432. https://doi.org/10.1080/13613324.2014.911166

Hudson, F. (1908a). Pioneers. *The song of manly men and other verses*, (pp. 38–39). David Nutt.

Hudson, F. (1908b) *Pioneers*. https://www.thefleece.org/felix/pioneer.html

Hund, W. D., Mills, C. W., & Sebastiani, S. (Eds.). (2015). *Simianization: Apes, gender, class, and race* (vol. 6). LIT Verlag Münster.

Khan, S., Allan, R., Pennington, J., & Richardson, L. (2015). Paying our dues: The importance of newcomer solidarity with the Indigenous movement for self-determination in Canada. *The Canadian Journal of Native Studies*, *35*(1), 145–153.

Keenan, J. (2016). *The terrible Indian wars of the West: A history from the Whitman massacre to Wounded Knee, 1846–1890*. McFarland.

Key, F. S. (n.d.). *The star spangled banner*. Smithsonian. https://amhistory.si.edu/starspangledbanner/the-lyrics.aspx

Ladson-Billings, G. (1995). Toward a theory of culturally relevant pedagogy. *American educational research journal*, *32*(3), 465–491. https://doi.org/10.3102%2F00028312032003465

Landow, G. P. (1990). History, his Story, and stories in Graham Swift's 'Waterland.' *Studies in the Literary Imagination*, *23*(2), 197–211.

Leerssen, J. (2013). 'Retro-fitting the past': Literary historicism between the Golden Spurs and Waterloo. In *The historical imagination in nineteenth-century Britain and the Low Countries* (pp. 111–131). Brill.

Maaka, R., & Andersen, C. (Eds.). (2006). *The indigenous experience: Global perspectives*. Canadian Scholars' Press.

MacLeod, A. L. (1998). Whitman in Australia and New Zealand. In J. R. LeMaster & D. D. Kummings (Eds.), *Walt Whitman: An encyclopedia*. Garland Publishing. https//whitmanarchive.org/criticism/current/encyclopedia/entry_367.html

Macintyre, S., & Clark, A. (2003). *The history wars*. Melbourne University Publishing.

Manne, R. (Ed.). (2003). *Whitewash: On Keith Windschuttle's fabrication of Aboriginal history*. Black.

Mar, T. B. (2010). Carving wilderness: Queensland's national parks and the unsettling of emptied lands, 1890–1910. In T. Mar & P. Edwards (Eds.), *Making settler colonial space: Perspectives on race, place and identity* (pp. 73–94). Palgrave Macmillan. https://10.1057/9780230277946_5

Marcus, S. (1976). Freud and Dora: Story, history, case history. *Psychoanalysis and Contemporary Science*, *5*, 389–442.

McCreanor, S. (2000). Australian heroes and saints. *Australian Religion Studies Review*, *13*(2).

McIntosh, P. (1992). White privilege: Unpacking the invisible knapsack. In A. Filor (Ed.), *Multiculturalism* (pp. 30–36.). New York State Council of Educational associations.

McIntosh, P. (2007). White privilege: Unpacking the invisible knapsack. *Race, class, and gender in the United States: An integrated study*, 177–182.

Micheal, S., Ogbeide, A. E., Arora, A., Alford, S., Firdaus, R., Lim, D., & Dune, T. (2021). Exploring tertiary health science student willingness or resistance to cultural competency and safety pedagogy. *International Journal of Environmental Research and Public Health*, *18*(17), 9184. https://doi.org/10.3390/ijerph18179184

Mignolo, W. D. (2007a). Introduction: Coloniality of power and de-colonial thinking. *Cultural Studies*, *21*(2–3), 155–167. https://doi.org/10.1080/09502380601162498

Mignolo, W. D. (2007b). Delinking: The rhetoric of modernity, the logic of coloniality and the grammar of de-coloniality. *Cultural Studies*, *21*(2–3), 449-514. https://doi.org/10.1080/09502380601162498

Mignolo, W. D. (2009). Epistemic disobedience, independent thought and decolonial freedom. *Theory, Culture & Society*, *26* (7–8), 159–181. https://doi.org/10.1177%2F0263276409349275

Mignon, C. (1998). Pioneers! O Pioneers (1895). In J. R. LeMaster & D. Kummings (Eds.), *Walt Whitman: An encyclopedia* (Entry 594). New York, Garland Publishing. https://whitmanarchive.org/criticism/current/encyclopedia/entry_594.html

Miller, J., Hyde, C. A., & Ruth, B. J. (2004). Teaching about race and racism in social work: Challenges for white educators. *Smith College Studies in Social Work*, *74*(2), 409–426. https://doi.org/10.1080/00377310409517724

Murphy, S., & Cuneen, C. (2018). *As Indigenous incarceration rates keep rising, justice reinvestment offers a solution*. The Conversation.

The New Community Bible. (2012). (International Edition). St Pauls.

O'Connor, J. E. (1993). The White Man's Indian. *Film & History: An Interdisciplinary Journal of Film and Television Studies*, *23*(1), 17–26. https://muse.jhu.edu/article/395797

O'Doherty, C. (2021, March 8th). Blowing up Nelson's Pillar and the fate of Nelson's head. *IrishCentral*. https://www.irishcentral.com/roots/history/blowing-up-nelsons-pillar-nelsons-head

O'Dowd, M. (2010). 'Ethical positioning' a strategy in overcoming student resistance and fostering engagement in teaching Aboriginal history as a compulsory subject to pre-service primary education students. *Education in Rural Australia*, 20(1), 29–42.

O'Dowd, M. (2011). Australian identity, history and belonging: The influence of white Australian identity on racism and the non-acceptance of the history of colonisation of Indigenous Australians. *International Journal of Diversity in Organisations, Communities & Nations*, *10*(6), (29–42).

O'Dowd, M. (2012a). Embodying the Australian nation and silencing history. *Arena Journal*, (37/38), 88–104.

O'Dowd, M. (2012b). Engaging non-indigenous students in indigenous history and 'un-history': An approach for non-indigenous teachers and a politics for the twenty-first century. *History of Education Review*, *41*(2), 104–118. https://doi.org/10.1108/08198691211269539

O'Dowd, M. (2020, February 5th). Explainer: What is systemic racism and institutional racism? *The Conversation*. https://theconversation.com/explainer-what-is-systemic-racism-and-institutional-racism-131152

Orser Jr., C. E. (1998). The challenge of race to American historical archaeology. *American Anthropologist, 100*(3), 661–668. https://doi.org/10.1525/aa.1998.100.3.661

Patrick, W. S. J. (2015). 'Pulya-ranyi': Winds of change. *Cultural Studies Review, 21*(1), 121–131.

Peters-Little, F., Curthoys, A., & Docker, J. (2010). *Passionate histories: myth, memory and Indigenous Australia*. ANU Press.

Pettit, B., & Western, B. (2004). Mass imprisonment and the life course: Race and class inequality in US incarceration. *American Sociological Review, 69*(2), 151–169. https://doi.org/10.1177%2F000312240406900201

Quaid, S., & Williams, H. (2021). Troubling knowledges and difficult pedagogical moments for students learning. *International Journal of Inclusive Education*, 1–19. https://doi.org/10.1080/13603116.2021.1916110

Quijano, A. (2000). Coloniality of power and Eurocentrism in Latin America. *International Sociology, 15*(2), 215–232. https://doi.org/10.1177%2F0268580900015002005

Reynolds, H. (1981). *The other side of the frontier: Aboriginal resistance to the European invasion of Australia*. James Cook University of North Queensland.

Reynolds, H. (1996). *Aboriginal sovereignty: Reflections on race, state, and nation*. Allen & Unwin.

Reynolds, H. (2000). *Why weren't we told? A personal search for the truth about our history*. Penguin Books.

Reynolds, H. (2006). *The other side of the frontier: Aboriginal resistance to the European invasion of Australia*. UNSW Press.

Rigney, A. (2008). Fiction as a mediator in national remembrance. In S. Berger, L. Eriksonas, & A. Mycock (Eds.), *Narrating the nation: Representations in history, media and the arts* (pp. 79–96). Berghahn Books.

Roberts, T. (2005). *Frontier justice: A history of the Gulf country to 1900*. University of Queensland Press.

Russell, L. (2001). *Savage imaginings: Historical and contemporary constructions of Australian Aboriginalities*. Australian Scholarly Publishing.

Salter, P. S., Adams, G., & Perez, M. J. (2017). Racism in the structure of everyday worlds: A cultural-psychological perspective. *Current Directions in Psychological Science, 27*(3), 150–155. https://doi.org/10.1177%2F0963721417724239

Sawyer, S. E. (2013). *Touch my tears: Tales from the trail of tears*. Rockhaven Publishing.

Said, E. (1995). *Orientalism: Western constructions of the orient*. Penguin.

Stanner, W. E. H. (1969). *After the dreaming: Black and white Australians—An anthropologist's view*. Australian Broadcasting Commission.

Statista. (2021). *Number of people killed by police in the United States from 2013 to 2021, by ethnicity*. https://www.statista.com/statistics/1124036/number-people-killed-police-ethnicity-us/

Straus, S. (2004). How many perpetrators were there in the Rwandan genocide? An estimate. *Journal of Genocide Research, 6*(1), 85–98. https://doi.org/10.1080/1462352042000194728

Sturgis, A. H. (2007). *The trail of tears and Indian removal*. Greenwood Publishing Group.

Tate, C. (2020). *Unsettled ground: The Whitman massacre and its shifting legacy in the American West*. Sasquatch Books.
Teichmann, M. (2005). Keith Windschuttle on White Australia. *National Observer*, (65), 38–43.
Thijs, K. (2011). The metaphor of the master: 'Narrative hierarchy.' In S. Berger & C. Lorenz (Eds.), *The contested nation: Ethnicity, class, religion and gender in national histories* (pp. 60–74). Palgrave Macmillan.
Upadhyay, N. (2019). Making of "model" South Asians on the Tar Sands: Intersections of race, caste, and Indigeneity. *Critical Ethnic Studies*, 5(1–2), 152–173. https://doi.org/10.5749/jcritethnstud.5.1-2.0152
Vaught, S. E., & Castagno, A. E. (2008). "I don't think I'm a racist": Critical Race Theory, teacher attitudes, and structural racism. *Race Ethnicity and education*, 11(2), 95–113. https://doi.org/10.1080/13613320802110217
Valluvan, S. (2019). The uses and abuses of class: left nationalism and the denial of working class multiculture. *The Sociological Review*, 67(1), 36–46. https://doi.org/10.1177%2F0038026118820295
Vickers, E. (Ed.). (2013). *History education and national identity in East Asia*. Routledge.
Vickery, P., & Dix, A. (2021). Amending the national anthem-from words of exclusion to inclusion: An interview with the Hon Peter Vickery QC. *Victorian Bar News*, (169), 54–59.
Vrasidas, C. (1997). The White Man's Indian: Stereotypes in film and beyond. *Journeys toward visual literacy. Selected readings, Annual Conference of the International Visual Literacy Association* (pp. 63–70). https://eric.ed.gov/?id=ED408950
Wagner, A. E. (2005). Unsettling the academy: Working through the challenges of anti-racist pedagogy. *Race Ethnicity and Education*, 8(3), 261–275.
Ward, R. (1958). *The Australian legend*. Oxford University Press
Western, B., & Wildeman, C. (2009). The black family and mass incarceration. *The ANNALS of the American Academy of Political and Social Science*, 621(1), 221–242. https://doi.org/10.1177%2F0002716208324850
White, R. (1981). *Inventing Australia: Images and identity 1688–1980*. Routledge.
Whitman, W. (1865). *Pioneers! O Pioneers! Leaves of grass* (pp. 229–232).
Wimmer, A. (2012). *Waves of war: Nationalism, state formation, and ethnic exclusion in the modern world*. Cambridge University Press.
Windschuttle, K. (2002). *The fabrication of Aboriginal history (vol. one): Van Diemen's Land 1803–1847*. Macleay Press.
Wintle, M. (2008). Personifying the Past: National and European history. In S. Berger, L. Eriksonas, & A. Mycock (Eds.), *Narrating the nation: Representations in history, media and the arts* (vol. 11, pp. 222–245). Berghahn Books.
Wolfe, P. (1999). *Settler colonialism*. A&C Black.
Wolfe, P. (2006). Settler colonialism and the elimination of the Native. *Journal of genocide research*, 8(4), 387–409. https://doi.org/10.1080/14623520601056240
Yang, D. (1999). Convergence or divergence? Recent historical writings on the rape of Nanjing. *The American Historical Review*, 104(3), 842–865. https://doi.org/10.2307/2650991
Yerushalmi, Y. Z. (1996). *Jewish history and Jewish memory*. University of Washington Press.

Zembylas, M. (2012). Pedagogies of strategic empathy: Navigating through the emotional complexities of anti-racism in higher education. *Teaching in Higher Education, 17*(2), 113–125. https://doi.org/10.1080/13562517.2011.611869

Zembylas, M. (2014). Theorizing 'difficult knowledge' in the aftermath of the 'affective turn': Implications for curriculum and pedagogy in handling traumatic representations. *Curriculum Inquiry, 44*(3), 390–412. https://doi.org/10.1111/curi.12051

CHAPTER 10

HOW IS RACISM A GLOBAL ISSUE?

Connecting Critical Global Education to the Teaching of Race

Hanadi Shatara and Gerardo Aponte-Safe

University of Wisconsin, La Crosse

> What if SNL had had an Iraqi choir? A Syrian choir? a Yemeni choir? An Afghan choir? A Palestinian choir? I want to join the collective grieving so badly but it's hard when the collective never grieves for me and mine.
> —*Randa Tawil, 2022*

As the world witnessed the February 24, 2022 Russian invasion of Ukraine, an outpouring of support for Ukrainians was manifested instantly. Only two days later, on February 26, 2022, the sketch comedy show *Saturday Night Live* (*SNL*) had a Ukrainian choir perform during its cold open. Soon after, blue and gold lights bathed buildings and monuments around the world, from the Eiffel Tower to the Empire State Building, the Sydney Opera House, Berlin's Brandenburg Gate, the Taipei 101 skyscraper, Tokyo's Municipal Building, and even Niagara

---

Out of Turmoil: Catalysts for Re-learning, Re-Teaching, and Re-imagining History and Social Science, pages 167–179.
Copyright © 2023 by Information Age Publishing
www.infoagepub.com
All rights of reproduction in any form reserved.

Falls (Reuters, 2022). Similar displays of solidarity were present in smaller communities throughout the United States, including Lansing, Michigan; Lexington, Kentucky; Muscatine, Iowa; and Sandusky, Ohio.

In the midst of such support, communities of Color,[1] immigrants, and Black and Brown refugees wrestled with the tension of seeing immediate and overwhelming support for Ukraine and its refugees considering the severe backlash that other refugee groups have experienced. These tensions are captured in the following tweet:

> Once & for all: Unless the victim is white, European, Xtian (& US-Israel friendly), resistance is terrorism, Int'l law doesn't apply, vetoes apply, refugees have no right to return (& are unwelcome), & the aggressor has the right to self defence & to acquire territory by war. (Ashrawi, 2022)

The Western/Global North (i.e., white[2] European, United States citizen, Australian, Canadian) reaction to the refugee crisis after the 2022 invasion of Ukraine contrasted significantly with its reaction to Syrian, Afghan, Yemeni, Somali, Tigrayans, Palestinian, and Rohingya refugee crises (to name a few) in the last decade. These reactions involved shock over how Russians could possibly invade, occupy, and devalue another European country. "They're like us" was clearly articulated; "those other refugees are not" was an important subtext, which was also verbalized in some instances.

In the February 28, 2022, episode of *The Daily Show*, Trevor Noah aggregated statements from reporters describing the invasion and its impact on people, which we include below:

> **Reporter 1:** This is not a developing third world nation, this is Europe
> **Reporter 2:** These are prosperous middle-class people. These are not people trying to get away from areas in North Africa. They look like any European family that you would live next door to.
> **Expert 1:** What could be a difference here from other conflicts you know that could seem very far away you know in Africa, the Middle East, whatever, I mean these are Europeans that we're seeing being killed.
> **Reporter 3:** This isn't a place, with all due respect, you know, like Iraq or Afghanistan, you know. This is a relatively civilized, relatively European, I have to choose those words carefully too, city where you wouldn't expect that or hope that it's going to happen.
> **Noah:** Wow, that was you, choosing your words carefully. That was the careful version. So what were you going to say if you weren't choos-

---

[1] Inspired by Jessica C. Harris (2017) and Lindsay Pérez Huber (2010), we capitalize Color in relation to people and communities of Color as a "form of linguistic empowerment" (Harris, 2017, p. 1055).

[2] Continuing to reference Pérez Huber, we intentionally do not capitalize white to "reject the grammatical representation of power capitalization brings to the term" (Pérez Huber, 2010, p. 93).

ing your words carefully? "I just hope the next time this happens, it happens back in the Middle East where it belongs? Here's the thing, beyond the racism...fighting crazy wars was Europe's thing?...Now people are gonna be like, "Oh to see this in Europe." Like, I'll tell you now—I don't know about you, but I was shocked to see how many reporters, around the world by the way, seem to think that it's more of a tragedy when white people have to flee their countries. Because I guess, what, the darkies were built for it? (Noah, 2022, 10:06–11:49)

As we see in these reactions to the Russian invasion of Ukraine, communication technologies and social media have facilitated the expansion of global interconnectedness. The world is constantly at our fingertips—we carry it in our pockets (our cell phones), in our workplaces, at our computers—and we depend on it to function. Young people in schools are also impacted by these technologies and the immediacy of information from media and about current events. As the world follows us around in our daily tasks, it is important that we, as members of global communities, develop skills for consuming, understanding, and producing quality and humanizing information (Andreotti, 2014; Breakstone et al., 2018; Lim & Tan, 2020; Menten, n.d.; Merryfield, 2012; Myers, 2010). Therefore, the development of global perspectives is an essential piece of education.

Just as global awareness and perspectives are essential skills for teachers and young people, critical global perspectives—the perspectives that extend our awareness of the world to uncover its power dynamics and challenge global systems of oppression—are imperative to building not just a globally interconnected society, but a more just and inclusive one (Andreotti, 2014; Aponte-Safe & Shatara, 2021; Busey & Coleman-King, 2020; Busey & Dowie-Chin, 2021; Subedi, 2013). Global issues are not neutral because global interconnectedness has often come through the pursuit of (neoliberal) empires resulting in the subjugation of communities around the world (Andreotti, 2014; Camicia & Franklin, 2011; Willinsky, 1998). In describing this lack of neutrality, we conceptualize global issues through a racial lens (Busey & Coleman-King, 2020). As the sample tweets and video in the introduction illustrate, digital media can allow people, especially young people and teachers, to access information beyond the filters of white supremacy and see the racialization of others, building critical global awareness and engagement, leading to justice movements calling for Black lives to matter, Indigenous rights to land, and an end to climate change. Yet, the impact of algorithms severely restricts who has access to such information (Krutka et al., 2020; Lim & Alrasheed, 2021).

In this chapter, we provide a framework for critical global education as a tool for teachers to assess curriculum materials and tools to approach global perspectives in their classrooms. This framework was developed based on our prior research and teaching experience in global education. Then, we present an Inquiry

Design Model (IDM; Grant et al., 2017) unit we developed for teachers to introduce the global issue of racism into their teaching. Our goal in this IDM is to unpack the ways that racism pervades communities around the world. Good anti-racist pedagogical materials are available to address U.S. contexts, but we hope to shed light on an approach that highlights how racism happens not only in the United States—as it is mostly contextualized in U.S. social studies classrooms (Adams & Busey, 2017)—but also around the world.

Engaging in anti-racism within global education is essential. While some work has been conducted, the field of global education lacks sustained engagement with racism as a global issue (Shatara & Kim, in press). Therefore, we offer this as a beginning place but certainly not as the ending. This chapter is born of many conversations during our work and teaching together, and we hope that more research and scholarship will go into thinking about race and racism globally.

DEFINING CRITICAL GLOBAL EDUCATION

Global perspectives are an essential part of being an active citizen in the 21st century. In social studies education, incorporating global dimensions of citizenship requires that we expand beyond covering local communities and nation-oriented traditions and trace connections beyond borders (Hanvey, 1982). Engaging in this work requires a critical disposition that brings an expansive lens to what and whose knowledge counts in the curriculum, which knowledge is prioritized, and which remains hidden or absent. The curriculum materials we discuss in this chapter expand an analytical framework for critical global curriculum analysis (Aponte-Safe & Shatara, 2021) to explore critical global perspectives. Below we discuss the work of critical global scholars that shape our thinking on critical global perspectives.

In previous work (Aponte-Safe & Shatara, 2021), we outlined a framework for analyzing curriculum materials through a global perspective, with an emphasis on critical global perspectives. This framework operationalizes Tye's (2014) definition of global education, which emphasizes issues of global interconnectedness that transcend national borders through multiple perspectives to build individual and collective action. The framework provides teachers with a process for connecting their curriculum to issues that transcend national borders, which are seldom included in the formal curriculum. See Table 10.1 for reference.

Additionally, the framework provides guidance for teachers to view curriculum through critical global perspectives, which uncover the power dynamics underlying and producing the interconnections between and among communities around the world. These critical perspectives are guided especially by the work of Subedi (2013) and Andreotti (2014).

In calling for decolonizing social studies curriculum, Subedi (2013) advocated for a "more nuanced and complex interpretation of global issues" (p. 629). He argued that a decolonizing curriculum actively pursues:

TABLE 10.1. Process of Analyzing Educational Texts with a Critical Global Perspective (Aponte-Safe & Shatara, 2021)

Step	Explanation
Step 1: Identify Explicitly Global Standards	Identify these terms in the text: "global," "world," "globe," and "international."
Step 2: Identify Globally Adjacent Standards	Identify these terms in the text: "human," "culture," "country/countries" and any specific countries/regions name.
Step 3: Reinterpreting through a Global Lens	Reinterpret and find opportunities for global perspectives in the text, specific to interconnectedness of issues and systems, perspective taking, and action.
Step 4: Challenging Dominant Narrative through a Critical Global Lens	Challenge dominant narratives and counter with attention to the larger inequitable and unequal systems in place as a result of colonization and imperialism in the text.

- Antiessentialism, which ensures that cultures are not presented as homogeneous or monolithic and challenges hierarchies between cultures;
- Contrapuntal perspectives, which challenges the otherization of colonized groups with narratives of resistance and thriving; and
- Ethical solidarity, which refers to authentic and empowering partnerships towards meaningful action to global challenges and issues.

Similarly, Andreotti's (2014) work challenged notions of global citizenship education promoting dominant narratives of the world. She argued for critical global citizenship education that exposes the colonial roots of global problems, tracing the systemic and complex origins of global issues and unmasking solutions that reify colonial power hierarchies. She used the example of poverty in the "developing world" to uncover the complex structures and systems of inequality and injustice tied to colonization that have led to and exacerbated poverty, especially uncovering who benefits from and controls such systems. Furthermore, Andreotti argued that discussions on this global issue should seek more than elusive harmony and equality and instead create grounds for meaningful and sustained dialogue that empower groups to have autonomy in defining their own development.

Critical global education requires special attention in social studies education, especially when reframing what is counted as global and whose frames are centered. Speaking on the making of global anti-blackness, Busey and Dowie-Chin (2021) challenged discourse in social studies education that reduces global citizenship to modern technology, global interdependency, and values of "good" and "bad" global citizens. They argued such discussions are continuations of the Euro-Western narratives that continue to reify racism by rendering racism and anti-blackness as invisible (p. 159). With their treatise on the exclusion of Blackness from humanness and citizenship, Busey and Dowie-Chin argued that social studies education and critical global education need to do more than address deepening racial divides or teaching about instances or incidents of racism on a global scale. Busey and Dowie-Chin challenged these fields to reconsider the very definitions of citizenship as linked to power.

Inspired by their work, we speak about the importance of critical global perspectives to achieve a more just society to ensure that social studies educators and global educators wrestle with the principles of who has defined citizenship and the power they continue to hold in the global sphere. In crafting our curriculum materials, we follow in the footsteps of these critical scholars and hope to help teachers explore ways to engage this work in their classrooms.

TEACHING CRITICAL GLOBAL EDUCATION ISSUES: EXAMPLE OF TEACHING RACISM AS A GLOBAL ISSUE

There is a plethora of global issues that can be discussed critically using the framework we have provided above. Yet, one global issue is not as developed within the global context: racism (Busey & Dowie-Chin, 2021). In the following IDM, we contextualize racism as a global issue and provide resources and essential questions that grant opportunities to incorporate global issues and discussions of race and racism into instruction. This IDM was developed with a secondary social studies context in mind, especially in world history or geography classes, though resources can certainly be adapted for younger audiences as well as other subjects such as English language arts, communications or media studies, and global studies.

We begin by framing the IDM around the concept of a global issue, centering around this compelling question: "How is racism a global issue?" This question allows students to think about how issues affect local and global communities and to think about how racism is an issue that plagues the world, not just the United States. We connected this IDM to two sets of standards from the National Council for the Social Studies' (2013) C3 Framework and the Social Justice standards from Learning for Justice (2016). We focus on the "Developing Claims and Using Evidence" component of the C3 Framework to provide opportunities for students to build on their claim of racism as a global issue using evidence from the sources provided. Each performance task asks students to practice this skill throughout the IDM. We also focus on Diversity and Justice strands from the Social Justice standards to allow students to understand the inequitable power dynamics within global racism while also understanding the history and current events concerning racial issues and justice within the world. We end the first section of the IDM introducing the concept of a global issue, defined in the Staging the Question section, asking students to think about how issues affecting the world also affect their local communities. In the different supporting questions, we discussed how teachers can include racism as an example of a global issue and proceed with the IDM in a critical way.

We divided the IDM into three sections with supporting questions, formative performance tasks, and resources. The first supporting question considers the definition of global racism and how it is connected to imperialism and colonialism. We provide five sources that tackle the supporting question in different ways. Source SQ1.A describes distortion in maps and how colonialism and imperialism relate to geography. Sources SQ1.B-SQ1.E are articles and media that focus on one region of the world and how racism and white supremacy have affected that area, including France (SQ1.C), South Africa (SQ1.D), and East Asia (SQ1.E).

The second supporting question goes further in investigating how racism is not just an issue in the United States. We provide three case studies with sources, allowing students to think about racism as a global concept through a much deeper dive into the issue as opposed to the previous supporting question concerning students' introduction to global racism, its definition, and existence. One of the case studies explores the racism present within the Ukraine crisis. Sources SQ2.A and SQ2.B provide two ways that this crisis connects with racism. Source SQ2.A discusses how the media has represented the situation in Ukraine and Ukrainian refugees versus similar situations and refugees from countries such as Iraq, Syria, and Afghanistan. Source SQ2.B discusses the treatment of Africans trying to flee Ukraine. These two perspectives offer students opportunities to unpack two types of racism: the contrast between coverage of white refugees from Ukraine versus Black and Brown refugees in other contexts, as well as discriminatory policies towards Africans escaping Ukraine. This connects to Busey and Dowie-Chin's (2021) question of who is considered human. The second case study looks at police violence as an issue that affects multiple areas of the world, not just the United States. Examining this source allows students to connect an issue familiar in the local setting (the United States) to global contexts. The third case study looks at the erasure of Indigenous languages in Latin America and how linguistic genocide is systemic within societies as a global issue. By providing these cases, teachers can demonstrate that racism is manifested within different regions of the world and through different means, whether it is through language, representations in media, or state actions.

Our last supporting question discusses the act of resistance. King's (2020) framework for Black historical consciousness includes a section called "Black Agency, Resistance and Perseverance" (p. 338). He emphasized that Black people are not just victims of oppression, but also have agency to resist oppressive structures; he challenged us to teach about agency, resistance, and perseverance in Black communities. In his words,

> [T]hroughout history, Black people could act independently, made their own decisions based on their interests, and fought back against oppressive structures. This concept recognizes that Black people have a spirit of freedom and revolt as each generation has fought against oppression. (p. 338)

Inquiry Design Model (IDM) Blueprint™ (Grant et al., 2017)

Compelling Question	How is racism a global issue?
Standards and Practices	**C3 Framework:** D3.3.9-12. Identify evidence that draws information directly and substantively from multiple sources to detect inconsistencies in evidence in order to revise or strengthen claims. D3.4.9-12. Refine claims and counterclaims attending to precision, significance, and knowledge conveyed through the claim while pointing out the strengths and limitations of both. **Social Justice:** DI.9-12.10 I understand that diversity includes the impact of unequal power relations on the development of group identities and cultures. JU.9-12.15 I can identify figures, groups, events and a variety of strategies and philosophies relevant to the history of social justice around the world.
Staging the Question	Question: What is a global issue? Define global issue: an issue or series of issues that can be economic, political, social, environmental that affects the world as a community and goes beyond national boundaries. Identify different global issues

Supporting Question 1	Supporting Question 2	Supporting Question 3
What is global racism? How is it connected to colonialism and imperialism?	Is racism only a United States issue? Based on three case studies, how is racism present in the world?	What are ways the global community has resisted racism?
Formative Performance Task	**Formative Performance Task**	**Formative Performance Task**
Describe racism in the global context and give evidence that shows how racism is connected to colonialism and imperialism.	Evaluate and give evidence on how racism is present in the world.	Summarize the ways different communities in the world resisted racist policies rooted in colonialism and imperialism
Featured Sources	**Featured Sources**	**Featured Sources**
Source SQ1.A: Vox (2016), "Why All Maps Are Wrong" **Source SQ1.B:** Last Week Tonight with John Oliver (2021), "Afghanistan" (Warning: Explicit Language) **Source SQ1.C:** Beaman (2021), "Race: Neverending Taboo in France" **Source SQ1.D:** Magaisa (2021), "The Legacy of Racism in South Africa"	**Case 1: Racism in relation to Ukraine** **Source SQ2.A:** Noah (2022), "Russia Punished & Media Shocked by Invasion in 'Relatively Civilized' Ukraine" **Source SQ2.B:** Pronczuk & Maclean (2022), "Africans Say Ukrainian Authorities Hindered Them From Fleeing"	**Source SQ3.A:** Avila (2016), "Two-Day Workshop Strengthens Ties Between Indigenous Language Digital Activists in Peru" **Source SQ3.B:** Silverstein (2021), "The Global Impact of George Floyd: How Black Lives Matter Protests Shaped Movements Around the World"

How is Racism a Global Issue? • 175

Featured Sources	Featured Sources	Featured Sources
Source SQ1.E: Baker (2020), "Examining Race in East Asian Studies"	**Case 2: Global Policing** **Source SQ2.C:** Leonard (2021b), "Defunding the Police is a Global Movement" **Source SQ2.D:** Leonard (2021a), "U.S. Policing is a Global Problem" **Case 3: Erasure of Indigenous Languages** **Source SQ2.E:** Robidoux (2019), "Linguistic Genocide in Colombia" **Source SQ2.F:** Óre & Diaz (2019), "In 21st Century, Threats 'From All Sides' for Latin America's Original Languages"	**Source SQ3.C:** Burton (2019), "The Young Activists of Color Who Are Leading the Climate Charge" **Source SQ3.D:** Underwood (2021), "Resistance and the 'War on Terror' in East Africa"
Summative Performance Task — **Argument**	How is racism a global issue? Construct an argument on how racism is a global issue. Cite from the featured resources and research to support how racism is a global issue.	
Extension	Research a global activist or a global activism organization who is taking action to combat racism in their context.	
Taking Informed Action	Create a social media post (IG, Facebook, Twitter, Snapchat, TikTok) or a presentation for the school community that addresses global racism.	

Inspired by King's work, we provide resources for teachers to discuss global resistance to racism in the world. In thinking about the sub-issues discussed in the first two supporting questions, we provided sources that discuss language activism to combat language erasure in Indigenous communities, Black Lives Matter activism around the world to combat anti-Blackness and state violence, and East African resistance to policing and the role of the United States within state violence. We also included sources on young activists of Color beyond Greta Thunberg to show students that communities of Color have agency to resist racism and tackle global issues within their local communities.

We end with the summative performance task as a traditional assignment in which students answer the compelling question and provide evidence from the listed sources and other sources if students choose to do more research. We also ask students to take informed action by using social media as a way to spread awareness on racism as a global issue. As Yee and El-Naggar (2021) described, social media has played a role in resistance movements; giving students opportunities to practice responsible social media use allows them to become informed members of society who take action in ethical ways. If schools, families, and students are uncomfortable using social media, students can create presentations to share with the larger school community on issues of global racism.

There are some limitations to this IDM that are connected to the intended audience of this book, who are United States educators and scholars. For one, the majority of the sources are in English and due to this reality that is rooted in colonialism, white supremacy, and U.S. exceptionalism, many perspectives that are in different languages are missing. Second, the majority of these sources are from Western media. Again, this is another ramification of colonialism and U.S. exceptionalism, while also a consequence as our work is situated in the United States.

Lastly, while this IDM can be perceived as a three-day lesson/mini unit, it is important to note that teachers need to be intentional with their framing of discussing race and racism in the classroom. This is only a brief IDM and an example of how racism is a global issue. More time and intention must be spent having conversations and discussions on identity, global social structures, colonialism, and imperialism to further students' understanding of the institutionally racist systems that are ingrained in the world. We recommend looking at lessons and materials around identity, race, and belonging within Learning for Justice resources, Rethinking Schools resources, and the forthcoming book *Critical Race Theory and Social Studies Futures: From the Nightmare of Racial Realism to Dreaming Out Loud* to support educators in their discussions of race and racism.

CONCLUSION

The summer of 2020 saw a pivotal shift in the conversation on racism in the United States which reverberated around the globe as we responded to the murder of George Floyd. The conversation on U.S. racism was heard around the world, and people from around the world joined the protests. The COVID-19 global pandemic also exposed the dividing lines of racial discrimination, not only in U.S. access to healthcare, but in how different countries of the world held the keys to health. This moment is an opportune time to contextualize the conversations on anti-racism that situate the United States within broader global movements. Our chapter provides ways in which teachers can begin to have these conversations in their classroom while also acknowledging the globalness of racial justice. We call for critical educators to incorporate the global in their teaching and scholarship. We reimagine global education to be more critical and attuned to the realities of anti-Blackness, Islamophobia, and other aspects that prevent this world from being a just place.

REFERENCES

Adams, M., & Busey, C. L. (2017). "They want to erase that past": Examining race and Afro-Latin@ identity with bilingual third graders. *Social Studies and the Young Learner, 30*(1), 13–18.

Andreotti, V. O. (2014). Soft versus critical global citizenship education. In S. McCloskey (Ed.), *Development Education in Policy and Practice* (pp. 21–31). Palgrave Macmillan UK. https://doi.org/10.1057/9781137324665_2

Aponte-Safe, G. J., & Shatara, H., (2021) Realities and possibilities: Critical global education in Wisconsin elementary social studies standards, *The Critical Social Educator 1*(1). https://doi.org/10.31274/tcse.11480

Ashrawi, H. (2022, February 27). Once & for all: Unless the victim is white, European, Xtian (& US-Israel friendly), resistance is terrorism, Int'l law doesn't apply, vetoes apply, refugees have no right to return (& are unwelcome), & the aggressor has the right to self defence & to acquire territory by war. [Tweet]. Twitter. https://twitter.com/DrHananAshrawi/status/1497957852517912586.

Avila, E. (2016, April 1). *Two-day workshop strengthens ties between Indigenous language digital activists in Peru.* Global Voices. https://globalvoices.org/2016/04/01/two-day-workshop-strengthens-ties-between-indigenous-language-digital-activists-in-peru/

Baker, B. (2020, September 29). *Examining race in East Asian Studies.* Penn Today. https://penntoday.upenn.edu/news/examining-race-east-asian-studies

Beaman, J. (2021, April 1). Race: A never-ending taboo in France. *Georgetown Journal of International Affairs.* https://gjia.georgetown.edu/2021/04/01/race-a-never-ending-taboo-in-france/

Breakstone, J., McGrew, S., Smith, M., Ortega, T., & Wineburg, S. (2018). Why we need a new approach to teaching digital literacy. *Phi Delta Kappan, 99*(1), 27–32. https://doi.org/10.1177/0031721718762419

Burton, N. (2019, October 11). *Meet the young activists of color who are leading the charge against climate disaster.* Vox. https://www.vox.com/identities/2019/10/11/20904791/young-climate-activists-of-color

Busey, C. L., & Coleman-King, C. (2020). All around the world same song: Transnational anti-Black racism and new (and old) directions for critical race theory in educational research. *Urban Education.* https://doi.org/10.1177/0042085920927770.

Busey, C. L., & Dowie-Chin, T. (2021). The making of global Black anti-citizen/citizenship: Situating BlackCrit in global citizenship research and theory. *Theory & Research in Social Education, 49*(2), 153–175. https://doi.org/10.1080/00933104.2020.1869632

Camicia, S. P., & Franklin, B. M. (2011). What type of global community and citizenship? Tangled discourses of neoliberalism and critical democracy in curriculum and its reform. *Globalisation, Societies and Education, 9*(3–4), 311–322. https://doi.org/10.1080/14767724.2011.605303.

Grant, S. G., Swan, K., & Lee, J. (2017). *Inquiry-based practice in social studies education: Understanding the inquiry design model.* Routledge.

Hanvey, R. G. (1982). An attainable global perspective. *Theory Into Practice, 21*(3), 162–167. https://doi.org/10.1080/00405848209543001

Harris, J. C. (2017). Multiracial campus professionals' experiences with multiracial microaggressions. *Journal of College Student Development, 58*(7), 1055–1073. https://doi.org/10.1353/csd.2017.0083.

King, L. J. (2020). Black history is not American history: Toward a framework of Black historical consciousness. *Social Education, 84*(6), 335–341.

Krutka, D. G., Heath, M. K., & Mason, L. E. (2020). Technology won't save us–A call for technoskepticism in social studies. *Contemporary Issues in Technology and Teacher Education, 20*(1), 108–120.

Last Week Tonight with John Oliver. (2021, August 23). *Afghanistan.* https://www.youtube.com/watch?v=dykZyuWci3g

Learning for Justice. (2016). *Social justice standards: The Teaching tolerance anti-bias framework.* https://www.learningforjustice.org/sites/default/files/2020-09/TT-Social-Justice-Standards-Antibias-framework-2020.pdf.

Leonard, S. (2021a, January 28). U.S. policing is a global problem. *AJ+.* https://www.ajplus.net/stories/us-policing-is-a-global-problem.

Leonard, S. (2021b, April 6). Defunding the police Is a global movement. *AJ+.* https://www.ajplus.net/stories/defunding-the-police-is-a-global-movement.

Lim, S. S., & Alrasheed, G. (2021, May 16). Beyond a technical bug: Biased algorithms and moderation are censoring activists on social media. *The Conversation.* https://theconversation.com/beyond-a-technical-bug-biased-algorithms-and-moderation-are-censoring-activists-on-social-media-160669

Lim, S. S., & Tan, K. R. (2020). Front liners fighting fake news: Global perspectives on mobilising young people as media literacy advocates. *Journal of Children and Media, 14*(4), 529–535. https://doi.org/10.1080/17482798.2020.1827817

Magaisa, T. (2021, March 9). The legacy of racism in South Africa: Institutional violence by security forces recalls apartheid abuses. *Human Rights Watch.* https://hrw.org/news/2021/03/09/legacy-racism-south-africa#

Menten, A. (n.d.). Five ways to use technology and digital media for global learning. *Asia Society.* https://asiasociety.org/education/five-ways-use-technology-and-digital-media-global-learning

Merryfield, M. M. (2012). Global education. In W. B. Russell III (Ed.), *Contemporary social studies: An essential reader* (pp. 57–76). Information Age.

Myers, J. P. (2010). The curriculum of globalization. In B. Subedi (Ed.), *Critical global perspectives: Rethinking knowledge about global societies* (pp. 103–120). Information Age.

National Council for the Social Studies. (2013). *College, career, and civic life (C3) framework for social studies state standards: Guidance for enhancing the rigor of K–12 civics, economics, geography, and history.* National Council for the Social Studies. https://www.socialstudies.org/system/files/2022/c3-framework-for-social-studies-rev0617.2.pdf

Noah, T. (2022, February 28). *Russia punished & media shocked by invasion in "relatively civilized" Ukraine* [Video: The Daily Show with Trevor Noah]. YouTube. https://youtu.be/6C38p7N5h9M

Óre, D., & Diaz, L. (2019, July 28). In 21st century, threats 'from all sides' for Latin America's original languages. *Reuters.* https://www.reuters.com/article/us-latam-indigenous-language/in-21st-century-threats-from-all-sides-for-latin-americas-original-languages-idUSKCN1UN04W.

Pronczuk, M., & Maclean, R. (2022, March 1). Africans say Ukrainian authorities hindered them from fleeing. *The New York Times.* https://www.nytimes.com/2022/03/01/world/europe/ukraine-refugee-discrimination.html.

Pérez Huber, L. (2010). Using Latina/o Critical Race Theory (LatCrit) and racist nativism to explore intersectionality in the educational experiences of undocumented Chicana college students. *Educational Foundations, 24,* 77–96.

Reuters. (2022, February 28). Cities around the world light up in Ukrainian Flag colors. *Reuters.* https://www.reuters.com/news/picture/cities-around-the-world-light-up-in-ukra-idUSRTS5S5HT

Robidoux, E. (2019, December 1). Combating linguistic genocide in Colombia. *The Borgen Project.* https://borgenproject.org/tag/linguistic-genocide-in-colombia/.

Shatara, H., & Kim, E. (in press). The global color-line: Critical Race Theory and Global Citizenship Education in conversation and in classrooms. In A. Vickery & N. N. Rodríguez (Eds.), *Critical race theory and social studies futures: From the nightmare of Racial Realism to dreaming out loud.* Teachers College Press.

Silverstein, J. (2021, June 4). The global impact of George Floyd: How Black Lives Matter protests shaped movements around the world. *CBS News.* https://www.cbsnews.com/news/george-floyd-black-lives-matter-impact/

Subedi, B. (2013). Decolonizing the curriculum for global perspectives. *Educational Theory, 63*(6), 621–638. https://doi.org/10.1111/edth.12045

Tawil, R. [@randa_tawil]. (2022, February 27). *what if SNL had had an Iraqi choir? A Syrian choir? a Yemeni choir? An Afghan choir? A Palestinian choir? I want to join the collective grieving so badly but its hard when the collective never grieves for me and mine.* [Tweet]. Twitter. https://twitter.com/randa_tawil/status/1497998239470997506.

Tye, K. A. (2014). Global education: A worldwide movement. An update. *Policy Futures in Education, 12*(7), 855–871.

Underwood, A. (2021, July 2). Resistance and the 'war on terror' in East Africa. *AJ+.* https://www.ajplus.net/stories/resisting-americas-secret-war-in-east-africa.

Vox. (2016, December 2) *Why all maps are wrong.* https://www.youtube.com/watch?v=kIID5FDi2JQ

Willinsky, J. (1998). *Learning to divide the world: Education at empire's end.* University of Minnesota Press.

Yee, V., & El-Naggar, M. (2021, May 18). 'Social media is the mass protest': Solidarity with Palestinians grows online. *The New York Times.* https://www.nytimes.com/2021/05/18/world/middleeast/palestinians-social-media.html

PART IV
RECONCEPTUALIZING CURRICULUM

CHAPTER 11

CENTERING INDIGENOUS VOICES

A Book and Film Study in a University Social Studies Content Course

Linda Doornbos
Oakland University

The dominant narrative of United States history tells the story of our country as settled by European immigrants and that Americans are White. This powerful narrative, embedded in our culture and told in our textbooks, misrepresents, marginalizes, or ignores the experiences of peoples of other races and ethnicities (Levstik & Barton, 2015; Loewen, 2018). In particular, recent social studies research reveals the lack of coverage of Indigenous peoples of the United States in classrooms across grade levels (Journell, 2009; Sabzalian, 2019; Shear, 2015; Wilmore, 1998). Their histories are marginalized, and the nations are portrayed as outsiders in the American quest for expansion and progress. Disrupting the dominant narrative is imperative in understanding and living into the complexities of our country. Transforming how we learn and teach about Indigenous people is of utmost importance as we seek to see, understand, and disrupt racism.

Out of Turmoil: Catalysts for Re-learning, Re-Teaching, and Re-imagining History and Social Science, pages 183–199.
Copyright © 2023 by Information Age Publishing
www.infoagepub.com
All rights of reproduction in any form reserved.

184 • LINDA DOORNBOS

However, research of elementary and secondary preservice teachers indicates not only a lack of content knowledge related to Indigenous peoples' histories but also the lack of opportunities given in teacher preparation programs to critically discern and disrupt preconceived notions of the history of the United States (Chandler & Branscombe, 2015; McCoy, 2018; Sabzalian & Shear, 2018). Furthermore, research highlights the necessity of dialogue on how centering Indigenous peoples' experiences can be used as a call for action in our classrooms (Shear et al., 2015; 2018).

Therefore, I designed a book and film study to center Indigenous experiences and expand preservice teachers' content knowledge and critical thinking about teaching Indigenous-related content in elementary and middle school classrooms. Specifically, this chapter will describe a study of the book, *An Indigenous Peoples History of the United States: For Young People* by Roxanne Dunbar-Ortiz (2019), coupled with the study of the documentary film *Dawnland* (Mazo & Pender-Cudlip, 2018) within a social studies content university course. Intentional instructional strategies engaged preservice teachers in the content to

- *critically discern* how they see and inhabit the world;
- *constantly disrupt* their assumptions regarding Indigenous peoples› past and present experiences; and,
- *continually develop* with others—as producers of knowledge—ways to (re)image and (re)define the way they think, learn, and act as teachers.

I first express the impetus for this work. Then I describe how I embedded the book and film study within my social studies content course. I conclude by inviting other teacher educators to support preservice teachers in the critical work of centering Indigenous voices in the elementary and middle school classrooms.

LEARNING TO "SHUT UP AND LISTEN"

"Don't you white people ever just shut up and listen?" This question—asked in love, yet charged with emotion—was said to me almost thirty years ago by a dear friend and colleague as we talked one day after school. This colleague, Diné[1], had much to teach me—of Dutch descent—about seeing, understanding, and acting differently in the world. He explained that silence from my Navajo students did not mean they were bored, incompetent, or defiant—and, yes, unfortunately, those

---

[1] In "A Note to Readers" (p. vii-ix) in Roxanne Dunbar-Ortiz (2019) *Indigenous Peoples' History of the United States for Young People,* explains to readers how naming groups of Native people is in a constant state of change. Diné is used here because this is my friend's preferred naming. Navajo, Zuni, and Hopi were, at the time, the most common names for the tribes living in the Southwest. Throughout the social studies content course and in the remainder of this paper, I use Indigenous peoples to acknowledge and honor those who called this land home long before the arrival of "settlers."

were some of my assumptions. Instead, silence in the Navajo culture is often a sign of respect as one first listens and then gives an opinion when the time is right. Additionally, silence is commonly an indication that individuals are not setting themselves apart or above their peers.

The above conversation is one of many necessary encounters I experienced while teaching at a former missionary boarding school in New Mexico. I am a cisgender White, middle-class, Protestant Christian who spent my first 25 years in a White world. In retrospect, it was in this place, this land of the Navajo, Zuni, and Hopi, that I came face to face with whiteness and began the journey of shutting up to listen. These encounters ignited my life-long commitment to constantly discern how I see and understand the world, disrupt the harm done by the silencing, omitting, or misrepresenting the histories and stories of people of color; and with others develop new ways of defining what it means to know, to teach, and to learn.

Influential in this journey was witnessing this former boarding school's commitment to making amends with its "White is right" past. While it is beyond the scope of this paper to recall the over 100 years of history regarding this particular missionary "Indian" boarding school, or the recent atrocities surfacing regarding the mistreatment of children in boarding schools in Canada and Michigan, suffice to say that much has and continues to change. As a boarding school, the primary goal of education was to assimilate "heathen Indians" into the White culture—thus, stamping out Indigenous identity and culture as part of the Christianizing process. Noteworthy is this school's humble recognition of its harmful past and its willingness to begin a path of reconciliation and renewal to create a better future. As of 2021, the school serves one of the most diverse student populations in terms of ethnic, economic, religious, and academic diversity of any Christian school in the country (Hoezee & Meehan, 1996).

Just as the school has and continues to be on a journey of reconciliation and renewal for harm done, living in the "White is right" narrative, so too have I. My experiences in New Mexico play a central role in my commitment to personally and professionally listen to voices disrupting the dominant narrative and join with them in actively making the world more just and equitable. Currently, my work as a teacher educator involves bringing critical counternarratives into my social studies content course. Through critical counternarratives, I seek to create opportunities to listen to voices that disrupt and challenge the dominant narrative.

PERSPECTIVES

The following three perspectives infused throughout the designing and enacting of the book club and film study: Tribal critical race theory (TribalCrit), critical whiteness pedagogy (CWP), and the teaching history for justice framework (Martell & Stevens, 2021). These perspectives support the intentional pedagogical decision to center Indigenous peoples' experiences and invite future teachers to take seriously the need to bring the historically silenced, omitted, or marginalized voices into the classroom.

Tribal Critical Race Theory

TribalCrit (Brayboy, 2005), as a theoretical framework, addresses Indigenous peoples' issues in the United States. With its roots in critical race theory, which highlights racism as pervasive in our society, TribalCrit highlights pervasive colonization—not as something that happened in the past, but rather structurally permeating our life as a nation. Brayboy (2005) stated, "It is my hope and belief that TribalCrit begins to allow us to change the ways that Indigenous students think about schools and, perhaps more importantly, the way that both schools and educational researchers think about American Indian students" (p.442). The framework's nine interrelated tenets provide the foundational work for this change. It supports teacher educators and researchers in understanding peoples' unique racialized and political state as members of sovereign nations. See Appendix A for a list of the nine tenets.

These nine tenets offered me ways to think, imagine, and create the educational space for addressing the often unknown or untold racism in teaching about Indigenous peoples and cultures in classrooms. Preservice teachers take the social studies content course early in our preparation program as a prerequisite for the social studies methods course. With intentionality, I embedded the book study to center Indigenous peoples' history of the United States.

Simultaneously, in the documentary film *Dawnland* (Mazo & Pender-Cudlip, 2018), Mazo & Pender-Cudlip exposed the "harmful, complex positioning of Indigenous peoples in the context of colonialism on the one hand and Indigenous traditions, knowledge, and inherent rights to self-government on the other" (Calderón, 2019, p. 2). TribalCrit provided the theoretical lens used in designing the book and the film study to expand students' content knowledge and critical thinking about teaching Indigenous-related content in elementary and middle school classrooms.

Critical Whiteness Pedagogy

Whereas TribalCrit provided the theoretical lens, CWP informed the pedagogical choice to embed the book and film study in the social studies content course. Whiteness—as a social construct of hierarchical and hegemonic power—informs a superior way of knowing and being that has created, contributed to, and systematically continues to dehumanize Black, Indigenous, and people of color (Doane & Bonilla-Silva, 2003; Kincheloe & Steinberg, 1998; Swartz, 2007). Systematic whiteness in education is pervasive through the "official knowledge"—constructed and consisting of white norms, white knowledge, and white common sense (Apple, 1993; Leonardo, 2009). The official knowledge that manifests itself in social studies is articulated in Chandler and Branscombe's (2015) White social studies (WSS). The ten components of WSS expose ways seen and unseen whiteness maintain the status quo through dominant racial thinking and dominant historical narratives. See Appendix A for a list of the ten components.

If left unexamined, teachers—who make content and pedagogical choices within the construct of the WSS approach—will continue to implicitly and explicitly cause harm. Challenging these choices is imperative, especially since most of the U.S. teaching force in K–12 is White, middle-class females (National Center for Education Statistics, 2020). Critical whiteness studies (CWS) provide the necessary framework to deconstruct—decenter—whiteness and interrogate how whiteness creates a "violent condition within which people of color must racially survive" (Matias & Mackey, 2016, p. 35). As an extension of CWS, critical whiteness pedagogy (CWP) opens up space for making the intentional content pedagogical choices needed to challenge the tenacity of WSS (Hawkman, 2018).

CWP informed the content chosen for the social studies course and the strategies selected to study the book, *The Indigenous Peoples' History of the United States* (Dunbar-Ortiz, 2019), along with the film *Dawnland* (Mazo & Pender-Cudlip, 2018). As counternarratives, the book and the film provided intentional spaces for Indigenous peoples to speak for themselves (Buchanan, 2015; Marcus & Stoddard, 2009). In doing so, I put forth the challenge to: "Shut up and listen" to Indigenous voices; to interrogate whiteness as property at the individual, group, and structural levels; and to expose what role we might play as future social studies teachers in systematically perpetuating white supremacy.

Justice in History Education

The third perspective informing my work as interwoven with TribalCrit and CWP was Martell and Stevens' (2021) justice-oriented teaching of history, specifically their "thinking like an activist" framework. The framework has three components: (a) *cultural preparation*—envisioning a better, more equal, and just society through (un)learning systematic structures of oppression and working with others to bring about lasting change; (b) *critical analysis*—recognizing the unequal power relationships that have created and maintained systematic oppression; and (c) *collective action*—understanding the confrontational and non-cooperative actions of past and present social movements to disrupt systematic inequality.

Putting these components into practice allows educators to understand justice and do the work of justice. Understanding justice involves exposing unequal power relationships that have created systemic racism, sexism, classism, ableism, homophobia, and other forms of oppression and discrimination. Doing the work of justice involves acting with others to disrupt oppression to create a more just and equitable future. Noteworthy is the framework's intentional move away from glorifying individual actors in history to centering the social movements needed (past, present, and future) to disrupt inequality and build a better world.

Therefore, so that we understood and did justice, I crafted the book and film study to incorporate the three pedagogical approaches needed to enact the "thinking like an activist" framework—social inquiry, critical multiculturalism, and transformative citizenship (Martell & Stevens, 2021). Through critical social inquiry, I sought to raise students' awareness and ability to identify the past and present social injustices towards Indigenous peoples in the United States. Critical multicultural pedagogy exposed institutional inequalities resulting in cultural genocide, intergenerational trauma, and the omission, silencing, or marginalization of Indigenous peoples' experiences in the social studies curriculum. Lastly, as we engaged in activities to examine echoes of the past in present-day realities, I challenged students to see the necessity of turning knowledge into action. Importantly, I wanted my preservice teachers to understand transformative citizenship—to see the necessity of collective activism to ensure the systematic changes needed for a more just and equitable future for Indigenous peoples.

OVERVIEW AND DESCRIPTION OF BOOK AND FILM STUDY

The book *Indigenous Peoples' History of the United States for Young People* (Dunbar-Ortiz, 2019) is adapted for upper elementary and middle school students. It reframes the origin of the history of the United States from Indigenous peoples› perspective, thereby correcting the dominant story. Unlike most books for children, textbooks, and curriculum, a distinguishing feature is that it tells the story from pre-European North America to the present. Students are presented with the doctrine of discovery, the U.S. origin story myth of being "discovered," and the central role settler colonialism and government policies played in forced assimilation and cultural genocide. Significantly, readers are challenged to join Indigenous peoples who always have and still are involved in resistance against imperialism.

In the documentary *Dawnland* (Mazo & Pender-Cudlip, 2018), viewers are taken behind the scenes of the first official United States Truth and Reconciliation Commission›s (TRC) investigation into the removal of Native children from their homes to "save them from being Indian." Powerful personal testimonies of Maine›s Wabanaki (People of the Dawn) and interviews of TRC members expose the complex "messiness" in unearthing harmful truths and in moving forward to heal the deeply embedded mistrust between state and tribal members.

In Winter 2021, I integrated the book and the film into my social studies content course. In doing so, we centered Indigenous peoples' experiences into the study of our state and then situated these experiences in a larger context. We grappled with two questions: "What does it mean to be civilized?"; and as suggested in the film's viewing guide (Lesser, 2019), "What is the relationship between the taking the land and the taking the children?" The goal was to increase our content knowledge and, as a result of these, at times, difficult encounters, consider how to turn knowledge into action and bring Indigenous peoples' experiences into the preservice teachers' future classrooms.

Due to COVID-19 restrictions, this content course was asynchronous, consisting of 14 weekly modules. However, I was pleased when all the students committed to meeting synchronously on Zoom four times for our book and film study. Given the large class size, I offered two-time slots per meeting so that a smaller group size would provide more opportunities for active participation. In advance of each book and film study, students completed reading and viewing guides developed with prompts to draw their attention before, during, and after reading and viewing to

- critically discern—investigate assumptions about how they have come to see and live in the world;
- critically disrupt those assumptions to make visible and problematic the inequalities they encounter, and be willing to
- continually develop with others ways to (re)define, (re)imagine, and act to create a more just and equitable, democratic society.

Each book and film study centered around a prominent theme drawn from the reading and viewing, and each followed a similar pattern. The study opened with our university land acknowledgment, a map activity, and a quote from the book to draw attention to the particular theme. Then exploring and analyzing primary and secondary sources provided us with opportunities to analyze, explore, and confront our nation's history to disrupt the narrow, dominant narrative and make sense of the encountered broader, more inclusive narrative. The final activity of each meeting included an additional quote to specifically draw our attention to Indigenous peoples' acts of resistance. In our 90 minutes together, we examined and explored; cried and celebrated; questioned and wondered about the encountered content. Appendix B provides the reader access to a Google Folder containing the reading and viewing guides, a Google Slides presentation of an overview of book and film study meetings, and other resources.

The book study began with an acknowledgment of the ancestral, traditional, and contemporary lands of the Anishinaabe, known as the Three Fire Council, comprised of the Ojibwe, Odawa, and Potawatomi—whose land on which we now work and live. Integrated into the university land acknowledgment was the

TABLE 11.1. Book Study #1 Overview: Introduction—Chapter 2

Theme	Sophisticated vs. Savage
Opening quote	Learning to ask questions about who tells a history, or a story, is an important goal of this book. What you read shapes how you think about the world, whether it is history or story. And it shapes how you look at and think about people in the world too (Dunbar-Ortiz, 2019, p. 20).
Explore, analyze, confront	Key topics—naming, land, doctrine of discovery, manifest destiny, settler colonialism, white supremacy through primary source image analysis, video/lecture clips, and small and whole group discussions
Resistance quote	Indigenous peoples resisted invasions of their homelands and centuries of destruction and exploitations by the colonizers. Today they speak back, as individuals and as sovereign nations, against ongoing trauma and the consequences of conquest and terminal narratives. With their bodies, their art, and their words, they tell a different story (Dunbar-Ortiz, 2019, p. 46).

analysis of a state map and other websites that provided a window into our state tribes' cultures, history, and current residency. This information, along with the opening quote, challenged us to consider the significant role the Indigenous communities had and continue to have in shaping this region. On the one hand, the opening quote initiated a robust conversation exposing students' frustration—and even some anger—regarding their lack of knowledge of past and present-day Indigenous experiences. On the other hand, it invited students to re-learn and re-examine historical narrative—to ask tough questions, disrupt harmful assumptions, and think differently about the world and their place in it. Together we took up the challenge to examine opposing concepts of sophistication versus savagery as we investigated the compelling question—"What does it mean to be civilized?"

We explored, analyzed, and confronted key topics of naming, land, doctrine of discovery, manifest destiny, settler colonialism, and white supremacy through the following activities. First, we watched two minutes of the short film, *A Conversation with Native Americans on Race* (The Learning Network, 2021) that profiles seven individuals' experiences of living, thriving, and resisting in a society where they are often invisible. Students drew on these personal testimonies in breakout rooms to share their thinking and discuss how "naming" (Dunbar-Ortiz, 2019, p. ix) invites us to embrace Indigenous identities and experiences.

During the subsequent activities, we explored, analyzed, and confronted the phrase, "Everything in U.S. history is about the land" (Dunbar-Ortiz, 2019, p. 1). We listened to a small section of a lecture on the doctrine of discovery by Mark Charles (2018)—a Native American activist, public speaker, and author. To deepen our knowledge of this doctrine that has profoundly shaped our nation, we engaged in a group analysis of an image on the doctrine of discovery and in a Padlet activity to bring attention to the significance of how the doctrine fueled white supremacy and settler colonialism—White European settlers claimed to be instruments of divine design and culturally superiority.

The remaining small group discussion pertained to land as private property, white supremacy, and terminal narratives. Together we unveiled the stark reality of Indigenous civilization's sophistication—not savagery. Specifically, we acknowledged Indigenous peoples' land stewardship, elaborate roads, advanced agriculture practices, and well-developed governance systems. Then, in conclusion, the resistance quote brought us back full circle to acknowledge that we reside on stolen land, have insufficient knowledge of the origin story of the United States, and need to unlearn our preconceived notions of savagery. We ended our time together celebrating how sophisticated Indigenous peoples—individually and communally—have been in the past and continue in the present to speak out, and in doing so, tell a different story.

Our second book and film study began with integrating the university land acknowledgment with an analysis of a state map depicting ceding treaties. This map, along with the opening quote, drew us into the conflicting concepts of culti-

TABLE 11.2. Book and Film Study #2 Overview: Chapters 3–5 and ACT I

Theme	Cultivate vs. Conquer
Opening quote	With utter disregard for the Indigenous ways of thinking about the land, both sacred and non-sacred, the colonizers viewed all the land and resources they saw as things to own and exploit. They believed that their god told them told them it was theirs for the taking, even if that meant blood would be spilled (Dunbar-Ortiz, 2019, p. 67).
Explore, analyze, confront	Key topics—bloody footprints, the cult of covenant, and American exceptionalism through maps, a video clip, a song analysis, and small and whole group discussions
Resistance quote	From the first moment Europeans stepped onto what came to be known as North America, they left bloody footprints wherever they went seeking land and resources. They found, however, that Indigenous people were not easily scared off or conquered. Even after the birth of the United States, Native peoples would not get out of the way. They were determined to fight for their homelands, their communities, and their nations (Dunbar-Ortiz, 2019, p. 87).

vating versus conquering. In doing so, we considered the dire consequences when conflicting cultures collide, as portrayed in Chapters 3–5 and Act I of *Dawnland*.

We explored, analyzed, and confronted the critical topics of the cult of covenant, bloody footprints, and American exceptionalism during the following activities. We began with document-based questions as we listened to the remaining four minutes of the video, *A Conversation with Native Americans on Race* (The Learning Network, 2021). Powerfully and effectively, these Indigenous voices speak about the harsh realities of broken treaties, colonization, and cultural genocide—while at the same time offering healing and hope through decolonizing acts of embracing Indigenous languages, cultures, and rights to sovereignty.

We then listened to "America the Beautiful" (Abby & Annalie, 2018) sung by two White female girls as they stroll through pristine neighborhoods, pause on the steps of a church, and reverently place flowers at a war memorial. In breakout rooms, students connected the words and images of the song to the book and film regarding the cult of covenant with its myth of the pristine wilderness, the Calvinist origin story, and the sacred land becoming real estate. As part of the discussion, students interrogated whiteness as property at the individual, group, and structural levels; then, as a whole group, we sought to expose what role we might play as future social studies teachers in either perpetuating or disrupting white supremacy.

Next, we dug into the roots of genocide by investigating the bloody footprints of European settlers conquering land and resources to own and exploit. Each of the four groups used Padlet to record the story of their assigned group—The Powhattan Confederacy, the Pequot Nation, the Cherokee Nation, and the Shawnee and Delaware Nation. In a gallery walk, we honored nations' location, uniqueness, and acts of resistance in fighting for the survival of their homelands and communities.

We then examined the relationship between the taking of land and the taking of children as we reviewed Act I of *Dawnland*. Students recalled the emotional testimonies of the Wabanaki tribal members that exposed atrocities of forced assimilation to "save them from being Indian" within boarding schools and forced foster care into "White" families. Noteworthy was how some students verbalized the significance of the Sacred Fire Ceremony as a space of healing and hope for intergenerational trauma caused by American exceptionalism that claims "White is right." The resistance quote captured well the consequences of cultures colliding—one seeking to conquer and control, and the other determined to cultivate and celebrate their connection to the land and each other.

We began the third book and film study with the land acknowledgment, followed by interacting with a time-lapse map of the transfer of Indigenous lands between 1776 and 1887 and the establishment of reservations. This map, along with the opening quote, highlighted the conflicting concepts of existence versus extinction. In doing so, Chapters 6–8 and Act II of *Dawnland* drew us back into our inquiry of what it means to be civilized and consider the relationship between the taking of the land and the taking of children.

We explored, analyzed, and confronted the critical topics of ethnic cleansing, government policies, and forced assimilation during the following activities. A co-constructed word cloud provided the impetus for a critical discussion of Thomas Jefferson's and Andrew Jackson's pursuit of Indigenous homelands. In breakout rooms, selected quotes and questions assisted students in discerning and disrupting romanticized, heroic representations of these past presidents. Chapter 6 exposed Jefferson and Jackson's raw, harsh realities of acquiring wealth and status through actions that directly or indirectly harmed others. Jefferson's ideas and government policies that cheated Indigenous nations out of their land paved the way for Jackson's horrific acts of forced removals and attempts at ethnic cleansing.

Next, an analysis of the song "My Country Tis of Thee" (Cedarmont Kids, 2015) allowed us to confront Jefferson's notion of building a country that spanned

TABLE 11.3. Book and Film Study #3: Chapters 6–8 and ACT II

Theme	Exist vs. Extinct
Opening quote	Every Indigenous nation on the continent eventually dealt with settlers who, with the help of the U.S. government, were bent on its destruction, removal, or assimilation (Dunbar-Ortiz, 2019, p. 121).
Explore, analyze, confront	Key topics—ethnic cleansing, government policies, and assimilation through the power of words, a song analysis, primary source analysis, and small and whole group discussions
Resistance quote	The long centuries of armed conflict in defense of the homeland ended. However, through innovation and persistence Indigenous people have continued to fight to protect and preserve their lands, their languages, and their ways of life (Dunbar-Ortiz, 2019, p. 156).

the continent from one coast to the other. In reality, through past encounters with Spain and Mexico, Indigenous peoples already connected the Atlantic to the Pacific through "networks of diplomacy and cultural exchange, predating Jefferson's idea by several thought years" (Dunbar-Ortiz, 2019, p. 122). In small groups, students used Jamboards to capture the particular experiences of Indigenous peoples of the southwestern United States. A gallery walk allowed us to listen and respond to each story. Noteworthy is how these counter stories disrupted the textbook version of westward expansion that promotes the settlers' belief that the "United States was preordained by a higher power to fill the continent" (Dunbar-Ortiz, 2019, p. 136).

We then examined the relationship between the taking of land and the taking of children as we reviewed Act II of *Dawnland*. Particularly salient was the tension rising between the testimonies shared by the social workers—revealing varying levels of awareness of the Native child welfare practices—and the Wabanaki individual recollections of being taken from parents, made to sit in bleach baths, forbidden to speak their Native language, and stripped of their "inferior" culture. These heart-wrenching stories exposed present-day realities of ethnic cleansing, government policies, and forced assimilation. We ended this meeting with a time of quiet reflection to decompress and ponder the harm of colonization—the theft of life and land—through acts that support the power of some people over others.

In our fourth and final book and film study our land acknowledgment was followed by "word" acknowledgments of the phrases "merciless Indian savages" as presented in the Declaration of Independence and "we the people" in the Preamble to the Constitution. Students reflected on the land and word acknowledgment as they analyzed the "America the Beautiful" YouTube video (2021, November 7)—a much more inclusive version than the one shown in our first meeting. This

TABLE 11.4. Book and Film Study #4: Chapters 9–Conclusion and ACT III

Theme	Embrace vs. erase
Opening quote	Indigenous nations had homelands and reservations where they continued their traditional ways. The existence of a people with a prior claim to the land whose values, languages, and lifeways differed from those of European American society was a constant source of anxiety to White settlers. (Dunbar-Ortiz, 2019, p. 158)
Explore, analyze, confront	Key topics—sovereignty, self-determination, and echoes of the past in the present through a song analysis, hexagonal thinking activity, case study analysis, and small and whole group discussions
Resistance quote	Their activism can be described as a persistent, organized, and increasing intertribal resistance to federal policies that undermined Indigenous self-determination and sovereignty (p.176). The persistence of the elders and the rising generation raised awareness of Indigenous peoples' concerns at many levels of U.S. society and led to the passage of laws that continue to galvanize and influence the work of Indigenous peoples today (Dunbar-Ortiz, 2019, p. 201).

song and the opening quote invited us to acknowledge our country's past injustices and past and present acts of resistance of Indigenous peoples.

Students participated in activities to explore, analyze and confront the critical topics of sovereignty, self-determination, and echoes of the past in the present. First, a hexagonal thinking activity allowed students to examine the persistence of sovereignty (Chapter 9) and specific acts of Indigenous activism from the 1960s through 2013 (Chapter 10). In small groups, students used the geometric shapes to connect ideas/concepts and from their assigned chapter—a process where the results look entirely different for each group. Students used their hexagonal designs to interact with the big ideas of Chapter 9—assimilation, white supremacy, sovereignty, allotment, and intergenerational trauma with the acts of intertribal resistance described in Chapter 10—Alcatraz, fish-in occupation, Trail of Broken Treaties caravan, and activism that led to the Indian Self-Determination and Education Assistance Act and the Indian Child Welfare Act. Then each group shared their designs and provided evidence to support the reasoning for their configurations.

The hexagonal activity set the stage for discussing Act III of *Dawnland*. Students drew from their viewing guide reflections to examine the contrasting views of existence—sovereignty, self-determination, and cultural identity—with those of extinction—institutional racism, termination, and cultural genocide. We then processed how the stories of the Wabanaki people mirrored the history of Indigenous peoples as presented in the book. The TRC uncovered past atrocities and exposed ways state power undermined Wabanaki sovereignty and cultural identity. Noteworthy is the rising tension and immense challenges that the commission faced as they worked toward truth and reconciliation to ensure the survival of the Wabanaki—People of the Dawn.

In the culminating activity students explored, analyzed, and confronted "echoes of the past in the present" (Dunbar-Ortiz, 2019, p. 220). In small groups, students investigated the case study of Indigenous peoples' resistance to the Dakota Access Pipeline as presented in the book. Using a graphic organizer, students analyzed and applied the nine key concepts and issues discussed throughout the book (p. 220) to Standing Rock in the twenty-first century. Then after a whole group discussion, students returned to breakout rooms to repeat the applied analysis. They choose to analyze the Wabanaki's experiences as presented in *Dawnland*, the Navajo Nation's disproportionate suffering of higher rates of infection and death from COVID-19, or Enbridge Line 5 and the Great Lakes Tunnel—a hot topic in our state.

We concluded our final book and film study contemplating the invitation presented by Dunbar-Ortiz (2019):

> While living persons are not responsible for what their ancestors did, they are responsible for the society they live in, which is a product of the past. As you've read through this book, you've seen many instances in which a country that sees itself as exceptional did not behave in exceptional ways. You learned a lot about the ways that Indigenous peoples view their encounters with colonizers. What does this mean

for you? You can turn your knowledge into action in situations that affect the lives of Native. (pp. 226–227)

Students shared ways the book and film had helped them discern and disrupt what they knew or did not know about Indigenous peoples' past and present. We then asked, "Now what?" and challenged ourselves to not only consider the necessity of individual action, but also to the collective activism needed to interrupt deeply embedded institutional racism.

While students recognized the need for action, they willingly admitted a lack of clarity on their next steps to challenge, interrupt, and counter the ever-present dominant narrative. Some talked of the need to continue expanding their content knowledge, and others suggested bringing children's literature books into the classroom. We acknowledged that the "struggle is real" and found hope in the fact that we could continue our work together in the additional two social studies methods courses required in our university's teacher preparation program.

A CALL TO COLLECTIVE ACTIVISM

Indigenous peoples' histories are marginalized, and the nations are portrayed as outsiders in the American quest for expansion and progress. Transforming how we learn and teach about Indigenous people is of utmost importance as we seek to understand and live into the complexities of our country. This chapter invites teacher educators to consider ways in which a book and film study can provide space for preservice teachers to discern how they see and inhabit the world, disrupt their assumptions regarding Indigenous peoples past and present experiences, and begin to develop with others how to ensure ways of centering Indigenous peoples' experiences in their future classrooms. Indigenous voices invite us to:

- experience their sophisticated (vs. savage) ways of knowing and being;
- examine the importance of cultivating and respecting the land (vs. conquer and control);
- acknowledge Indigenous peoples' existence (vs. extinction); and
- embrace (vs. erase) their sovereignty and right to self-determination.

Heeding these voices is imperative as collectively we take action to support preservice teachers in including Indigenous peoples' history and present-day joys and challenges into elementary and middle school classrooms.

APPENDIX A

Nine tenets of Tribal Critical Race Theory (Brayboy, 2005, pp. 429–430).

1. Colonization is endemic to society.
2. U.S. policies toward Indigenous peoples are rooted in imperialism, White supremacy, and desire for material gain.
3. Indigenous peoples occupy a liminal space that accounts for both the political and racialized natures of our identities.
4. Indigenous peoples have a desire to obtain and forge tribal sovereignty, self-determination, and self-identification.
5. The concepts of culture, knowledge, and power take on new meaning when examined through an Indigenous lens.
6. Governmental policies and educational policies toward Indigenous peoples are intimately linked around the problematic goal of assimilation.
7. Tribal philosophies, beliefs, customs, traditions, and visions for the future are central to understanding the lived realities of Indigenous peoples, but they also illustrate the differences and adaptability among individuals and groups.
8. Stories are not separate from theory; they make up theory and are, therefore, real and legitimate sources of data and ways of being.
9. Theory and practice are connected in deep and explicit ways such that scholars must work towards social change.

10 Components of White Social Studies (Chandler & Branscombe, 2015, pp. 63–64).

1. Employs common sense, essentialized understandings of race to reify the historical status quo,
2. Has enacted (pedagogical) and personal (philosophical) traits that impact classroom pedagogy,
3. Assumes that dominant narratives and paradigms of thinking in the social sciences, particularly historical investigation, are unproblematic,
4. Has a deep, personal, and racial investment in the symbolic, fictive imaginary of the United States as a polity,
5. Is inherently contradictory and self-reinforcing,
6. Is 'raceproof' (i.e., historical/social phenomena can be explained without race),
7. Ignores contemporary, current events that cast into question historical narratives' legitimacy and, more importantly, their meaning,

8. Utilizes selective use of aspects of historical thinking to support prior claims (i.e., The selective use of chronology: Declaration of Independence is important, slavery is not),
9. Rest squarely in the transmission camp of social studies theory,
10. Protects dominant, European/White narratives from criticism.

APPENDIX B

The following Google Folder (https://bit.ly/ExistenceasResistance) contains:

1. *Dawnland* (Mazo & Pender-Cudlip, 2018): Documentary Viewing Guides and streaming rights information.
2. Existence as Resistance: Google Slide Overview of Book/Film Study Meetings.
3. *Indigenous Peoples' History of the United State for Young People* (Dunbar-Ortiz, 2019): Guided Reading Guides.
4. Additional Resources.

REFERENCES

Abby & Annalie. (2018, July 1). *America the beautiful* [Video]. YouTube. https://www.youtube.com/watch?v=bGzvyhEfrdo

America the Beautiful. (2021, November 7). [Video]. YouTube. https://www.youtube.com/watch?v=xJc_SRsbGS0&t=1s

Apple, N. W. (1993). *Official knowledge: Democratic education in a conservative age*. Routledge. https://doi.org/10.1080/1085566032000074940

Brayboy, B. (2005). Toward a tribal critical race theory in education. *The Urban Review*, *37*(5), 425–446. https://doi.org/10.1007/s11256-005-0018-y

Buchanan, L. B. (2015). Fostering historical thinking toward civil rights movement counter-narratives: Documentary film in elementary social studies. *The Social Studies*, *106*(2), 47–56. https://doi.org/10.1080/00377996.2014.973012

Calderón, D. (2019, June). *Tribal critical race theory: Origins, applications, and implications*. (Research Briefs Series, Issue 19). Center for Critical Race Studies in Education at UCLA. https://issuu.com/almaiflores/docs/dc_tribalcrit

Cedarmont Kids. (2015, July 2). *My country tis of thee.* [Video]. YouTube. https://www.youtube.com/watch?v=D2JUvKZoAsI

Chandler, P., & Branscombe, A. (2015). White social studies: Protecting the white racial code. In P. Chandler (Ed.), *Doing race in social studies: Critical perspectives* (pp. 61–87). Information Age Publishing.

Charles, M. (2018, May 20). The Doctrine of Discovery: A lecture by Mark Charles [Lecture recording]. https://wirelesshogan.com/2018/05/31/the-doctrine-of-discovery-a-lecture-by-mark-charles/

A conversation with Native Americans on race. (2021). *The Learning Network*. https://www.nytimes.com/2021/10/21/learning/film-club-a-conversation-with-native-americans-on-race.html

Doane, A. W., & Bonilla-Silva, E. (2003). *White out: The significance of racism*. Routledge.

Dunbar-Ortiz, R. (2019). *Indigenous peoples' history of the United States for young people*. Beacon Press.

Hawkman, A. M. (2018). Exposing whiteness in the elementary social studies methods' classroom: In pursuit of developing anti-racist teacher education candidates. In S. B. Shear, C. M. Tschida, E. Bellows, L. Brown Buchanan, & E. E. Saylor (Eds.), *(Re)Imagining elementary social studies: A controversial reader* (pp. 49–71). Information Age Publishing.

Hoezee, S., & Meehan, C. H. (1996). *Flourishing in the Land: A hundred-year history of Christian reformed missions in North America*. Eerdmans Publishing Company.

Journell, W. (2009). An incomplete history: Representations of American Indians in state social studies standards. *Journal of American Indian Education, 48*(2), 18–32.

Kincheloe, J. L., & Steinberg, S. R. (1998). Addressing the crisis of whiteness: Reconfiguring white identity in a pedagogy of whiteness. In J. L. Kincheloe, S. R. Steinberg, N. M. Rodriguez, & R. E. Chennault (Eds.), *White, reign: Deploying whiteness in America* (pp. 3–29). St. Martin's Press.

The Learning Network. (2021). *A conversation with Native Americans on race*. https://www.nytimes.com/2021/10/21/learning/film-club-a-conversation-with-nativeamericans-on-race.html

Leonardo, Z. (2009). *Race, Whiteness, and education*. Routledge.

Lesser, M. (2019). *Dawnland teacher's guide*. Upstander Project. https://upstanderproject.org/dawnland

Levstik, L. S., & Barton, K. C. (2015). *Doing history: Investigating with children in elementary and middle school* (5th ed.). Routledge.

Loewen, J. W. (2018). *Lies my teacher told me: Everything your American textbook got wrong*. The New Press.

Marcus, A. S., & Stoddard, J. D. (2009). The inconvenient truth about teaching history with documentary film: Strategies for presenting multiple perspective and teaching controversial issues. *The Social Studies, 100*(6), 279–284. https://doi.org/10.1080/00377990903283957

Martell, C. C., & Stevens, K. M. (2021). *Teaching history for justice: Centering activism in students' study of the past*. Teachers College Press.

Matias, C. E., & Mackey, J. (2016). Breakin' down whiteness in antiracist teaching: Introducing whiteness pedagogy. *The Urban Review, 48*(1), 32–50. https://doi.org/10.1007/s11256-015-0344-7

Mazo, A., & Pender-Cudlip, B. (Directors). (2018). *Dawnland* [Documentary film]. Upstander Project.

McCoy, M. L. (2018). Preparing social studies educators to teach American Indian boarding schools. In S. B. Shear, C. M. Tschida, E. Bellows, L. Brown Buchanan, & E. E. Saylor (Eds.), *(Re)Imagining elementary social studies: A controversial reader* (pp. 255–277). Information Age Publishing.

National Center for Education Statistics. (2020). *Race and ethnicity of public school teachers and their students*. https://nces.ed.gov/pubs2020/2020103/index.asp

Sabzalian, L. (2019). The tensions between Indigenous sovereignty and multicultural citizenship education: Toward an anticolonial approach to civic education. *Theory &*

Research in Social Education, 47(3), 311–346. https://doi.org/10.1080/00933104.2019.1639572

Sabzalian, L., & Shear, S. B. (2018). Confronting colonial blindness in citizenship education. In. S. B. Shear, C. M. Tschida, E. Bellows, L. Brown Buchanan, & E. E. Saylor (Eds.), *(Re)Imagining elementary social studies: A controversial reader* (pp. 153–176). Information Age Publishing.

Shear, S. B. (2015). Cultural genocide masked as education. In W. B. Russell (Ed.), *Doing race in social studies: Critical perspective* (pp. 13–40). Information Age Publishing.

Shear, S. B., Knowles, R. T., Soden, G. J., & Castro, A. J. (2015). Manifesting destiny: Re/presentations of Indigenous peoples in K–12 U.S. history standards. *Theory & Research in Social Education, 43*(1), 68–101. https://doi.org/10.1080/00933104.2014.999849

Shear, S. B., Sabzalian, L., & Buchanan, L. (2018). Affirming Indigenous sovereignty: A civics inquiry. *Social Studies and the Young Learner, 31*(1), 12–18.

Swartz, E. (2007). Stepping outside the master script: Re-connecting the history of multicultural America. *The Journal of Negro Education, 76*(2), 173–186.

Wilmore, L. (1998). First peoples first. *Poverty & Race, 71*(1), 11-12 .

CHAPTER 12

JOURNEY BOX PROJECTS FOR A POST-PANDEMIC WORLD

How the Experiences of Teacher Candidates Invite the (Re)imagination of Culturally Relevant Social Studies Education

Kaitlin E. Popielarz
University of Texas at San Antonio

The system of schooling in the United States continues to (re)produce racist, classist, and sexist systems of oppression in which the country itself was founded upon (Ladson-Billings, 2006; Love, 2019). This is particularly transparent in social studies education which often perpetuates a biased view of the world through a white, Eurocentric, patriarchal, and heteronormative gaze (Morrison, 2019). Ladson-Billings (1995, 2001b) has called for a culturally relevant approach to interdisciplinary social studies education to foster social studies education as collaborative, empowering, and meaningful. To respond to this call, I guide elementary teacher candidates (TCs) in the (re)learning of history and social science education through the curation of multi-modal journey box projects (Alarcón et al., 2015; Labbo & Field, 1999; Salinas et al., 2016). TCs critically analyze the state-mandated social studies standards and the National Council for the Social Studies

(NCSS) C3 Framework to learn about a specific person, time period, or event that is typically marginalized within social studies education. TCs then build a journey box project filled with primary and secondary sources, narrative storytelling, and differentiated curricular resources to situate critical counter narratives in the elementary social studies classroom (Ladson-Billings & Tate, 1995). TCs present their journey box projects to peers, family members, faculty, and community members through a gallery walk.

Social studies as an interdisciplinary anchor to enact culturally relevant learning experiences within PreK–12 classrooms and teacher education programs (TEPs). Through the framework and practice of culturally relevant pedagogy (CRP), this chapter suggests how social studies may emerge as an essential foundation for teachers and learners to cultivate a socio-political/critical consciousness that is necessary for purposeful and meaningful education during and beyond the time of pandemic (Ladson-Billings, 2001b, 2021b). Ladson-Billings (2021a) spoke of the four intersecting pandemics currently facing many students and educators: systemic racism, capitalism, climate crises, and the COVID-19 pandemic. Advocating for "the hard re-set" to education, Ladson-Billings (2021b) invites educators to imagine and enact a post-pandemic pedagogy in which the classroom becomes a space to engage in CRP.

To respond to Ladson-Billings' lifelong work to revitalize education through CRP, this chapter shares how TCs experience the curation of multi-modal journey box projects as they (re)learn, (re)examine, and (re)imagine the elementary social studies classroom. More specifically, the insight from TCs demonstrates how the journey box project was pivotal in the growth of their critical socio-political/ critical consciousness as future elementary educators who practice CRP (Ladson-Billings, 1999). I utilize this chapter to provide a guide for the development of culturally relevant journey box projects in PreK–12 social studies classrooms and social studies teacher education. In turn, the chapter invites educators and students to utilize journey box projects to (re)create social studies classrooms as spaces that center the vibrancy and multiplicity of shared histories in collective efforts to transition into a post-pandemic world.

CULTURALLY RELEVANT PEDAGOGY

Through her foundational scholarship on culturally relevant pedagogy, Ladson-Billings has addressed and revealed how African American students are marginalized in PreK–12 and higher education classrooms. Ladson-Billings (2006) has refused deficit narratives that label Black, Indigenous, Asian, Latinx, Pacific Islander, and students of color as "failing" or "at-risk" based upon the harmful and oppressive achievement measures of high stakes standardized tests. Rather, Ladson-Billings posits the critical framework and practice of CRP to assert the multiplicity of students' identities as inherent assets for classroom teaching and learning in efforts to eradicate systemic inequities in schools and communities (Ladson-Billings, 1995). Inspired by her research on eight successful teachers of African American children, Ladson-Billings (2009, 2021b) grounded CRP in three principles. The first principle is a focus on academic achievement which measures students' knowledge growth through meaningful formative assessment during the school year as opposed to scores on high stakes standardized tests. The second principle, cultural competence, is the ability for students and educators to be fluent in their own culture (e.g., history, language, heritage, traditions, knowledge, etc.) while also developing the capacity to be fluent in another culture. The third principle is socio-political/critical consciousness, or "the 'so what' factor" (Ladson-Billings, 2014, p. 145), which invites students and educators to be deeply knowledgeable about the world around them in order work toward social change in schools and communities.

Ladson-Billings (2014) has noted how "every one of these key components is corrupted in most applications of CRP" (p. 142). CRP is often utilized to reinforce assimilation, low expectations of students of color, disengagement from sociopolitical/critical issues, or to enhance scores on high stakes standardized tests. In turn, Ladson-Billings (2014) has advocated for the application of CRP in teacher education programs for two explicit reasons: (1) to invite teacher candidates to conceptualize, practice, and enact the principles of CRP before they enter their own classrooms and (2) to dismantle the systemic roadblocks (e.g., admissions, student teaching, standardized exams, and certification) that prevent teacher candidates of color from accessing and being successful in teacher education. In this context, the research study presented in this chapter examines how teacher candidates engage in CRP through the development of journey box projects. Such learning experiences supported teacher candidates in their practice as social studies educators and to prepare them for content-based standardized exams necessary for certification. Through such paradigm shifts within TEPs, CRP may be utilized to ensure access, equity, and transformation in PreK–12 and higher education classrooms.

CULTURALLY RELEVANT PEDAGOGY IN THE SOCIAL STUDIES

A growing number of social studies scholars and teacher educators continue to apply culturally relevant pedagogy within their research and teaching practices (Burgard et al., 2021; Busey & Walker, 2017; Clay & Rubin, 2020; King, 2014; Martell, 2017; Milner, 2014; Popielarz, 2020; Shear et al., 2018). As an interdisciplinary subject matter, social studies is uniquely poised to utilize the three principles of CRP to enhance learning environments for all students (Ladson-Billings, 2001b). Through a culturally relevant approach to social studies education, educators and students may grow in historical consciousness to understand various perspectives within history while examining the present and anticipating the future (Ryan et al., 2020). For students and educators who are often marginalized in the classroom due to race/ethnicity, language, religion, dis/ability, socio-economic status, sexuality, gender, and/or immigration status, culturally relevant social studies education is a doorway to more intimately know themselves, their communities, and the world around them. Such teaching and learning experiences actively disrupt the standardization of social studies education in an era that must urgently address systemic racism, capitalism, climate crises, and COVID-19.

An example of culturally relevant pedagogy in social studies is the journey box project, which is a cumulative representation of learning through the creation of a literal, conceptual, and/or digital box. What began as a student-led and interactive learning experience for elementary students (Labbo & Field, 1999) has now expanded to teacher preparation and educator professional development within social studies, English Language Arts, and bi/multilingual education (Alarcón et al., 2015; Valdez & Omerbasic, 2015). Whether in PreK–12 classrooms, teacher education programs, or professional development settings, journey box projects invite learners and educators to conceptualize, analyze, and interpret social studies content outside of conventional norms (Salinas et al., 2015). Journey box projects purposefully use critical and historical inquiry in order to examine diverse, multifaceted, and nuanced perspectives of history, social sciences, and current events/issues (Salinas et al., 2012).

Journey box projects actively disrupt the dominant narrative of social studies which often perpetuates the prominence of whiteness, Eurocentrism, patriarchy, and heteronormativity (Salinas & Blevins, 2013). By unsettling and interrogating the dominant narratives within social studies education, learners and educators are able to amplify and celebrate the voices, perspectives, and experiences of those marginalized in the curriculum due to race/ethnicity, language, religion, dis/ability, socioeconomic status, sexuality, gender, and/or immigration status (Franquiz et al., 2011; Vickery & Salinas, 2019). In turn, the use of critical counter narratives in the curation of journey box projects invites educators and students to engage in culturally relevant pedagogy as they grow in academic achievement/learning, cultural competence, and critical-historical consciousness (Ladson-Billings & Tate, 1995).

Journey box projects have evolved through their use in teacher education to explicitly provide TCs the opportunity to examine narratives, stories, and perspectives that are often marginalized or erased in the social studies (Ender, 2022; Franquiz et al., 2011; Valdez & Omerbasic, 2015). Due to the predominantly white teacher workforce, such efforts by teacher education programs are necessary for TCs to examine their own identities, engage in critical inquiry regarding their teaching practices, and gain content knowledge for diverse social studies education (Ladson-Billings, 2021b). For example, Salinas et al. (2015) examined how the Tejano History Curriculum Project invited future and current bilingual educators to critically analyze Tejano/a history in Texas. Through the use of critical historical inquiry, participants in the Tejano History Curriculum Project inspected dominant narratives in Texas history for educators to envision and create social studies education that is culturally relevant for students and educators (Salinas et al., 2015).

Importantly, journey box projects are also utilized to provide Black, Indigenous, Asian, Latinx, Pacific Islander and teacher educators and TCs of color the opportunity to learn about, share in, and recenter their identities for classroom teaching and learning. Such experiences have the potential to be a site of healing and transformation for future and current educators, as well as students (Vickery & Salinas, 2019). For example, through the use of Black and endarkened feminism, Vickery (2020) restyled journey box projects within an elementary social studies methods course to recenter family histories and stories within social studies and civics curriculum. Relatedly, Salinas et al. (2016) developed journey box projects that amplified the multiplicity of identities and experiences within Latinx communities. Vickery (2020) and Salinas et al. (2016) demonstrate how the use of culturally relevant pedagogy in teacher education are an invitation for teacher candidates to engage in transformative learning experiences that will benefit PreK–12 students.

CULTURALLY RELEVANT PEDAGOGY AS A HARD RESET

The ground-breaking framework and research of culturally relevant pedagogy are often applied in the classroom simply to "use the language and culture of the students to teach them part of the 'acceptable' curricular cannon" (Paris, 2012, p. 95). Ladson-Billings (2021b) has directly noted that many educators often forego the true essence of CRP in their curricular design and instructional practice when they do not include all three principles. CRP continues to be appropriated by corporate education reformers and far-right legislatures through content standards and high-stakes testing that further oppress and harm marginalized students (Love, 2019). Many classroom teachers, teacher educators, and teacher candidates reinforce white middle class norms within PreK–12 schooling rather than engage in the critical and justice-based frameworks defined in CRP.

In response, Ladson-Billings (2014) has advocated for the remix of CRP to recenter the principles of achievement/student learning, cultural competence, and socio-political/critical consciousness in PreK–12 classrooms and teacher education programs. Ladson-Billings (2021b) has encouraged CRP to be a framework and practice to directly respond to the ongoing and intensified systemic oppressions that impact Black, Indigenous, Asian, Latinx, Pacific Islander and students of color in the U.S. educational system. By embedding CRP as Ladson-Billing intended within TEPs, teacher educators and TCs have the opportunity to cultivate classroom communities where the fullness of their students' identities, knowledge, communities, strengths, and desires are centered within teaching and learning. Such efforts are challenging and complex, yet necessary in efforts to reckon with the ongoing impact of systemic racism, capitalism, climate crises, and COVID-19. The use of journey box projects within teacher education programs, as demonstrated by the research study offered in this chapter, are an invitation for students and educators to engage in culturally relevant social studies education, which is necessary for a post-pandemic world.

METHODS

From April to August 2019, I engaged in a critical qualitative research project informed by humanizing methodologies (Paris & Winn, 2014). One of the primary purposes of this research project was to analyze the use of culturally relevant pedagogy in an elementary social studies methods course. This chapter focuses specifically on the learning experiences related to the use of journey box projects in the course. As a teacher educator and critical qualitative scholar, I engage in humanizing methodologies due to the relationships and community I foster with teacher candidates as we learn and grow together. Much like the intention of journey box projects, humanizing methodologies aim to center, amplify, and celebrate a multiplicity of voices, perspectives, and experiences that are often marginalized in university-based classrooms and research. Humanizing approaches to teaching, learning, and research invites me to join TCs "in further exploring the interconnected terrain of worthiness, witnessing, friendship, vulnerability, shortcomings, and positive social change as it occurs across the research process in our professional lives" (Paris & Winn, 2014, p. xiv).

Positionality

As a white, cis-gender woman who is a teacher educator-scholar-community organizer, I understand that my viewpoint is bound in whiteness and my positionality is always present in my facilitation of teacher education courses and research projects (Picower & Kohli, 2017). In turn, I engage in anti-racist and anti-bias practices by frequently learning from and connecting with the people, places, and ecosystems of local communities. As the instructor of record for the social studies methods course, I invited TCs to join me in fostering a sense of responsibility and accountability to the students they teach through culturally relevant pedagogy. I mediated the complex terrain of being a participant-researcher as I led the design, data collection, and data analysis of the research project. I continuously reflected upon the analysis of data sources with participants, as well as mentors, colleagues, and collaborators to check myself and my positionality (Matias, 2013). Due to the humanizing focus of the social studies methods course and research project, I remain in relation with many of the participants of this research project to provide support and guidance in their continued growth as social studies educators.

Participants and Setting

Eleven teacher candidates volunteered to participate in the research project and are from a social studies methods course with 22 students total (see Table 12.1). Pseudonyms were used and chosen by the participants. TCs were enrolled in a college of education (COE) at a public research university in a Midwestern urban setting and were relatively halfway through earning their teacher certification in elementary education. TCs in the COE aiming to become certified in elementary education must take an elementary social studies methods course and participate in classroom field placements.

TABLE 12.1. Teacher Candidate Participant Information

Pseudonym	Race/Ethnicity	Pronouns	Major	Journey Box Project Topic
Renee	White	She/Her	Elementary Special Education	Women's Reproductive Rights
Fay	White	She/Her	Elementary Special Education	Disability Civil Rights Movement
Amy	White	She/Her	Early Childhood	Operation Desert Storm (Perspective of Veterans)
Kramer	White	She/Her	Elementary ELA Education	Rwandan Genocide
Maya	Asian American/White	She/Her	Elementary Science Education	Hidden Figures of the Space Race
Eleanor	White	She/Her	Elementary ELA Education	Beyond the First Lady (Edith Wilson and Eleanor Roosevelt)
Tyrone	African American	He/Him	K–12 Special Education	Motown Museum
Gabrielle	Latina	She/Her	Elementary ELA Education	Chicano Movement of the 1960s and 1970s
Rosalina	White	She/Her	K–12 Special Education	Black Women Leaders of the Civil Rights Movement
Christopher	White	She/Her	Early Childhood	The Black Panthers

Context

The social studies methods course at the focal point of this research project took place before the COVID-19 pandemic. Teacher candidates contextualized the cultural, geographic, historical, anthropological, and sociological components of the social studies through a socio-culturally aware and critically conscious lens. The structure of readings, digital media, assignments, and collaborative inquiry throughout the semester prompted TCs to learn through the guiding principles of culturally relevant pedagogy. The goal of the course aimed to prepare TCs to become effective social studies educators for the multilingual and multicultural learners they will teach. To prompt the critical inquiry and analysis of social studies, TCs developed journey box projects in which they examined the state-mandated K–8 Social Studies Standards and the NCSS C3 Framework to learn about and then center a person, time period, or event that is typically marginalized within social studies education (see Table 12.1). The journey box project provided TCs the opportunity to experience and practice culturally relevant social studies education. The TCs hosted a community celebration in which they presented their journey box projects to peers, family members, COE faculty, and community members. For details on the journey box project assignment, please see Table 12.2.

TABLE 12.2. Journey Box Project

Introduction and Directions to Project
Informed by Alarcón et al. (2015), Salinas et al. (2016), and Vickery (2020), you will cultivate a "Journey Box" as a cumulative representation of your understanding and practice of social studies education. Based upon your critical inquiry and analysis of the state-level content standards and National Council for the Social Studies C3 Framework, you will choose a topic that will demonstrate your learning journey throughout the semester. You will present and share your Journey Box at the end of the semester with your peers and various community partners. You will also upload your Journey Box materials to a shared Google Drive folder to engage in professional collaboration with your peers. For your Journey Box, you will learn about a person (ex: Yuri Kochiyama), a time period (ex: Reconstruction Era), and/or event (ex: 1968 Chicanx/Latinx student walkouts) that could be taught in a social studies class. The Journey Box should center someone and/or something that is marginalized in U.S. social studies education. You are encouraged to create a Journey Box that focuses on a person, time period, and/or event from your local context. Your Journey Box will share a counter narrative that is useful to imagine and enact social studies education that is meaningful and empowering for educators and students. The development of your Journey Box will invite you to conceptualize, experience, and practice the principles of Culturally Relevant Pedagogy in social studies education: academic achievement/student learning, cultural competence, and socio-political/critical consciousness (Ladson-Billings, 2001). Your Journey Box will include a variety of primary and secondary sources in order to portray a holistic and thorough counter narrative about your topic. You will respond to specific questions and share information/resources for each source of your Journey Box in order to discuss how your peers could teach the topic in the social studies classroom. In addition, your Journey Box will include a reflective paper that will summarize and connect your topic to cumulative learning opportunities throughout the semester.

Components to Journey Box Project	
Creative box display or format selected	Your Journey Box may be displayed through a literal box, a tri-fold poster, specific technology platform, social media too, etc. Your display should be reflective of your own (re)learning journey and your topic of choice.
Index of items	The index should act as a "table of contents" and outline each component of your Journey Box.
Narrative	The narrative should be a 1 to 2-page double-spaced summary of the documents provided in your Journey Box. The narrative should include how the Journey Box could be taught within the classroom.
Connection to content standards, learning goals, and objectives	You will provide specific content standards from both the specific state-level standards and NCSS C3 Framework that will support the use of your Journey Box topic in social studies education. You will also provide learning goals and objectives that will explain key expectations and outcomes for student learning.
Importance, relevance, and universal design for learning	You will provide a 1 to 2-page double-spaced summary about why students and educators need to know about the specific Journey Box topic. This summary should include a description of how the Journey Box topic is culturally relevant to students and their communities. The summary should incorporate a discussion of potential accommodations and differentiated learning opportunities through Universal Design for Learning to support all students in their learning.
3 to 5 DBQs for each source	You will develop 3 to 5 data/document-based questions (DBQs) to accompany each source in your Journey Box. The DBQs should encourage critical inquiry and higher order thinking. DBQs should (1) solicit prior knowledge, (2) prompt analysis and comparison, and (3) encourage meaningful connections.

Journey Box Projects for a Post-Pandemic World • **209**

TABLE 12.2. Continued

	Components to Journey Box Project
4 Visual/image primary sources	Utilize a variety of sources and artifacts that will construct the counter narrative of your Journey Box. At least 4 sources should be visual/image primary sources.
4 Text/participant account primary sources	Utilize a variety of sources and artifacts that will construct the counter narrative of your Journey Box. At least 4 sources should be text/participant account primary sources.
4 Your choice of primary or secondary sources	Utilize a variety of sources and artifacts that will construct the counter narrative of your Journey Box. At least 4 sources can be your choice of either primary sources or secondary sources.
Reflection	Your reflection should be a 2 to 4-page reflection of your (re)learning experiences this semester. Your reflective paper should directly connect your Journey Box to various assignments and learning experiences from the course.
Presentation	You will present and share your Journey Box to peers and community partners. Your presentation should include a thorough discussion of your Journey Box. You will also share your Journey Box to a collaborative Google Drive folder for your peers to potentially utilize your Journey Box Project as a classroom teacher.
APA format	Your Journey Box should be developed using APA format.
	Guide to Creating Journey Box Project
Choose a topic	What is your topic? Why did you choose this topic? How does this topic have the potential to be taught in social studies? How is this topic typically situated, if at all, in social studies? How will your Journey Box present a counter narrative of this topic?
Connection to content standards, learning goals, and objectives	What are the main state-level social studies standards to be covered? What are the main NCSS C3 Framework components to be covered? What are the learning goals for students? What are the objectives of this Journey Box? How do the objectives thread between the standards, narrative, DBQs, and sources?
Importance, relevance, and universal design for learning	How is the learning experience relevant to students? How does this topic connect to the students' identities and communities? How will students be invited to grow in socio-political/critical consciousness? How will you incorporate accommodations and differentiated learning opportunities through Universal Design for Learning? What are the multiple modes of engagement, representation, and expression for all students to achieve the desired goals of the learning experience(s)?
Selection of sources	What 4 visual/image primary sources, 4 text/participant primary account primary, and 4 additional primary or secondary sources will you be using? Where did you locate these sources? How do these sources contribute to the counter narrative of this topic? How will you be organizing and displaying your sources?
Developing data/document-based questions	Do you have 3–5 DBQs for each source that engage in and prompt critical inquiry and higher order thinking? Do your 3–5 DBQs for each source invite students to: connect prior knowledge and experiences, analyze and compare sources, and make connections?

continues

TABLE 12.2.   Continued

	Guide to Creating Journey Box Project
Narrative	Why is your topic relevant to social studies education? What story are you trying to tell through your Journey Box? How would you teach this topic in a social studies classroom? How is this topic relevant and meaningful to your students? In what ways does this topic parallel your socio-political/critical consciousness growth this semester?
Reflection	What did you learn about yourself through the development of the Journey Box? Provide specific examples and references. What did you learn about social studies education through the creation of your Journey Box? Provide specific examples and references. How has the Journey Box project heartened your perceptions of social studies as teaching and learning for social justice and social change? How has the Journey Box encouraged you to develop culturally relevant approaches to social studies education? What are the possibilities you envision for social studies after developing your Journey Box?

Data Sources and Analysis

The research project implemented a variety of qualitative data collection methods to report on the impact of culturally relevant pedagogy in a social studies methods course (LeCompte & Schensul, 2010; Maxwell, 2013). For the purposes of this chapter, the data sources include curricular artifacts and semi-structured interviews with participants. The primary sources of data are the journey box projects that were developed by TCs and reflections they later provided on the assignment during interviews. The data sources were cross-analyzed to establish emerging themes and subsequent findings pertaining to the TCs' understanding and practice of CRP within the social studies through the use of journey box projects. I began by organizing the data sources by the guiding principles of CRP to examine where TCs may have grown in and/or demonstrated (a) academic achievement/student learning, (b) cultural competence, and (c) sociopolitical/critical consciousness. I then examined the data sources for TCs who actualized CRP through their own growth as educators and the curriculum they developed for current or future students in their journey box projects. Through this ongoing and emergent process, I located three TCs—Amy, Gabrielle, and Maya—who clearly demonstrated CRP through the curation of their journey box projects.

FINDINGS

The findings share how Amy, Gabrielle, and Maya's journey box projects exhibit their collective growth as educators through their understanding and use of culturally relevant pedagogy in elementary social studies education. First, the TCs excelled academically as they grew in curricular and pedagogical knowledge in the development of their journey box projects. By experiencing a purposeful student-led assignment, the TCs came to understand how they may implement similar learning opportunities in the classroom. Second, Amy, Gabrielle, and Maya grew in cultural competence as they came to understand an event, person, or time period that is typically marginalized in social studies education. The TCs demonstrated how learning from an array of voices, places, and people are an invitation to grow as responsible and accountable educators, community members, and citizens.

Third, and perhaps most significantly, is the growth of Amy, Gabrielle, and Maya's socio-political/critical consciousness as they curated their journey box projects. All three TCs entered the course disliking social studies and hesitant to implement current events/issues in the elementary classroom. The journey box project invited the TCs to (re)imagine the possibilities of social studies education through culturally relevant pedagogy as they practice how to read the word and the world (Ladson-Billings, 2021; Freire, 2005). The following descriptions, images, and tables demonstrate Amy, Gabrielle, and Maya's (re)learning and (re)imagination of culturally relevant social studies through their journey box projects.

Amy

Amy's journey box project centered a critical counter narrative to Operation Desert Storm by addressing the experiences of her dad who served in the military and was a veteran of the Gulf War (see Figure 12.1). For many children and family members of veterans, Amy often struggled to understand the immense and challenging effects war had on her father. In turn, Amy utilized the journey box project

FIGURE 12.1   Amy's Journey Box Project on Operation Desert Storm.
(Source: K. Popielarz, 2019)

to better understand her family history and learn how to center difficult subjects within elementary social studies (see Table 12.3).

Gabrielle

Gabrielle's journey box project amplified the critical counter narrative of the Chicano/a Movement by celebrating her own identity as a Mexican American and learning more about the predominantly Latinx students from her classroom field placement (see Figure 12.2). This experience encouraged Gabrielle to better understand how she might bring local and national current events into the elementary social studies classroom. As such, Gabrielle employed the journey box project to understand how she might connect historical events and social movements of the past to contemporary issues and social justice initiatives (see Table 12.4).

Maya

Maya's journey box project magnified the critical counter narrative of Hidden Figures of the Space Race by focusing on historical and contemporary fig-

TABLE 12.3. Culturally Relevant Pedagogy in Action: Amy's Journey Box Project on Operation Desert Storm

Academic achievement and student learning	I can connect my Journey Box (Operation Desert Storm) through my knowledge and understanding of culturally relevant pedagogy in the elementary social studies by providing students with the opportunity to explore different approaches to learning history from the historical point of view so they may interpret their world now along with the world of others from the past. I would provide my students with real life artifacts from Operation Desert Storm. It would also be beneficial for my students if I were to bring in a guest speaker from that time period. Including awesome and real resources will help them remember and enjoy the material they are learning.
Cultural competence	I now believe that teaching current and past events in the social studies classroom can establish a foundation of awareness and inquiry. Current and past events offer the social studies teacher countless opportunities to help make the curriculum relevant to our everyday lives. I've also learned that it's important to bring all students' cultures together within the classroom. I've really enjoyed working on our Journey Box Project. I have gained so much knowledge about Operation Desert Storm and how my dad probably felt. He is my hero.
Sociopolitical and critical consciousness	My relearning process has encouraged me to help students develop the knowledge, skills, attitudes, and values to actively participate in life through learning and exercising their rights and responsibilities as citizens at school and in their community. Students should not be afraid to stand up for what they believe. If they see that something should be changed around their community, then they should be given the support and resources needed to put a plan into action. When students give back to their community, it will help them build long-term relationships with other people around them, their academic skills will increase, and they will feel good about actively changing things.

Journey Box Projects for a Post-Pandemic World • **213**

FIGURE 12.2. Gabrielle's Journey Box Project on the Chicano/a Movement. (Source: K. Popielarz, 2019)

TABLE 12.4. Culturally Relevant Pedagogy in Action: Gabrielle's Journey Box Project on the Chicano/a Movement

Academic achievement and student learning	Being Mexican American, I learned a lot more about myself that I didn't realize I was missing. It helped me connect to my culture and heritage. This topic is relevant because it was a very large civil rights movement that happened in the United States during the 1960s and 1970s. I truly believe that this type of history is beneficial for all students to know. It is a major part of American history and there are many ways that you can connect what was happening back then to current events that are going on today. This makes it even more meaningful and relevant to students in the classroom. I think that if I were in an elementary room, I would teach this topic through picture books and then expand on that by using primary and secondary sources. I think I would utilize role-playing scenarios and classroom discussion to further my students thinking on the topic. A great way to talk about this topic would also be tying it into current events.
Cultural competence	I think studying the Chicano/a Movement could really impact students in different ways. For me, it made me connect to my culture, identity, and heritage more. I was able to learn more about the struggles that members of my family went through, and it made me really proud to be a Mexican American. This is the kind of feeling that I hope the studying of this movement can bring to students in the classroom. It is also very easy to connect this to the local community. There were times when Cesar Chavez came [here] which is something studies can learn about.
Sociopolitical and critical consciousness	Throughout our course I have learned quite a few things about myself that I was not aware of. Before taking this class, I was not aware of the real impact you can have on children when talking about social studies and social justice topics at the elementary school level. I also doubted that these topics were appropriate for students in elementary classes. I doubted their ability to comprehend topics and their ability to initiate change at such a young age. After this class, I cannot believe that I ever doubted their abilities and what children are capable of.

FIGURE 12.3. Maya's Journey Box Project on Hidden Figures of the Space Race. (Source: K. Popielarz, 2019)

TABLE 12.5. Culturally Relevant Pedagogy in Action: Maya's Journey Box Project on Hidden Figures of the Space Race

Academic achievement and student learning	The Journey Box project has shown me how much I can discover and relearn just by putting in some research effort. I actually didn't even know about Katherine Johnson and the other women who worked at NASA when I first picked my topic. I just thought the Space Race would be a good topic and it turned out to be more meaningful and important than I ever expected. My major is science education, so being able to connect science and social studies in a project was very special and eye-opening for me. Now I can't stop reading tweets of former and current astronauts and reading articles about future space exploration plans.
Cultural competence	I found multiple ways that my topic connects to science, mathematics, art, racial and gender diversity, the past, present, future, and to the community. I can use this Journey Box to have my students reflect on how the events in the past have shaped what their community looks like and is today. I can have my students look for art dedicated to these events as well as create their own in their community. I can take my students to the science center to deepen their understanding of space exploration. I can have students relate what is happening currently in space exploration to that of the past.
Sociopolitical and critical consciousness	My Journey Box ended up connecting to culturally relevant pedagogy in more ways than I thought. As I researched, I continued to find hidden stories of figures that persevered through racial and gender barriers while working for NASA during the Space Race. These figures had a tremendous impact on space exploration and the civil rights movement. There are now many schools and programs that encourage all cultures, races, and genders in STEM careers. STEM careers have been held by predominantly white men and we are now seeing this statistic change. There is more diversity in STEM than ever before and we look up to brave people like Katherine Johnson and now Leland Melvin for tipping the scales and empowering all races, cultures, and genders to find their place in social change and human advancement.

ures of NASA such as Katherine Johnson and Leland Melvin (see Figure 12.3). By sharing in the major contributions of African Americans throughout the history of space exploration, Maya explicitly connected space travel to past and present civil rights movements. In this way, Maya viewed the journey box project as an opportunity to highlight careers in STEM for her students while also connecting ongoing social justice causes to elementary social studies education (see Table 12.5).

DISCUSSION

It is important to note that each of the teacher candidates were not social studies majors and did not have positive social studies learning experiences within their PreK–12 education. In turn, I approached the design and the instruction of the social studies methods course as an opportunity to embrace the contradictory past experiences by joining TCs in (re)learning the social studies and its possibilities for the classroom. For these reasons, the course assignments modeled how TCs may be learners alongside their students and engage in the lifelong process of disrupting the dominant narrative of conventional social studies education (Ladson-Billings, 2001a). In particular, the framework and practice of culturally relevant pedagogy in the methods course invited TCs to interrogate their own experiences in social studies classrooms. This process of inquiry and analysis was essential to the development of their journey box projects, which prompted TCs to (re)imagine social studies as a culturally relevant practice.

The journey box projects served as a vehicle for the TCs to grow in culturally relevant approaches to elementary social studies education that actively move away from conventional norms and dynamics within many classrooms. This is exhibited in Amy's interview reflection on her journey box project: "It made me want to learn more about social studies because I was never into social studies. After that journey box project, I learned so much about that topic and [I] actually want to share that information with the world or students." Amy's excitement and purpose demonstrates how the use of culturally relevant pedagogy in teacher education fosters TCs' self-efficacy and confidence to initiate similar practices in their own social studies classrooms. The journey box project thus represents one curricular and pedagogical tool to support TCs in their growth as educators who intimately understand and practice culturally relevant pedagogy in social studies.

Amy, Gabrielle, and Maya chose journey box projects that were personal to them which informed their passion and dedication to the assignment. While all of the TCs chose journey box projects with topics that interested them, Amy, Gabrielle, and Maya engaged in the assignment to explicitly learn more about their identities in order to discover how this may impact teaching and learning. This is revealed in Gabrielle's interview: "My family came from Texas, they were migrant workers, and learning about where Chicano/a comes from helped me learn about myself. This is [how] I want [my students] to feel." Gabrielle's reflections demonstrate the potential for transformative learning experiences when TCs engage in culturally relevant pedagogy through the use of journey box projects. In particular, Gabrielle's journey box project centered her own familial history and identity, which invited her to experience and practice how to replicate similar opportunities for students. Gabrielle's journey box project thus demonstrates the impact of meaningful and purposeful critical counter narratives in culturally relevant social studies education (Salinas et al., 2016; Vickery, 2020).

The journey box projects were also an opportunity for TCs to practice developing an interdisciplinary curriculum, which is essential for CRP in social studies education (Ladson-Billings, 2001b). Because many of the TCs were not social studies majors, the journey box project invited them to connect their specific content area expertise to the social studies through interdisciplinary approaches. For TCs like Maya, the journey box project was a medium to bridge the worlds of art, science, and social studies education: "I really enjoy creating and that inspired me to teach. I can collaborate with students and help them tap into their creativity and express it." Due to the multimodal approach to the journey box projects (Valdez & Omerbasic, 2015), TCs were provided differentiated and relevant opportunities for engagement, representation, action, and expression (Annamma & Handy, 2019). Maya and the other TCs were not restricted in the curation of their journey box projects with the intention that they would implement similar practices in classroom field placements and their own future classrooms. This is a particularly innovative implication for teacher educators interested in utilizing journey box projects in a variety of subject area methods courses as the assignment nor culturally relevant pedagogy are limited to social studies education.

CONCLUSION

Educators and students continue to endure unprecedented times due to the four intersecting pandemics of systemic racism, capitalism, climate crises, and the COVID-19 pandemic. Teaching practices and learning opportunities must respond to provide educators and students the ability to understand and address the times in which we live. In turn, this chapter joins Ladson-Billings' call to reset education by enacting culturally relevant pedagogy in social studies education through journey box projects. Rather than a "return to normal," such learning experiences provide educators and students the ability to grow in socio-political/critical consciousness that is needed for inclusive, affirming, and revitalizing futures. By sharing in the transformative learning experiences of TCs like Amy, Gabrielle, and Maya, this chapter demonstrates the possibilities of interdisciplinary and multimodal social studies education that is grounded in the framework and practice of culturally relevant pedagogy. In this way, Amy, Gabrielle, and Maya model the everyday culturally relevant practices that may imagine and enact education anew for a post-pandemic world.

REFERENCES

Alarcón, J., Holmes, K., & Bybee, E. (2015). Historical thinking inside the box: Preservice elementary teachers use journey boxes to craft counter narratives. *The Social Studies*, *106*(4), 186–192.

Annamma, S. B. & Handy, T. (2019). DisCrit solidarity as curriculum studies and transformative praxis. *Curriculum Inquiry*, *49*(4), 442–463.

Burgard, K., O'Quinn, C., Boucher, M., Pinnix, N., Trejo, C., & Dickson, C. (2021). Using photographs to create culturally relevant classrooms: People of San Antonio, Texas in the 1930s. *Social Studies and the Young Learner*, *33*(3), 3–7.

Busey, C., & Walker, I. (2017). A dream and a bus: Black critical patriotism in elementary social studies standards. *Theory & Research in Social Education*, *45*(4), 456–488.

Clay, K. L., & Rubin, B. C. (2020). "I look deep into this stuff because it's part of me": Toward a critically relevant civics education. *Theory & Research in Social Education*, *48*(2), 161–181.

Ender, T. (2022). *Dialogue with T. Ender* (personal communication, February 28, 2022).

Franquiz, M. E., Carmen Salazar, M., & DeNicolo, C. P. (2011). Challenging majoritarian tales: Portraits of bilingual teachers deconstructing deficit views of bilingual leaners. *Bilingual Research Journal*, *34*, 279–300.

Freire, P. (2005). *Pedagogy of the oppressed* (30th Anniversary ed.). Continuum.

King, L. J. (2014). Learning other people's history: Pre-service teachers' developing African American historical knowledge. *Teaching Education*, *25*(4), 427–456.

Labbo, L. D., & Field, S. L. (1999). Journey boxes: Telling the story of place, time, and culture with photographs, literature, and artifacts. *The Social Studies*, *90*(4), 177–182.

Ladson-Billings, G. (1995). Toward a Theory of Culturally Relevant Pedagogy. *American Educational Research Journal*, *32*(3), 465.

Ladson-Billings, G. (1999). Preparing teachers for diverse student populations: A critical race theory perspective. *Review of Research in Education*, *24*, 211–247.

Ladson-Billings, G. (2001a). Lies my teacher still tells: Developing a critical race perspective toward the social studies. In G. Ladson-Billings (Ed.), *Critical Race Theory Perspectives on social studies: The profession, policies, and curriculum* (pp. 1–11). Information Age Publishing.

Ladson-Billings, G. (2001b). Crafting a culturally relevant social studies approach. In E. Wayne Ross (Ed.), *The social studies curriculum* (pp. 201–216). University of New York Press.

Ladson-Billings, G. (2006). From the achievement gap to the education debt: Understanding achievement in U.S. schools. *Educational Researcher*, *35*(7), 3–12.

Ladson-Billings, G. (2009). *The dreamkeepers: Successful teachers of African American children*. Jossey-Bass.

Ladson-Billings, G. (2014). The (R)Evolution will not be standardized: Teacher education, hip hop pedagogy, and culturally relevant pedagogy 2.0. In D. Paris & H. S. Alim (Eds.), *Culturally sustaining pedagogies: Teaching and learning for justice in a changing world* (pp. 141–156). Teachers College Record.

Ladson-Billings, G. (2021a). *Justice matters: Reclaiming a fundamental right* [Video]. YouTube. https://www.youtube.com/watch?v=m3W8_zt7V_4

Ladson-Billings, G. (2021b). I'm here for the hard re-set: Post pandemic pedagogy to preserve our culture. *Equity & Excellence in Education, 54*(1), 67-78.

Ladson-Billings, G., & Tate, W. F. (1995). Toward a critical race theory of education. *Teachers College Record, 97*(1), 47–68.

LeCompte, M., & Schensul, J. (2010). *Designing and conducting ethnographic research: An introduction*. AltaMira Press.

Love, B. (2019). *We want to do more than survive: Abolitionist teaching and the pursuit of Educational freedom*. Beacon Press.

Martell, C. C. (2017). Approaches to teaching race in elementary social studies: A case study of preservice teachers. *The Journal of Social Studies Research, 41*, 75–87.

Matias, C. (2013). Check yo'self before you wreck yo'self and our kids: Counterstories from culturally responsive white teachers? ... To culturally responsive white teachers! *Interdisciplinary Journal of Teaching and Learning, 3*(2), 68–81.

Maxwell, J. (2013). *Qualitative research design: An interactive approach*. SAGE Publishing.

Milner, H. R. (2014). Culturally relevant, purpose-driven learning & teaching in a middle school social studies classroom. *Multicultural Education, 21*(2), 9–17.

Morrison, T. (2019). Race matters. In T. Morrison, *The source of self-regard: Selected essays, speeches, and meditations* (pp. 131–139). Alfred A. Knopf.

Paris, D. (2012). Culturally sustaining pedagogy: A needed change in stance, terminology, and practice. *Educational Researcher, 41*(3), 93–97.

Paris, D., & Winn, M. T. (2014). *Humanizing research: Decolonizing qualitative inquiry with youth and communities*. SAGE Publications.

Picower, B., & Kohli, R. (2017). *Confronting racism in teacher education: Counternarratives of critical practice*. Routledge.

Popielarz, K. (2020). [Book Review] We want to do more than survive: Abolitionist teaching and the pursuit of educational freedom by Bettina Love. *Journal of Social Studies Research, 44*(1), 1–5.

Ryan, A. M., Tocci, C., & Moon, S. (2020). *The Curriculum Foundations Reader*. Palgrave Macmillan.

Salinas, C., & Blevins, B. (2013). Critical historical inquiry: How might pre-service teachers confront master historical narratives? *Social Studies Research and Practice, 9*(3), 35–50.

Salinas, C., Blevins, B., & Sullivan, C. (2012). Critical historical thinking: When official narratives collide with *other* narratives. *Multicultural Perspectives, 14*(1), 18–27.

Salinas, C., Rodriguez, N. N., & Lewis, B. A. (2015). The Tejano history curriculum project: Creating a space for authoring Tejanas/os into the social studies curriculum. *Bilingual Research Journal, 38*(2), 172–189.

Salinas, C. S., Franquiz, M. E., & Rodriguez, N. N. (2016). Writing Latina/o historical narratives: Narratives at the intersection of critical historical inquiry and LatCrit. *Urban Review, 48*, 419–439.

Shear, S., Tschida, C., Bellows, E., Buchanan, L. B., Saylor, E. (2018). *(Re)Imagining elementary social studies: A controversial issues reader*. Information Age Publishing.

Vickery, A. E. (2020). "This is a story of who America is:" Cultural memories and black civic identity. *Journal of Curriculum and Pedagogy, 17*(2), 103–134.

Valdez, V. E., & Omerbasic, D. (2015). Multimodal self-authoring across bi/multilingual educator and student learning spaces. *Bilingual Research Journal, 38,* 228–247.

Vickery, A. E., & Salinas, C. S. (2019). "I question America ... is this America?" Learning to view the civil rights movement through an intersectional lens. *Curriculum Inquiry, 49*(3), 260–283.

CHAPTER 13

AFRICAN AMERICAN HISTORY AND ITS VISUAL PORTRAYAL IN TEXTBOOKS

Tina L. Heafner
University of North Carolina at Charlotte

Antoinette M. L. Rochester
California Charter Schools Association

Social studies as a discipline is often criticized as teaching history and historical events inaccurately (Brown & Brown, 2010; Ladson-Billings, 2003; Sleeter & Stillman, 2005); this not to be wrongly interpreted as educators intentionally teaching history inaccurately. Rather, educators rely on accessible, persistent curriculum, which presents history from a white-Eurocentric[1] stance, omitting the voices and experiences of historically marginalized communities (Brown & Au, 2014; King, 2014; King & Brown, 2014). Consequently, there is a growing need for social studies practitioners to select resources to supplement these shortcomings; this includes reevaluating the most used resources in all academic disciplines, textbooks. Textbooks are meant to support classroom instruction; however, textbooks persist as students' primary source of information (Cuban, 1982; Heafner, 2020; Wade, 1993). Since textbooks tend to hold the position of present-

---
[1] Due to the nature of this chapter and the continued oppression of Black narratives in textbooks, we have chosen not to capitalize white.

Out of Turmoil: Catalysts for Re-learning, Re-Teaching, and Re-imagining History and Social Science, pages 221–242.
Copyright © 2023 by Information Age Publishing
www.infoagepub.com
All rights of reproduction in any form reserved.

ing incomplete narratives versus constructing and/or challenging knowledge of a complex and layered history, social studies is not only made boring but also whitewashed of a racialized, oppressive past and legacy of inequality and injustice (Berry & Gross, 2020; Gregory, 2021; Kendi, 2016; Rothstein, 2017). This insufficient narrative robs students of the "capacity to make sense of an uncomfortable past, a chaotic present, and inchoate future" (Heafner, 2020, p. 4). Hence, it is imperative that information within its pages presents *all* aspects of American history from a perspective that does not dismiss or omit uncomfortable aspects of American history because it does not support a commonly known larger, progressive national narrative (Rochester & Heafner, 2021).

Layers of complexity emerge as students interact with images not from their own cultural frames and/or images [mis]represent a marginalized person or racialized event, issue, or value. Historically, African American history is taught from a deficit perspective, leaving students to have a limited and/or negative perception of African Americans as a people and misguided when it comes to the history of African Americans in the United States (King, 2014; King & Brown, 2014); this misguidance can also be found in the imagery used to show aspects of African American history. Thus, images can have a positive or negative impact on students' understanding of history. Moreover, imagery such as photographs or paintings, used in social studies are tools that encourage inquiry while showing a physical representation of an event, person, or time. Images are significant meaning markers because they carry and interpret the social (Werner, 2002). Pictures not only frame the events, issues, and values of the collective human experience, they are intimately connected with profound changes in the social relations between those who make or curate images and those who engage with the image and text (Bezemer & Kress, 2010). Additionally, because the use of images is central to historical inquiry and its discipline, social studies practitioners are faced with the challenge of teaching students how to identify an author's perspective and contextualize images based on their time period of development (Werner, 2000). Interpretations tend to draw upon existing background knowledge or text narrative.

The aim of this chapter is to investigate the visual portrayal of African American history within a state-developed textbook focusing specifically on the tone in which said history is presented. The chapter begins with a review of the literature which addresses how African American history is represented in social studies textbooks and the use of imagery in social studies. Following is the theoretical framework which is combined theory consisting of tenets from critical race theory (CRT) and Black critical theory (BlackCrit) to create anti-Blackness education theory (a-BET) to examine the visual portrayal of African American history in a state-adopted textbook. To conclude, the chapter will discuss the possible effect of the imagery used in the state-adopted textbook regarding students' understanding of African American history. This research seeks to give more clarity in understanding how African American history is negatively depicted through imagery which then has a negative impact on students' understanding of African American history.

LITERATURE REVIEW

Paul Ortiz (2018) said, "As other racial minorities grow, it becomes increasingly important to address the fundamental question of fairness for African Americans, which affects the fortunes of the other groups" (p. 11). African American history is a part of American history; yet, African American history specifically is often only taught when it benefits the larger narrative of American history (King & Simmons, 2018). As a result, diverse aspects of African American history, specifically the direct contributions of African Americans in American society, are frequently silenced, leaving limited opportunities for other historically marginalized communities' history to be taught (Brown & Au, 2014). Learning the history of non-European Americans allows all students, especially Students of Color, to feel empowered and it reminds students that the United States is a pluralistic society.

Within the United States, states can adopt state-designed textbooks in social studies (Apple, 2013; Gordy & Pritchard, 1995; Hicks, 2013; Loewen, 2018). The use of state-designed textbooks allows students to learn their state history, but it does also present limitations. Specifically, the level of oversight regarding the perspective in which the information is presented differs, i.e., the state history can overpower the national narrative (Rochester & Heafner, 2021). Hence, depending upon the state, the *manner* and *tone* in which African American history is shown can either encourage or discourage positive dialogue and understanding of the experiences of African Americans in the United States (Eargle, 2015; Hancoc, 2021; Rochester & Heafner, 2021). Therefore, before conducting an analysis on imagery within a state-developed textbook, it is imperative to distinguish how African American history is currently presented on a macro-level. Likewise, imagery is used for a distinct purpose within social studies and is a key component of classroom instruction, thus, identifying the use of imagery is necessary before the tone and manner of images in a state-adopted textbook can be explored.

Social Studies Textbooks and African American History

Limited federal regulation is put on the development of social studies textbooks allowing states to either adopt textbooks that encourage racist ideologies and/or neglect to discuss America's past from the non-dominant perspective (Czerniak & Macias-Gonzalez, 2006). Although these shortcomings are known, textbooks are the main resource in classroom instruction (Czerniak & Macias-Gonzalez, 2006). Since African American history is often negatively portrayed in textbooks, it results in students who have jaded and/or skewed perceptions of the contributions of African Americans in the United States. (King et al., 2012).

Traditionally, African American history narratives are dominated by messages of oppression, inferiority to white people, and being stupid or unclean (Solórzano, 1997). Likewise, when African American history is portrayed positively, it is repeatedly done through the Civil Rights Movement causing students to have an overly simplified understanding of African American history and African American leaders (Banks, 2008). More specifically, when surveying nineteen social studies textbooks, Woodson (2015) found that alongside the information presented in textbooks being misleading regarding African Americans, they also promote the notion that only *particular* African American leaders are worth acknowledging and remembering because those individuals are viewed as "heroes" due to their role in achieving "racial progression" (Busey & Walker, 2017; Woodson, 2015). Meaning, there is distinct intentionality that can be seen when discussing historical African American figures to acknowledge those who were willing to work alongside white people for reform to occur versus those who unapologetically expressed disdain for how African Americans were treated to the masses.

Various states within the United States have intentionally included historically marginalized communities' history to be a part of standards and/or curriculums (Camicia & Zhu, 2019; Warner, 2015; Yoo et al., 2020). However, when analyzed in greater depth, the depiction of African Americans specifically, remains to be increasingly poor, leaving them to be seen as "bad people" even when the acts of violence are being done towards them (Martell & Stevens, 2017). Thus, Vasquez Heilig et al. (2012) states one of the major challenges when textbooks are used to support curriculum is it creates an *illusion of inclusion*; the idea that because the standards and/or curriculum supports the inclusion of diverse perspective it will inherently be reflected in classroom instruction and resources to support classroom instruction (Davis, 2019; Journell, 2009; Warner, 2015).

Social Studies and Imagery

Imagery has always been a part of history (Desai et al., 2010). Photographs specifically provide three in-depth outlooks in history (Danzer & Newman, 1992). First, photographs provide content that contains its background, subject, activity, and title. Next, photographs provide context which includes its historical value, setting, photographer's perspective, date, type, audience, purpose, and impact. Lastly, photographs show technology through black and white versus color, time/light/limits, and the camera itself (Danzer & Newman, 1992). Consequently, photographs become more than just an image, photographs become a representation of a historical time. Yet, "images are part of a whole culture and cannot be understood without a knowledge of that culture" (Burke, 2001, p. 36). Every image is a product of time and place and carries assumptions that may include or exclude viewers based upon social class, ethnocultural, religious, and educational backgrounds. Hence, interpretations are varied and depend upon the readers of the image, their identities, and the narrative context (Werner, 2000, 2002). For example, students with roots in Western traditions would be challenged to access images that draw allusions from colonized histories or Islamic cultural traditions (Werner, 2004).

Students have mixed experiences when contextualizing images. Fitchett et al. (2015) conducted an exploratory study on lynching images with preservice teachers and students. They were able to conclude that the responses of preservice teachers varied based on their students' race and content background. Fitchett et al. (2015) indicated that empathy from preservice teachers was either lacking/

superficial or their empathy became confused with "visceral emotion" (p. 260). Meaning, pre-service teachers struggled to accurately conceptualize the "why" of lynching images. The importance of these findings is vital to consider because teachers are viewed and act as gatekeepers of knowledge (Thornton, 2005) and meaning makers of images when students lack requisite background knowledge. Therefore, if they are unable to understand the "why" associated with images, especially with violent imagery, and know-how to approach it within classroom instruction, students are then left to their own devices which can have adverse effects on their understanding of historical events, time periods, and the necessity of including the voices of African Americans in historical teachings.

CRT and BlackCrit tackle the complexities of race and more importantly how narratives normalize racism. Additionally, an aim of both is to identify visual forms of racism. Images are powerful tools and are indicators of racialization (Weiner, 2016). Racialization occurs when those in positions of power maintain their power otherizing or erasing the experiences of non-dominate groups. For example, textbooks teach students that racism consists of incidental acts of violence by malicious individuals (Brown & Brown, 2010) or racist actions are portrayed as out of the ordinary (Araújo & Maeso, 2012). These depictions distort students' views of systemic racism and omit anti-racist discourses; they evade the most important element, namely power relations. The visual narrative is Eurocentric, stereotypes of African American people persist, race and racism remain tethered to certain locations and historical moments in time, and a settler social amnesia of enslavement and colonialism justify and lionize outsider intervention. Given images are essential tools for learning in social studies, critically examining how these images convey narratives of race, racism, and racialization is needed. Apart from the realized emotive responses noted above, students who view images in textbooks are more accepting of the visual frames portrayed, without questioning the images reality or truth (Rodriguez & Dimitrova, 2011), than written text narratives. In the absence of a critical frame, students fail to see racialized visual representations of history furthering color-blindness racism. Color-blind racism reinforces the curricular illusion that omits structural racism and racial privilege while avoiding accountability. Drawing upon intersecting tenets of CRT and anti-Blackness, we utilized a-BET as a tool for visual analysis to examine textbook representations of African American history in four eras whereby this history is most commonly found in the U.S. history curriculum.

METHODOLOGY

Through an exploratory study, the following research question was developed, how is African American history visually portrayed in images within a state-adopted textbook?

To answer this question, a qualitative case study methodology was used to analyze the images within the state-adopted textbook. The selection of the images was based on Lozenski (2017) research in which he stated African American history is taught in four timeframes, "the mid-nineteenth century (slavery statutes and antiliteracy laws), Reconstruction, post-*Brown v. Board*, and today, the early twenty-first century" (pp. 170–171). Consequently, two images were selected to evaluate the "mid-nineteenth century (slavery statutes and antiliteracy laws)," followed by one image for "Reconstruction," one image for "post-*Brown v. Board*," and no direct image, but rather a description of "today, the early twenty-first-century" image. a-BET, which is a hybrid of CRT and BlackCrit, was used as the premise of evaluation.

Anti-Blackness Education Theory

a-BET is a theory created that comprises tenets and ideas from CRT and Black-Crit (see Appendix A; Rochester & Heafner, 2021). From CRT, a-BET encompasses tenets two, three, and five,

> (2) the notion of colorblindness is counterproductive to achieving racial emancipation (Sleeter, 2017), (3) the deconstruction of racism and any negative impact it has on individuals of color can only be undone through the inclusion of experiential knowledge of all groups (Bell, 1992; Tate IV, 1997), and (5) the incorporation of a social justice praxis, that is intentional and pragmatic, shall dismantle systemic oppression for all historically marginalized groups (Ladson-Billings, 2014).

From BlackCrit, a-BET emphasizes the three ideas presented within the theory,

> (1) anti-blackness is endemic to, and is central to how all of us make sense of the social, economic, historical, and cultural dimensions of human life (Dumas & ross, 2016), (2) Blackness exists in tension with the neoliberal-multicultural imagination, and (3) BlackCrit should create space for Black liberatory fantasy, and resist a revisionist history that supports dangerous majoritarian stories that disappear white people from a history of racial dominance (Leonardo, 2004).

The rationale for creating a hybrid theory versus using CRT or BlackCrit individually is that although each of these theories explains shortcomings within education, primarily related to racial disparities, neither fully addresses the aim of our research. Hence, through integrating these theories together, imagery within the state-adopted textbook can be investigated critically and analytically.

Critical Race Theory in Education

CRT in education is primarily a critique of white supremacy and distinguishes the various ways white supremacy makes itself prevalent in the educational experiences of African Americans and other Students of Color (Ladson-Billings & Tate IV, 1995; Ladson-Billings, 2014). Originally developed by legal scholars, CRT is the analysis of race, law, and power which leads to privilege (Bell, 1992; Tate IV, 1997). Consisting of five tenets (see Appendix A, Figure 13.1), CRT teaches that race, racism, and white supremacy is a foundational component of America's identity as well as being interwoven into every aspect of American life, specifically the legal system (Bell, 1992). Thus, CRT indicates white people are naturally awarded power and privilege through their whiteness. However, because the power and privilege white people are inherently granted is not limited to one area, scholars found it necessary to address the influence race and privilege have on the United States' educational system (Ladson-Billings & Tate IV, 1995). The expansion of CRT in education emphasizes whiteness and how the power of whiteness impacts the educational experiences of Students of Color (Ladson-Billings & Tate IV, 1995). Specifically, Ladson-Billings and Tate IV (1995), indicate that words such as "urban" and "suburban" have a deeper meaning than solely identifying the characteristics of locations; these two words, in particular, are frequently used as a method to represent and categorize racial groups, i.e., white, Latinx, and African American students along with solidifying stereotypes. The effect of this on a child's educational experience is vast and often leaves African Americans and other Students of Color disenfranchised.

Black Critical Theory in Education

Developed as an extension of CRT, BlackCrit emphasizes societal desire to remove Blackness from America's identity (Dumas & ross, 2016). Consisting of three ideas (see Figure 13.1), BlackCrit addresses how Black *bodies* or Black people as a people are disregarded and marginalized even in spaces that aim to be inclusive under the idea of multiculturalism and diversity (Dumas & ross, 2016; King, 2016). Likewise, BlackCrit identifies the need for both educational and social policies to dismantle anti-Blackness ideologies through the acknowledgment of said policies being more inclusive and intentionally formulated to support the advancement of African Americans (Dumas & ross, 2016). In education, BlackCrit states that there is a reinforcement of white supremacy ideologies that uphold educational inequities and racializes the distribution or lack thereof, in educational resources (Dumas & ross, 2016). Specifically, echoing the scholarship of Ladson-Billings and Tate IV (1995) with CRT, BlackCrit indicates that division or lack thereof of resources reiterates whiteness as a form of power, resulting in Students of Color experiencing lower than satisfactory educational experiences and outcomes.

Analysis

Using the scholarship of Lozenski (2017), images were randomly selected based on the defined timeframes within the state-adopted textbook. Based on the images selected, a-BET was then used as the basis of analysis to evaluate the tone and way (manner) African American history is visually represented. For this process, we used an inductive approach with discursive tactics for historical textbook research. Acknowledging the hidden curricula of images and the formal curriculum (e.g., captions) we examined norms and power structures within social, cultural, historical contexts. The tone was defined as either positive, negative, or neutral representation and manner was defined as what they are seen doing within the image. The latter interrogated power relations. We offer a discussion of how the portrayed knowledge may be viewed by students. The rationale for categorizing tone as either positive, negative, or neutral and manner as actions occurring in the images was based on previous scholarship by Rochester and Heafner (2021) where excerpts from the same state-adopted textbook were analyzed during the same timeframes. Specifically, within their analysis, Rochester and Heafner (2021) used a-BET to evaluate the representation of African American history and experiences within social studies standards and developed four categories to explain how African American history is represented: oppression, statehood and identity, power struggle and resistance, and omission. Thus, using the said framework, the researchers aimed to place images in a similar categorization based on a-BET and whether images provided either positive, negative, or neutral representation based on what was occurring in the image.

RESULTS

Mid-Nineteenth Century (Slavery Statutes and Antiliteracy Laws)

In Chapter 4: Antebellum South Carolina, Lesson 1: Cotton is King (see Appendix B, Figure 13.2), a wood engraving of African American adults, children, and two white men is presented. This image appeared in *Harper's Weekly* in 1869 and is available through the Library of Congress (see https://www.loc.gov/pictures/item/91784966/). In the center of the frame are two African American men, one who is wildly smiling while turning a lever, on a machine that appears to clean or take apart cotton. Another African American man appears as if he is singing while carrying a bucket of cotton and an African American woman is carrying a basket full of cotton on her head while the African American children appear to be observing. Elites, specifically white "gentlemen" dressed in suits and top hats, inspect the cotton as shadows in the background. Under the image a caption states, "This wood engraving depicts the first cotton gin. The machine immediately skyrocketed cotton production in the South and made South Carolina planters some of the richest people in the world" (p. 119).

Based on the caption, it could be inferred that the men in top hats represent southern planters. They are also the only people mentioned in the caption. Moreover, the caption conveys a sense of state pride due its recognized economic global wealth. Yet, the words do not capture the immense impact on slavery the creation of the cotton gin generate. What is missed by this commodification of labor are the profits plantation owners were able to yield from rapidly increasing cotton production; a result of the innovation of the cotton gin which made picking cotton "easier" (Whitney, 1812). Students, readers of the text, are confronted with an economic narrative of slavery that omits the expanding trade in enslaved peoples, the growth of chattel slavery, and the insatiable need for slave labor fueled by an unprecedented global demand for cotton. In the first half of the 19th Century, southern cotton production more than doubled each decade until the Civil War and the rise of the Antebellum era of enslavement brought horrific treatment of enslaved. The image depicts white power without acknowledging whites as oppressors. A tenet of a-BET suggests a need to dismantle systemic oppression within the curriculum. A pedagogical intervention is needed whereby teachers unpack the hidden meaning of this image and reveal the role of white plantation owners in the commodification of the enslaved.

Drawing upon a-BET, the deconstruction of racism and any negative impact it has on individuals of color can only be undone through the inclusion of experiential knowledge of all groups. What is silenced in this visual portrayal is the effect of the cotton gin on enslaved African Americans—increased expectations for cotton picking. This omission could lead to misinterpretation of "easier" as making slavery more enjoyable or less brutal. The caption under the wooden engraved image of enslaved African Americans additionally does not acknowledge that the African Americans in the image *are enslaved*. Moreover, the pictorial representation of one of the African American men smiling and appearing joyful while using the cotton gin, diminishes and encourages false pretenses that enslaved African Americans were "happy" to use the cotton gin; "happy" to work for free; "happy" with the conditions surrounding their existence in the United States. These stereotypical myths of the contended slave are not contradicted nor is there discussion of the taking of freedom or enslaved resistance. The harshness, brutality, and realities of slavery are not presented in the narrative or in the textbook images supporting Woodson's (2015) research.

A-BET argues this type of imagery and cultural erasure is to be expected. While the caption aligns with the agricultural and economic interests of the state legislated policy, it completely ignores African Americans and enslavement. It presents African American history from the perspective of "planters" and "rich people"; commodifying African American history to uplift the economic fortitude of the state. This narrative promulgates a lens of oppression (Brown & Au, 2014), misrepresentations of African Americans (Woodson, 2015), and a white-centric American history (King & Simmons, 2018). Moreover, to acknowledge the harsh realities of slavery and the depths it is rooted in American history requires policymakers, textbook developers, and other stakeholders to recognize, that both any imagery showing enslaved people being joyful while "working" is an inaccurate depiction and, the economic benefits of slavery was only part of the reason slavery persisted in the South. Race is an important aspect of slavery and a key component to rationalizing its continuation in the South. Therefore, a-BET suggests using said imagery is another way of ignoring systematic racist ideologies and minimizing the experiences of African Americans in the United States.

The second image is a painting (see Appendix B, Figure 13.3) from Chapter 5: A Nation Divided, Lesson 2: The Battlefield, depicting the Massachusetts 54th Voluntary Infantry Regiment (Hicks, 2013). It is a freely accessible image available through the Library of Congress (see: https://www.loc.gov/resource/pga.01949/). In comparison to the previous image, African Americans are presented differently; specifically, the Massachusetts 54th African American Voluntary Infantry is seen charging Fort Wagner on Morris Island, South Carolina.

There are many things about this particular infantry that makes it unique and monumental, but one attribute that is of utmost importance, it was an all-African American Union Army troop during the Civil War (Massachusetts Historical Society, Founded 1791, n.d.).

Within the lithographic print, African American soldiers are seen charging the shore banks while proudly waving the American flag high. On the opposing side of the painting, Confederate soldiers raise the Confederate flag while preparing to resist the Union Armies' invasion. Some of the African American soldiers within the painting are shown as violently killing members of the Confederate Army while their officer, Colonel Robert Gould Shaw, holds his sword up high above his head. Underneath the painting, it states,

> Black soldiers from the 54th Massachusetts voluntary infantry regiment storm Fort Wagner in July 1863. Colonel Robert Gould Shaw, a white Union officer, led the men in battle. What do you think was the artist's view about Gould and the all-black 54th?

The Civil War was not a referendum on mechanisms for regional economic practices and wealth. It was a fight for equality and equity that was readily denied to African Americans based on southerners' and northerners' perception of them, their worth, and intelligence. Furthermore, African Americans were an instrumental component to the Union Army's victory in the Civil War. Thus, the use of this image would be deemed transformative according to a-BET because it uses imagery not only of a different perspective on the events of the Civil War, but also the resistance African Americans exhibited fighting for freedom, equity, and justice. Moreover, the painting and the history associated with the 54th Massachusetts Infantry allows students to rethink how they contextualize African Americans' involvement in the Civil War because it affirms the bravery and loyalty of the African American soldiers as they fought to their death for freedom and offers evidence of the respect, albeit constrained, they gained from Union military leaders. Frequently, the involvement of African American Union soldiers remains in the margins. Examining Carney's role and efforts of African Americans to engage in the military conflict are entry points for African American joy and pride.

Under a-BET, it is necessary for students to have the opportunity to see and read depictions of African Americans that put their needs, struggles, joys, and triumphs at the forefront. While promising, this image and the caption fail to acknowledge that official African American regiments were not formed by the U.S. federal government until after the Emancipation Proclamation was issued on January 1, 1863. This was despite the efforts of African American intellectuals and freedom-fighters, such as Fredrick Douglass. When the southern states seceded in 1860, Douglass and other prominent African Americans petitioned President Lincoln and Congress to allow African American men to enlist in the military. African American recruitment in 1863 was overwhelmingly successful with over one thousand men volunteering within the first five months in Massachusetts alone. The missed information marginalized the potential merit of disrupting the white narrative to include African American resistance and influence in U.S. history.

Additionally, the lithographic print reveals the presence of racial hierarchies in the Union Army. The first infantry units to storm the beach are African American and are led by white officers. From a-BET, this observation could encourage discussion(s) for students to explore the social stratification and racism in the North which is an aspect of the United States that is often omitted. More specifically, racial conflict during the Civil War, in particular, is frequently interpreted as the North being "pro-equality" so much so African Americans were treated as equals whereas in the South the opposite occurred (Lawson, n.d.). However, a distinct difference between the North and South's racial relations in the past is the North had de facto segregation versus the South had de jure segregation (Lawson, n.d). The valiant and brave efforts of the 54th proved African American troops were valuable and effective soldiers which challenged racialized notions of inferiority pervasive in the North. However, this is notwithstanding the significance of the year 1863, and the three-year gap for the U.S. government to officially authorize the recruitment of African American troops. Thus, this image could debunk myths of racial inequality as *only* a Southern creation because under a-BET said image can prompt inquiry in regard to historical perspective/subjectivity and counternarratives leading to incorporating primary sources that expound or depict the experiences of American Americans in both regions. Moreover, this image could be used by teachers to complicate assumptions that the motives of African Americans and Northern whites were the same. African Americans were not merely on the same side as Union soldiers engaged in acts of patriotism, they were fighting for freedom and the end of enslavement. They were also constantly required to prove their bravery and military effectiveness, and political value.

Reconstruction

Figure 13.4 from Chapter 7: Expansion and Reform, Lesson 2: The Tillman Era is a photograph of twenty-four young African American schoolchildren neatly dressed in suits and dresses with white aprons in front of their schoolhouse with their teacher (see Appendix B; Hicks, 2013). Next to the photograph, there is the caption, "The students and teacher of this turn-of-the-century black school are photographed outside their building. Knowing what you know about Jim Crow education, how do you think this school compared to most black schools in the South?" This image is available from the Library of Congress (see https://www.loc.gov/item/2007676239/); it was published by the Detroit Publishing Company between 1900–1910.

Similar to Figure 13.3, a-BET encourages the use of photographs such as these to dismantle the misrepresentation of African American history. Once slavery ended and the Reconstruction Era began, Northern philanthropists and missionaries rushed to the south to create schools for the newly freed African Americans (Anderson, 1988). Although Northern philanthropists may have had ulterior motives for coming to the South, this does not take away from their contributions to assist in the development of the south and progression of African Americans; never showing imagery of African Americans obtaining an education, voting at polls, and etc., only encourages a deficit minded narrative well documented in social studies textbooks (Brown & Au, 2014; King & Brown, 2014; Woodson, 2015). Education was a means of empowerment for the African American community. This image could be an inquiry entry point into studying collaborations and the critical role of education in the African American community. It is also a story of education as a central focus of human and civil rights.

Education in the rural South was a community-based movement among African Americans. A good example is the rise of Rosenwald Schools, a partnership between Booker T. Washington and Julius Rosenwald, which educated almost three-quarters of a million Black children over four decades including leaders of the Civil Rights Movement. Education becomes a path toward social and economic opportunities as well as grassroots community activism. Rosenwald alumni include Medgar Evers, May Angelou, Congressman John Lewis, and members of the Little Rock Nine. Rosenwald schools also revealed disenfranchisement and the racialized economic disparities of the Jim Crow South in which African American schools received less than a third per pupil as compared to white schools (Hanchett, 2022). Drawing upon the strong community unity and commitment to education, African Americans successfully fought against institutionalized educational segregation. In alignment with the aims of a-BET, the legacy of African American schools in forming an American education revolution offers Students of Color the opportunity to see and read depictions of African Americans that put their needs, struggles, joys, and triumphs at the forefront.

Examining the connection between the image and its suggested pedagogical integration reveals a nuanced problem under a-BET. Asking students to form a comparison between the school in the photograph against others indicates that some schools were in better conditions than others which implies that although schools were segregated due to Jim Crow laws, *all* segregation was not horrible, or even problematic. This creates a message that although the educational conditions African American children were experiencing were not equal to white children, it could have been worse depending on location. This perspective under a-BET highlights the continuous tension found when discussing the African American experience. Images such as this pacify discriminatory practices under the notion "things could have been worse" as well as project false messages that when discussing and teaching about Jim Crow South, it can be taught with minimal discussion of its lingering implications (Chafe et al., 2001).

Post-Brown v. Board of Education (1954)

Figure 13.5 from Chapter 9: Turbulence and Change, Lesson 2: The Movement of Democracy is a photograph of the Friendship Nine activist being arrested for protesting Jim Crow segregation laws (see Appendix B; Hicks, 2013). Following reconstruction, to limit African Americans from being able to advance within southern society and solidify racial hierarchy, Jim Crow laws were created (Chafe et al., 2001; Edwards & Thompson, 2010; Guffey, 2012). Jim Crow laws were a form of legal segregation that many southern states adopted to prevent the integration of African Americans in southern societies, i.e., ability to vote, attend a quality school, job opportunities, where they could eat and sit in public places, where they sat on public transportation and more (Chafe et al., 2001; Edwards & Thompson, 2010; Guffey, 2012). The effects of these laws were vast and deep and within every aspect of their life, African Americans were treated as second-class citizens and were terrorized through enforcement of this racialized system of segregation. Nonetheless, African Americans resisted and fought tirelessly for equality and equity but experienced countless amounts of discrimination and oppression during their fight for change (Chafe et al., 2001). The image of the Friendship Nine activists is an example of African American resistance in the Jim Crow South. The photograph shows four of the Friendship Nine leaving McCrory's establish under arrest for sitting-in. They are being escorted out by white police officers who charged them with trespassing. Two of the Friendship Nine are looking sternly at the camera and the self-controlled face of a third member of the student-activists is captured in the image. Under the photograph, it states,

> The Friendship Nine activist file out of McCroy's as they are arrested for defying Jim Crow segregation laws. Notice the three students' expressions. How are their moods different, and what does each mood tell you about what standing against segregation was like?

While this picture attempts to convey forms of resistance within the American Civil Rights Movement, it has limitations in interpretation based on a-BET. First, the image presents the caste system of the Jim Crow South. By including a picture focused on the arrest and law-breaking actions of African-Americans, this image has the potential to maintain racialized stereotypes of white power and the criminalization of African American young men. A simple google search yields many other, more empowering images of the Friendship Nine by positioning them as student-activists engaged in a national sit-in movement. Juxtaposing this image with others available through google would provide fodder for discussions and inquiries to explore the contrasting ways media presented the efforts of the African American community's fight for freedom and justice. Second, a-BET pushes students and teachers to understand the willingness of a generation of African American youth to bear personal and physical repercussions in their collective efforts to challenge oppression and injustice by studying these events through the voices of student activists. Teachers might direct students to anti-segregationist forms of protest (see Bettmann, 1961), archived videos at the Library of Congress (e.g., Finney et al., 2011), and Student Nonviolent Coordinating Committee publications (e.g., *The Student Voice*). For example, in a letter to his parents published in *The Student Voice* (1961), Clarence Graham wrote,

> Try to understand that what I am doing is right. It's not like going to jail for a crime like steaming, killing, etc., but we're going for the betterment of all colored people...So try to see things my way and give us, the younger generation, a chance to prove ourselves. (p. 1)

As part of the unfinished revolution of lunch counter, bus, library, and school protests for freedom and equality, the story of the Friendship Nine is monumental in the long struggle for civil rights. Their legacy demonstrates the ongoing fight against anti-Blackness and systems of oppression deeply rooted in American society.

The Friendship Nine included eight men who attended Friendship College in Rock Hill, South Carolina, and a field organizer for the Congress of Racial Equality. These men were jailed and charged for trespassing after a non-violent, sit-in protest at a lunch counter of McCrory's whites-only establishment. Inspired by the wave of sit-in protests spearheaded by the Greensboro Four in North Carolina, the Friendship Nine sought to economically and legally challenge systemic inequalities. It is unique in that it inspired a relatively new *jail, no bail* method of resistance supported by Dr. Martin Luther King, Jr., and Student Nonviolent Coordinating Committee. Their decision to refuse bail, concedes no guilt or wrongdoing, and going to jail for thirty days of hard labor set afire national discontent and boosted civil rights protests. Pairing the textbook image with how the town of Rock Hill remembers the Friendship Nine (see Figure 13.5) generates an entry point to examining various tactics used in the Civil Rights Movement and the need to turn collective attention to media-induced political pressure (see https://www.knowitall.org/collections/friendship-nine) and legal battles (see https://www.zinnedproject.org/news/tdih/jail-no-bail/). In the long road to justice, a marker was erected in honor of the Friendship Nine in Rock Hill, SC in 2007 (see Figure 13.5), their conviction was overturned by a South Carolina Supreme Court Justice in 2015 in an effort to *right* history, and the final member of the Friendship Nine was exonerated in 2015.

In addition, this image conveys a rich story of organized African American resistance and documents the long struggle of the African American community for equality, justice, and freedom. Educating students about the connections between the past and the present and the deep roots of racism embodies central tenets of a-BET. Under a-BET, imagery such as Figure 13.5, is necessary and needed when teaching African American history similar to Figure 13.2 and 13.3. Likewise, the inclusion of the Friendship Nine activist being arrested for refusing to comply with Jim Crow laws shows not only the dark past and experiences of African Americans but also highlights the endless desire for change and willingness to fight for said change. Yet, the question that Hicks (2013) posed under a-BET would be deemed questionable, or in others, a-BET would ask what the intent of the question is.

While it is important for students to contextualize images, consider the perspective of those within the image, and attempt to put themselves in their shoes, without accurate knowledge of Jim Crow South and segregation, students are liable to be left with a limited perspective on the experiences of those arrested when protesting Jim Crow laws. Asking students solely about the "mood" and "what each mood" implies there are differing opinions of the said experience as well as diminishing how other African Americans were treated when being arrested for protesting. No attention is given to the jail, no bail strategy or the risk this decision imposed, such as beatings, rapes, and ultimately murder. Additionally, the photograph of the Friendship

Nine activist further implies an appeal to the idea that racist ideologies are a part of the southern past, solely, and even then, the rationale behind racial differences was merely for the economic benefit of the states. Nonetheless, a-BET indicates instead of this approach encouraging racial progression, it furthers the divide because of the refusal to acknowledge African American history, resistance, and activism post-slavery, reconstruction, and post-*Brown v. Board of Education* (1954). To find curriculum which disrupts racialized history, teachers might look to resources Counter Histories (see https://southernstudies.olemiss.edu/projects/counter-histories/) and other resources available at the Zinn Education Project, Learning for Justice's *Teaching Hard History*, the *1619 Project* Curriculum, the #FergusonSyllabus, and www.CarolinaK-12.org. We also recommend curricular resources available through the Library of Congress exhibit the *Civil Rights Act of 1964: A Long Struggle for Freedom* (https://www.loc.gov/exhibits/civil-rights-act/civil-rights-era.html)

DISCUSSION AND CONCLUSION

Contemporary textbooks used to teach African American history, while not overtly racist, still remain oppositional spaces in which the humanity and status of African Americans is contested. Racism is embedded in American history, particularly Southern History. When discussing the racial history of the United States it is vital for there to be a level of awareness regarding the tone in which it is conveyed. A-BET indicates the need for education and every aspect of society to create and solidify a space for Blackness to be recognized and accepted as more than a part of America's past, present, and future (Rochester & Heafner, 2021). Scholarly research as well as our analysis on the imagery used within a state-adopted textbook showcases how images can either accurately or inaccurately retell and represent history. Hence, it is vital for educators to exercise intentionality when selecting visual portrayals of history (Fitchett et al., 2015) and to provide pedagogical narratives to redirect meaning when students are exposed to racialized images within required, policy-mandated course texts. Intentional evidence-based reframing is necessary to complicate assumptions that African Americans' reasoning for their actions was the same as white peoples. Although the images used within the state-adopted textbooks are representations of history, each image selected has a meaning and purpose when discussing South Carolina's history. The imagery used in the latter portions of the textbook, e.g., post-*Brown v. Board of Education* (1954), showed a mixture of racial progression as well as racial omission; racial progression by displaying how African Americans partook in resisting racial oppression and racial omission conveying present-day as a post-racial society. Although African Americans are no longer living through legal segregation, omitting current struggles African Americans continue to encounter overlooks the fact that race is still a part of America's fabric and being. Moreover, if the United States is to advance a "post-racial society," the only way that can be done successfully is through acknowledging that systematic racism exists and has been integral to our collective history. Imagery allows students the ability to better contextualize and understand the perspective of individuals during any given time period (Werner,

2000). Being that African American history is a history that is ignored, erased, and whitewashed, it becomes that much more important for the imagery used to show said history to be done with care and intention. Educators also bear a responsibility in asking how we might transform current depictions of African American history in textbooks through our teaching and our research. Our task is to bring to light racialized discourses and to critically evaluate what is seen and not seen in images as well as how these images are narrated within text and pedagogical supports (e.g., questions for evaluating images). We also have to seek additional resources to share counternarratives that lift up and honor African American resistance and lived experiences in holding the United States accountable to the democratic principles of freedom, equality, and justice.

APPENDIX A

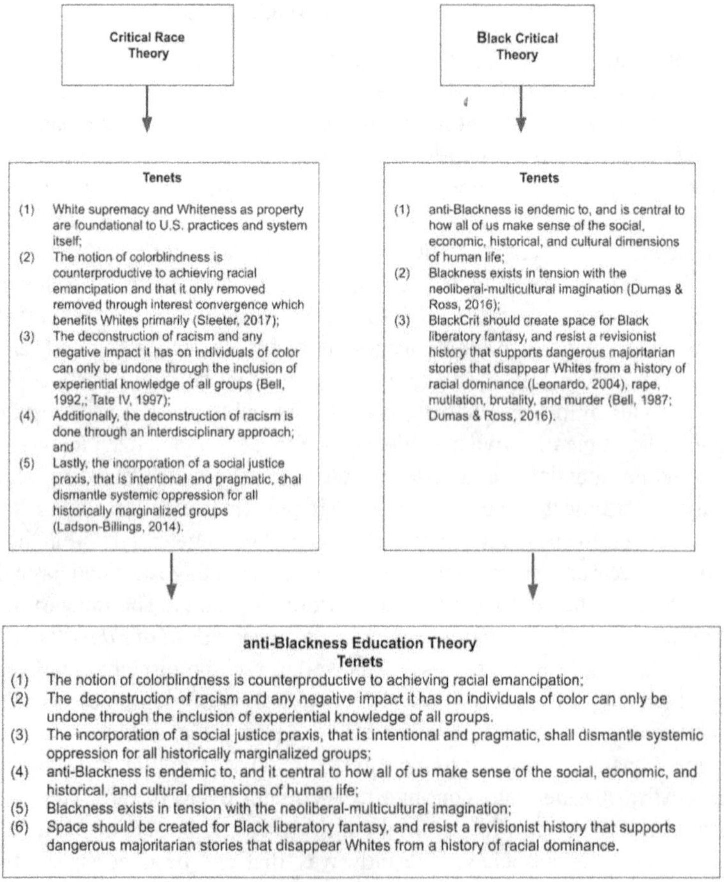

Critical Race Theory

Tenets
(1) White supremacy and Whiteness as property are foundational to U.S. practices and system itself;
(2) The notion of colorblindness is counterproductive to achieving racial emancipation and that it only removed removed through interest convergence which benefits Whites primarily (Sleeter, 2017);
(3) The deconstruction of racism and any negative impact it has on individuals of color can only be undone through the inclusion of experiential knowledge of all groups (Bell, 1992.; Tate IV, 1997);
(4) Additionally, the deconstruction of racism is done through an interdisciplinary approach; and
(5) Lastly, the incorporation of a social justice praxis, that is intentional and pragmatic, shal dismantle systemic oppression for all historically marginalized groups (Ladson-Billings, 2014).

Black Critical Theory

Tenets
(1) anti-Blackness is endemic to, and is central to how all of us make sense of the social, economic, historical, and cultural dimensions of human life;
(2) Blackness exists in tension with the neoliberal-multicultural imagination (Dumas & Ross, 2016);
(3) BlackCrit should create space for Black liberatory fantasy, and resist a revisionist history that supports dangerous majoritarian stories that disappear Whites from a history of racial dominance (Leonardo, 2004), rape, mutilation, brutality, and murder (Bell, 1987; Dumas & Ross, 2016).

anti-Blackness Education Theory
Tenets
(1) The notion of colorblindness is counterproductive to achieving racial emancipation;
(2) The deconstruction of racism and any negative impact it has on individuals of color can only be undone through the inclusion of experiential knowledge of all groups.
(3) The incorporation of a social justice praxis, that is intentional and pragmatic, shall dismantle systemic oppression for all historically marginalized groups;
(4) anti-Blackness is endemic to, and it central to how all of us make sense of the social, economic, and historical, and cultural dimensions of human life;
(5) Blackness exists in tension with the neoliberal-multicultural imagination;
(6) Space should be created for Black liberatory fantasy, and resist a revisionist history that supports dangerous majoritarian stories that disappear Whites from a history of racial dominance.

FIGURE 13.1. Anti-Blackness Education Theory

African American History and Its Visual Portrayal in Textbooks • 237

APPENDIX B

FIGURE 13.2. *The First Cotton Gin* (1869). Note. Enslaved African Americans using the cotton gin.
Note. By William L. Sheppard, 1869, p. 119 (https://digital.gibbssmitheducation.com/SC8_SE/119). This image appeared in *Harper's Weekly* in 1869 and is available through the Library of Congress (https://www.loc.gov/pictures/item/91784966/).

FIGURE 13.3. *Storming Fort Wagner* (c.a. 1890).
Note. Print shows Union soldiers storming the walls of Fort Wagner on Morris Island, South Carolina, and engaging some Confederate soldiers in hand-to-hand combat. By Kurz & Allison, p. 166 (https://digital.gibbssmitheducation.com/SC8_SE/166). This lithographic print is a freely accessible image available through the Library of Congress (https://www.loc.gov/resource/pga.01949/).

FIGURE 13.4. *African American School Children Posed With Their Teacher Outside a School, Possibly in South Carolina* (1900–1910).
Note. African American school children posed with their teacher outside a school, possibly in South Carolina. From the Detroit Publishing Company, between 1900–1910 (p. 236, https://digital.gibbssmitheducation.com/SC8_SE/236). This image is available from the Library of Congress (see https://www.loc.gov/item/2007676239/).

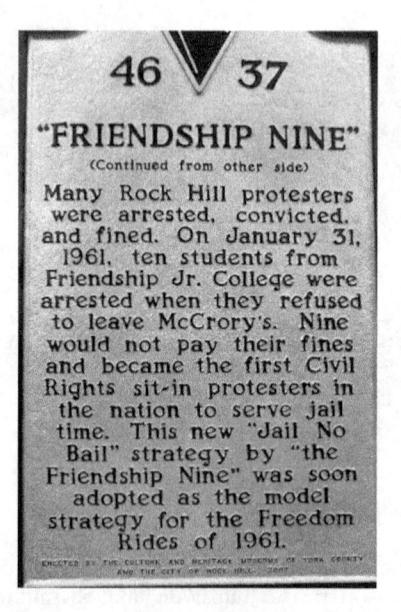

FIGURE 13.5. The Friendship Nine Historic Marker in Rock Hill, South Carolina

REFERENCES

African American school children posed with their teacher outside a school, possibly in South Carolina. Southern States, None. [Detroit publishing company, between 1900 and 1910] [Photograph]. https://www.loc.gov/item/2007676239/.

Anderson, J. (1988). *The education of blacks in the south, 1860–1935*. University of North Carolina Press.

Apple, M. W. (2013). *Knowledge, power, and education*. Routledge.

Araújo, M., & Maeso, S. R. (2012). History textbooks, racism and the critique of Eurocentrism: Beyond rectification or compensation. *Ethnic and Racial Studies, 35*(7), 1266–1286.

Banks, J. A. (2008). *An introduction to multicultural education*. Pearson/Allyn and Bacon.

Bell, D. (1992). *Faces at the bottom of the well*. Basic Books.

Berry, D. R., & Gross, K. N. (2020). *A Black women's history of the United States.* Beacon Press.

Bettmann, O. (1961, February 11). *Anti-Segregationists holding up signs*. [Photograph] From http://www.gettyimages.com/detail/news-photo/negro-student-carrying-a-sign-walks-past-mccrorys-store-news-photo/515550722

Bezemer, J., & Kress, G. (2010). Changing text: A social semiotic analysis of textbooks. *Designs for Learning, 3*(1–2), 10–29.

Brown, A. L., & Au, W. (2014). Race, memory, and master narratives: A critical essay on U.S. curriculum history. *Curriculum Inquiry, 44*(3), 358–389. http://doi:10.1111/curi.12049

Brown, K. D., & Brown, A. L. (2010). Silenced memories: An examination of the sociocultural knowledge on race and racial violence in official school curriculum. *Equity & Excellence in Education, 43*(2), 139–154. https://doi.org/10.1080/10665681003719590

Burke, P. (2001). *Eyewitnessing: Uses of images as historical evidence* (p. 36). Cornell University Press.

Busey, C. L., & Walker, I. (2017). A dream and a bus: Black critical patriotism in elementary social studies standards. *Theory & Research in Social Education, 45*(4), 456–488. http://doi:10.1080/00933104.2017.1320251

Camicia, S., & Zhu, J. (2019). LGBTQ inclusion and exclusion in state social studies standards: Implications for critical democratic education. *Curriculum and Teaching Dialogue, 21*(1–2), 7–20.

Chafe, W. H., Gavins, R., Korstad, R., Ortiz, P., Parrish, R., Ritterhouse, J., & Waligora-Davis, N. (2001). *Remembering Jim Crow: African Americans tell about life in the segregated south*. The New Press.

Cuban, L. (1982). Persistent instruction: The high school classroom, 1900–1980. *Phi Delta Kappan, 64*(1), 113–118.

Czerniak, J., & Macias-Gonzalez, V. (2006). Black slave revolt depiction and minority representation in U.S. history textbooks from 1950–2005. *UW-L Journal of Undergraduate Research IX*. https://www.uwlax.edu/globalassets/offices-services/urc/jur-online/pdf/2006/czerniak.pdf

Danzer, G. A., & Newman, M. (1992). Excerpt from tuning in, a curriculum development project. *The Social Studies, 83*(3), 134–134. http://doi:10.1080/00377996.1992.9956218

Davis, E. (2019). (Mis)representation of Latinxs in Florida social studies standards. *Social Studies Research and Practice*, *14*(1), 1–13. https://doi.org/10.1108/ssrp-01-2018-0004

Desai, D., Hamlin, J., & Mattson, R. (2010). *History as art, art as history: Contemporary art and social studies education*. Routledge.

Dumas, M. J., & ross, k. m. (2016). "Be real Black for me." *Urban Education*, *51*(4), 415–442. http://doi:10.1177/0042085916628611

Eargle, J. C. (2015). The dominant narrative of slavery in South Carolina's history standards. *The Journal of Social Studies*, *40*, 295–307. https://doi.org/10.1016/j.jssr.2015.08.001

Edwards, F. L., & Thomson, G. B. (2010). The legal creation of raced space: The subtle and ongoing discrimination created through Jim Crow laws. *Berkeley Journal of African-American Law & Policy*, *12*(1), 145–167. http://doi:10.15779/Z38XC8T

Finney, E. A., Mosnier, J., & Civil Rights History Project, U. S. (2011). *Ernest Adolphus Finney oral history interview conducted by Joseph Mosnier in Columbia, South Carolina*. [Video]. Library of Congress, https://www.loc.gov/item/2015669124/

Fitchett, P. G., Merriweather, L., & Coffey, H. (2015). "'It's not a pretty picture': How preservice history teachers make meaning of America's racialized past through lynching imagery. *The History Teacher*, *48*(2), 245–269.

Gordy, L., & Pritchard, A. M. (1995). Redirecting our voyage through history: A content analysis of social studies textbooks. *Urban Education*, *30*(2), 195–218. http://doi:10.1177/0042085995030002005

Gregory, J. R. (2021). Social work as a product and project of whiteness, 1607–1900. *Journal of Progressive Human Services*, *32*(1), 17–36. https://doi.org/10.1080/10428232.2020.1730143

Guffey, E. (2012). Knowing their space: Signs of Jim Crow in the segregated south. *Design Issues*, *28*(2), 41–60. http://doi:10.1162/desi_a_00142

Hanchett, T. (2022). *History south: Rosenwald school history*. https://www.historysouth.org/schoolhistory/

Hancoc, P. (2021). *Lame duck look back: Education bill to revamp social studies classes*. https://Capitolnewsillinois.com

Heafner, T. (2020). Agency, advocacy, activism: Action for social studies. *Social Education*, *84*(1), 4–12.

Hicks, T. E. (2013). *The South Carolina journey*. Gibbs Smith Education.

Journell, W. (2009). An incomplete history: Representation of American Indians in state social studies standards. *Journal of American Indian Education*, *48*(2), 18–32.

Kendi, I. X. (2016). *Stamped from the beginning: The definitive history of racist ideas in America*. Nation Books.

King, L. (2014). When lions write history: Black history textbooks, African-American educators, & the alternative Black curriculum in social studies education, 1890-1940. *Multicultural Education*, *22*(1), 2–11. https://doi.org/10.7709/jnegroeducation.84.4.0519

King, L., & Brown, K. (2014). Once a year to be Black: Fighting against typical Black history month pedagogies. *Negro Educational Review*, *65*(1–4), 23–43.

King, L., Davis, C., & Brown, A. (2012). African American history, race and textbooks: An examination of the works of Harold O. Rugg and Carter G. Woodson. *Journal of Social Studies Research*, *36*(4), 359–386.

King, L. J. (2016). Teaching Black history as a racial literacy project. *Race Ethnicity and Education, 19*(6), 1303–1318. http://doi:10.1080/13613324.2016.1150822

King, L. J., & Simmons, C. (2018). Narratives of Black history in textbooks. In *The Wiley International Handbook of History Teaching and Learning* (pp. 93–116). http://doi:10.1002/9781119100812.ch4

Kurz & Allison. (ca. 1890). *Storming Fort Wagner*. South Carolina United States Fort Wagner Morris Island, ca. 1890. Chicago: Kurz & Allison-Art Publishers, 76 & 78 Wabash Ave., July 5. [Photograph] Retrieved from the Library of Congress, https://www.loc.gov/item/2012647346/.

Ladson-Billings, G. (2003). Lies my teacher still tells. In G. Ladson-Billings (Ed.), *Critical race theory perspectives on the social studies: The profession, policies, and curriculum* (pp. 1–11). Information Age Publishing.

Ladson-Billings, G. (2014). They're trying to wash us away: The adolescence of critical race theory in education. In A. D. Dixon & C. K. Rosseau (Eds.), *Critical race theory in education: All God's children got a song* (pp. v–xiii). Routledge.

Ladson-Billings, G., & Tate, W. F., IV. (1995). Toward a critical race theory of education. *Teachers College Record, 97*(1), 47–68.

Lawson, S. F. (2022, September 27). "Segregation:" *Freedom's story*. National Humanities Center. http://nationalhumanitiescenter.org/tserve/freedom/1865-1917/essays/segregation.htm

Leonardo, Z. (2004). The color of supremacy: Beyond the discourse of 'white privilege.' *Educational Philosophy and Theory, 36*, 137–152. https://doi.org/10.1111/j.1469-5812.2004.00057.x

Loewen, J. W. (2018). *Teaching what really happened: How to avoid the tyranny of textbooks and get students excited about doing history*. Teachers College Press.

Lozenski, B. D. (2017). Beyond mediocrity: The dialectics of crisis in the continuing miseducation of black youth. *Harvard Educational Review, 87*(2), 161–185. https://doi.org/10.17763/1943-5045-87.2.161

Martell, C. C., & Stevens, K. M. (2017). Equity-and tolerance-oriented teachers: Approaches to teaching race in the social studies classroom. *Theory & Research in Social Education, 45*(4), 489–516. http://doi:10.1080/00933104.2017.1320602

Massachusetts Historical Society. Founded 1791. (n.d.). 54th Regiment. https://www.masshist.org/online/54thregiment/index.php

Ortiz, P. (2018). *An African American and Latinx history of the United States*. Beacon Press.

Rochester, A. M. L., & Heafner, T. L. (2021). Policy, standards, textbooks, and their role in students' understanding of African American history: An anti-Blackness Education Theory case study. In G. Samuels (Ed.), *Social science education consortium book series* (pp.101–125). Information Age Publishing Inc.*

Rodriguez, L., & Dimitrova, D. (2011). The levels of visual framing. *Journal of Visual Literacy, 30*(1), 48–65.

Rothstein, R. (2017). *The color of law: A forgotten history of how our government segregated America*. Liveright Publishing Corporation, a division of W.W. Norton & Company.

Sleeter, C. E. (2017). Critical race theory and the Whiteness of teacher education. *Urban Education, 52*(2), 155–169. https://doi.org/10.1177/0042085916668957

Sleeter, C. E., & Stillman, J. (2005). Standardizing knowledge in a multicultural society. *Curriculum Inquiry, 35*(1), 27–46. https://doi.org/10.1111/j.1467-873X.2005.00314.x

Solórzano, D. (1997). Images and words that wound: Critical race theory, racial stereotyping, and teacher education. *Teacher Education Quarterly, 24*(3), 5–19. https://www.jstor.org/stable/23478088

The Student Voice. (1961, February). Three protest groups elect jail. Call comes from Rock Hill for help. *The Student Voice* (p. 1). http://content.wisconsinhistory.org/cdm/ref/collection/p15932coll2/id/50093

Tate, W. F., IV. (1997). Critical race theory and education: History, theory, and implications. *Review of Research in Education, 22*, 195–247. http://doi:10.2307/1167376

Thornton, S. J. (2005). *Teaching social studies that matters: Curriculum for active learning.* Teachers College Press.

Vasquez Heilig, J., Brown, K., & Brown, A. (2012). The illusion of inclusion: A critical race theory textual analysis of race and standards. *Harvard Educational Review, 82*(3), 403–424. http://doi:10.17763/haer.82.3.84p8228670j24650

Wade, R. C. (1993). Content analysis of social studies textbooks: A review of ten years of research. *Theory & Research in Social Education, 21*(3), 232–256. http://doi:10.1080/00933104.1993.10505703

Warner, C. K. (2015). A study of state social studies standards for American Indian education. *Multicultural Perspectives, 17*(3), 125–132. https://doi.org/10.1080/15210960.2015.1047930

Weiner, M. (2016). Colonized curriculum racializing discourses of Africa and Africans in Dutch primary school history textbooks. *Sociology of Race and Ethnicity, 2*(4), 450–465.

Werner, W. (2000). Reading authorship into texts. *Theory & Research in Social Education, 28*(2), 193–219, http://doi:10.1080/00933104.2000.10505904

Werner, W. (2002). Reading visual texts. *Theory & Research in Social Education, 30*(3), 401–428, http://doi:10.1080/00933104.2002.10473203

Werner, W. (2004). On political cartoons and social studies textbook: Visual analogies, intertextuality, and cultural memory. *Canadian Social Studies, 38*(2) (online). www.quasar.ualberta.ca/css

Whitney, E. (1812). *Petition requesting the renewal of his patent on the cotton gin; 4/16/1812.* Referred to the the Select Committee on the Renewal of Eli Whitney's Patent on the Cotton Gin; Records of Early Select Committees, 1793–1909; Records of the U.S. House of Representatives, Record Group 233; National Archives Building. https://www.docsteach.org/documents/document/patent-renewal-cotton-gin

Woodson, A. (2015). "What you supposed to know": Urban Black students' perspectives on history textbooks. *Journal of Urban Learning, Teaching, & Research, 11*, 57–65. https://files.eric.ed.gov/fulltext/EJ1071418.pdf

Yoo, M. S., Mendez, S. L., Frischmann, N. E., Noeller, S., & Wallner, D. (2020). What our secondary textbooks miss: Infusing Mexican American history into U.S. social studies curricula. *Understanding and Dismantling Privilege, 10*(2), 40–49.

CHAPTER 14

RE-IMAGINING HEROES AND HOLIDAYS

Possibilities for Folkloristics in History and Social Science Education

Mark E. Helmsing
George Mason University

What comes to mind when you read the word *folklore*? Do you picture a village elder, dispensing wisdom to people of the community? Perhaps you imagine a group of teenagers sitting around a campfire telling urban legends about a ghostly spirit that allegedly haunts the summer camp? As it turns out, folklore is a vast, complicated, and culturally rich concept. Readers of *The Penguin Dictionary of American Folklore* (Axelrod & Oster, 2000) will find an array of folklore examples within the United States. The dictionary's entries help bring forward what it is we encounter when we encounter folklore.

Take for example just some of the entries for the letter "A": Johnny Appleseed, April Fools' Day, astrology, Area 51, and verbal lore associated with the AIDS crisis. In my life alone, I have immediate connections with all of these. My grandmother claimed to have seen an extraterrestrial alien aircraft in the sky one evening in the 1950s, not far from Wright Patterson Airforce Base, a place

---

Out of Turmoil: Catalysts for Re-learning, Re-Teaching, and Re-imagining History and Social Science, pages 243–257.
Copyright © 2023 by Information Age Publishing
www.infoagepub.com
All rights of reproduction in any form reserved.

indirectly associated with the lore of Area 51. I have both pranked others and been pranked myself on April Fools' Day every year since I can remember. I am from Indiana, which has several places purported to have been visited or traveled by Johnny Appleseed, such as Fort Wayne, the city near where the real-life inspiration for Johnny Appleseed, John Chapman, died in 1845, which now hosts the annual Johnny Appleseed Festival commemorating the real person and the folk history surrounding him. I know that my birthday, January 26, is associated with the astrological sign of Aquarius, which, no matter what science may suggest otherwise, feels hard to ignore as I identify strongly with my astrologically preordained personality traits and dispositions as an Aquarius.

However, not all folklore is fun. As a young person growing up during the height of the AIDS crisis in the 1980s and 1990s, I learned and recirculated many cultural expressions my peers and I transmitted about the lore of AIDS, through tasteless jokes about "being positive" and urban legends that mosquitos transmit HIV. To the aims and purposes of formal education, all of these examples could be considered the enemy: fake news or fake information, misinformation, superstition, conspiracy, untruths, or less harmful but equally undesirable trivial curiosities. However, this is the kind of learning that almost every person partakes through all aspects of their cultural life, both socially and individually, publicly and privately, outside of the boundaries of formal learning and schooling. To ignore folklore is to ignore the expressions of culture that give our social worlds meaning, which, in turn, is at the heart of social education.

While it does not receive as much attention as other history and social science disciplines that comprise the social studies, folklore is a field of study that has a place within social studies education. However, much like folklore itself, the place it occupies within social studies education is not always clear or easy to ascertain. Its place within our field may initially seem conservative, tired, outdated, and out of step with contemporary cultural critique and analysis shaping so much of current work in history and the social sciences. It may seem odd for a book about contemporary, reimagined approaches in history and social science education to include a chapter about one of the oldest academic disciplines in existence. The first two professional organizations devoted to the formal study of folklore, The Folklore Society in Great Britain and the American Folklore Society, appeared in 1878 and 1888, respectively. Both of these learned societies took inspiration for their study of folklore from the fieldwork on beliefs, legends, and cultures that brothers Jacob and Wilhelm Grimm published in the early 1800s, studies on what they termed *das Volk*, the German phrase for "the people," or, "the folk" (Bronner, 1986, 2017).

Not only is folklore an old discipline itself, but the content of that which folklorists study is often assumed to be old itself: old customs, old tales, old traditions, and old stuff in general. This very assumption is exemplified unironically in the title of a book *The Old Traditional Way of Life: Essays in Honor of Warren E. Roberts,* the first person in the United States to be granted a Doctor of Philosophy degree in folklore (Walls & Shoemaker, 1989; Zumwalt, 1988). More importantly, this chapter may seem out of place in this book because for many history and social science educators, folklore may be considered something we must teach against or to actively dispel from our students' historical understanding, such as myth of the Alamo, the folk hero Davy Crocket, the fakelore surrounding George Washington as a young boy, and folk histories that complicate our understanding of what is real and what is false. Why, then, would we want to carve space within the already crowded social studies, social science, and history curriculum to study things that may be derided as old, false, or just plain folksy? The reasons are many and this chapter aims to help make a case for including the ideas, methods, concepts, and content of folklore studies within social studies. As our field continues to think through the possibilities of disciplinary thinking, such as thinking like a historian, or thinking like a geographer, the disciplinary possibilities of thinking like a folklorist offer rich connections and new directions for the social studies.

This chapter provides readers with an overview of folkloristics (the academic field and methodology for studying folklore) as an area of knowledge not normally considered central to K–12 curricula. My reason for providing this overview of folkloristics is to consider new possibilities for educators in history, social sciences, the social studies, as well as allied fields such as language arts education, all of which I will collectively refer to as social education. More importantly, I aim for social educators to consider how folkloristics can further our commitments to teach for diversity, equity, and inclusion through practices of culturally sustaining pedagogies. After defining the field of folkloristics through what I refer to as the 3 C's of folklore, and explaining why folklore matters to social education, I discuss its ability to support and affirm culturally sustaining curriculum and pedagogy as a particularly special purpose for including folklore in social education. I then discuss four key examples that illustrate these claims in the service of having learners in history and social science contexts sustain their own dynamic community practices while also drawing from them. These four examples correlate to four approaches social educators can use when teaching with a folkloristic perspective: (a) investigating and analyzing traditional actions, behaviors, and practices; (b) questioning and situating personal, social, and community narratives (such as histories, but also legends, tales, commemorations, and memorials); (c) evaluating and appraising expressive forms of traditional culture; and (d) creating and preserving forms of traditional culture.

SOCIAL SCIENCE APPROACHES TO TEACHING AND LEARNING FOLKLORISTICS

Folklore can be a complicated process of definition, similar to the challenges and complexities of defining and distinguishing amongst social studies, social education, and social science education. In contemporary practice, the study of folklore, along with folklife, folk art, and folk culture, is referred to with the technical term *folkloristics*, which uses social science and humanities-oriented tools, methods, and practices to analyze and interpret traditional culture and the traditions that help folks produce, distribute, and consume their local, or vernacular, culture (Fivecoate et al., 2021). At times in this chapter, I will refer to folkloristics in the technical, academic sense, but other times will refer to folklore as both the subject and object of its study, in much the same way that 'history' refers both to the subject of study and the object which it studies (i.e., history is the study of history and folklore is the study of folklore).

Folkloristics is a discipline, a theory, and a methodology that studies "informal, traditional culture" in everyday life (McNeill, 2013, p. 13) often in the form of "traditional knowledge put into, and drawing from, practice" (Bronner, 2019, p. 76). When folklorists talk about practice, they are referring to the acts of producing, transmitting, circulating, consuming, performing, and preserving cultural expressions. Cultural expressions can take on a seemingly infinite array of forms. William John Thoms published one of the first systematic considerations of what constitutes folklore in 1846, defining folklore as "manners, customs, observances, superstitions, ballads, proverbs, etc., of the olden time" (Bauman, 1992, p. 29). Over a century later, in the first edition of one of the first academic textbooks on folklore, Brunvand (1968) echoes this definition by organizing chapters on proverbs, riddles, rhymes, folk poems, myths, legends, folktales, folksongs, ballads, superstitions, customs, festivals, folk dances, folk games, folk costumes, and gestures. Half a century later, these cultural expressions remain vibrant areas to study, as exemplified in *The Oxford Handbook of American Folklore and Folklife Studies* (Bronner, 2019), which includes many of the same forms (e.g., rituals, jokes, legends, games, crafts), but also new forms raising contemporary consciousness, such as the internet in folklore and folklife, the folklore and folklife of LGBTQIA+ and queer culture, and the folklore and folklife of neurodiverse and ability-centered identities.

At this point in our attempts at defining folklore, social educators would be right to ask what the difference is between folklore and some of the social sciences such as anthropology and sociology. I offer one crude way of contemplating this distinction. Sociologists study society and human behavior within large structural and social configurations, studying social issues, problems, and practices that are often approached from a macro perspective, such as social dimensions of aging, crime, healthcare, and religion. Anthropologists also study from a macro perspective, attempting to explain all things "anthro"–the human–through the study of human-ness, from language patterns to kinship patterns to patterns of belief, farming, migration, and sexuality. To see this point metaphorically, Fivecoate (2020) encourages us to think of sociology and anthropology as studying the conceptual physics of culture, society, and humans at large, on a universal, cosmological scale, whereas we can think of folklore as the study of the particle physics of culture, the atomized "stuff that makes up the day-to-day lives of individuals within communities" which often take the form of "small, almost imperceptibly minute building blocks of social reality" (n.p.).

FOLKLORE IN THE SOCIAL SCIENCE CLASSROOM: AN EXAMPLE FROM A HIGH SCHOOL CLASSROOM

To see what folklore can look like in classroom practice, I offer one pedagogical example. In a former study I conducted of high school social studies teachers, I spent time in a ninth-grade U.S. History course during an instructional unit on the history of different minority groups in the United States throughout the twentieth century. During instruction on the history of gay, lesbian, bisexual, and trans communities, the teacher provided sociological analyses of gay male communities in the United States, using a sociological perspective to explain patterns of discrimination and criminalization gay, lesbian, bisexual, and trans communities experienced in the United States throughout much of the twentieth century, including quantitative analyses of arrest records, police raids, and court challenges of legal precedents. The teacher used an anthropological perspective to explain the cultural significance of celebrity Judy Garland's death in 1969 that could be a causal explanation of the tensions and conflict that gave rise to the gay and trans rebellion that occurred at the Stonewall Inn in New York City later that year, using anthropological insight to explain the significance of forming private bonds of kinship and community in spaces that needed to be safe for gay and trans people, such as the Stonewall Inn. Surprisingly to me, the teacher also used folkloristic insight to illuminate for the students many colloquial, communal, and common cultural features of what we could term gay folklore, including teaching the class about the different variations of the rainbow flag, cultural practices at Pride parades and festivals, the cultural meaning of folk phrases such as "friend of Dorothy" that reinforced an earlier aspect of the lesson on the cultural significance of Judy Garland and the events leading up to the event referred to as "Stonewall." One student asked if it was a slur to refer to a gay man as "a friend of Dorothy," and the teacher carefully explained in a manner consistent with a folkloristic approach how the phrase exited and operated to work as a form of safe coding and identification within communities of gay men.

This U.S. History course lesson allowed students to see how folklore associated with gay men can illuminate aspects of queer life and queer history that may be "otherwise ignored, invisible, and in many ways seemingly untellable" (Thorne, 2021 p. 293). The inclusion of these expressive forms in the classroom signal ways teachers can be alert and attentive for folklore in many 'hidden' or unexpected regions of the history, social science, and social studies curriculum. In the following sections, I discuss some ways social studies educators can begin the search for folklore in their teaching.

THE 3'CS OF FOLKLORE

Folklorists would argue against the idea that everything we encounter in everyday life constitutes folklore. What folklorists call attention to are the specific practices, objects, materials, and behaviors that help "people keep tradition in mind as they navigate modern everyday life" (Bronner, 2019, p. ix). Folkloric actions, concepts, or expressions are "repeated, variable social actions that might be perceived, or constructed, as traditional" (Bronner, 2019, p. ix). This means folklore is observable and often repeated or replicated. Because folklore is not merely everything we encounter in life, understanding it becomes a productive and useful objective for social education. Social educators and their students can use folklore as an opportunity for inquiry into approaching, examining, analyzing, and interpreting informal traditional and expressive culture. There are three features I find helpful when I am engaged in teaching and learning about folklore, which I casually refer to as the "3 C's" of folklore. The 3 C's refer to how folklore is (a) colloquial; (b) communal; and (c) common (Ben-Amos, 2020; Feintuch, 2003; Georges & Jones, 1995; Oring, 1986).

Folklore Is Colloquial

Folklore can generally be considered knowledge about things learned in colloquial ways, most often in informal spaces beyond the formal spaces of learning such as schools and museums. Even though I learned a great deal about life and the various cultures of which I am a part while attending school, this learning happened informally in the spaces of learning where knowledge is colloquial and conversational: on the bus ride to school, on the walk home from school with friends, in the locker room before and after P.E. class, at sleepovers and parties, shopping malls, parking lots, summer camps, field trips, dances, playing basketball in the city park. Today these spaces are extended and enhanced digitally through social media, mobile phone and computer technology, and the virtual spaces we inhabit in our lives. Other informal spaces of learning are contextually specific and culturally significant to colloquial transformation of knowledge often through conversation, occurring in spaces such as barbershops for men, especially in African American communities; salons and beauty shops for women, especially in communities of the U.S. South; kitchens for learning traditional foodways; rectories and temples for learning religious traditions; barns and farmyards for learning agricultural traditions; the garage and junkyard for learning automobile folk culture and folklife.

Folklore Is Communal

One can read numerous available encyclopedias and dictionaries of urban legends, folk tales, and folk sayings, but that is not how a person first encounters knowledge of such things authentically. All folklore can be traced back to some origin with a particular group, community, or collective. It is the "learning of the people" in which "the people" are part of a specific communal form (Burne, 1914, p. 1).

Because folklore is communal, it must be learned through a community. One learns folklore communally from and within the community of which one is a part, or, in the case of academic folklorists, a community of which one is studying. I learned different types and kinds of folklore from each of the different cultural communities of which I have belonged in my life: white culture, Protestant culture, Hoosier culture, Midwest culture, "American" culture, working-class culture, cultures of masculinity, to name a few. Gaming culture, sports culture, bar culture, drug culture, youth culture, military culture, nudist culture, Mormon culture, French culture are of course all types of communities with their own types of culture. The folklore of that culture, however, is produced, transmitted, and consumed communally.

On the other hand, folklore can even be a part of smaller communities. A school community can have its own folklore and customs, such as the folkloric tradition of Sunnyslope High School, a school where I taught in Phoenix, Arizona, in which each fall freshmen walk up the slope of Sunnyslope Mountain across the street from the school to paint a large letter "S," a tradition that marks the ritual beginning of a new school year. Families can have their own folklore that is communal to their traditions passed down from one generation of the family to another.

Folklore Is Common

Some may approach the study of folklore as seeming unacademic or unintellectual because the material of folklore is clearly visible. Although ideological issues may exist deep within the personal meanings and cultural significance of folklore, as in the adage that underneath every joke is a kernel of truth, folklore is very much an intellectual pursuit of surfaces, of seeing and appreciating what is visible and conspicuous and less oriented towards trying to determine what is inconspicuous, abstract, or conceptual. This makes the knowledge that both goes into folklore and comes out of folklore appear to some as the 'common' sense of a community, its own 'common' knowledge. This common sense of what Boggs (1943) terms the "knowledge or teaching of a folk" (p. 8). Bayard (1953) argues that the materials of folklore are the only true, real "common property" shared by a community or group. Because folklore is common knowledge, some may have disdain for folklore as being marginal knowledge or trivial knowledge, particularly peoples and groups engaged in highly specialized pursuits of knowledge that distinguish 'folk' culture from erudite and refined 'high' or 'elite' culture. The attitude of defining anything 'folk' as common, insignificant knowledge appears in numerous historical examples such as the connotation folklore has in French to mean something with "a picturesque aspect but without importance or without deep significance" (Ó Giolláin, 2000, p. 1).

The colloquial, communal, and common characteristics that typify folklore is what makes folklore distinct from other forms of culture we may teach and study about with our students, such as mass media and popular culture, both of which employ some form of commercial context to produce and distribute the culture that is then consumed by the masses at large (the population that makes up the "popular" of popular culture). Folklore, on the other hand, is transmitted and circulated informally, often orally, and resists being copywritten, trademarked, and, to a lesser extent, commercialized. Various aspects of folklore may merge into, or become appropriated, by mass media and popular culture, but it lives its own life independent of it. For example, *Spider-Man* appears in, and is consumed through, comic books, television series, and Hollywood films. Spider-Man, in all of his forms as object, text, and idea, belongs to popular culture, whose own popularity waxes and wanes and appears, at the time of this writing in 2022, to be spanning a new and renewed height of his popularity. But human interactions with spiders help inform the mythos of Spider-Man and that comes from folklore. Humans have long had complicated relationships with spiders, a relationship that appears in many cycles of myths, folktales, and legends across cultures, such as Anansi, a trickster character who often takes the form of a spider in West Africa, African American, and Caribbean folklore (Klintberg, 1985). In some cases, the folkloric attributes of spiders spinning webs appear across multiple cultural contexts, from Arachne, a doomed weaver in Greek mythology transformed into a spider, to Uttu, an ancient Sumerian god of weaving, and to Neith, an ancient Egyptian god of spinners, weavers, and the woven tapestry of human time and destiny (Weigle, 1992). These ancient folkloric forms of spider-human interaction appear in more modern folklore, such as urban legends people have passed down and circulated for years about spiders hatching eggs in human faces and hair (Holt & Mooney, 1999), and in connections to historical accounts of epidemics and diseases extending back to the Middle Ages (Davey, 1994). These are examples of folklore, not popular culture, but it illustrates how popular culture (such as Spider-Man) makes use of existing sources of (quite old) folklore. Including this form of knowledge can richly shape students' historical and social scientific thinking through how folkloristic ways of knowing position students to construct and use "knowledge that is part of the cultural commons" in their everyday lives and communities (Bowman & Hamer, 2011, p. 220).

HEROES AND HOLIDAYS: CRITICALLY CONSIDERING FOLKLORE AS SOCIAL STUDIES

These definitions and perspectives on folklore and folklife derived from folkloristics have immediate relevance for social education. A brief case study can show us this relevance in practice. The influential book *Beyond Heroes and Holidays,* first published in 1998, and now, over two decades later, in a revised second edition, calls educators' attention to the facile, parochial, and ethnocentric approaches to teaching about and with diverse cultures and histories (Lee et al., 2011). The book, and others like it published since the growth of critical approaches to multicultural education, has corrected many problems and pitfalls throughout school curricula in the United States, especially problems that have long troubled social education. The title refers in part to how it was at one time common in classroom instruction to see students dress up as "Pilgrims" and "Indians" to reenact the U.S. settler colonial fantasy of the "First Thanksgiving" each November, or to see instruction on ethnic diversity, community history, and cultural conflicts flattened and reduced to banal activities relegated to special holidays or particular lessons during the academic year, such as substituting substantive instruction on the histories of African civilizations with an hour spent making masks out of construction paper.

Activities such as these inappropriately skirt around acts of cultural appropriation and trivialization in that they take the 'real' of folklore, folklife, and folk culture and reduce it to a craft, a game, or an opportunity for diversion and play. It is not the case that play is inherently wrong or bad, but that the way educators frame this content should use the same level of intellectual inquiry and investigation as with other aspects of history and social science learning, approaching the cultural examples as sources of knowledge, and as venerable representations of a community or culture that cannot be reduced to the form often seen in activities such as role playing, mask making and other arts and crafts, and games (Banks, 2015; Hyland, 2009).

An educator, however, may wonder why not to engage in these teaching activities when folklore itself studies things such as mask making as a culturally relevant practice, along with games, play, and crafts itself. Indeed, the study of crafts and crafters, makers, such as mask makers, and folk artists is a large subgenre of folkloristic inquiry (Glassie, 2010, 2020). The answer to this is to consider the purpose of the inquiry occurring in the first place. Brown-Jeffy and Cooper (2011) identify a core principle of culturally relevant pedagogy as the focus on identity and achievement of both students themselves and the content which they are studying, which includes highlighting and supporting "cultural heritage" and "affirmation of diversity" (p. 72). To do these effectively, the social educator must frame and approach cultural heritage with the same level of care, concern, and priority as other academic subjects and inquiry, which means taking the step to ensure any activity does not reduce this learning to trivializing activities and maintains the same level of skill that is found in other dominant forms of learning in social education, such as contextualizing primary sources, developing, and supporting arguments with claims, and evaluating, analyzing, and interpreting human and social behavior.

The use of folklore as something that is merely fun, creative, or novel is what in part developed a customary approach to teaching about heroes and holidays within social education. Almost every form of traditional culture has its own heroes and its own holidays and its own histories, beliefs, traditions, and rituals. Helping students and educators conceptualize traditional knowledge that rejects essentialism, exoticism, and ethnocentrism is a key component of making social education a form of "culturally sustaining" curriculum and pedagogy. This is a characteristic Paris and Alim (2017) would identify in the effort to educate through "sustaining dynamic community practices" (p. 7).

Critical approaches developed in multicultural education, social education, and related fields throughout the 1990s, 2000s, and 2010s began to show how parochializing and provincializing cultural heritage, a key feature of culturally responsive, relevant, and sustaining pedagogies, occurred through classroom celebrations of holidays that often turned into an occasion to make and eat treats and throw a party. In other instances, lessons on cultural heroes can lead to simplistic hagiographic celebration and veneration of the hero without connecting the hero to cultural elements worthy of sustained social and historical inquiry. For example, many social studies lessons position Rosa Parks as a hero of the U.S. Civil Rights movement, which can have an effect of flattening the complex dimensions of her life, in a way that borders on patronizing Parks's legacy and memory (Gilbert, 2018). Similarly, a lesson plan that centers Martin Luther King Jr. Day as a day to do diversional games and activities for fun, as opposed to meaningful, enriching inquiry into Dr. King's life and legacy, often ends up reinforcing the idea holidays are meant to be an occasion for fun and taking a break from what may be regarded as regular learning.

As a result, a social educator would not be questioned or criticized for choosing to eschew and avoid lessons on holidays or heroes altogether in their curriculum for concerns over patronizing the hero or holiday itself or using recognition of said heroes and holidays as an excuse for parties and time excused from instruction. But in doing so, the social educator inadvertently forecloses the opportunity to achieve what McCarthy (1994) singles out as an important element of a critical social education, namely how "radically diverse cultural knowledge(s) rooted in the social bases and experiences of oppressed groups should be introduced into the school curriculum" which can work to create and teach through "an organic link to other experiences and struggles within society" (p. 95). The organic link McCarthy has in mind seems well suited to be supported through different approaches to using folkloristic inquiry, including inquiry into holidays and heroes.

Investigating and Analyzing Traditional Actions, Behaviors, and Practices

A first approach would be for social educators to arrange instruction in which their learners are investigating and analyzing traditional actions, behaviors, and practices, a goal supported by many of the themes found in the national standards from the National Council for the Social Studies, such as its first theme, "Culture," and its fifth theme, "Individuals, Groups, and Institutions" (National Council for the Social Studies (NCSS), 2010). In a study on using Danish folklore and folktales in education, Virtue (2007) found that lessons on Danish folk heroes, such as Alexander in the Danish folk tale of the Golden Bird, opened up productive spaces for students to learn about equality, social responsibility, cooperation and compassion (p. 26). In doing so, students were able to make connections between traditional actions, behaviors, and practices dramatized in the folk tale and reflect on what place those ideals had in Danish culture of the past and present. In a similar study, Fry (2009) examines opportunities for multicultural education through "folklore-rich" literature, which she documents in using the legend of St.

Ann's flood for students to inquire into topics such as the Hindu religion, the history and culture of Trinidad, and the trans-Atlantic African diaspora.

In my U.S. History and U.S. Literature courses I taught to eleventh-grade high school students, I used the holiday of Thanksgiving as an opportunity to teach about the folkloric practices surrounding Thanksgiving celebrations in the United States. Mindful of what Shear (2015) points out as problematic approaches to teaching Thanksgiving as a peaceful diplomatic encounter between the settler colonial Pilgrims and the Indigenous peoples the Pilgrims encountered, I always want to approach the teaching of Thanksgiving in a way that does justice to historical truths and also engages students in 'thinking like a folklorist' about the holiday. One activity involved making a large list of food items I asked my students to share that they enjoyed and looked forward to eating at Thanksgiving. In every instance, some students would be surprised by what other students claimed as Thanksgiving foods (e.g., oyster dressing for some, deviled eggs for others). This is an engagement with a kind of folklore termed foodways, the rules, customs, and traditions surrounding foods and how food plays a role in the development of cultures (Thursby, 2008).

Because Thanksgiving has long been a part of the U.S. "national mythology since the seventeenth century and has been formally sponsored by presidential decrees since the time of Abraham Lincoln," it allows for a deep historical examination of the folkloric changes Thanksgiving has had in the United States (Santino, 1994, p. 168). I explored with my students the connections between European harvest festivals and Thanksgiving in the United States, looking back to Roman harvest festivals honoring Ceres, which lead to traditions of a later iteration of Ceres and the Roman festival in medieval England with a festival honoring the Corn Maiden (Santino, 1994).

Questioning and Situating Personal, Social, and Community Narratives

A second approach would be for social educators to arrange instruction in which their learners are questioning and situating personal, social, and community narratives, such as histories, but also legends, tales, commemorations, and memorials, in existing social education curricula. This can be done in support of different NCSS themes, such as the second theme "Time, Continuity, and Change," and the third theme, "People, Places, and Environments" (NCSS, 2010). Using a systematic framework for studying stories of specific figures in social movements and histories of social injustice, Jewett (2007) argues for drawing upon folkloristic approaches that support critical media literacy skills in learning why certain communities and cultures tell and share the stories they do for particular narrative purposes. Arguing that questions such as "what was life like?" can be problematic because students "cannot know what life was like for everyone in a particular group to live in a time and place or to participate in a particular movement or event" (Jewett, 2007, p. 167). What students can engage in, however, is questioning stances, using active questioning and inquiry strategies, to consider causes for and consequences of which narratives (personal, social, and/or community narratives) tend to cohere around particular individuals, lending a heroic status and why such heroic statues tend to become a part of a group's traditional narratives, such as the folklore surrounding George Washington and Abraham Lincoln that promulgate particular myths of whiteness and American exceptionalism.

Evaluating and Appraising Expressive Forms of Traditional Culture

A third approach would be for social educators to arrange instruction in which their learners are evaluating and appraising expressive forms of traditional culture. Consider the many rich and culturally varied examples of U.S. folk music as an expressive form of traditional culture throughout different regions of the United States. Lovorn (2009) argues for social educators to make use of the "connections between history and folk music," ranging from study inquiry into "African American spirituals, stirring Civil War battle cries, and lonely cowboy yodels" (p. 173). Using a classroom example of teaching about the Dust Bowl in the United States during the Great Depression of the 1930s, students can evaluate and appraise the expressive form of folk songs about this particular historical experience in the music and lyrics of Woody Guthrie's song "Dust Bowl Disaster," which, Lovorn (2009) illustrates, can become a cultural connection to examining folk music about the Dust Bowl and Great Depression from other regions in the United States, as well as from Indigenous cultures and communities located in North America, such as the Cherokee in Oklahoma and the Sioux in South Dakota. Rather than singing the songs because doing so may be fun or novel, engaging in critical analysis of the music and lyrics of such songs, and engaging in evaluating and appraising the roles and features of expressive forms of traditional culture during this period in history can engage students in a more productive and, hopefully, respectful inquiry into culture. This relationship to folklore enacts what Gutiérrez and Johnson (2017) explain as a key reason to teach with about culture in classrooms, namely that "celebrating, affirming, sustaining, and accounting for culture is the central object of pedagogies that seek to redress educational inequities and histories of curricular exclusion and pedagogical malpractice for youth from nondominant communities" (p. 249).

Creating and Preserving Forms of Traditional Culture

Finally, a fourth approach to consider would be for social educators to arrange instruction in which their learners are creating and preserving forms of traditional culture. I find many useful folkloristic resources in museums and cultural organizations, especially due to the fact that in the United States almost every state has an official state folklorist or a center devoted to folklore, folklife, and traditional culture within that state. One example is found in the Country Music Hall of Fame Museum in Nashville, Tennessee. In 2010, the museum began a program for educators titled "Words and Music" in which songwriters, folk singers, folk musicians, as well as commercial musical artists, engage with students to consider, reflect upon, and ultimately create lyrics that would serve to document local life in their communities, creating and preserving community narratives, histories, and cultures through traditional expressive forms of culture such as song lyrics and the act of songwriting.

Similarly, the Junior Appalachian Musicians program uses folkloristic study of music making, traditional music and instruments, and traditions of singing in the Appalachian region to more respectfully, responsibly, and responsively teach about Appalachian peoples, places, and environments, utilizing several NCSS themes in an interdisciplinary fashion. In doing so, social educators can uphold what Paris and Alim (2017) view as a primary goal of culturally sustaining pedagogies, which is to seek those moments in which "education sustains the lifeways of communities who have been and continue to be damaged and erased through schooling" (p. 1). Social educators can use folk narratives and folklore of Indigenous peoples in North America to help center the perspectives and histories of Indigenous peoples and their cultures as vital and central to any conceptions of U.S. cultural identity, working to use folklore not as a means of exoticizing or othering Indigenous peoples in the work of a white gaze in the classroom, but to instead push back on colonizing curriculum in schools.

These examples are shared in the hopes that they can empower social educators to consider the materials, practices, and approaches of folkloristics to legitimate, support, and better educate learners about the vicissitudes of so much that makes teaching about ethnicities, cultures, and communities vitally necessary and in need of thoughtful and reflective practice. Rather than relegating folklore to nostalgic, old-fashioned dimensions of the false, the marginal, and the irrelevant, social educators can use such materials to sustain cultural traditions their students may not even know exist in their communities and in the histories of these communities. The cultural and social configurations of the communities our students belong require that we take them seriously, and to do so we can turn to the ideas, methods, and practices of folkloristics.

REFERENCES

Axelrod, A., & Oster, H. (2000). *The penguin dictionary of American folklore*. Penguin.

Banks, J. (2015). *Cultural diversity and education: Foundations, curriculum, and teaching* (6th ed.). Routledge.

Bauman, R. (1992). Folklore. In R. Bauman (Ed.), *Folklore, cultural performances, and popular entertainments: A communications-centered handbook* (pp. 29–40). Oxford University Press.

Bayard, S. P. (1953). The materials of folklore. *Journal of American Folklore, 66*(262), 1–17.

Ben-Amos, D. (2020). *Folklore concepts: Histories and critiques*. Indiana University Press.

Boggs, R. S. (1943). Folklore: Materials, science, art. *Folklore Americas, 3*(1), 1–8.

Bowman, P., & Hamer, L. (Eds.). (2011). *Through the schoolhouse door: Folklore, community, curriculum*. Utah State University Press.

Bronner, S. J. (1986). *American folklore studies: An intellectual history*. University Press of Kansas.

Bronner, S. J. (2017). *Folklore: The basics*. Routledge.

Bronner, S. J. (2019). *The practice of folklore: Essays towards a theory of tradition*. The University Press of Mississippi.

Brown-Jeffy, S., & Cooper, J. E. (2011). Toward a conceptual framework of culturally relevant pedagogy: An overview of the conceptual and theoretical literature. *Teacher Education Quarterly*, 4, 65–84.

Brunvand, J. H. (1968). *The study of American folklore: An introduction*. W. W. Norton & Company.

Burne, C. S. (1914). *The handbook of folklore*. Sidgwick and Jackson.

Davey, G. C. L. (1994). The "disgusting" spider: The role of disease and illness in the perpetuation of fear of spiders. *Society & Animals, 2*(1), 17–25.

Feintuch, B. (Ed.). (2003). *Eight words for the study of expressive culture*. University of Illinois Press.

Fivecoate, J. A. (2020). *A brief history of folkloristics &/+/vs. anthropology*. https://jessefivecoate.com/2020/06/26/a-brief-history-of-folkloristics-vs-anthropology/

Fivecoate, J. A., Downs, K., & McGriff, M. A. E. (2021). The politics of trivialization. In J. A. Fivecoate, K. Downs, & M. A. E. McGriff (Eds.), *Advancing folkloristics* (pp. 59–76). Indiana University Press.

Fivecoate, J. A., Downs, K., & McGriff, M.A.E. (Eds.). (2021). *Advancing folkloristics*. Indiana University Press.

Fry, S. W. (2009). Exploring social studies through multicultural literature: Legend of the St. Ann's Flood. *The Social Studies, 100*(2), 85–92.

Georges, R. A., & Jones, M. O. (1995). *Folkloristics: An introduction*. Indiana University Press.

Gilbert, L. (2018). Putting Mrs. Rosa Parks front and center of an elementary methods course. In S. B. Shear, C. M. Tschida, E. Bellows, L. B. Buchanan, & E. E. Saylor (Eds.), *(Re)imagining elementary social studies: A controversial issues reader* (pp. 199–218). Information Age Publishing.

Glassie, H. (2010). *Prince Twins Seven-Seven: His art, his life in Nigeria, his exile in America*. Indiana University Press.

Glassie, H. (2020). *Daniel Johnston: A portrait of the artist as a potter in North Carolina*. Indiana University Press.

Gutiérrez, K. D., & Johnson, P. (2017). Understanding identity sampling and cultural repertoires: Advancing a historicizing and syncretic system of teaching and learning in justice pedagogies. In D. Paris & H. S. Alim (Eds.), *Culturally sustaining pedagogies: Teaching and learning for justice in a changing world* (pp. 247–260). Teachers College Press.

Holt, D., & Mooney, B. (1999). *Spiders in the hairdo: Modern urban legends*. August House Publishers.

Hyland, N. (2009). One White teacher's struggle for culturally relevant pedagogy: The problem of the community. *The New Educator, 5*(1), 95–112.

Jewett, S. (2007). The stories of people's lives: Thematic investigations and the development of a critical social studies. *The Social Studies, 98*(4), 165–171.

Klintberg, B. (1985). *Fabula, 26*(3–4), 274–287.

Lee, E., Menkart, D., & Okazawa-Rey, M. (Eds.). (2011). *Beyond heroes and holidays: A practical guide to K–12 antiracist, multicultural education and staff development.* Teaching for Change.

Lovorn, M. G. (2009). Folk in the history classroom: Using the music of the people to teach eras and events. *Social Education, 73*(4), 173–178.

McCarthy, C. (1994). Multicultural discourses and curriculum reform: A critical perspective. *Educational Theory, 44*(1), 81–98.

McNeill, L. S. (2013). *Folklore rules: A fun, quick, and useful introduction to the field of academic folklore studies.* Utah State University Press.

Ó Gilláin, D. (2000). *Locating Irish folklore: Tradition, modernity, identity.* Cork University Press.

Oring, E. (1986). On the concept of folklore. In E. Oring (Ed.), *Folk groups and folklore genres: An introduction* (pp. 1–22). Utah State University Press.

Paris, D., & Alim, H. S. (Eds.). (2017). *Culturally sustaining pedagogies: Teaching and learning for justice in a changing world.* Teachers College Press.

Santino, J. (1994). *All around the year: Holidays and celebrations in American life.* University of Illinois Press.

Shear, S. B. (2015). Cultural genocide masked as education: U.S. History textbooks' coverage of Indigenous education policies. In P. T. Chandler (Ed.), *Doing race in social studies: Critical perspectives* (pp. 13–40). Information Age Publishing.

Thorne, C. W. (2021). Hidden thoughts and exposed bodies: Art, everyday life, and queering Cuban masculinities. In S. Otero & M. A. Martínez-Rivera (Eds.), *Theorizing folklore from the margins: Critical and ethical approaches* (pp. 293–312). Indiana University Press.

Thursby, J. S. (2008). *Foodways and folklore: A handbook.* Greenwood Press.

Virtue, D. C. (2007). Folktales as a resource in social studies: Possibilities and pitfalls using examples from Denmark. *The Social Studies, 98*(1), 25–27.

Walls, R. E., & Schoemaker, G. H. (Eds.). (1989). *The old traditional ways of life: Essays in honor of Warren E. Roberts.* Trickster Press.

Weigle, M. (1992). *Spiders & spinsters: Women and mythology.* University of New Mexico Press.

Zumwalt, R. L. (1988). *American folklore scholarship: A dialogue of dissent.* Indiana University Press.

BIOGRAPHIES

ABOUT THE EDITORS

Dr. **Dean P. Vesperman** is an assistant professor of education at the University of Wisconsin-River Falls and editor of the *Iowa Journal for the Social Studies*. Dr. Vesperman teaches courses in secondary and elementary social studies methods. He earned his doctorate at Indiana University in Curriculum and Instruction, minoring in Learning Sciences. Before earning his doctorate Dean taught junior high and high school social studies for eleven years in southeastern Wisconsin and CTY for 18 summers. Dr. Vesperman has published articles on pedagogical methods for teaching social studies. He lives in Western Wisconsin with his wife, daughter, and dog.

Dr. **Anne Aydinian-Perry** is a recent graduate in Curriculum & Instruction at the University of Houston, specializing in Social Education. She is a National Board Certified Teacher in History/Social Studies. She taught secondary social studies for 11 years in public, charter, and private schools in Houston, Texas. Her research interests include popular culture, social education, underrepresented narratives & hidden histories, primary source usage, and program evaluation in teacher education and the social sciences. Anne, her husband, and rescue pup Luna split time between Klein and their family farm in La Grange, Texas.

Matthew T. Missias, PhD, is a School Support Specialist and Part-Time Faculty at Grand Valley State University. His research examines how both pre-service and in-service teachers imagine their practice and salient pedagogical and developmental moments, and how those intersect with curricular choices to create possibilities and barriers to innovative practices. Additionally, he works in the social science education field providing professional development for, and generating research on, how teachers understand and teach social studies and citizenship with focus on critical examinations of diverse identities, interrogations of our shared past, and how imagined dimensions of citizenship engage teachers and learners.

Whitney G. Blankenship currently teaches US History at San Antonio College. She earned her doctorate at The University of Texas at Austin in Social Studies Education and was an Associate Professor at Rhode Island College as a joint appointment to the Departments of Educational Studies and History. Her research interests include historical thinking, curriculum history, and technology integration in the social studies classroom. She lives in Austin with her husband, Loyd and two very bad tuxedo cats.

ABOUT THE CONTRIBUTORS

Mary Adu-Gyamfi is a teacher educator and doctoral candidate at the University of Missouri-Columbia in Learning Teaching and Curriculum with a focus on social studies education and teacher education. She teaches elementary social studies methods courses at the university and engages in research with pre-service and in-service teachers toward critical consciousness and racial literacies development in collaborative spaces.

Gerardo Aponte-Safe, PhD, is Assistant Professor of Global Education at the University of Wisconsin-La Crosse, teaching courses in global and multicultural education. His research broaches the fields of teacher education and social studies education, considering how teachers navigate conflicting cultural lenses in curriculum and pedagogy for teaching diverse learners. Recent work examines how secondary teachers implement pedagogies for global education across different subject disciplines, and how those practices can be brought to teacher preparation contexts. Dr. Aponte-Safe has worked as a social studies teacher in Florida and a teacher educator in Michigan, Texas, and the Dominican Republic.

Sheila F. Baker, PhD, is an Associate Professor and Coordinator for the School Library and Information Science program at the University of Houston-Clear Lake. She is a 20-year veteran teacher and school librarian and has been certified by the National Board for Professional Teaching Standards. Her research interests include school librarian preparation, children's literature, and the promotion of diversity, equity, and inclusion in K–12 settings.

Trustin Dinsdale is a fifth grade mathematics and science teacher at a charter school in Denver, Colorado. He has a bachelor's in elementary education and a master's in educational leadership and policy analysis from the University of Missouri.

Linda Doornbos is an Assistant Professor of Elementary Social Studies at Oakland University in Rochester, Michigan. She works within collaborative communities to better see, understand, and disrupt systematic racism in education. She is interested in developing practices where students critically engage with material that inspires them to wonder about the world and their place in it; exposes them to multiple perspectives of power, privilege, and identity; and instills a desire to act and facilitate change. Before being at Oakland, Linda was an elementary and middle school social studies and language arts teacher for twenty-eight years in multiple contexts and settings.

Antony Farag, EdD—a social studies teacher at Westfield High School in Westfield, NJ and a lecturer at the Rutgers Graduate School of Education. As a teacher of color, he is one of the few teachers of color serving that demographic. He is an early career scholar focused on critically examining the teachers of white students and their pedagogies. He is also co-founder of Global Consciousness Consulting which provides professional development, curriculum writing, and other services informed by critical race theory, and other social theories with the aim of preparing students, teachers, and organizations for a continually globalizing world.

Tina Lane Heafner, PhD, is a Professor in the Department of Middle, Secondary, and K–12 Education at the University of North Carolina at Charlotte. Her administrative responsibilities include Directing the PhD in Curriculum and Instruction. Tina is the 2019–2020 National Council for the Social Studies (NCSS) President and NCSS College and University Faculty Assembly (CUFA) 2015–2016 Chair. Tina's publications include seven co-authored books and six edited books including recent titles such as: *The divide within: Intersections of realities, facts, theories, and practices,* and the *Handbook of research on emerging practice and methods for K–12 online and blended learning.*

Mark E. Helmsing, PhD, is an assistant professor of education, history, and folklore at George Mason University. His research examines how people learn and feel about the past through engagements with history, heritage, historical culture, historical memory, tourism, and folklore. His published work includes studies of topics ranging from ghost stories and murder ballads, Disney movies and television shows, Vietnam War veterans and Civil War reenactors, and town festivals and museum exhibitions. As a member of George Mason's Reconciling Conflicts and Intergroup Divisions Lab, Mark has engaged in international teaching and research experiences in Germany and Poland, Cyprus, and Greece.

Lightning Peter Jay, PhD, is an assistant professor at Binghamton University in New York in the Department of Teaching, Learning, and Teacher Education. His research works at the intersection of social studies, teacher education, and student learning with a particular interest in how teacher educators can support the development of responsive and effective new teachers. Prior to joining the Binghamton faculty, Lightning was a classroom teacher in Brooklyn, New York and Minneapolis, Minnesota before attending the University of Pennsylvania's Graduate School of Education for his doctorate.

Rylie Kever is a second grade teacher at a public school in Kansas City, Missouri and master's student at the University of Missouri-Columbia studying elementary education.

Joey Laurx is a fifth grade teacher of language arts, science, and social studies at a charter school in Denver, Colorado and a doctoral student studying education reform at the University of Northern Colorado. She holds a bachelor's degree in elementary education and a master's degree in educational Leadership and policy analysis from the University of Missouri.

Ian McGregor is Assistant Professor at the University of Nevada, Reno. His scholarship and teaching focus on social studies teacher preparation, human rights education, and civics/citizenship education with an emphasis on teaching difficult history. His current research explores how teachers and students conceptualize citizenship in human rights education and the use of virtual interactive technologies in Holocaust museum education. He was a high school social studies teacher in Louisiana for six years.

Glenn Mitoma is Managing Director of the Institute for Social Transformation at the University of California Santa Cruz, where he leads efforts to advance human rights and social justice through partnership, collaboration, and community engaged research. Glenn's writing has focused on the history of human rights and human rights education. As a scholar-practitioner, he has developed engaged research and teaching projects designed to promote a culture of human rights, including initiatives in K–12 human rights education, business and human rights, democracy and dialogues, and human rights film & digital media.

Dr. **Mary O'Dowd** is a non-Indigenous Australian academic and activist. She specialises in the cultural interface of Indigenous and non-Indigenous education in settler colonial contexts. Her research foci in this context include: history, human rights, racism, nationalism and ethics. Her scholarship evidences reflective research on effective praxis to reduce racism by engaging non-Indigenous students/citizens in deep critical engagement and ethical thinking to enable capacity to be respectful non-Indigenous citizens on Indigenous land, with Indigenous peoples and Indigenous cultures, histories, spiritualities and ontologies. She has won teaching awards in three universities, including a teaching fellowship. She lives in Darumbal Country .

Mariah Pol is a first-generation Latina doctoral student studying Curriculum and Instruction at Indiana University. Prior to pursuing her doctoral studies, she was an award-winning social studies educator in Northwest Indiana. She was the recipient of 11 domestic and international teaching fellowships, the 2019 Gilder Lehrman Institute of American History Indiana History Teacher of the Year, and the 2020 Caleb Mills Indiana History Teacher of the Year award through the Indiana Historical Society.

Kaitlin Popielarz is an Assistant Professor in the Department of Interdisciplinary Learning and Teaching at UTSA. Dr. Popielarz is a former secondary and adult education social studies teacher, which is where she developed her passion for empowering learning communities. Her research and teaching interests include connecting teacher education programs to youth-centered and intergenerational grassroots community movements, knowledges, and organizations to provide future and current educators the opportunity to learn community-based and culturally sustaining pedagogies. She is energized by collaborating with colleagues, students, and community members in the development of critical qualitative research projects that inform possibilities for transformative social change.

Antoinette (Toni) Rochester is a doctoral candidate in the Department of Middle, Secondary, and K–12 Education (Urban Education) at the University of North Carolina Charlotte. She is the Associate Director of Research at the California Charter Schools Association and a former Graduate Research Assistant at the University of North Carolina Charlotte. Her interests include addressing equity issues amongst minority students and the intersection between race, policy, and education.

Amy J. Samuels, EdD, is an associate professor of instructional leadership and program coordinator for instructional and teacher leadership at the University of Montevallo. She instructs courses on curriculum, educational equity, mentoring, and professional development. Her research interests include critical multicultural and culturally responsive practices to foster increased equity. Amy has authored peer-reviewed articles and book chapters, and presented sessions at national and international conferences, about culturally responsive pedagogy, racial (in)equity, racial literacy, and whiteness. Amy also works collaboratively with school districts and organizations to design and facilitate staff development to support and advance diversity, equity, and inclusivity.

Gregory L. Samuels, PhD, is an associate professor of secondary education at University of Montevallo and past-president of the Social Science Education Consortium. Gregory teaches courses on classroom management, diversity, and instructional strategies. Additionally, he is a co-principal investigator for GEAR UP Jefferson County. A grant focused on increasing access and opportunities for students in Birmingham school districts. His research interests include social justice education, critical pedagogy, and inclusive practices throughout the social studies curriculum. He has authored several peer-reviewed articles and book chapters with the most recent on Black Lives Matter, racial literacy, and inequities of rural education.

Dr. **Hanadi Shatara** is an Assistant Professor of Social Studies Education at University of Wisconsin-La Crosse. Her research focuses on critical global education, teacher positionalities, the representations of Southwest Asia and North Africa, Arab Americans, and Palestine in education, and teacher education. Some of her goals are to incorporate critical global perspectives and social justice into K–12 classrooms. Dr. Shatara was also a middle school social studies teacher for seven years in Philadelphia, PA, where she became a National Board-Certified Teacher and a Fulbright scholar.

Dr. **Debby Shulsky**, EdD, is an Associate Professor in Curriculum and Instruction and Coordinator for the Teacher Education Program at the University of Houston-Clear Lake. As a Social Studies educator of over 20 years standing, her teaching and research explore pedagogies that engage learners in experiences that cultivate the essential literacies and habits of mind required of critically engaged global citizens.

Sandra Sirota is Assistant Professor in Residence of Human Rights and Experiential Global Learning at the University of Connecticut. Sandra's work explores human rights and social justice education in the U.S. and South Africa. She is Executive Committee Member of the University and College Consortium for Human Rights Education, Book Review Co-Editor for the *Journal of Human Rights*, and Human Rights Faculty Coordinator with UConn's Early College Experience program. Sandra has consulted with the United Nations and other human rights organizations. Recent publications appear in the *International Journal of Human Rights Education, Journal of Human Rights,* and *Comparative Education Review.*

Aaron Teo is a PhD Candidate and Sessional Academic in the School of Education at the University of Queensland, Australia, and a Business and Law teacher at a Brisbane-based Independent School. Aaron's research focuses on the raced and gendered subjectivities of migrant teachers from "Asian" backgrounds in the Australian context, as well as critical pedagogies in white Australian (university and school) classroom spaces. He is interested in qualitative research methods, particularly the use of critical autoethnography as a form of reflexive, emancipatory inquiry.

Bailey Verdone, EdM, is an ELA and Humanities educator at Westfield High School in Westfield, NJ and a lecturer at the Rutgers Graduate School of Education. She completed her master's degree studying Indigenous ways of knowing and its inclusion within public school curricula. She is multiracial with Indigenous, Latinx and European ancestry. As a multiracial individual she is especially interested in expanding the scope of curricula, revising policy and pedagogy. Along with Antony, she is a co-founder of Global Consciousness Consulting.

CPSIA information can be obtained
at www.ICGtesting.com
Printed in the USA
JSHW011254271222
35305JS00001B/2